This book is dedicated to all SQL Server DBAs and IT professionals who, for years, are stuck on the belief that they don't have what it takes to succeed – that you're not good enough, not smart enough, not technical enough, not talented enough.

It's about time to let go of those lies and start living the life you were meant to live.

This book was written by a person who was told he would not amount to anything.

Table of Contents

About the Author

Edwin M Sarmiento is the Managing Director of 15C, a consulting company that specializes in designing, implementing, and managing high-availability infrastructures. Proud of his heritage as a Filipino, Edwin now lives in Ottawa, Canada, and specializes in high availability, disaster recovery, and system infrastructure. He is a former Microsoft Data Platform MVP of 12 years standing and is a Microsoft Certified Master for SQL Server. He is very passionate about technology and has interests in music, neuroscience, social psychology, professional and organizational development, leadership, and management matters when not working with databases. Edwin strives continually to live up to his primary mission statement: to help people and organizations grow and develop their full potential.

About the Technical Reviewer

Borbala Toth-Apathy is a database professional who's been fascinated with SQL for more than 15 years. She is currently a SQL Server database architect. She enjoys digging deep into anything and everything data related, especially about performance.

Acknowledgments

To my Creator, Jesus Christ. Your absolute belief in me compels me to believe in myself.

To my parents. You should have told me earlier that I won't be able to read my own handwriting. I should have invented a speech-to-text app years ago for people who don't have a sense of humor.

To my mom… who sent us to private school but couldn't take us to McDonald's. I wouldn't be able to tell the stories in Chapters 5 and 9 if you could.

To my dad… who didn't want me to become a pilot. I wouldn't be able to appreciate the complexities of flight travel and tell stories about them in Chapter 4 if I was flying the plane.

To Daniel, Earl, and Nerisse. I'm surrounded by your extraordinary creativity every single day. It's no wonder we end up making crazy stuff up like the "idea generator." I've learned so much about developing my own creativity just by hanging out in the *D.E.N.*

To the Worship Team at myChurch Canada… who urged me to use a digital audio workstation before I can play keys with the team. I really needed an introductory story for Chapter 6.

To my editors at Apress – Jonathan, Laura, and Jill. You make your authors look like rockstars (OK, just the writing part because I owe my parents for my good looks).

To my technical editor, Borbala. Your reviews and comments kept me tight on the technical details and helped make them clearer.

To Audi, Locky, Lexy, and Lodgi. You'll have others joining you soon.

Introduction

The year was 1999. My ex-girlfriend (now wife) and I were wrapping up the final touches in preparation for a new Internet cafe that we were about to open. I unboxed my brand-new US Robotics Sportster 56K dial-up modem, plugged it into my main computer, and waited to test my Internet connection. This was the moment that I had been waiting for.

During this time, I was still relatively new to the Internet. Having been introduced to it during my university days, I understood how powerful it was. My classmates and I used it to send physics lab reports to each other, either through email or simple FTP. I skipped libraries and started using Lycos and AltaVista to do my research. I used it to create a simple website on GeoCities that functioned like a resume. I knew I chanced upon a gold mine that no one in my university (nor my city) was fully aware of. But this was nothing quite like what I saw when I turned on my computer and connected to the Internet.

An ad on my Yahoo Mail popped up about a new service offering from Dialpad: free international phone calls worldwide from the comforts of your own desk. I initially thought this was insane. You see, back in those days, to make international phone calls, you would have to dial a number that connects you to a trunk line or an operator who will make the call on your behalf. Plus, it costed an average of $5/minute to call a phone in San Francisco, United States, from Manila, Philippines. This Dialpad thing didn't make sense.

But I had got nothing to lose. I connected my headset to the computer, launched the Dialpad applet inside Netscape Navigator, and dialed my aunt's phone number in San Francisco. Within a few minutes, we were talking – I can hear her, she can hear me. I could not believe it. What I thought was an insane idea had become reality. And I couldn't wait to tell my parents. No more expensive phone calls to the United States.

But…

It's interesting how a technological innovation such as the Voice over Internet Protocol (VoIP) that started more than four decades ago (it was invented in 1973 but wasn't commercialized until the late 1990s) has created an entire industry. It has created job opportunities like VoIP engineers, network engineers, developers who write apps that leverage VoIP, and the like. It allowed applications that run on top of VoIP to go mainstream – the friend you called on Instagram, the conference call you hosted on Zoom or Skype, or that aunt you talked to on WhatsApp.

Every technological innovation that solves a major business pain point goes through the same process of conception, adoption, and, finally, becoming common. In the case of VoIP, the expensive and cumbersome task of making an international phone call. We technology professionals should be on the constant lookout for the next new thing, applying critical thinking as to how it can create the next industry. We need to learn how to observe the winds, watch where it is going, and adjust our sails. Or else, we run the risk of becoming obsolete and not able to advance in our careers. Mainframes and FORTRAN, anyone?

But that doesn't mean you'll be recognized by your peers as the Oracle of Tech. In fact, quite the opposite. You'll be ridiculed, mocked, scorned, or even considered crazy. When I told my mom I could call the United States for free using the Dialpad service, she literally laughed. When I told my classmates in 1996 that robots and artificial intelligence will become mainstream, I was ridiculed. When I told my peers back in 2003 that they should look forward to having a Linux exam option added to the Microsoft Certified Systems Engineer certification, they called me crazy. It didn't help that Steve Ballmer called Linux a cancer in 2001.

This is why I described the lifecycle of a technological innovation. Because if you know how it works, it wouldn't matter what other people think or say. You are absolutely sure that it will work the way it does. Look back at the technological innovations in the last four decades. Virtualization was born out of a need to share expensive computer resources among a large group of users back in the days of the mainframe. Today, every organization leverages virtualization to run applications. The public cloud was born out of a need to treat IT as a business model to generate revenue instead of merely a cost of doing business. Today, public cloud providers are used instead of building private data centers and buying hardware.

This brings us to 2017, the year Microsoft released SQL Server 2017. It was the first version of SQL Server that ran on top of Linux. Yes, the same Linux that Steve Ballmer called a cancer in 2001 is now running the world's most popular operational database management system, according to Gartner. Even the Microsoft Azure certification exams have Linux components in them. Microsoft plus Linux is no longer a topic of April Fool's jokes. This is real. And just like the lifecycle of any technological innovation, this will become mainstream. The question is, "will you be ready when that time comes?"

Alongside the launch of SQL Server on Linux came another technological innovation already emerging: the container technology. While originally designed for the Linux operating system, containers solve a unique business problem that every IT organization has: reliably run software when moved from one computing environment to another. Imagine upgrading or migrating from a physical machine to another physical machine or to a virtual machine or to a public cloud. Even moving code from a developer's laptop to a production environment. I'm sure you've heard your developers say "but it worked in my laptop" more than a dozen times. Containers are here to eliminate these challenges.

With both technologies already available, it's not surprising to see Microsoft not only support SQL Server on Linux running in container technologies but also leverage it in their own internal development and build processes. It's only a matter of time when SQL Server on Linux running on containers becomes more common than the SQL Server on Windows that we've known for the past two-and-a-half decades.

And that's the goal of this book. SQL Server database administrators and developers like yourself who have been working with SQL Server for a while already know a thing or two about the relational database engine. You already know how SQL Server stores data on data pages, how indexes speed up (or not) queries, and how it achieves high availability. I want you to take the same knowledge and experience as you prepare yourself for the next wave of technological innovation in container technologies. Imagine you're on a journey and this book will be your guide, each chapter laying out steps along the way toward your final destination.

How This Book Is Structured

This book consists of 11 chapters with an Appendix and is structured in the following way:

- **Chapter 1** introduces you to container technologies, a bit of a history of how it started and how Microsoft adopted it for the Windows Server operating system as well as SQL Server on Linux.

- **Chapter 2** walks you through how to configure a Windows Server operating system as a container host, allowing you to leverage your existing knowledge of Windows.

- **Chapter 3** covers a bit of what you need to know to get started with the Linux operating system in preparation for configuring it to run as a container host.

- **Chapter 4** covers the Docker ecosystem to better understand how container technologies work.

- **Chapter 5** introduces you to Docker images and containers but with a focus on using them with SQL Server.

- **Chapter 6** is where managing and administering containers come in, introducing the most common operational tasks that you need to perform when working with containers.

- **Chapter 7** introduces the concept of persisting data with containers since SQL Server is designed to store and persist data.

- **Chapter 8** covers a bit of working with SQL Server on Linux, the installation and management experience to get you started with administering SQL Server on Linux and, eventually, building custom SQL Server on Linux container images.

- **Chapter 9** walks you through building a custom SQL Server on Windows container image that you can use for standardized deployments.

- **Chapter 10** walks you through building a custom SQL Server on Linux container image.

- **Chapter 11** covers a bit of Docker networking so you can better configure SQL Server on containers for interaction with other applications.

I highly recommend that you start with the **Appendix.** While it is very easy nowadays to spin up a lab environment on a public cloud infrastructure such as Amazon AWS, Microsoft Azure, or Google Cloud Platform, I don't want you to miss the experience of setting everything up from start to finish. I'm surprised to hear from senior SQL Server DBAs who have no experience installing a Windows Server operating system and configuring TCP/IP. There's nothing wrong with that. But, oftentimes, it's what determines whether an issue can easily be resolved or not.

Plus, because the network infrastructure in public cloud environments is offered as a service, there are several layers that abstract what's really going on. It can be very frustrating to try and test out something new in a safe environment only to find out that you wasted so many hours solving a problem that you have no control over or can only be solved by providing your credit card information. You're here to learn container technologies, not get into financial debt.

So, let's get started and dive into the world of container technologies.

CHAPTER 1

Introduction to Containers

Those who cannot remember the past are condemned to repeat it.

—George Santayana

Container technologies are changing the way we develop, deploy, and run software. While it may seem like a technology that came out of nowhere and is now taking over IT organizations, nothing could be further from the truth.

In this chapter, we'll travel back in time to look at a bit of the history around container technologies and how it evolved. You might be thinking: "I hated history in high school." And I can totally relate. I only read history in high school and college for the sole purpose of answering test questions. I hated memorizing names and dates. So, why even bother with the history of container technologies?

History gives us the benefit of hindsight, something you don't have when you are experiencing something for the very first time. When somebody else has already done what you are trying to accomplish, you have the benefit of the lessons they have learned, their mistakes that you can avoid, and possibly the patterns that seem to appear out of nowhere. These history lessons are full of insights that can help you better understand the technology or the world, in general. Over the years, I've learned to appreciate history and how it shaped our current reality – better yet, how I can change my present so I can shape the future.

We'll also look at the company – Docker, Inc. – behind the development of the most widely used and recognized container technology today.

Conversations around container technologies wouldn't be complete without comparing it with virtualization technologies. We'll spend a little bit of time looking at the similarities and differences between the two.

Finally, we'll look at how Microsoft adopted the container technology for both Windows and SQL Server.

1

© Edwin M Sarmiento 2020
E. M. Sarmiento, *The SQL Server DBA's Guide to Docker Containers*,
https://doi.org/10.1007/978-1-4842-5826-2_1

The Latest 30-Year-Old Technology

I was surprised when I learned that container technologies date back to 1979. It was the Unix V7 that allowed processes to run in isolation – the ability to isolate and protect one process from another – at the operating system level. The idea came about due to the need to share very expensive computing resources among many users at the same time. Think back to the days when mainframes can only do one specific task that can take days or even weeks to run.

However, like any other technological innovation that didn't get as much adoption, process isolation technologies became stagnant. It wasn't until the year 2000 when the Unix-like operating system FreeBSD introduced Jails – a mechanism to partition a computer system into several independent mini-systems, each with its own files, processes, and security. You can think of this as the early days of the virtualization technologies that we know of today.

Several variations of implementing process isolation technologies evolved afterward, including the Linux VServer in 2001 (a patch to the Linux kernel that allowed operating system–level virtualization), Solaris Containers in 2004 (former Sun Microsystems' implementation of operating system–level virtualization), and Open Virtuozzo in 2005. In 2006, Google came up with their own addition to the Linux kernel and named it Process Containers, later renaming it to Control Groups (*cgroups*) to avoid confusion with the word container in the context of the Linux containers.

The year 2008 became the pivotal moment for the evolution of container technologies when the Linux Containers (LXC) project was created, merging the work that Google engineers have done in cgroups into the Linux kernel. It allowed for running multiple isolated Linux systems on a host using a single Linux kernel – without the need for an additional patch.

The LXC became the building block of the modern container technologies that came after it. In 2011, VMWare with EMC and General Electric started an open source initiative named Cloud Foundry Warden for managing a collection of containers across multiple hosts. In 2013, Google created yet another open source version of their container stack called lmctfy (which stands for Let Me Contain That For You) and have since collaborated with Docker, Inc. for the development of the container runtime environment, *libcontainer*.

Container technologies may seem like the latest technology that is sweeping the IT world. The fact of the matter is that it isn't new. It was just way ahead of its time. And now that its time has arrived, you just cannot afford to ignore it.

Docker – The Company and the Container Runtime

Docker is to container runtime engine much like how VMWare is to virtualization or Red Hat is to Linux – it has become a huge brand name in the IT world. The Docker runtime engine was developed by the company Docker, Inc. The company didn't start out as a development company. In fact, they started as a platform-as-a-service company that allowed developers to build and run apps without worrying about the underlying infrastructure. Unfortunately, the company was struggling to generate revenue and pay their bills. The good thing about it is that they learned how to make the most out of the situation they were in.

While Docker, Inc. was having financial difficulties, the engineers decided to open source the underlying technology – Docker, the container runtime engine – behind their platform-as-a-service offering in 2013. They didn't expect it to take off. And when it did, the company pivoted their business and focused on Docker. They even changed their name from dotCloud, the original name when the company was founded, to Docker, Inc. Thus, the modern container technology was born. Early versions of Docker leveraged LXC as the container runtime engine. Later versions use libcontainer.

It's interesting to see how Docker pivoted from a struggling business to what can now be considered a profitable software company. We, IT professionals, need to learn from their example. We need to learn how to pivot when the need arise. Learn emerging technologies instead of settling for old ones so long as they meet business objectives. We need to learn how to pivot our roles from purely technical to more of leadership. And since technology is constantly evolving, we need to evolve with it, changing roles whenever necessary.

This is key to success in the IT industry.

The Case for Containers

We IT professionals like to geek out on technology because they are cool and fun. It's easy to fall into the trap of focusing on technology for technology's sake. But realize that every successful technology is meant to solve a business problem. To be successful as an IT professional, we need to focus on the business problem that a technology solution is meant to solve.

So what business problem does container technology solve? Reliably run software when moved from one computing environment to another. SQL Server administrators deal with this every time a database is migrated or upgraded from one platform to another – from physical machine to another physical machine, from physical machine to virtual machine, from older version to newer version, or from on-premises to the cloud. A more common scenario is when a developer writes T-SQL code from their development environment and promotes the code in staging environment and even production. Even with a proper change management process, this can still be an issue because there is no guarantee that the different computing environments will be the same. Configuration drift accounts for many high availability and disaster recovery system failures that I have to deal with as a consultant.

Container technology addresses this problem. It does so by packaging an application and all of its dependencies like binaries, kernel libraries, configuration files, system tools, and so on and creating an entire runtime environment. A container image is created and packaged with the application and all of its dependencies. The image is then deployed as a container at runtime.

Containers vs. Virtualization

At first glance, it may seem that containers look a lot like virtualization given their nature and functionality. Don't be confused. Have a look at the diagram of the hypervisor architecture in Figure 1-1.

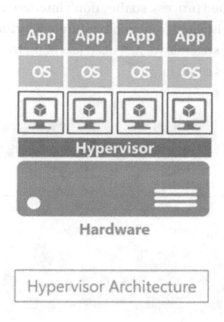

Figure 1-1. *Hypervisor architecture*

In the world of virtualization, you run a hypervisor – VMWare, Hyper-V, Xen, and so on – on top of a hardware. You, then, create a virtual machine with its own operating system before you can install and run your application. Each virtual machine is configured to use a portion of the hardware's CPU, memory, network, and storage resources. For years, virtualization solved a major business problem that the IT organization faced: overprovisioning physical hardware. In the past, we simply guessed and overprovisioned the specifications of the physical machine, letting it run while barely using even a quarter of the hardware resources. Virtualization allowed us to create multiple virtual machines on a single physical machine to maximize every bit of hardware resource available. It also allowed for process and application isolation – they run within the boundaries of the virtual machine. This made the finance people very happy. But not us.

We spend a huge amount of time managing operating systems – patching, securing, monitoring, updating, auditing, licensing, and even allocating resources for them. It's like managing operating systems has become a business unit on its own. We're not in the business of managing operating systems, but our day-to-day tasks sure seem like we are. Wouldn't it be great if you only had one operating system that runs the different applications but in an isolated process, so they don't interfere with one another, much like how one application is isolated from another through virtual machines? We don't need to get rid of operating systems, we just need less of them.

This is where containers come in.

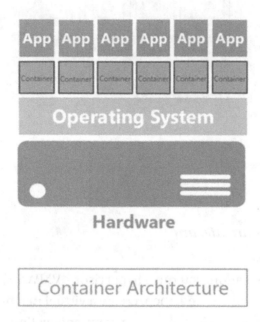

Figure 1-2. *Container architecture*

In Figure 1-2, you only have one operating system. The containers share the same operating system kernel with other containers, each one running as isolated processes in user space. Containers abstract the operating system kernel instead of abstracting the hardware like what virtualization does. Imagine the impact this has on your resources. Instead of having multiple copies of the operating system running on guest virtual machines, you only have a single copy, thus reducing the amount of storage space requirement. You are also reducing the amount of administrative overhead necessary with managing operating systems. If you have ever had to work during the weekends and holidays just to install that critical security patch on all of your servers, you know how big of a deal this is. Plus, given the resource requirements for containers, you can run more of them in a single host compared to virtual machines.

Microsoft, Containers, and SQL Server on Linux

In the short period that I had working as an Oracle DBA, I made my own decision to pivot. Back then, Oracle was the name when it comes to relational databases. My peers were moving into Oracle and Java. But I decided to go the opposite way – I switched to Microsoft SQL Server and .NET. I did it because I saw how Microsoft did software, focusing more on the users rather than merely the technology. They created user interfaces, accessible documentation, tutorials, blog posts, online communities, and the like. The hard-core geeks made fun of it. But customers loved it. So, I pivoted.

The year was 2015. At the annual Microsoft MVP Summit, I was listening to Microsoft executives from the database systems group talk about a project that they were working on. They called it Project Helsinki. The mission is to bring SQL Server to Linux. Microsoft had customers asking whether they would make SQL Server available on Linux. The executives talked about how the next generation of developers didn't really care about the underlying operating system – they just want a data platform. Microsoft was still focusing on the customers.

When SQL Server 2017 was released, it was made available for both Windows and Linux. It was no longer an April Fool's joke (I wish they did not release it on April 1st). This was real. SQL Server 2017 was the first version that ran on Windows, Linux, and Docker containers. I immediately downloaded and installed SQL Server on my CentOS Linux virtual machine, and within a few minutes, I was able to connect to it remotely using my SQL Server Management Studio installation on my Windows 8 machine.

Tip   The Apress book *Pro SQL Server on Linux* by Bob Ward provides a back story on how Microsoft managed to make this seemingly impossible task a reality.

It was also during this time that Microsoft incorporated the Docker engine in the Windows Server 2016 operating system – Windows Server Containers. They partnered with Docker, Inc. to create a container runtime engine that is native inside the Windows Server operating system. Since Docker is open source, it allowed Microsoft to make modifications to it and make it work on Windows.

Open source, Microsoft, SQL Server on Linux, Containers. I'm sure the Steve Ballmer of 2001 didn't see this coming.

Summary

As container technology is taking over the IT landscape, administrators need to be prepared to modernize their SQL Server databases and deploy them on newer platforms like Linux, specifically Docker containers. This is the goal of this book.

In the next chapter, we will look at how to leverage container technologies in a platform that SQL Server administrators are familiar with – the Windows Server operating system.

CHAPTER 2

Install and Configure Docker on Windows Server

Learning is the creation of a relationship between the known and the unknown.

—Tony Robbins

The previous chapter introduced the container technology, its origins, and how SQL Server now runs on Linux and Docker containers. But for someone who has minimal to no experience with Linux, this can be a bit overwhelming. So, instead of jumping straight into Linux, this chapter will help you get started with Docker containers using a platform that you are already familiar with – the Windows Server operating system. Microsoft partnered with Docker, Inc. to bring Docker containers on the Windows Server operating system, making it easy for Windows and SQL Server administrators to learn and deploy Docker containers.

We will be using Windows Server 2016 Build 1607 for this chapter, but later versions such as 1709 and 1803 can be used as well. However, you certainly don't want to be learning container technologies while having to deal with the issues of prerelease software. Trust me, I lost a lot of hair in the early 2000s dealing with prerelease software.

© Edwin M Sarmiento 2020
E. M. Sarmiento, *The SQL Server DBA's Guide to Docker Containers*,
https://doi.org/10.1007/978-1-4842-5826-2_2

Note   This chapter does not go into the process of installing the Windows Server operating system. It is assumed that an existing clean installation of a Windows Server 2016 is available and has Internet connectivity. For a walk-through of installing Windows Server 2016, refer to *Appendix A*.

Also, the default Windows Server installation will opt for Server Core, unless you specifically choose Desktop Experience. You will be working with the command line when you start working with Docker and Linux so just stick with the graphical user interface on Windows for now.

Minimum System Requirements

Like any software installation, you need to meet the minimum system requirements to successfully use a Windows Server operating system as a *Docker container host*. A Docker container host is the operating system that runs the Docker *daemon* (a daemon is simply the Linux equivalent of a service in Windows).

- *RAM*: At least 4GB. You don't want to end up spending a lot of time troubleshooting a container deployment issue only to find out that you don't have enough memory resources. Plus, a SQL Server instance will use up as much memory resource as it possibly can. It's the same behavior when running it in a container.

- *Operating system*: Just because we're using Windows Server 2016 doesn't mean that's all you need to know. Remember, containers share the same operating system kernel. This means the operating system of the container host should support the operating system of the container image. Since we're deploying a Windows Server 2016 container host, you can only deploy a Windows Server 2016 container image running Server Core or Nano Server. We'll skip Nano Server since SQL Server is not supported to run on top of Nano Server.

- *Disk space*: The bare minimum is 32GB. Much like virtual machines, each container image requires its own disk space. Allocate enough disk space so you can run multiple containers at the same time.

Enable Containers Feature in Windows Server 2016

Installing and configuring a Docker container host on a Windows Server 2016 machine is a three-step process. You need the machine to be connected to the Internet to download the binaries, the PowerShell packages, and the Windows-based container images.

The first step is to enable the Containers feature on Windows Server 2016:

1. From the *Start* menu, select *Server Manager.*

2. In Server Manager Dashboard, click the *Add roles and features* link. This will run the *Add Roles and Features Wizard.*

3. Click Next until you get to the *Select features* dialog box. Select the *Containers* checkbox as shown in Figure 2-1 and click Next. Note that the *.NET Framework 4.6 Features* checkbox is selected by default on Windows Server 2016 Build 1607. If it isn't, expand the *.NET Framework 4.6 Features* checkbox and make sure that *.NET Framework 4.6 (Installed)* is shown.

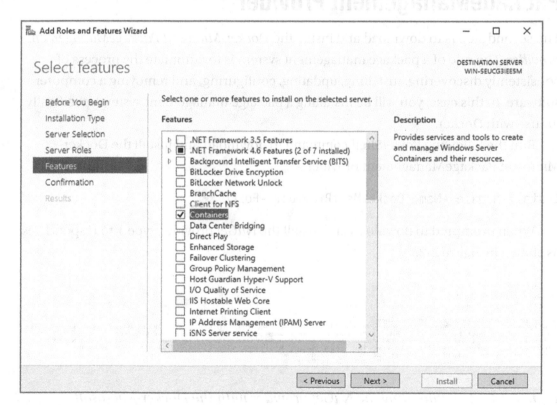

Figure 2-1. *Check the Containers checkbox in the Select features dialog box*

4. In the *Confirm installation selections* dialog box, click Install.

Since you will be working with Docker commands via the command line – both on Windows and Linux – this is a great opportunity to start working with the command line from within a Windows environment. Embrace the blinking cursor and get comfortable with it. An alternative to enabling the Containers feature is by using the `Install-WindowsFeature` PowerShell cmdlet. Open an elevated administrative PowerShell command shell and run the following command:

```
Install-WindowsFeature –Name Containers
```

You will be prompted to restart the machine after enabling the Containers feature to complete the installation process. Either you perform the restart using the method you're familiar with or use the `Restart-Computer` PowerShell cmdlet.

Download and Install the Docker-Microsoft PackageManagement Provider

The second step is to download and install the *Docker-Microsoft PackageManagement provider*. The role of a package management system is to automate the process of consistently discovering, installing, updating, configuring, and removing a computer software. In this case, you will be installing a package management system specifically for use with Docker.

Run the following PowerShell command to download and install the Docker-Microsoft PackageManagement provider:

```
Install-Module -Name DockerMsftProvider -Force
```

When prompted to download and install the *NuGet* provider, type *Y* to respond Yes, as shown in Figure 2-2.

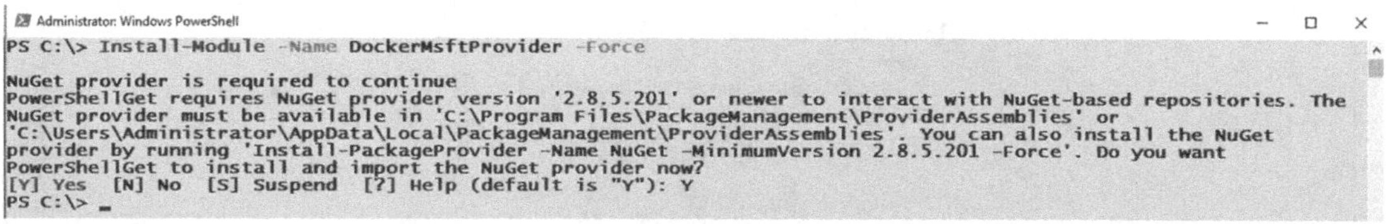

Figure 2-2. *Downloading the NuGet provider with the Docker-Microsoft PackageManagement provider*

Note   The topic of package management systems can be a bit confusing for IT professionals who mainly work on the Windows platform. For years, software on Windows was distributed through EXE, MSI, and MSU files – just download the installation file, double-click, and install. This isn't the case with Linux. Given the open source nature of Linux and the availability of software from different sources, package managers are used to install and manage software. PowerShell 5.0 introduced the capability to leverage a package manager to simplify the complexity of installing software and PowerShell modules.

If you want to geek out on the details of how the Docker-Microsoft PackageManagement provider is implemented, check out the GitHub repository at *https://github.com/OneGet/MicrosoftDockerProvider.*

Download and Install the Docker Package

The third step is to download and install the Docker software package. Run the following PowerShell command to download and install the Docker software package using the Docker-Microsoft PackageManagement provider that you downloaded in the previous step. Figure 2-3 shows a successful installation of Docker Enterprise Edition (EE).

```
Install-Package -Name docker -ProviderName DockerMsftProvider -Force
```

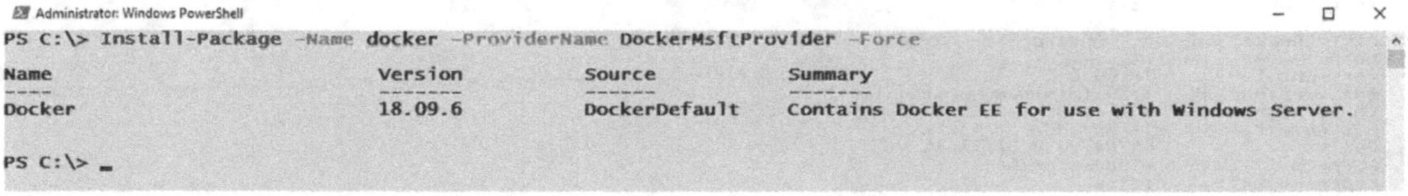

Figure 2-3. Downloading and installing the Docker software package

This will create a Windows service named *Docker Engine* that calls the command "C:\Program Files\Docker\dockerd.exe" --run-service

The service is configured to automatically start when the server starts, but the installation process does not explicitly start the service. This is where you need to do the unpopular server reboot to update the environment variables so you can run Docker commands from either the command prompt or the PowerShell command shell. Don't worry. This will be the last time you need to reboot your server.

Verifying the Docker Engine Installation

I did say you need to start being comfortable working with the command line. From here onward, you will be working with the command line – either the command prompt or PowerShell command shell. I prefer using PowerShell so I can leverage the available PowerShell cmdlets alongside the Docker commands. Just remember that the output of a PowerShell command or cmdlet is either an object or a collection of objects, while the output of a Docker command is text. Also, run every command in an elevated administrative PowerShell command shell.

Run the following command to check the version of Docker installed on the server:

```
docker version
```

Figure 2-4 shows the output of the command, displaying the version of the Docker client and the Docker engine running on the machine.

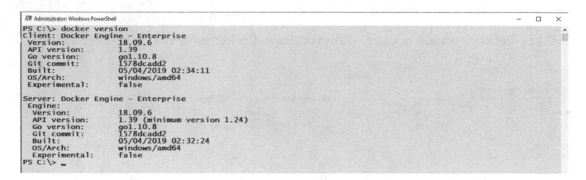

Figure 2-4. *Displaying the version of Docker client and Docker engine*

The *OS/Arch:* properties for both client and server show *windows/amd64* since the Docker engine is running on a Windows Server 2016 machine. Also, what was installed is the Docker Engine – Enterprise Edition. This means that you have full support from both Microsoft and Docker when you deploy containers on your Docker host. In fact, even though the Docker engine is the one responsible for running containers on a Windows Server machine, Microsoft is the first point of contact for support. Chapter 4 describes the difference between Docker Enterprise Edition and Docker Community Edition in more detail.

Run the following command to display system-wide information regarding the docker installation on the server. Figure 2-5 shows the output of the command.

```
docker info
```

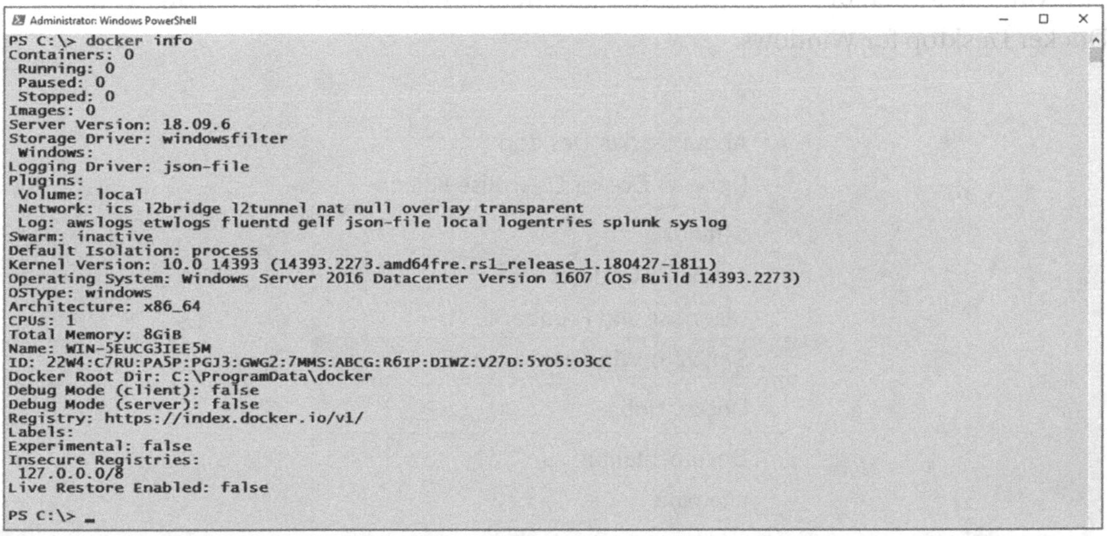

Figure 2-5. *Displaying the system-wide information of the Docker installation*

At this point, your Windows Server 2016 machine is a fully functional Docker container host.

Docker Desktop for Windows

The idea behind using a server operating system for deploying a Docker container host instead of a desktop operating system like Windows 10 is to get you to experience how it is like to deploy Docker in "the real world," much like how data center engineers would deploy it in a production environment. Understanding the underlying infrastructure that runs an application helps you become a more well-rounded IT professional.

Docker Desktop for Windows is what most developers use to get started with learning Docker on a Windows operating system. It is a native Windows application that leverages Hyper-V virtualization. I like to think of it as some form of nested virtualization – it will create a MobyLinux virtual machine inside the Hyper-V host. The MobyLinux virtual machine will run as a Docker container host to run Linux-based containers. But because it's a native Windows application, you can run Windows-based containers directly on the host. You can switch between running Linux-based and Windows-based containers with Docker Desktop for Windows. Figures 2-6 and 2-7 show how you can switch between Windows containers and Linux containers from within Docker Desktop for Windows.

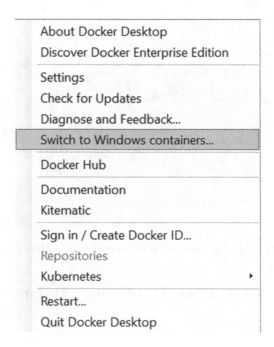

Figure 2-6. *Switching to Windows containers*

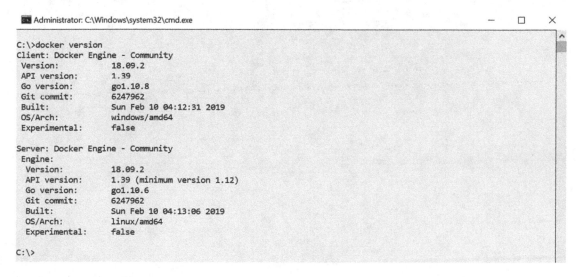

About Docker Desktop
Discover Docker Enterprise Edition

Settings
Check for Updates
Diagnose and Feedback...
Switch to Linux containers...

Docker Hub

Documentation
Kitematic

Sign in / Create Docker ID...
Repositories

Restart...
Quit Docker Desktop

Figure 2-7. *Switching to Linux containers*

Running the docker version command displays different results depending on whether you're running Linux or Windows containers. Figure 2-8 shows the output of the command when running Linux containers. Notice that the OS/Arch: property of the client is *windows/amd64* while that of the server is *linux/amd64* (this is the MobyLinux virtual machine that was created to run on top of Hyper-V).

```
Administrator: C:\Windows\system32\cmd.exe                               —    □    ×

C:\>docker version
Client: Docker Engine - Community
 Version:           18.09.2
 API version:       1.39
 Go version:        go1.10.8
 Git commit:        6247962
 Built:             Sun Feb 10 04:12:31 2019
 OS/Arch:           windows/amd64
 Experimental:      false

Server: Docker Engine - Community
 Engine:
  Version:          18.09.2
  API version:      1.39 (minimum version 1.12)
  Go version:       go1.10.6
  Git commit:       6247962
  Built:            Sun Feb 10 04:13:06 2019
  OS/Arch:          linux/amd64
  Experimental:     false

C:\>
```

Figure 2-8. *Docker Desktop on Windows – client and server details (Linux containers)*

The installation of Docker Desktop on Windows is straightforward. Just download and run the installation file from the Docker Hub.

Should any of your developer colleagues want to try out Docker, Docker Desktop on Windows is what you recommend. We big boys play with real toys – servers, that is.

Summary

This chapter walked you through the process of installing and configuring a Windows Server 2016 as a Docker container host. The server is now ready to run any Windows-based containers that have the same operating system kernel as Windows Server 2016. Note that this is the same setup as you would deploy in a production environment, minus all custom configuration that your organization requires for security, reliability, and standardization.

And while Docker was initially created for the Linux operating system, you didn't have to learn anything Linux – yet. That's what's up in the next chapter. So, buckle up. It's time to dive into the world of Linux.

CHAPTER 3

Install and Configure Docker on Linux

The key to life is accepting challenges. Once someone stops doing this, he's dead.

—Bette Davis

I still cannot believe I'm writing this chapter – about Linux, for SQL Server DBAs. In Chapter 1, I mentioned how Microsoft brought SQL Server to Linux in 2017. That came as a big surprise to a lot of SQL Server DBAs who have only known SQL Server as a relational database engine that runs on a Windows operating system. But just like any technological innovation, you can either choose to embrace it or ignore it. Embracing it gives you an opportunity to grow and take your career to a whole new level.

I'm assuming you have very little to no experience with Linux. So, we'll start with getting yourself familiar with Linux – knowing the simple and basic commands that you need to work with the operating system, the filesystem, and Docker. That means spending majority of the time working with the command line. You also need to change your way of thinking when it comes to security. You'll see that in action when we get to the section on updating your Linux system.

Once you've gotten a little bit comfortable with Linux, we will go ahead and install and configure the Docker engine on Linux. Unlike Windows, Linux has so many distributions (or distros, as they are commonly known) available, making it challenging to know every single one of them. We will only focus on two Linux distros – CentOS and Ubuntu. Apart from consistently being in the top ten list of the most popular Linux server distros, these are two out of three that Microsoft support for running SQL Server on Linux. CentOS is a free, enterprise-class, community-supported distribution based

© Edwin M Sarmiento 2020
E. M. Sarmiento, *The SQL Server DBA's Guide to Docker Containers*,
https://doi.org/10.1007/978-1-4842-5826-2_3

on Red Hat Enterprise Linux (RHEL). You get the experience of working on a RHEL-like Linux distribution without the price of an enterprise support agreement. Ubuntu, on the other hand, is a popular Linux distro for developers that is based on Debian GNU/Linux. We still need to keep developers happy, don't we?

To make learning Linux a little bit easier, pick a distro and stick to it. You can learn other distros once you feel comfortable with your first choice.

Note   Same as Chapter 2, this chapter does not go into the process of installing a Linux operating system. That is what *Appendix A* is for. This chapter assumes that you already have a clean installation of either a CentOS or Ubuntu Linux server with a secure shell (SSH) client configured to connect remotely to the machines.

Minimum System Requirements

Unlike Windows, Linux does not require a lot of system resources to run. So, if you follow the minimum system requirements for running Docker on Windows Server, you'll be fine.

- *RAM*: At least 4GB. The reason why I always start with 4GB of RAM even on a Linux machine is because I assume it will be running SQL Server. My Linux sysadmin colleagues laughed at me years ago for doing this. I can't blame them. But, back then, nobody dreamed of running SQL Server on Linux. Besides, 2GB is the minimum memory requirement for running SQL Server on Linux.

- *Operating system*: There are other supported Linux distros you can use. Docker supports a minimum of CentOS 7 (you need at least version 7.4 for RHEL) and Ubuntu Server Xenial 16.04 (LTS). To get you started on running Docker on Linux, we will be using CentOS 7.6 (1810) and Ubuntu Server Xenial 16.04 (LTS). You can download the CentOS ISO image from *www.centos.org/download/* and the Ubuntu Server Xenial ISO image from *http://releases.ubuntu.com/16.04/*. Be sure to select the *Server install image* and not the *Desktop image* for Ubuntu.

- *Disk space*: You will be surprised at the disk space requirements for Linux – even when running SQL Server. You will see in *Chapter 5* the difference in disk space requirements between a container running SQL Server on Linux and SQL Server on Windows. 20GB is my bare minimum for any Linux installation.

Note   There really isn't an official supported minimum system requirement for running the Docker engine on a Linux operating system. I spent hours searching the Docker documentation for what they consider a supported minimum system requirement. What you'll find, however, is the minimum system requirements for running Docker Universal Control Plane – the cluster management solution for multi-host Docker clusters. Save that for a more advanced configuration since you're in the early stages of learning Docker.

Basic Linux Commands You Need to Get Started

This is not a book about Linux. The purpose of this book is not to turn you into a full-blown Linux geek (although I'm not going to stop you from being one). However, since you will be deploying Docker on a Linux operating system, you need to learn a few basic commands, just enough to get you started. Once you're comfortable working with Linux, you can get deeper on some of these commands.

I used to refer to the Linux man (short for manual) pages for documentation on any command that I would like to use. Now, a few keystrokes and your favorite search engine are all you need – the Internet has everything you need.

The goal in this chapter is to install and configure Docker on Linux. The following are the Linux commands that you need to accomplish this task:

> *sudo*: Short for "substitute user, do." A security best practice in Linux is to log in as an ordinary user, not the superuser (or root). *Root* is like the local administrator account in Windows – it can do just about anything. Since you're not going to log in using the *root* account, you must prefix all administrative commands with *sudo* (nobody's going to stop you from logging in as *root* but, please, I beg you not to). By default, this will switch the security context of your interactive shell user to that of *root*.

yum: Short for Yellow Update Manager, a package management utility developed by Red Hat for installation, updates, and removal for Red Hat package manager (RPM) systems. This is the package management utility available on both RHEL and CentOS.

yum-config-manager: A utility to manage package repositories, commonly on RHEL/CentOS systems.

apt-get: Used with the Advanced Package Tool (APT). It's Ubuntu and other Debian-based Linux's version of yum. For managing packages on Ubuntu, this is the tool of choice.

add-apt-repository: Utility for adding a repository on Ubuntu and other Debian-based Linux distros.

ls: Linux's version of *dir* on Windows, used to list directories and the files in them.

grep: Comes from the name **g**lobally search a **r**egular **e**xpression and **p**rint. A tool for searching plaintext data sets for lines that match a regular expression. I use this mostly to search either a text file or an output of a command for specific text.

cat: Short for catenate. A utility used to process files such as reading a text file and displaying its contents, copying contents of a text file into another file, or combining contents of multiple files. I use this a lot for displaying contents of files on the screen.

systemctl: A command used to manage *systemd* – a system and service management utility on Linux. You use this to stop, start, restart, and check status of daemons on Linux.

Also be sure to learn the pipe operator (|). You use the *pipe* operator to send output from one command to another. It's like the *pipe* operator in PowerShell.

Be sure to remember your password! You will be running *sudo* a lot to run other commands, so you had better remember your password. And, please don't write it on a Post-it note or a piece of paper for everyone to see. I'll shoot you with a Nerf gun if I see you. I recommend using a password manager to store your login information. LastPass is a popular password manager for Windows that stores encrypted password online.

There are other Linux packages that you need to install, and each one of them has their own syntax. Usage of these packages will be covered later in the chapter where they are needed.

Installing Docker on CentOS Linux

The process of installing Docker on CentOS is a little bit different from that of Ubuntu. So, I decided to break the installation process down into two sections – one for CentOS and one for Ubuntu. Should you decide to install Docker on a CentOS machine, this section outlines the process for you.

Update the CentOS System Packages

Use the following *yum* command to update all installed packages with available updates. The following example command demonstrates the use of the Linux commands you've learned in the previous section:

```
sudo yum update
```

Here, you prefix the *yum* command with the *sudo* command, so you can run it in the security context of the root user. And like most Linux commands, the *yum* command has several subcommands that you can use to perform tasks. The *update* subcommand is used to update all installed packages. Think of this as the CentOS equivalent of running Windows Updates.

Notice the prompt for password when you run the command in Figure 3-1. This is the password of the currently logged in user who wants to run the command, not of the root user.

Figure 3-1. *Password prompt for running Linux commands with sudo*

As a security best practice, this is how you will be running commands in Linux.

Depending on the state of your CentOS machine, running yum update may require you to download all the necessary updates. Figure 3-2 shows a prompt to install and upgrade all the necessary packages on the system.

```
selinux-policy                    noarch          3.13.1-229.el7_6.12           updates          484 k
selinux-policy-targeted           noarch          3.13.1-229.el7_6.12           updates          6.9 M
shadow-utils                      x86_64          2:4.1.5.1-25.el7_6.1          updates          1.1 M
systemd                           x86_64          219-62.el7_6.6                updates          5.1 M
systemd-libs                      x86_64          219-62.el7_6.6                updates          407 k
systemd-sysv                      x86_64          219-62.el7_6.6                updates           84 k
tuned                             noarch          2.10.0-6.el7_6.3              updates          254 k
tzdata                            noarch          2019a-1.el7                   updates          494 k
util-linux                        x86_64          2.23.2-59.el7_6.1             updates          2.0 M
xfsprogs                          x86_64          4.5.0-19.el7_6                updates          897 k

Transaction Summary
================================================================================
Install    1 Package
Upgrade   66 Packages

Total download size: 133 M
Is this ok [y/d/N]: 
```

Figure 3-2. *Prompt to download all the necessary packages*

Type *y* to download and install all the updates.

Install the Required Dependencies

One thing I like about Linux is that using package managers will install what you tell it to, including the required dependencies. This practice reduces the disk space requirements and potential attack surface. So, when you have a package like Docker that depends on other packages, you need to either manually install those other packages or install Docker using a package manager that automates the installing of dependent packages. You only have to do the installation of all the packages once, though.

You need to install several packages that Docker depends on. These other packages are

> *yum-utils*: This is more of an extension to the *yum* command. It's a collection of tools that integrate with *yum* to perform tasks such as managing repositories, installing debugging packages, cleaning up packages, and the like. You can think of this as *yum* on steroids.

> *device-mapper-persistent-data*: This package provides storage virtualization and abstraction capabilities for Linux. Docker's own Device Mapper storage driver leverages this package's capabilities for advanced volume and storage management. *Chapter 5* covers how the filesystem works when working with Docker containers in more detail.

lvm2: The LVM2 or Logical Volume Manager package provides common logical volume management for the Linux kernel such as RAID configuration, volume resizing, volume snapshots, and the like. Think of this as Linux's version of Windows' Disk Management utility.

Run each of the following yum `install` commands to install the required dependencies:

```
sudo yum install yum-utils
sudo yum install device-mapper-persistent-data
sudo yum install lvm2
```

If you're as lazy as I am, you can run the following single yum `install` command to do the same:

```
sudo yum install yum-utils device-mapper-persistent-data lvm2
```

Add the Docker Stable Repository to Your System

In Linux, a repository (or repo) is a location from which your machine retrieves and installs OS and application updates. Think of *yum* as Apple iTunes and repos as the Apple App Store. When you install an app on your phone, the package manager takes care of locating the repo, installing, updating, and even deleting the app. You don't have to worry about where the app can be downloaded from.

But since your system is not aware of additional packages that you want to install other than those that came preinstalled, you must define the repo. This tells Linux where to find the package during installation.

Run the following *yum-config-manager* command to add the Docker stable repository to your system:

```
sudo yum-config-manager --add-repo https://download.docker.com/linux/
centos/docker-ce.repo
```

Figure 3-3 shows the docker-ce.repo file being downloaded from the URL source and added to the */etc/yum.repos.d/* directory.

```
emsarmiento@CENTOSDOCKER01:~                                                    —  σ  ×
[emsarmiento@CENTOSDOCKER01 ~]$ sudo yum-config-manager --add-repo https://download.docker.com/linux/centos/docker
-ce.repo
Loaded plugins: fastestmirror
adding repo from: https://download.docker.com/linux/centos/docker-ce.repo
grabbing file https://download.docker.com/linux/centos/docker-ce.repo to /etc/yum.repos.d/docker-ce.repo
repo saved to /etc/yum.repos.d/docker-ce.repo
[emsarmiento@CENTOSDOCKER01 ~]$ █
```

***Figure 3-3.** Adding the Docker Community Edition repo*

Run the following *cat* command if you're curious to know what's inside the docker-ce.repo file:

```
sudo cat /etc/yum.repos.d/docker-ce.repo
```

Figure 3-4 displays the content of the docker-ce.repo file. It shows you the URL sources of the Docker CE packages for CentOS Linux.

***Figure 3-4.** The docker-ce.repo file*

Note   You might be wondering why we're working with Docker CE (Community Edition) on Linux instead of the Docker EE (Enterprise Edition) like on a Windows Server machine. Docker CE is the free, open source version of Docker that you can use without having to pay for licenses nor support. This means you can deploy a Docker container host on an open source Linux distro like CentOS with no software-related cost. Deploying a Docker container host on a Windows Server machine requires a Windows Server license. And since you're already paying for a Windows Server license, Microsoft decided to bundle Docker EE instead of Docker CE.

Install Docker CE

After updating your system and adding the Docker CE repo, you can now install the Docker CE package. Run the following command to download and install the Docker CE installation package for CentOS:

```
sudo yum install docker-ce
```

Type *y* when prompted to download the GPG key for CentOS from the Docker repo.

There are other dependent packages that will be installed alongside Docker. Figure 3-5 shows a list of package dependencies that will be installed as part of installing Docker. The two packages worth noting are *docker-ce-cli*, the Docker client command-line interface, and *containerd.io*, the one responsible for managing the complete lifecycle of a container on the Docker host.

```
emsarmiento@CENTOSDOCKER01:~                                              –  □  ×

Dependencies Resolved

================================================================================
 Package                Arch       Version            Repository          Size
================================================================================
Installing:
 docker-ce              x86_64     3:18.09.7-3.el7     docker-ce-stable    19 M
Installing for dependencies:
 audit-libs-python      x86_64     2.8.4-4.el7         base                76 k
 checkpolicy            x86_64     2.5-8.el7           base               295 k
 container-selinux      noarch     2:2.99-1.el7_6      extras              39 k
 containerd.io          x86_64     1.2.6-3.3.el7       docker-ce-stable    26 M
 docker-ce-cli          x86_64     1:18.09.7-3.el7     docker-ce-stable    14 M
 libcgroup              x86_64     0.41-20.el7         base                66 k
 libsemanage-python     x86_64     2.5-14.el7          base               113 k
 policycoreutils-python x86_64     2.5-29.el7_6.1      updates            456 k
 python-IPy             noarch     0.75-6.el7          base                32 k
 setools-libs           x86_64     3.3.8-4.el7         base               620 k
```

Figure 3-5. *List of dependent packages when installing Docker*

The installation will create a Linux daemon named *docker* on the system. By default, the *docker* daemon is disabled. Run the following *systemctl* command to check the status of the *docker* daemon. Figure 3-6 shows the status of the *docker* daemon after installation. A status of *Active: inactive (dead)* is a giveaway.

```
sudo systemctl status docker
```

```
[emsarmiento@CENTOSDOCKER01 ~]$ sudo systemctl status docker
å docker.service - Docker Application Container Engine
   Loaded: loaded (/usr/lib/systemd/system/docker.service; disabled; vendor preset: disabled)
   Active: inactive (dead)
     Docs: https://docs.docker.com
[emsarmiento@CENTOSDOCKER01 ~]$ 
```

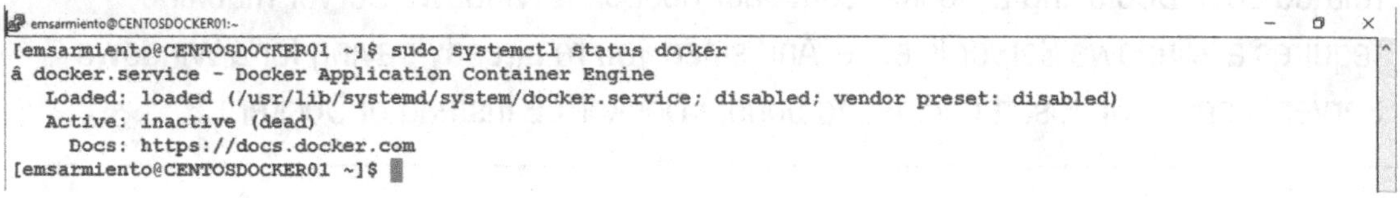

Figure 3-6. *Status of Docker daemon*

Starting the Docker Daemon and Enabling on Startup

Run the following command to start the *docker* daemon:

```
sudo systemctl start docker
```

And much like on a Windows Server installation, you want the *docker* daemon to automatically start on server reboot. Run the following command to enable the *docker* daemon to automatically start when the server starts or is rebooted:

```
sudo systemctl enable docker
```

This time, when you rerun the same command to check the status, you'll see a status of *Active: active (running)*. Figure 3-7 shows the status of the *docker* daemon with a snippet of the log.

```
emsarmiento@CENTOSDOCKER01:~                                                         -   □   ×
[emsarmiento@CENTOSDOCKER01 ~]$ sudo systemctl status docker
â docker.service - Docker Application Container Engine
   Loaded: loaded (/usr/lib/systemd/system/docker.service; enabled; vendor preset: disabled)
   Active: active (running) since Fri 2019-06-28 11:51:55 EDT; 3min 33s ago
     Docs: https://docs.docker.com
 Main PID: 1828 (dockerd)
   CGroup: /system.slice/docker.service
           ââ1828 /usr/bin/dockerd -H fd:// --containerd=/run/containerd/containerd.sock

Jun 28 11:51:52 CENTOSDOCKER01 dockerd[1828]: time="2019-06-28T11:51:52.712188511-04:00" level=info msg="pi...grpc
Jun 28 11:51:52 CENTOSDOCKER01 dockerd[1828]: time="2019-06-28T11:51:52.712365516-04:00" level=info msg="pi...grpc
Jun 28 11:51:53 CENTOSDOCKER01 dockerd[1828]: time="2019-06-28T11:51:53.097790637-04:00" level=info msg="Gr...nds"
Jun 28 11:51:53 CENTOSDOCKER01 dockerd[1828]: time="2019-06-28T11:51:53.098826766-04:00" level=info msg="Lo...rt."
Jun 28 11:51:54 CENTOSDOCKER01 dockerd[1828]: time="2019-06-28T11:51:54.242727787-04:00" level=info msg="De...ess"
Jun 28 11:51:54 CENTOSDOCKER01 dockerd[1828]: time="2019-06-28T11:51:54.939488570-04:00" level=info msg="Lo...ne."
Jun 28 11:51:55 CENTOSDOCKER01 dockerd[1828]: time="2019-06-28T11:51:55.235062592-04:00" level=info msg="Do...09.7
Jun 28 11:51:55 CENTOSDOCKER01 dockerd[1828]: time="2019-06-28T11:51:55.235566306-04:00" level=info msg="Da...ion"
Jun 28 11:51:55 CENTOSDOCKER01 dockerd[1828]: time="2019-06-28T11:51:55.671973346-04:00" level=info msg="AP...ock"
Jun 28 11:51:55 CENTOSDOCKER01 systemd[1]: Started Docker Application Container Engine.
Hint: Some lines were ellipsized, use -l to show in full.
[emsarmiento@CENTOSDOCKER01 ~]$
```

Figure 3-7. *Status of Docker daemon with the log*

We'll save the verification of the Docker installation for later.

Installing Docker on Ubuntu Linux

Should you decide to install Docker on an Ubuntu machine, this section outlines the process for you. While there are some differences in commands used between Linux distros, the process is similar.

Update the Ubuntu System Packages

If CentOS uses *yum* for package management, Debian-based Linux distros such as Ubuntu use *apt-get*. Prior to installing Docker and other dependent packages, you need to update the system. Run the following command to update your Ubuntu system:

```
sudo apt-get update
```

The next command is to install the newest versions of all packages currently installed on the system:

```
sudo apt-get upgrade
```

I got a little bit confused the first time I ran these two commands. And maybe you were asking the same question that I had: *what's the difference between update and upgrade?* The apt-get update command doesn't actually install new versions of the packages installed on the system. It merely updates package information so the system knows which ones need upgrading. It's like updating your phone contact list with new numbers and addresses before calling them to verify the new information. Since packages and their dependencies can change over time – maybe due to bug fixes, security updates, or even metadata changes – your system might try to download a package that no longer exists or has been moved to a different location. The `apt-get upgrade` command is the one that does the actual upgrade of all the packages installed on the system to their newest version. If new packages are required because of package dependencies, they will be installed as well. This is the reason why `apt-get update` should always be performed before `apt-get upgrade`.

Install the Required Dependencies for Connecting to a Repository over HTTPS

Similar to CentOS, you need to install several packages that Docker depends on. These are for use with connecting to a repo over HTTPS.

apt-transport-https: Ubuntu uses this to allow apt-get to download packages via HTTPS.

ca-certificates: This package contains a list of common certificate authorities, also used in combination with *apt-transport-https*.

curl: Short for Client URL Request Library, a tool to get or send files using a URL syntax. I use this mostly to download files from the Internet, such as repo files for a package.

gnupg-agent: This is used to manage secrets (or private keys). You need to add Docker's official GPG key on your system and that needs to be handled properly.

software-properties-common: A tool used to manage package sources. Without this, you would have to manually add and/or remove package repos on your system.

Run the following command to install the required dependencies:

```
sudo apt-get install apt-transport-https ca-certificates curl gnupg-agent
software-properties-common
```

Don't be surprised if not all of the packages will be installed. Some of them may have already been updated via the `apt-get upgrade` command.

Add the Official GPG Key from Docker

Validating the integrity of a software package before installation is one way to guarantee that it is indeed what the developer originally distributed. You certainly don't want to download a file that has been maliciously modified and redistributed. Of course, this assumes that the developer signs the package and makes the public key available.

Most Linux packages are validated by verifying its GPG key. Docker created their own GPG key that they use to create their package so you can validate its integrity before installing.

Use the following *curl* command to download and add the official GPG key from Docker into the Ubuntu system:

```
curl -fsSL https://download.docker.com/linux/ubuntu/gpg | sudo apt-key add -
```

Using the pipe operator, the output of the *curl* command is piped to the *apt-key* command to add the downloaded key to the list of trusted keys in the system.

It wouldn't make sense for you to simply accept the key as it is without verifying whether or not it is the original key from Docker. This is where fingerprints are useful. Docker provided the fingerprint in their documentation so you can verify it with the key you downloaded:

```
9DC8 5822 9FC7 DD38 854A E2D8 8D81 803C 0EBF CD88
```

You can use the following *apt-key* command to verify the fingerprint, passing the fingerprint value without spaces. Figure 3-8 displays the key with the matching fingerprint that you passed.

```
sudo apt-key finger 9DC858229FC7DD38854AE2D88D81803C0EBFCD88
```

```
emsarmiento@ubuntudocker01: ~                                                    —  □  ×
emsarmiento@ubuntudocker01:~$ sudo apt-key finger 9DC858229FC7DD38854AE2D88D81803C0EBFCD88
pub     rsa4096 2017-02-22 [SCEA]
        9DC8 5822 9FC7 DD38 854A  E2D8 8D81 803C 0EBF CD88
uid           [ unknown] Docker Release (CE deb) <docker@docker.com>
sub     rsa4096 2017-02-22 [S]

emsarmiento@ubuntudocker01:~$ ▊
```

Figure 3-8. *Displaying the Docker GPG key fingerprint*

Add the Docker Stable Repository to Your System

Same as with CentOS, you need to add the Docker stable repository to your Ubuntu system. Use the following *add-apt-repository* command to do this. The *lsb_release* command with the *-cs* parameter appended to the repo information displays the Linux Standard Base (LSB) information containing the short format of the codename. In the case of this Ubuntu distro, it's *xenial*.

```
sudo add-apt-repository "deb [arch=amd64]
https://download.docker.com/linux/ubuntu $(lsb_release -cs) stable"
```

This command will add the information in the */etc/apt/sources.list*. You can verify this by displaying the contents of the */etc/apt/sources.list* using the following *cat* command. Figure 3-9 displays the URL source of the Docker CE package repo for Ubuntu.

```
sudo cat /etc/apt/sources.list
```

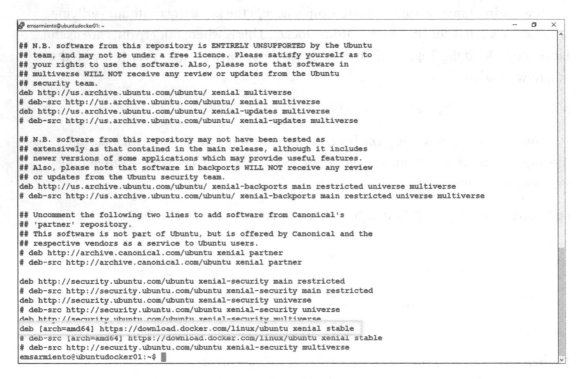

Figure 3-9. *Docker CE repo added to the /etc/apt/sources.list*

Because you have made modifications to your Ubuntu system by installing additional packages and adding the Docker CE repo, you need to rerun the `apt-get update` command:

```
sudo apt-get update
```

Now, you're ready to install the Docker CE package.

Install Docker CE

While CentOS uses `yum install` to download and install the Docker CE package, Ubuntu uses `apt-get install`.

```
sudo apt-get install docker-ce
```

Type *y* when prompted to continue. Like when you installed Docker CE on CentOS, other package dependencies will be installed alongside *docker*, including *docker-ce-cli* and *containerd.io*, as shown in Figure 3-10.

```
emsarmiento@ubuntudocker01:~$ sudo apt-get install docker-ce
Reading package lists... Done
Building dependency tree
Reading state information... Done
The following additional packages will be installed:
  aufs-tools cgroupfs-mount containerd.io docker-ce-cli libltdl7 pigz
Suggested packages:
  mountall
The following NEW packages will be installed:
  aufs-tools cgroupfs-mount containerd.io docker-ce docker-ce-cli libltdl7 pigz
0 upgraded, 7 newly installed, 0 to remove and 3 not upgraded.
Need to get 53.2 MB of archives.
After this operation, 253 MB of additional disk space will be used.
Do you want to continue? [Y/n]
```

Figure 3-10. *List of dependent packages when installing Docker*

Unlike with CentOS, you don't have to manually configure the Docker daemon to start and enable on server reboot. That has been done for you as part of the installation process.

Verifying the Docker Engine Installation

Now that Docker CE has been installed on your Linux machine, it's pretty much the same as with any operating system. The Docker command-line interface and the Docker commands are the same across the board. You can run the following command to check the version of Docker installed on the server:

```
sudo docker version
```

Figure 3-11 shows the output of the command on an Ubuntu machine side by side with a CentOS machine, displaying the version of the Docker client and the Docker engine. I used the command cat /etc/os-release | grep PRETTY_NAME to display the friendly name of the Linux distro. As you can see, the versions are the same.

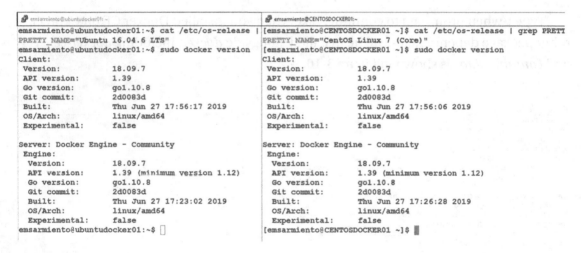

Figure 3-11. *Displaying the version of Docker client and Docker engine*

Don't make the mistake of running *docker* commands on Linux without *sudo*. Oftentimes, administrators coming from the Windows platform bring their practices and way of thinking as they come into the Linux world. And they wonder why something isn't working. Running *docker version* without *sudo* will return an error message such as the one in Figure 3-12.

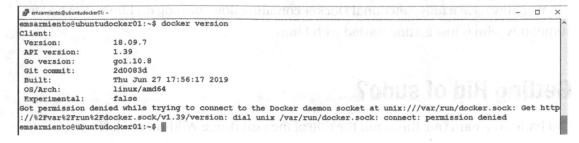

Figure 3-12. *Running Docker commands without sudo*

You don't want to end up troubleshooting a perceived installation issue like this and spending hours trying to figure out what's wrong only to realize that you simply did not run the command with elevated privileges.

Run the following command to display system-wide information regarding the docker installation on the server. Figure 3-13 shows the output of the command. And there's clearly more information provided on a Linux system than there is on the Windows system.

```
sudo docker info
```

```
emsarmiento@ubuntudocker01:~$ sudo docker info
Containers: 0
 Running: 0
 Paused: 0
 Stopped: 0
Images: 0
Server Version: 18.09.7
Storage Driver: overlay2
 Backing Filesystem: extfs
 Supports d_type: true
 Native Overlay Diff: true
Logging Driver: json-file
Cgroup Driver: cgroupfs
Plugins:
 Volume: local
 Network: bridge host macvlan null overlay
 Log: awslogs fluentd gcplogs gelf journald json-file local logentries splunk syslog
Swarm: inactive
Runtimes: runc
Default Runtime: runc
Init Binary: docker-init
containerd version: 894b81a4b802e4eb2a91d1ce216b8817763c29fb
runc version: 425e105d5a03fabd737a126ad93d62a9eeede87f
init version: fec3683
Security Options:
 apparmor
 seccomp
  Profile: default
Kernel Version: 4.4.0-142-generic
Operating System: Ubuntu 16.04.6 LTS
OSType: linux
Architecture: x86_64
CPUs: 1
Total Memory: 7.788GiB
Name: ubuntudocker01
```

Figure 3-13. *Displaying the system-wide information of the Docker installation*

You now have a fully functional Docker container host running on Linux. Not bad for somebody who is just getting started with Linux.

Getting Rid of sudo?

Old habits die hard (no, this is not the title of the next Bruce Willis movie). Having worked with Windows for most of my career, I still forget to use *sudo* every time I run a command on Linux. And I'm sure you will, too. Remember the error message in Figure 3-12? It can be annoying. However, it is a good security practice to avoid logging in using *root* and always use *sudo* in every command you run.

But since you're still getting started with Linux, I'll give you a temporary pass to work around this subtle annoyance. No, I'm not going to let you get away with logging in as *root* – that's a deadly sin in my book. I'll only allow you to run *docker* commands without *sudo* – for now.

Note   The reason why you need to run *docker* commands with *sudo* is because the docker daemon binds to a Unix socket instead of a TCP/IP port (Unix sockets make interprocess communications within the same machine much faster by eliminating some checks and operations – like routing – that TCP/IP uses). By default, the *root* user owns that Unix socket, and the only way that other users can access it is by using *sudo*. This is why the docker daemon always runs as *root*.

To run *docker* commands without *sudo*, you need to

1. Create a group named *docker*

2. Add your user account to it

When the docker daemon starts, members of the *docker* group will have access to the Unix socket. It's like the old *SQLServerMSSQLUser$instancename* local Windows group in older versions of SQL Server – members of this group have access to the SQL Server service.

Run the following *groupadd* command to create a group named *docker*:

```
sudo groupadd docker
```

You'll get a message like the one in Figure 3-14 if the *docker* group already exists.

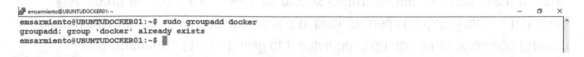

Figure 3-14. *Creating the group named docker*

If that's the case, proceed to add your user account to the *docker* group. Run the following *usermod* command to do so:

```
sudo usermod -aG docker $USER
```

The *-a* parameter is used to append (or add) a user to a group (the *G* parameter following). The *$USER* environment variable is for the currently logged on user (that's you).

Just like in Windows, you must log out and log back in for the changes to take effect. You can then rerun the *docker version* and *docker info* commands without having to use *sudo*. Figure 3-15 shows the output of running the *docker info* command using the user account that I added to the *docker* group.

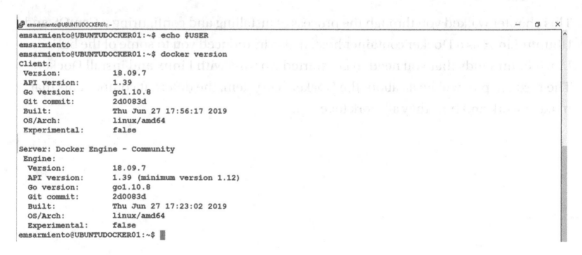

Figure 3-15. *Running docker commands without sudo*

Caution   Be warned – security is a serious matter and I don't take it lightly. Only trusted users such as administrators should be added to the *docker* group. Any member of this group has permissions to control the docker daemon. This means adding someone to this group is equivalent to giving them permanent, non-password-protected *root* access. This is more dangerous than the permissions of the *SQLServerMSSQLUser$instancename* local Windows group because it has *root* access. Scary, isn't it?

Be sure to read the documentation on Docker security, particularly the section on Docker daemon attack surface at `https://docs.docker.com/engine/ security/security/`.

And don't forget to document all users added to this group so you can keep track of who the members are.

Summary

This chapter walked you through the process of installing and configuring a CentOS and Ubuntu Linux as a Docker container host. It also introduced you to some of the basic Linux commands that you need to get started working with Linux and install Docker. The next chapter will be all about the Docker ecosystem, the different components that make it work and how they all work together.

CHAPTER 4

The Docker Ecosystem

Interdependence is and ought to be as much the ideal of man as self-sufficiency.

—Mahatma Gandhi

I've always been fascinated by airplanes. When I was a kid, I wanted to become a pilot and travel around the world. Maybe it's the excitement of traveling to a new place or the challenge of figuring out how a complex system works. Or maybe it was both.

While I was waiting to board my flight on the Thanksgiving of 2008, I couldn't help but wonder how complex the whole flight travel experience is. If you've been on a commercial flight before, you know what I'm talking about. When you check in to the counter, the airline agent will hand you a boarding pass and tag your luggage so it reaches your final destination. Your boarding pass has details of the flight – the gate information, your seat assignment, boarding and departure times, passenger details, and the like. A gate will be assigned to the plane for passengers to go to and board the flight. As you are getting ready to board, the gate attendant will check your identity based on your boarding pass. As the plane is about to leave the gate, the pilot will check their flight data plan and verify if it is in accordance with the air traffic controller instructions. If everything goes according to plan, the flight leaves the gate and heads off to its destination (one of the ground crew was kind enough to share this information as we were passing time waiting for our delayed flight).

Every complex system is composed of different parts working together. If you're just a consumer of a product or service (like that of a flight), it's fine not knowing the intricate details of how it works. You only need to know enough on how to properly use it. But if you will be responsible for delivering even a part of that product or service, you owe it to yourself and the people using it to understand how it works, specifically your part.

© Edwin M Sarmiento 2020
E. M. Sarmiento, *The SQL Server DBA's Guide to Docker Containers*,
https://doi.org/10.1007/978-1-4842-5826-2_4

The goal of this chapter is to get you acquainted with the complex system that is Docker. To achieve this goal, I will introduce you to the different components that make up the entire ecosystem while, at the same time, introducing the most common commands that you need to start working with Docker. So, be ready for a more keyboard-banging approach to learning.

Note   The sample commands covered in this chapter will be shown in either a Windows PowerShell command shell or a Linux secure shell – CentOS or Ubuntu – without the inclusion of the *sudo* command (refer to the section on "Getting Rid of sudo?" in Chapter 3). This is to illustrate the interoperability of the *docker* command. But this doesn't mean I'm giving you the permission to ignore the security practices of running commands on both Windows Server and Linux server operating systems. Remember, only the *docker* commands will run without *sudo* on Linux. All the other commands that require elevated privileges will still require *sudo*.

Hello World: Docker Edition

I'm sure you've had your share of "hello world" while learning a computer programming language. I got introduced to "hello world" more than two-and-a-half decades ago while learning computer programming for the first time in my sophomore year in university. I wish I could say that it was the beginning of my journey into computer programming (the only reason I passed the course was because my best friend wrote my final project). But it did open my eyes to what "hello world" was and what it was for – a test as to whether or not the operator knows how to use it. It's no wonder every programming language starts out with displaying "hello world" as a standard output.

Docker is no different. And while it isn't really a programming language, they embraced the "hello world" concept and came up with their own. But the way they created their version of "hello world" is amazingly brilliant, in my opinion. More than displaying a simple "hello world" message on your screen, their version gave you an idea of how Docker works. On your Linux system, run the following command to see what I mean:

```
docker run hello-world
```

Figure 4-1 shows the Docker's version of "hello world". Brilliant, isn't it?

```
emsarmiento@CENTOSDOCKER01:~
[emsarmiento@CENTOSDOCKER01 ~]$ docker run hello-world
Unable to find image 'hello-world:latest' locally
latest: Pulling from library/hello-world
1b930d010525: Pull complete
Digest: sha256:6540fc08ee6e6b7b63468dc3317e3303aaae178cb8a45ed3123180328bcc1d20f
Status: Downloaded newer image for hello-world:latest

Hello from Docker!
This message shows that your installation appears to be working correctly.

To generate this message, Docker took the following steps:
 1. The Docker client contacted the Docker daemon.
 2. The Docker daemon pulled the "hello-world" image from the Docker Hub.
    (amd64)
 3. The Docker daemon created a new container from that image which runs the
    executable that produces the output you are currently reading.
 4. The Docker daemon streamed that output to the Docker client, which sent it
    to your terminal.

To try something more ambitious, you can run an Ubuntu container with:
 $ docker run -it ubuntu bash

Share images, automate workflows, and more with a free Docker ID:
 https://hub.docker.com/

For more examples and ideas, visit:
 https://docs.docker.com/get-started/

[emsarmiento@CENTOSDOCKER01 ~]$
```

Figure 4-1. *Hello World: Docker edition*

Unfortunately, the same command – `docker run hello-world` – no longer works for Docker on Windows Server 2016. It has nothing to do with the command, it has everything to do with the version of the container image as we will cover at a later section. Even when you follow Docker's documentation on installing Docker Enterprise on Windows Servers, running the same command will still return a message like the one in Figure 4-2.

```
Administrator: Windows PowerShell
PS C:\> docker run hello-world:nanoserver
Unable to find image 'hello-world:nanoserver' locally
nanoserver: Pulling from library/hello-world
C:\Program Files\Docker\docker.exe: no matching manifest for windows/amd64 10.0.14393 in the manifest list entries.
See 'C:\Program Files\Docker\docker.exe run --help'.
PS C:\>
```

Figure 4-2. *Running Hello World: Docker edition on Windows Server*

That's because of the introduction of Microsoft's semi-annual channel (SAC) servicing model. The image used to build Microsoft's version of Docker's *hello-world* container image has been deprecated for Windows Server 2016 (refer to *https:// github.com/docker/for-win/issues/3775*). Don't get me started on how confusing this servicing model to businesses is.

To get the same output as the container image you ran on Linux, run the following command instead. Note the use of a tag, a label specifically defining what image to use to run the container. Usage of tags will be covered in more detail at a later section.

```
docker run hello-world:nanoserver-sac2016
```

Figure 4-3 shows the output of Docker's version of "hello world" on Windows Server 2016. Don't be surprised if the Windows Server image takes much longer to download compared to the Linux image.

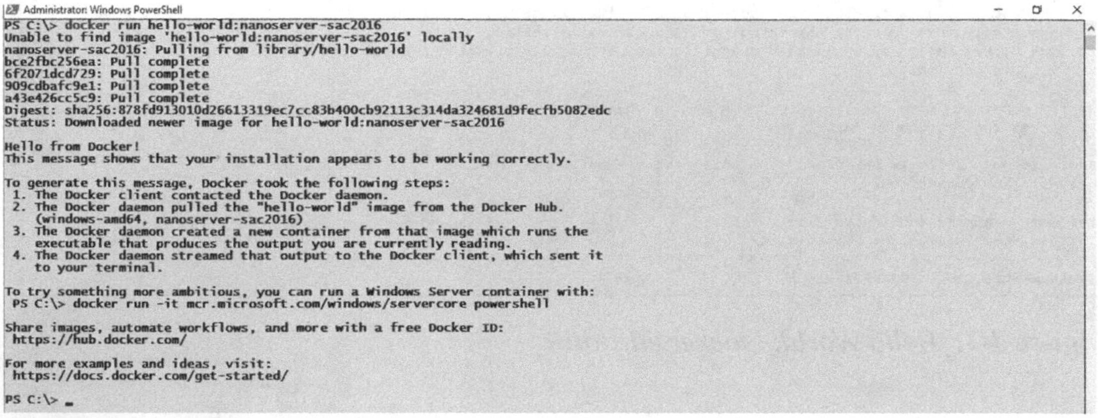

Figure 4-3. The working Hello World: Docker edition on Windows Server

Beyond the output of the `docker version` and `docker info` commands you ran in previous chapters, if you get this result, you're guaranteed that Docker is working correctly on your system. You've passed the simple sanity check. But that's not the goal of this chapter. Let's have a look at the output of Docker's "hello world" to understand how Docker works and identify the different components that make up this complex system.

How Docker Runs Containers

The `docker run hello-world` command you ran is a very simple example of how to run a Docker container. Docker's version of "hello world" explains how Docker actually does it. Figure 4-4 illustrates the processes involved in running a Docker container.

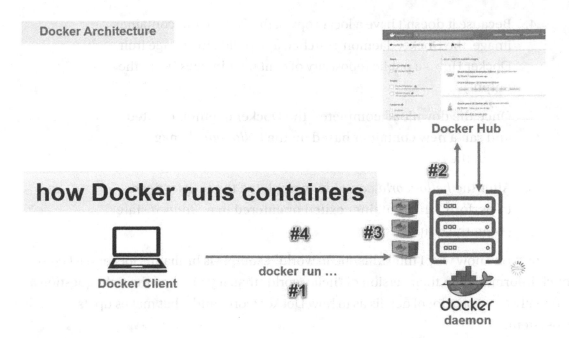

Figure 4-4. *How Docker runs containers*

The following is an explanation of the process by which Docker runs containers. The *hello-world* container is used for purposes of example, but the process is the same no matter the container.

1. You run the `docker run hello-world` command from the Docker CLI client.

2. The Docker CLI client makes API calls to the Docker daemon. In this case, it passes the *run* subcommand to run a new container based on the *hello-world* container image as a template (#1 in the output).

3. The first thing that the Docker daemon does when it receives a request to run a container is to check whether it already has a local copy of the *hello-world* container image in its local filesystem. Since this is a brand-new installation, no local copy of the image is available.

4. Because it doesn't have a local copy of the *hello-world* container image, the Docker daemon searched and pulled the image from Docker Hub – a public repository of container images (#2 in the output).

5. Once the download completes, the Docker daemon created and ran a new container based on the *hello-world* image (#3 in the output).

6. After the *hello-world* container completed the tasks it needs to perform, the container exited or entered in a *Stopped* state (#4 in the output).

Now you know why I think this "hello world" example is brilliant. Docker packed so much information in their version of "hello world" that, if you asked the right questions, can really give you a lot of details as to how Docker works and what makes up its ecosystem.

The Docker Ecosystem

I've used several names, terms, and keywords in the previous section to describe how Docker runs a simple container. But I haven't defined those terms yet, so I'll do just that in the following sections.

Docker CLI

Let's start with what you can infer from #1 in the output in Figure 4-4: what is the Docker CLI? The Docker CLI (command-line interface) is your point of interaction with the Docker daemon. Docker commands are executed through the Docker CLI client and sent to the Docker daemon. You can think of this as SQL Server Query Analyzer (I wish Microsoft will bring back this lightweight tool) or SQL Server Management Studio. By default, this is installed on the machine together with the Docker daemon. All the *docker* commands you ran from the previous chapters were executed locally from the point of view of the Docker host machine. On the Windows Server machine, you logged in via Remote Desktop, opened Windows PowerShell, and ran the *docker* commands – locally. On the Linux machine, you initiated an SSH session to connect remotely, but, once logged in, you ran the *docker* commands locally. This is the approach we will be using throughout the book. However, nobody is stopping you from configuring the Docker CLI client to connect to a remote Docker host, similar to installing SQL Server Management Studio on your Windows client workstation and connecting to a remote SQL Server instance.

Docker Daemon

Docker daemon (or service in Windows) is a client-server application and the runtime engine responsible for creating and running Docker objects. It is the center of your interactions with Docker and the best place to start understanding all the moving parts in the Docker ecosystem. You can think of it like the SQL Server relational database engine. The Docker daemon interacts with the Docker CLI client through a REST API. Because of the default installation where the Docker CLI client is installed on the same machine as the Docker daemon, the Docker engine is often referred to having these three major components – the Docker daemon, the REST API, and the Docker CLI client.

Docker Commands

The *docker* command is the base command that you use when interacting with the Docker daemon through the Docker CLI client. To perform Docker administrative tasks, you either use subcommands or management commands with their corresponding parameters. A great way to explore all the different subcommands or management commands is to run the `docker` or `docker help` commands. Figure 4-5 shows all the available options and commands. A complete list of docker commands is available on the Docker documentation *https://docs.docker.com/engine/reference/commandline/docker/*.

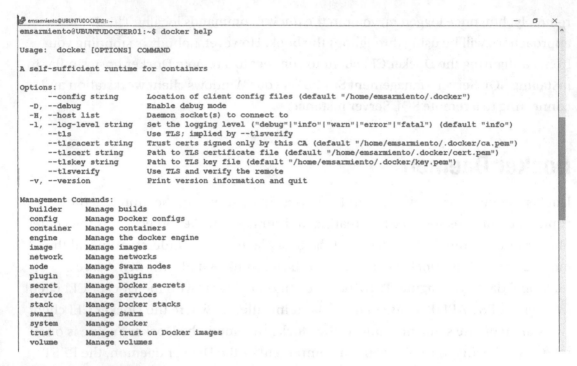

Figure 4-5. *Display all available Docker options and commands*

You've already used some of these commands like *docker run*, docker version, and docker info.

Don't get ahead of yourself. We will be using several of these options and commands throughout the book to perform Docker administrative tasks.

Docker Images and Containers

I got confused the first time I've seen the term *Docker image* as it usually appears together with the term *Docker containers*. I'll save you the hassle that this confusion might cause.

A Docker image is a static, *read-only* template for creating application containers. It's a non-running representation of all the various components required to run the application. A Docker container, however, is a runtime instance of the image. When you ran the docker run hello-world command, *hello-world* is the name of the Docker image. You can think of a Docker image as a blueprint, like a technical drawing for a car. You create the blueprint (Docker image) based on how you want the car (Docker container) to look like and function. Once the blueprint has been finalized, you can create as many instances as you want of the car based on the blueprint. You have the freedom to make changes to the aesthetic of the car – color, accessories, interiors, and the like – without the need to modify the blueprint. Should you decide to make major modifications to the car, you have to go back to the drawing board and rewrite the blueprint.

This is just a high-level overview of what Docker containers and Docker images are, just enough to get you started with understanding the components of the Docker ecosystem. *Chapter 5* dives deeper into the internals of what they are and how they are stored in the filesystem.

Docker Hub

Docker Hub is a container registry. It's a cloud-based, public repository from Docker, Inc. used for creating, testing, storing, and distributing Docker images. Think of it as the Apple App Store or the Google Play store of Docker images. Docker Hub provides several services and features:

- *Repository*: It is where you can store your Docker images, either for private or public use.

- *Teams and organizations*: This is a way to manage permissions and access to Docker images stored on your repository. You can create teams and assign users to them as well as create an organization that consists of teams and different repositories.

- *Official images*: These are a curated set of Docker repositories hosted on Docker Hub for providing base operating system images, a download-and-use image for popular programming languages and platforms, and reference for best practices on how to use them. These images are stored in the top-level repositories (more of this in the section on "Docker Image Naming Convention"), and it's safe to assume that they are from reliable and trustworthy sources.

- *Publisher images*: Docker Hub hosts Docker images from software vendors like Microsoft, Oracle, Red Hat, IBM, and so on. These images are maintained and supported by the corresponding vendors. The SQL Server on Linux and SQL Server on Windows containers that we will be using in later chapters are examples of publisher images.

- *Builds*: This allows you to automatically build and upload Docker images from a Git repository like GitHub, GitLab, and Bitbucket.

- *Webhooks*: This allows you to integrate with other services through automation, such as triggering an automation server when you successfully uploaded a Docker image to Docker Hub.

Docker Hub is accessible through *https://hub.docker.com/* and is the default container registry that the Docker engine uses to search, push, or pull Docker images. This is your first stop if you want to search for specific Docker images that you want to use. Figure 4-6 displays the search results for SQL Server on Docker Hub.

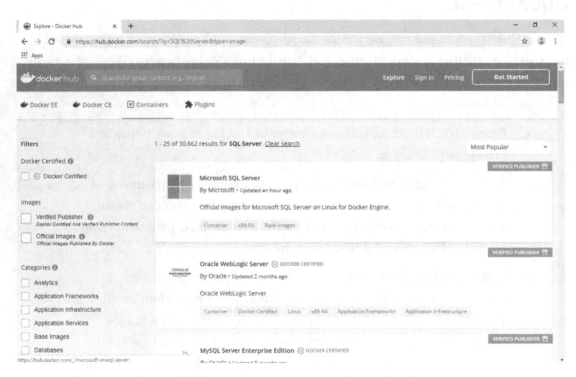

Figure 4-6. *Search results for SQL Server on Docker Hub*

There are available public container registries other than Docker Hub that you can use. The more popular ones are from the major cloud providers like Amazon Elastic Container Registry (ECR), Microsoft Container Registry (MCR), and Google Container Registry (GCR). You can tell Docker to override the default configuration and work with a different public container registry. An example will be shown at a later section. In case you don't want to use public container registries, you can deploy your own private container registry on-premises.

A term associated with container registries is *pull*. Pull is simply a fancy word for download. When the Docker daemon pulled the *hello-world* image, it just means it downloaded the image from Docker Hub and into its own local filesystem. And with the term pull comes its counterpart - *push*. Again, it's just a fancy word for upload.

Since Docker Hub is a public repository, you can pull available Docker images without the need to create a Docker ID. However, should you decide to push your own custom Docker images to Docker Hub, you need to sign up for a Docker ID (and have your credit card information available if you go beyond the FREE tier).

Exploring Docker Hub

I did mention that Docker Hub is your first stop if you want to search for specific Docker images that you intend to use. But nowhere in the output of when you ran Docker's version of "hello world" did you see a web browser open up, searched for the *hello-world* image on Docker Hub, and initiated a pull. Besides, you don't have a graphical user interface on Linux. How do you explore what images are available on Docker Hub? Use the *docker search* command and pass it the appropriate search term and parameters. For example, you can run the following command if you want to search Docker Hub for all images that contain the name "microsoft", as shown in Figure 4-7:

```
docker search microsoft
```

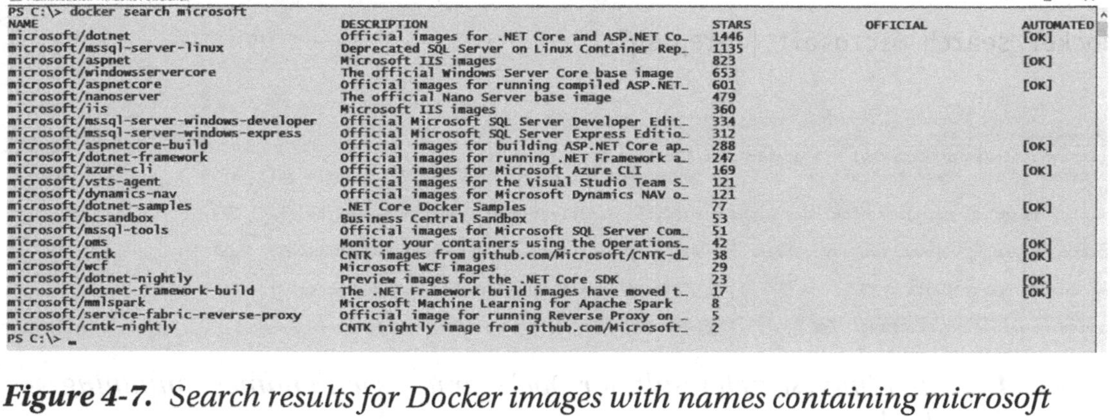

```
Administrator: Windows PowerShell
PS C:\> docker search microsoft
NAME                                         DESCRIPTION                                     STARS     OFFICIAL   AUTOMATED
microsoft/dotnet                             Official images for .NET Core and ASP.NET Co…   1446                 [OK]
microsoft/mssql-server-linux                 Deprecated SQL Server on Linux Container Rep…   1135
microsoft/aspnet                             Microsoft IIS images                            823                  [OK]
microsoft/windowsservercore                  The official Windows Server Core base image     653
microsoft/aspnetcore                         Official images for running compiled ASP.NET…   601                  [OK]
microsoft/nanoserver                         The official Nano Server base image             479
microsoft/iis                                Microsoft IIS images                            360
microsoft/mssql-server-windows-developer     Official Microsoft SQL Server Developer Edit…   334
microsoft/mssql-server-windows-express       Official Microsoft SQL Server Express Editio…   312
microsoft/aspnetcore-build                   Official images for building ASP.NET Core ap…   288                  [OK]
microsoft/dotnet-framework                   Official images for running .NET Framework a…   247
microsoft/azure-cli                          Official images for Microsoft Azure CLI         169                  [OK]
microsoft/vsts-agent                         Official images for the Visual Studio Team S…   121
microsoft/dynamics-nav                       Official images for Microsoft Dynamics NAV o…   121
microsoft/dotnet-samples                     .NET Core Docker Samples                        77                   [OK]
microsoft/bcsandbox                          Business Central Sandbox                        53
microsoft/mssql-tools                        Official images for Microsoft SQL Server Com…   51
microsoft/oms                                Monitor your containers using the Operations…   42                   [OK]
microsoft/cntk                               CNTK images from github.com/Microsoft/CNTK-d…   38                   [OK]
microsoft/wcf                                Microsoft WCF images                            29
microsoft/dotnet-nightly                     Preview images for the .NET Core SDK            23                   [OK]
microsoft/dotnet-framework-build             The .NET Framework build images have moved t…   17                   [OK]
microsoft/mmlspark                           Microsoft Machine Learning for Apache Spark     8
microsoft/service-fabric-reverse-proxy       Official image for running Reverse Proxy on …   5
microsoft/cntk-nightly                       CNTK nightly image from github.com/Microsoft…   2
PS C:\>
```

Figure 4-7. *Search results for Docker images with names containing microsoft*

The results of the command are sorted according to "stars" or popularity. Looking at the ranking, it seems the SQL Server on Linux image is more popular than the ASP.NET Core on Windows image, considering that .NET Core has been released a year earlier than SQL Server on Linux.

I wish the *docker search* command is as feature rich as the Docker Hub website where I can search by name of publisher, whether or not it's a Docker certified image, or it's a Windows or Linux container. But that shouldn't stop you from leveraging your PowerShell or Linux scripting superpowers to manipulate and further filter the results you get from *docker search*. Let's say you only want to list all the SQL Server–specific images. Since the results of the *docker search* command are a stream of text, you can use the *Select-String* PowerShell cmdlet to find specific string values. Run the following *docker search* command on your Windows Server host, using the PowerShell pipe character with the *Select-String* cmdlet to filter the results for anything with "sql". Figure 4-8 shows all Docker images with names containing "microsoft" filtered to only display those with "sql". As a SQL Server DBA, these are the ones we're more interested in.

```
docker search microsoft | Select-String sql
```

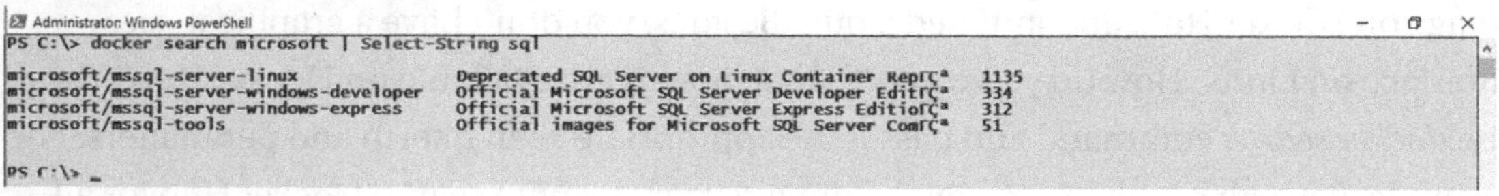

Figure 4-8. *On Windows, search results for Docker images with names containing microsoft and sql*

You can do the same with Linux by using the *grep* command, as shown in Figure 4-9.

```
docker search microsoft | grep sql
```

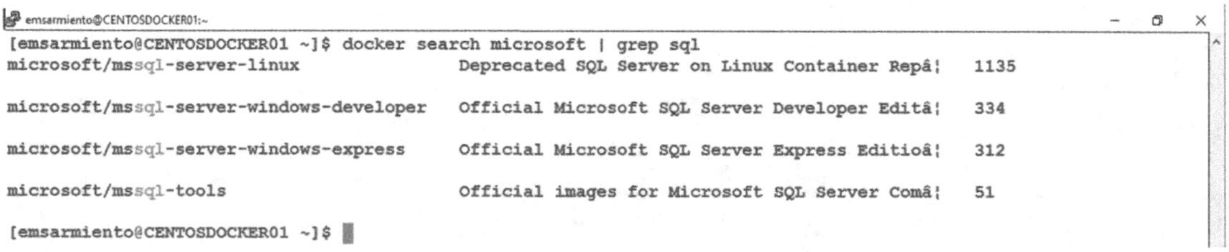

Figure 4-9. *On Linux, search results for Docker images with names containing microsoft and sql*

Tip   This is where you need to be cautious of the environment – Windows or Linux – that you're working on. Keep in mind, containers virtualize the underlying operating system. Unlike other relational database management systems that only have Linux-based images available on Docker Hub, SQL Server is available on both Windows and Linux. You don't want to make the mistake of pulling and running a SQL Server on Linux image on a Windows Server host and vice versa. It's not going to work.

Docker Image Naming Conventions

You might be itching to work with SQL Server on containers but bear with me for a moment. We'll get there soon. Let's first look at container naming conventions because it helps set you up for the win when it comes to searching, pulling, building, or even pushing Docker images.

Similar to working with SQL Server, there are default Docker configuration settings that have been provided for you during installation. Take, for instance, the default container registry that is Docker Hub. When you ran the *docker run* command to run Docker's version of "hello world", you didn't have to provide the registry name. It simply used Docker Hub. You can opt to use other public container registries. But to do so, you need to understand the naming conventions used when working with Docker images.

Docker images are referenced using a standard naming convention. This is to provide predictability for users consuming the images. The standard naming convention is similar to GitHub repository names, using the following format:

REGISTRY[:PORT]/REPO/IMAGE[:TAG]

An image name is made up of slash-separated name components, optionally prefixed by a registry hostname. The registry hostname must comply with standard DNS rules. If a registry hostname isn't provided, it defaults to Docker Hub. Docker Hub's fully qualified hostname is *https://index.docker.io* or simply *docker.io*. You can see this in the *Registry:* field when you run *docker info*, as shown in Figure 4-10.

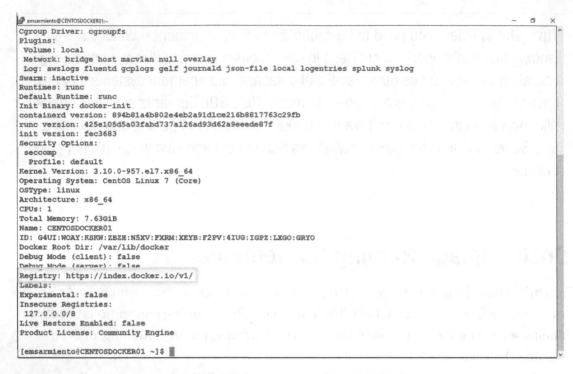

```
emsarmiento@CENTOSDOCKER01:~                                                    —    □    ×
Cgroup Driver: cgroupfs
Plugins:
 Volume: local
 Network: bridge host macvlan null overlay
 Log: awslogs fluentd gcplogs gelf journald json-file local logentries splunk syslog
Swarm: inactive
Runtimes: runc
Default Runtime: runc
Init Binary: docker-init
containerd version: 894b81a4b802e4eb2a91d1ce216b8817763c29fb
runc version: 425e105d5a03fabd737a126ad93d62a9eeede87f
init version: fec3683
Security Options:
 seccomp
  Profile: default
Kernel Version: 3.10.0-957.el7.x86_64
Operating System: CentOS Linux 7 (Core)
OSType: linux
Architecture: x86_64
CPUs: 1
Total Memory: 7.63GiB
Name: CENTOSDOCKER01
ID: G4UI:WOAY:KSKW:ZBZH:N5XV:FXRM:XEYB:F2PV:4IUG:IGPZ:LXGO:GRYO
Docker Root Dir: /var/lib/docker
Debug Mode (client): false
Debug Mode (server): false
Registry: https://index.docker.io/v1/
Labels:
Experimental: false
Insecure Registries:
 127.0.0.0/8
Live Restore Enabled: false
Product License: Community Engine

[emsarmiento@CENTOSDOCKER01 ~]$
```

Figure 4-10. *Fully qualified DNS hostname of Docker Hub*

You can use any available public container registries other than Docker Hub with their corresponding registry hostname in your *docker* commands. The following is a list of some that you may choose from. Usage will depend on how the public container registries are accessed.

- *Microsoft Container Registry (MCR)*: mcr.microsoft.com

- *Amazon Elastic Container Registry (ECR)*: dkr.<region>. amazonaws.com

- *Google Container Registry (GCR)*: gcr.io

After the registry hostname comes the repository (or repo, for short) name. The repo structure varies depending on how the images are stored on the container registry. With so many software vendors using Docker Hub as a public container registry, the first-level repo name is the name of the software company. For example, *docker.io/microsoft* is Microsoft's official repo on Docker Hub.

The image name comes next after the repo and it is what identifies the contents of the Docker image. Looking at the results of the docker search command in Figure 4-7, you can see the following:

- *mssql-server-linux* is the image that contains SQL Server on Linux.

- windowsservercore is the official Windows Server Core base image.

- *mssql-server-windows-express* is the image that contains SQL Server Express Edition on Windows.

But given the numerous versions, editions, and operating system combinations that SQL Server now has – even excluding versions earlier than SQL Server 2016 – relying solely on the image name isn't enough. What if you need a Docker image running SQL Server 2017 with Cumulative Update 5 on Windows Server 2016?

This is where *tags* come in. Tags further identify the contents of the Docker image, providing additional detail whenever possible. If you don't provide the tag when you run a container or pull an image from a repo, Docker will assume that you want the image that has the *latest* tag and that the image exists. Refer to the *docker run* command that you ran on Linux:

```
docker run hello-world
```

This is the same as running the command `docker run hello-world:latest` since you didn't provide the tag with the image name, whereas the *docker run* command you ran on Windows has a tag on the image name.

```
docker run hello-world:nanoserver-sac2016
```

That's because the *hello-world* Windows container image with the *latest* tag no longer exists – hence, the error message earlier in Figure 4-2.

As you can see, tags make it easier for users to further identify the Docker image. This becomes more relevant when you start creating your own custom images. You want to provide as much information as possible for users to identify the right image that they need. Refer to Figure 4-11 for a list of available tags that you can use for the SQL Server on Linux image, available at *https://hub.docker.com/_/microsoft-mssql-server*.

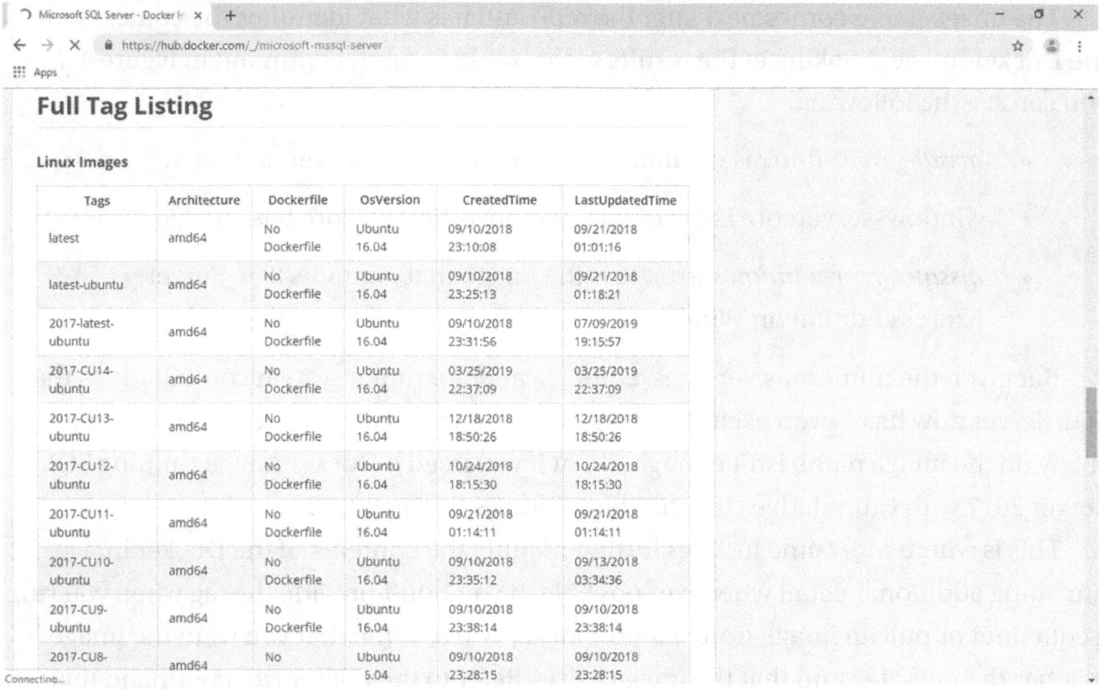

Full Tag Listing

Linux Images

Tags	Architecture	Dockerfile	OsVersion	CreatedTime	LastUpdatedTime
latest	amd64	No Dockerfile	Ubuntu 16.04	09/10/2018 23:10:08	09/21/2018 01:01:16
latest-ubuntu	amd64	No Dockerfile	Ubuntu 16.04	09/10/2018 23:25:13	09/21/2018 01:18:21
2017-latest-ubuntu	amd64	No Dockerfile	Ubuntu 16.04	09/10/2018 23:31:56	07/09/2019 19:15:57
2017-CU14-ubuntu	amd64	No Dockerfile	Ubuntu 16.04	03/25/2019 22:37:09	03/25/2019 22:37:09
2017-CU13-ubuntu	amd64	No Dockerfile	Ubuntu 16.04	12/18/2018 18:50:26	12/18/2018 18:50:26
2017-CU12-ubuntu	amd64	No Dockerfile	Ubuntu 16.04	10/24/2018 18:15:30	10/24/2018 18:15:30
2017-CU11-ubuntu	amd64	No Dockerfile	Ubuntu 16.04	09/21/2018 01:14:11	09/21/2018 01:14:11
2017-CU10-ubuntu	amd64	No Dockerfile	Ubuntu 16.04	09/10/2018 23:35:12	09/13/2018 03:34:36
2017-CU9-ubuntu	amd64	No Dockerfile	Ubuntu 16.04	09/10/2018 23:38:14	09/10/2018 23:38:14
2017-CU8-	amd64	No	Ubuntu 16.04	09/10/2018 23:28:15	09/10/2018 23:28:15

***Figure 4-11.** Available tags for SQL Server on Linux image*

Tip Another reason why you need to specify a tag is because you'll never know what *latest* image you actually get from the public container registry. If you look at the SQL Server on Linux image tags in Figure 4-11, the image with the *latest* tag shows the LastUpdatedTime as 09/21/2018 01:01:16. However, in the image with the *2017-latest-ubuntu* tag, the LastUpdatedTime shows 07/09/2019 19:15:57. So, which one really is the latest? You can pull and run both the *latest* and *2017-latest-ubuntu* images to find out. At the time of writing, the image with the *latest* tag is running SQL Server 2017 with CU13, whereas the image with the *2017-latest-ubuntu* tag is running SQL Server 2017 with CU15 with security update (KB4505225). You don't want to be pulling and deploying a SQL Server image that is incompatible with what you want to use both for testing and production. Using tags make sure that you get what you really need.

Now that you understand how the naming conventions work with Docker images, let's examine the *docker* commands you ran earlier in this chapter. The *docker run* command you ran on Windows can be written as

```
docker run docker.io/library/hello-world:nanoserver-sac2016
```

while on Linux,

```
docker run docker.io/library/hello-world:latest
```

with *library* as the repo name.

To make this even more relevant, let's say you want to pull a SQL Server on Linux image on your Linux Docker host. To do so, run the following command. Pulling the image does not create and run a container. It just stores it in the local container registry's filesystem. You have the option to pull all of the images you need and store it in the local filesystem. This has the advantage of running containers quickly because the Docker daemon no longer has to wait for the image to be fully downloaded.

```
docker pull microsoft/mssql-server-linux
```

This can be written as

```
docker pull docker.io/microsoft/mssql-server-linux:latest
```

You can also refer to Microsoft Container Registry (MCR) to download the image:

```
docker pull mcr.microsoft.com/mssql/server:latest
```

Given that this is a dedicated public registry for Microsoft and that they have several products available as Docker images, the repo name now represents the product name (in this case, *mssql*) instead of the software vendor's name.

Note   Because Docker Hub was the pioneer in public container registries, almost all software vendors have their images and documentation up on their portal. It has become the go-to public container registry for Docker images – Docker Hub hosts both the metadata and the images. As software vendors started creating forks to the Docker source code and created their own versions, they also created their own public container registries. In an effort to avoid any breaking changes and still provide a seamless user experience, most software vendors leveraged the syndication model to keep the content on Docker Hub up to date. This is what Microsoft did with MCR. MCR hosts all of the Microsoft images and syndicates the metadata to Docker Hub. Anytime Microsoft adds or updates a SQL Server on Windows or Linux image, they will syndicate the metadata to Docker Hub. When you pull a SQL Server image from Docker Hub, you get redirected to MCR for the image files. Unfortunately, there is no portal-like experience for MCR like that of Docker Hub. So, you still need Docker Hub to search for Microsoft images. You can read more about the creation of the MCR in this blog post: *https://azure. microsoft.com/en-ca/blog/microsoft-syndicates-container- catalog/*

Enough with these concepts. With the knowledge of how the different components work in the Docker ecosystem, it's time to see them in action – SQL Server DBA style.

Running SQL Server on Windows Containers

There are two ways to run a Docker container:

- Pull the image first using the *docker pull* command and, then, run it using the *docker run* command.

- Use the *docker run* command. If the image doesn't exist in the local filesystem, the docker daemon will implicitly pull the image first before running.

Run the following command to pull and run the *SQL Server 2017 Developer Edition on Windows* with the *latest* tag image on your Windows Docker host. Go grab a snack as the process to pull and run will take some time.

```
docker run -e "ACCEPT_EULA=Y" -e "SA_PASSWORD=mYSecUr3PAssw0rd" -p
1433:1433 --name sqldevwincon01 -d -h winsqldev01 microsoft/mssql-server-
windows-developer
```

Now, this *docker run* command is a little bit more than the "hello world" image that we started with in this chapter. This is where the real fun starts.

The following parameters are used with the *docker run* command. They will be the same parameters that you'll use for your Linux server host:

- *-e*: Set required environment variables; these are specific to SQL Server. The *ACCEPT_EULA* and *SA_PASSWORD* parameters are self-explanatory. I'm sure you've read the EULA every time you installed SQL Server.

- *-p*: Publish a container's TCP port (or a range of ports) to the host using this format *ip:hostPort:containerPort*. This allows you to connect to the SQL Server instance in the container from a remote client, mapping port 1433 on the host to port 1433 on the container.

- *--name*: A unique custom name to help identify the container instead of a system-generated one. This helps you easily identify the container when performing additional tasks.

- *-d*: Run the container in detached mode (background process) and print the container ID. This means that after running the *docker run* command, the container still runs in the background. Use this parameter since SQL Server runs as a service. Without this parameter, the container will run, complete its task, and exit.

- *-h*: Server hostname that you want to assign to the container. Assigning the same value to the *-h* and *--name* parameters makes it easy to identify the container.

Figure 4-12 shows the result of running the *docker run* command on your Windows Server host.

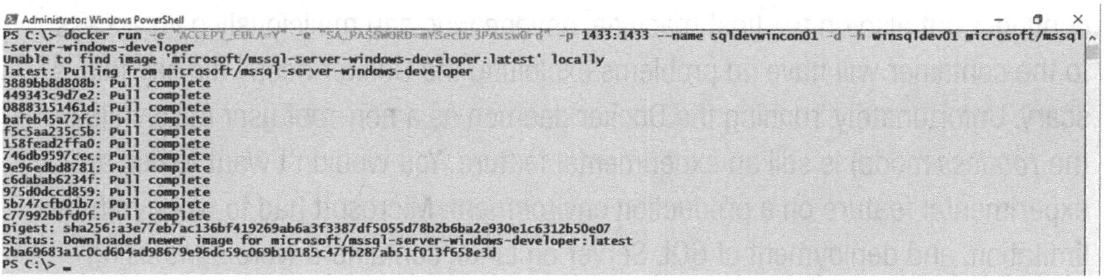

Figure 4-12. *Pulling and running SQL Server on Windows container*

You will see later why it took some time to pull the image.

Running SQL Server on Linux Containers

Run the following command to pull and run a *SQL Server 2017 Developer Edition with CU14 on Ubuntu Linux* image on your Linux Docker host. We'll also use the MCR for the public container registry since only the image with the *latest* tag is available on Docker Hub. Don't worry, you can run this on either an Ubuntu or CentOS Linux Docker host. And you don't have to wait as long as when you pulled the SQL Server on Windows image. Figure 4-13 shows the result of running the docker run command on your Linux Docker host.

```
docker run -e "ACCEPT_EULA=Y" -e "SA_PASSWORD=mYSecUr3PAssw0rd" -p
1433:1433 --name sqldevlinuxcon01 -d -h linuxsqldev01 mcr.microsoft.com/
mssql/server:2017-CU14-ubuntu
```

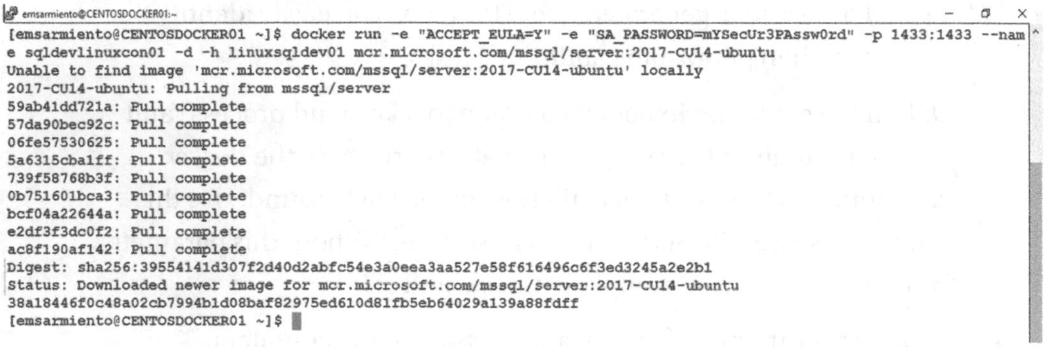

Figure 4-13. *Pulling and running SQL Server on Linux container*

Note In *Chapter 3*, I talk about the security implications of adding users to the *docker* group. That's because the Docker daemon runs as *root*. This means any container you run on your Docker host has *root* privileges, not only inside the container but also on the host machine. Anyone who can maliciously gain access to the container will have no problems exploiting the Docker host. I did say this is scary. Unfortunately, running the Docker daemon as a non-root user (also called the *rootless* mode) is still an experimental feature. You wouldn't want to use an experimental feature on a production environment. Microsoft had to work with this limitation, and deployment of SQL Server on Linux containers were done using *root*. SQL Server 2019 changed that and allowed running a SQL Server on Linux container as a non-root user. I'll cover how to build and run a SQL Server on Linux container as either *root* or non-root user in *Chapter 10*.

Beginning to Explore Containers and Images

So, you pulled and ran the SQL Server on container images. You didn't see any error message. Or maybe you did. If you want to start exploring the images you pulled, run the docker images command. This will give you an idea as to why the SQL Server on Windows image took ages to pull compared to the SQL Server on Linux image, the same reason why Docker's version of "hello world" took longer to run on Windows than it did on Linux. Figure 4-14 may shock you – it shows the results of the docker images command on both my Windows Server host and Linux Server host.

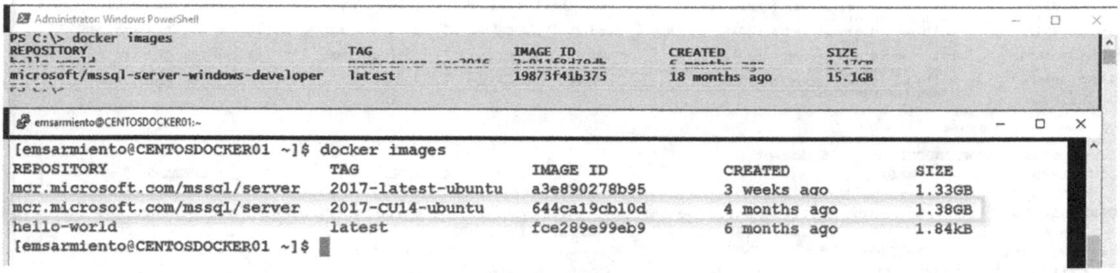

Figure 4-14. *Comparing SQL Server on Windows vs. SQL Server on Linux images*

Just because you didn't see any error message when you ran a container doesn't mean everything is fine. To find the status of all the running containers, run the docker ps command. Figure 4-15 shows the currently running containers on my Windows Server and Linux server hosts.

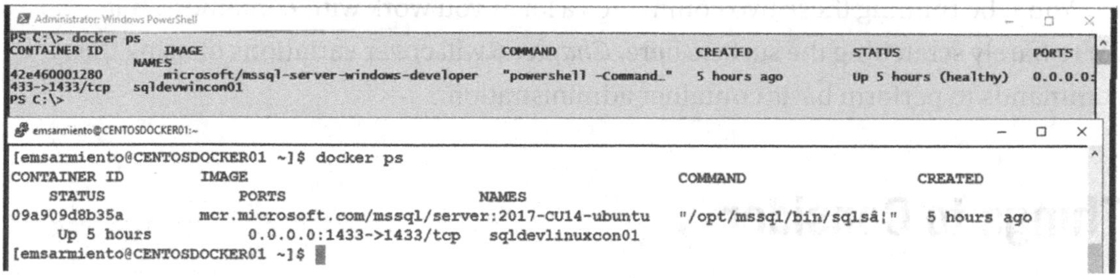

Figure 4-15. *Docker containers currently running*

The *STATUS* column tells you whether your container is currently running. If the container you just ran doesn't appear in this list and you didn't get any error message, it could mean that it ran for a while and got terminated afterward. A container that has been terminated could mean that the job it was supposed to do has already been completed (like the *hello-world* container) or that a fatal error occurred inside the container that forced it to stop. It's important to know what the container does so you know what to expect from it.

Running the docker ps -a command displays all containers – whether running or terminated. Figure 4-16 shows a list of all the containers I ran, including the *hello-world* containers that have terminated – those with *STATUS* value of Exited (0).

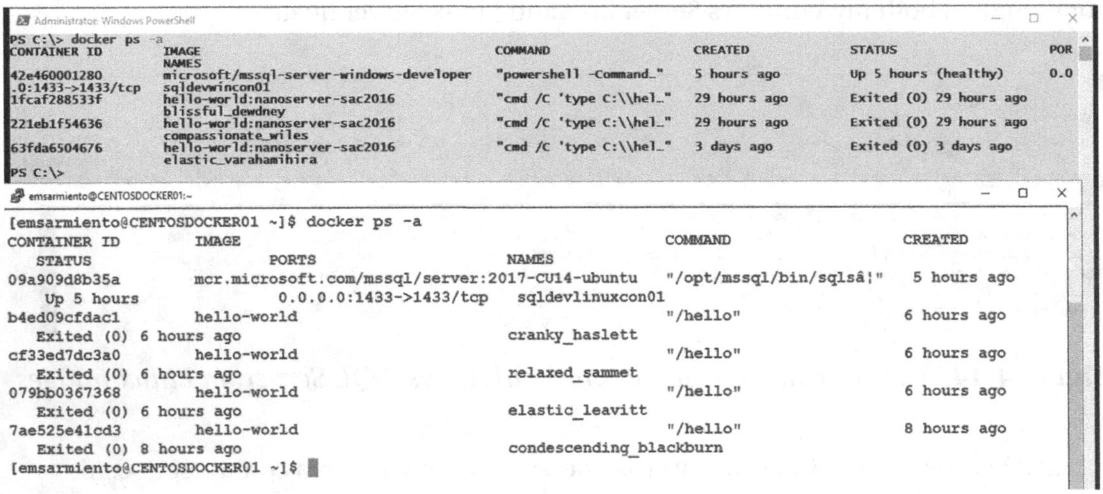

Figure 4-16. *Displaying all Docker containers – both currently running and terminated*

You'll be running these two commands a lot as you work with containers. But we're barely scratching the surface here. *Chapter 6* will cover variations of using these commands to perform basic container administration.

Things to Consider

Doesn't it feel good to pull and run a SQL Server on Windows and Linux containers just by running the commands provided? Of course, it does. But don't get too excited. Working with a new environment like Docker presents new challenges that you need to be aware of.

The first one is licensing. I'm not going to pretend to be a licensing expert, but I've dealt with SQL Server licensing for years that I know how to talk about it. You might be wondering what edition of SQL Server on Linux is available on the image you pulled. The name nor the tag doesn't mention anything unlike the SQL Server on Windows container. The image defaults to the free Developer Edition. For any testing or learning purposes, I stick with the free editions – Developer and Express. You can't go wrong with that. You can choose other editions by including the *MSSQL_PID* environment variable in your *docker run* command provided you have a valid license for them. And be sure to talk to your Microsoft licensing expert for deploying SQL Server on containers in a production environment. They have the last say on this.

The second one is the *SA_PASSWORD* environment variable. The *sysadmin* password should meet the SQL Server password complexity requirements as described in *https://docs.microsoft.com/en-us/sql/relational-databases/security/ password-policy*. Since this is a required parameter in the installation process, failing this policy would cause the installation to fail and the container to stop.

I found out about this the hard way when I first ran the preceding commands to run a SQL Server on Linux container. After running the *docker run* command and expecting it to work, I couldn't figure out why I cannot connect to the SQL Server instance remotely (I'll cover this in more detail in the next section). I thought it was due to firewall ports not being opened. So, I did the usual PING and TELNET tests. Zilch. I can connect to port 1433 for a while, but after a few minutes, the port was no longer responding. I checked if the container was still running, and I noticed that it terminates and exits after a few minutes. That got me curious about what's really going on. After reading the logs, I saw the SQL Server error message shown in Figure 4-17.

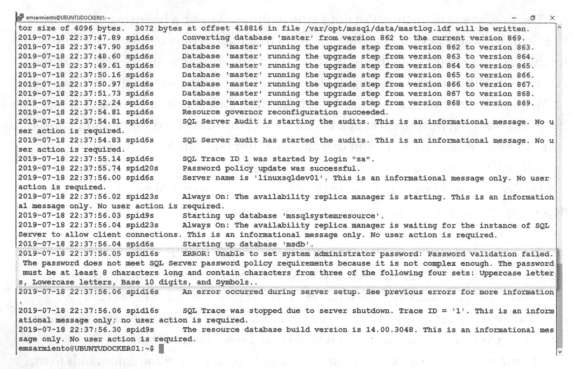

Figure 4-17. *SQL Server error log from the container logs*

I spent hours trying to figure out why the container would terminate immediately after running only to find out that my *sysadmin* password did not meet the password policy.

Similarly, the use of special characters that may mean something to your shell environment like PowerShell or SSH can potentially cause issues, especially when used with single quotes instead of double quotes like the following example:

```
docker run -e 'SA_PASSWORD=$Qlu=j&Q7aoN' ...
```

I wrote a simple PowerShell script years ago that generates complex passwords. Occasionally, the script would generate a password that starts with a special character, one that means something to the shell environment that I was using. Here's one of the passwords I used to create a SQL Server on Linux container. Note that it starts with the $ character.

$Qlu=j&Q7aoN

Because the $ character has a special meaning in both PowerShell and Linux (the $ character represents a variable expression), it was interpreted as a variable expression when passed as a value in the *SA_PASSWORD* environment variable. It also failed SQL Server's password policy requirements.

Last is the assigning of names to containers using the *--name* parameter. Not only is it a good practice to properly name your containers, it also avoids scrambling around trying to figure out what container *cranky_haslett* is and what is it for. I ran the *hello-world* container several times on my Linux host to show the different names that the system automatically generated. If not for the image name, there's no way I can figure out what *relaxed_sammet* container is. Refer to Figure 4-18 for a list of really interesting system-generated names.

```
CONTAINER ID   NAMES                     IMAGE                                                 COMMAND
b4ed09cfdac1   cranky_haslett            hello-world                                           "/hello"
cf33ed7dc3a0   relaxed_sammet            hello-world                                           "/hello"
079bb0367368   elastic_leavitt           hello-world                                           "/hello"
41f3b4e1a860   sqldevlinuxcon01          mcr.microsoft.com/mssql/server:2017-latest-ubuntu     "/opt/mssql/bin/
7ae525e41cd3   condescending_blackburn   hello-world                                           "/hello"
[emsarmiento@CENTOSDOCKER01 ~]$
```

Figure 4-18. *System-generated Docker container names*

If you're curious about how Docker generates these names, refer to the source code at *https://github.com/moby/moby/blob/master/pkg/namesgenerator/names-generator.go*. There's no reason to not have fun doing your job.

Connecting to the SQL Server Instance Remotely

I don't like installing anything unnecessary on production servers, including client tools. In fact, I try to convince my customers to install the SQL Server database engine on Windows Server Core since the day it became supported (I have very few successes but at least I tried). My goal is to minimize the surface area of the servers and prevent people from logging in directly to them. This reduces the attack surface and minimizes human error and administrative overhead. I can't count the number of times somebody accidentally rebooted a production server because they thought they were logged in to a test server – or somebody using the dedicated Terminal Services session to run a simple query and preventing other administrators from logging in.

What I do is install all the client tools I need to manage servers – Remote Server Administration Tools (RSAT), TELNET client, SFTP client, SQL Server Management Studio, and so on – on a client workstation. Use the client workstation to connect to and manage servers remotely. Besides, this is how you'll deploy enterprise applications anyway, with the client remotely connecting to the service.

In a single server deployment, the simplest way to connect to the container is to leverage the IP address or the DNS name (if you have a DNS server) of the Docker host. The *-p* parameter you used with *docker run* allows you to use the Docker host's IP address to access the container remotely and maps the specified port on the Docker host to the specified port on the container. In the example *docker run* command, we're mapping port 1433 on the host to port 1433 on the container.

To find out the IP address of the host machine, you could run

- `ipconfig` on Windows

- `ip addr` on CentOS or Ubuntu

Before attempting to connect to the SQL Server instance inside the container, perform basic networking tests like PING and TELNET. I always start with these two to make sure connectivity issues have nothing to do with SQL Server. I don't want to waste a lot of time troubleshooting SQL Server only to find out that a port has been blocked by a firewall rule. If I don't get a response from a PING test, I don't always assume that the service is down. It might just be that the network administrators have disabled ICMP responses as part of their security policy. A TELNET test on the SQL Server port number would tell me if SQL Server is listening. If I don't get a "could not open a connection to the host" error message, that's the only time I proceed to test using a client application.

Launch SQL Server Management Studio and connect to the SQL Server Docker container using the IP address and the *sysadmin* credentials you specified. Figure 4-19 shows the results of a simple query to display the instance name and SQL Server version. I used SQLCMD mode when running queries so I don't have to constantly provide instance names and credentials when connecting to remote SQL Server instances.

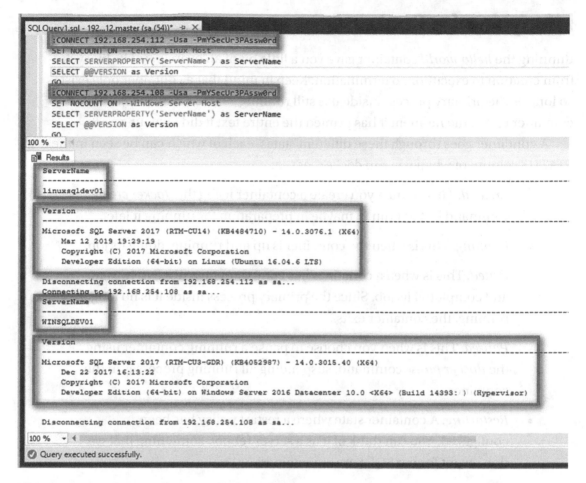

Figure 4-19. Connecting remotely to SQL Server on containers using SSMS

Recall the use of the *-h* parameter to reflect the server hostname – the server hostname is the instance name of a default SQL Server instance. Also, the available SQL Server on Linux container runs on Ubuntu Linux 16.04.6 LTS, even when you're running CentOS Linux 7 as your Docker host.

Once you're inside SQL Server Management Studio, the user experience is the same. You don't have to be in the command line or learn all the new SQL Server command-line tools. You can perform all the management tasks you've ever done in the comforts of a familiar environment.

Lifecycle of a Container

Running the *hello-world* container gave you a little bit of an overview of its lifecycle – from creation to execution to termination. Keep in mind that a container only exists so long as the primary process inside it is still running – hence, why the *hello-world* container exited the moment it has printed the entire text it did on your screen.

A container goes through these different states, each of which can be seen in the *STATUS* column of when you run `docker ps -a`:

- *Created*: This is when you create a container using the *docker create* command but not run it, maybe in preparation for running it later.

- *Running*: This is when the container is up and running, doing its job.

- *Exited*: This is when a container has gone through a RUNNING state and completed its job. Since the primary process inside it is no longer running, the container exits.

- *Paused*: This is when you choose to pause a running container using the *docker pause* command, suspending all running processes in the container.

- *Restarting*: A container state where a restart policy has been configured. You can think of it as a server reboot, something that we don't want for our SQL Server containers.

- *Dead*: This is when the Docker daemon attempted to stop a container but failed.

Think of running the *docker run* command as a combination of running the *docker create* command and *docker start* command. Let's say you want to use both the *docker create* and *docker start* command for the *hello-world* container:

```
docker create hello-world
```

Like the *docker run* command, this will return the container ID value. You pass this as a parameter to the *docker start* command, including the *-a* parameter, to attach the output of the container to your terminal console. I usually just pass the first 12 characters of the container ID in my *docker* commands. Figure 4-20 shows running *docker create* and *docker start* as an alternative to running *docker run*.

```
docker start -a 3df6324e4c12
```

```
emsarmiento@CENTOSDOCKER01:~                                                    —  □  ×
[emsarmiento@CENTOSDOCKER01 ~]$ docker create hello-world
3df6324e4c12bbe9dab45284bec320b0386903bde3b3dd337069b84ce3db25b7
[emsarmiento@CENTOSDOCKER01 ~]$ docker start -a 3df6324e4c12bbe9dab45284bec320b0386903bde3b3dd337069b84ce3db25b7

Hello from Docker!
This message shows that your installation appears to be working correctly.

To generate this message, Docker took the following steps:
 1. The Docker client contacted the Docker daemon.
 2. The Docker daemon pulled the "hello-world" image from the Docker Hub.
    (amd64)
 3. The Docker daemon created a new container from that image which runs the
    executable that produces the output you are currently reading.
 4. The Docker daemon streamed that output to the Docker client, which sent it
    to your terminal.

To try something more ambitious, you can run an Ubuntu container with:
 $ docker run -it ubuntu bash

Share images, automate workflows, and more with a free Docker ID:
 https://hub.docker.com/

For more examples and ideas, visit:
 https://docs.docker.com/get-started/

[emsarmiento@CENTOSDOCKER01 ~]$ ▌
```

Figure 4-20. *Running docker create and docker start commands*

I rarely use these two commands separately and just rely on the *docker run* command for creating and running containers.

Container states are similar to the different states that virtual machines (VM) go through – you can start, stop, or pause them whenever you like. And much like VMs, the processes running inside a container become unavailable when you stop the container. The container remains – together with the data associated with it – in the filesystem of the Docker host until you explicitly remove it. Removing the container does not remove the image. Recall that a container is a runtime instance of the image. You can create, start, stop, and remove as many containers as you want from the reference image – it's not going to affect the image. You could delete the image from the Docker host. Doing so will trigger the Docker daemon to pull the image from the configured container registry when you decide to run it again. We'll cover the internals of images and containers in more detail in *Chapter 5*.

Summary

An understanding of the different components that make up the Docker ecosystem can help you become aware of what goes into running a container. This prepares you for when you start deploying containers in a production environment.

We've looked at the roles of the Docker CLI client and how to use it to run Docker commands. We've explored how the Docker daemon is the center of your interactions with Docker. We also looked at the difference between images and containers and how the Docker daemon interacts with Docker Hub for pulling (and pushing when you start creating your own custom) images. And an understanding of the image naming convention can help you work with both publicly available images and the ones that you'll create.

Running a SQL Server on container and connecting to it remotely are no big deal, especially when Microsoft has already provided images available for use. And there really isn't any difference once you've connected to the SQL Server instance inside the container. You can use the tools and commands that you've already known for years working with SQL Server.

I've introduced you to a couple of *docker* commands in this chapter to get you started working with containers. You definitely need to get these under your belt since you will be using them a lot:

- *docker version*: Displays the Docker version information; used for verifying your installation

- *docker info*: Displays system-wide information; also used for verifying installation and checking configuration

- *docker run*: Runs a command in a new container or, from SQL Server's point of view, runs a container with a SQL Server instance

- *docker search*: Searches Docker Hub for available container images

- *docker pull*: Pulls an image or a set of images from a container registry

- *docker images*: Displays all images stored in the Docker host's local filesystem

- *docker ps*: Lists available containers

Get ready for the next chapter as we'll be looking at images and containers – from the point of view of the filesystem – in more detail.

CHAPTER 5

Docker Images and Containers

Beauty: the adjustment of all parts proportionately so that one cannot add or subtract or change without impairing the harmony of the whole.

—Leon Battista Alberti

Being born and raised in a developing country has its own challenges, interesting ones, to say the least. Our family was in the lower-middle class with a single wage earner. So, things like snacks and movies were considered luxury. Imagine how it felt like entering a McDonald's store for the first time when I was 8 years old.

Our "tita" brought me and my elder brother to a McDonald's store one summer afternoon in 1984. My first ever encounter with the Happy Meal was uneventful – the regular burger coupled with fries and a drink came with the Lego building set. As far as an 8-year-old is concerned, it was a feast that came with a toy set (the fact is the servings were also huge back in those days). I saw from my aunt's face that she was more than happy to oblige if we asked for more. I didn't need any convincing. The menu displayed an enticing picture of a chocolate milkshake, a perfect beverage for the scorching hot summer day.

As the server was preparing my milkshake, I couldn't help but notice a large soda dispenser beside it. Every server preparing orders with drinks would place an empty cup below one of the dispensers, pressed one of those cute little buttons, and out comes the drink. My little kid brain was immediately flooded with questions. Where was the drink coming from? How does it know where to get water or Coca-Cola or root beer? How can it fit all the drinks in that small machine? Was there a guy behind the machine whose only job is to fill up the soda dispenser? Does it really rain cheeseburgers?

© Edwin M Sarmiento 2020
E. M. Sarmiento, *The SQL Server DBA's Guide to Docker Containers*,
https://doi.org/10.1007/978-1-4842-5826-2_5

When you're working for a global fast food chain that sells a dozen or more beverages, it helps to know how a machine like the soda dispenser works. You want to know who the beverage supplier is, how to connect the right beverage tank to the soda dispenser, and what to do in case the machine stopped dispensing drinks. My 8-year-old questions were as valid as they were with that soda machine as they are working with Docker images and containers.

This chapter will cover the internals of working with Docker images and containers from a storage point of view. We'll be exploring what images are made of, how they are described, and how they are stored in the filesystem. The more you understand how Docker deals with images, the better equipped you are at designing your own custom images.

Note   Most of the examples shown in this chapter will pertain to Linux unless otherwise specified. This will give you a chance to improve your skills working with the Linux filesystem while learning about Docker images and containers at the same time.

A Quick Review (And Then Some...)

In the previous chapter, I gave you a high-level overview of the difference between an image and a container. I'm going to repeat it because repetition is key to mastery. But since this is more of a deep dive coverage into images and containers, we're going to explore the concepts in more detail. So, here goes.

A Docker image is a static, *read-only* template for creating application containers. It's a non-running representation of all the various components required to run the application. An image consists of a set of files structured in a filesystem layer that contains application files, operating system–dependent files like libraries that your application needs, and metadata that describes what it is. Each filesystem layer is only a set of differences from the layer before it, much like a series of SQL Server transaction log backups that make up a log sequence chain with the full database backup being the base image. Think back to when you ran the *docker pull* command in the previous chapter. Figure 5-1 illustrates this layered filesystem corresponding to the output of the *docker pull* command for the SQL Server on Linux image. Don't think that the bunch of system-generated, 64-character – represented by short 12-digit – hex strings are meaningless. Each *Pull complete* message represents a filesystem layer that makes up the entire image.

| a9dca2f6722a |
| 6b5009e4f470 |
| bcf04a226444a |
| 0b751601bca3 |
| 739f58768b3f |
| 5a6315cba1ff |
| 06fe57530625 |
| 57da90bec92c |
| 59ab41dd721 |
| Build time |

```
root@CENTOSDOCKER:/
[root@CENTOSDOCKER /]# docker pull microsoft/mssql-server-linux
Using default tag: latest
latest: Pulling from microsoft/mssql-server-linux
59ab41dd721a: Pull complete
57da90bec92c: Pull complete
06fe57530625: Pull complete
5a6315cba1ff: Pull complete
739f58768b3f: Pull complete
0b751601bca3: Pull complete
bcf04a22644a: Pull complete
6b5009e4f470: Pull complete
a9dca2f6722a: Pull complete
Digest: sha256:9b700672670bb3db4b212e8aef841ca79eb2fce7d5975a5ce35b7129
Status: Downloaded newer image for microsoft/mssql-server-linux:latest
[root@CENTOSDOCKER /]#
```

Figure 5-1. *SQL Server on Linux image with image layers*

A Docker container, however, is a runtime instance of the image. Every Docker container you create and run will be based on the read-only image template. You can think of a Docker image as a blueprint, like a technical drawing for a car. You create the blueprint (Docker image) according to how you want the car (Docker container) to look like and function. Once the blueprint has been finalized, you can create as many instances as you want of the car from the blueprint. You have the freedom to make changes to the aesthetic of the car – color, accessories, interiors, and the like – without the need to modify the blueprint. Should you decide to make major modifications to the car, you have to go back to the drawing board and rewrite the blueprint.

If a Docker image is a read-only template, how can you possibly run containers that require making changes to the filesystem? Writing to a read-only media is like trying to write data to a write-once CD-ROM. It doesn't work the second time (and who still uses CD-ROMs in today's world?). Surely, there's some magic happening under the covers if we need to make changes to the files inside the read-only template. Besides, how useful will a read-only database be outside of reporting and analytics? Even a simple configuration change to the SQL Server instance requires making changes to the *master* database data files.

The secret lies in the fact that a container is really a thin, read-write filesystem layer that sits on top of the read-only layer. Figure 5-2 illustrates how a Docker container functions as a thin, read-write filesystem layer sitting on top of the read-only layer. The *docker run* command returns the container ID representing the thin, read-write layer.

71

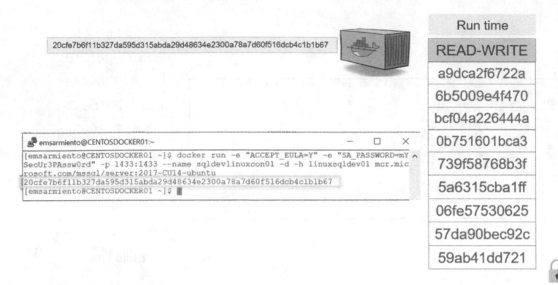

Figure 5-2. *SQL Server on Linux container as a read-write filesystem layer*

This read-write filesystem layer is similar to how differencing disks work in Microsoft Hyper-V and linked clones in VMWare. You can create as many containers as you want from the same image, creating a one-to-many relationship between the image and the container. Any change you make to the container only happens in the read-write filesystem layer and does not affect the base read-only layer. This thin, read-write layer also explains why containers start up quickly compared to physical or virtual machines. Unlike with virtual machines, you are not booting up an entire system with containers. You are simply starting them up, skipping all the processes required to boot up an operating system. Since the base operating system of the Docker host is already started, all the container has to do is create the read-write filesystem layer and load all the necessary files to start the app inside it.

Now that we've established the fact that a Docker container is really a thin, read-write filesystem running on top of a read-only filesystem layer, let's start digging a little bit deeper.

Behind the Scenes of Pulling Images

In the previous chapter, the section on "How Docker Runs Containers" gave you an idea of how the different components in the Docker ecosystem work together to run a container. Step #4 is where the Docker daemon would reach out to Docker Hub to search for and pull an image in preparation for running it. But have you ever wondered how Docker Hub knew what platform your Docker host is running on and how to give it the correct image? And I mean the platform information that you get when you run the `docker info` command, like the one shown in Figure 5-3.

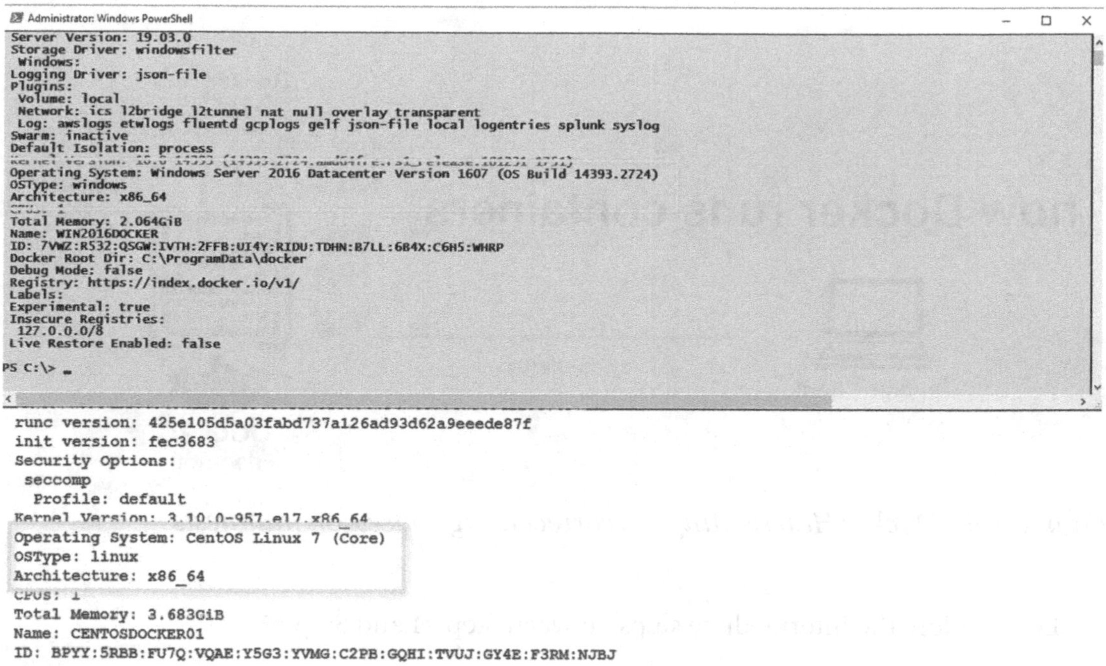

Figure 5-3. *Platform information of your Docker host from the docker info command*

Recall that prior to Microsoft deprecating their version of the *hello-world* image, I can run the same `docker run hello-world` command on both Windows Server and Linux Docker hosts and would get the same output. Docker Hub will give your Docker host the correct image based on the platform information so long as there is an available image.

In between the previous chapter's Step #4 and Step #5 are intermediate steps that deal with *manifests*. Don't get confused about what a manifest is. It's just a fancy term for a JSON file that describes what the image is: the filesystem layers that make up the image, their sizes, and the digest. Figure 5-4 introduces those intermediate steps.

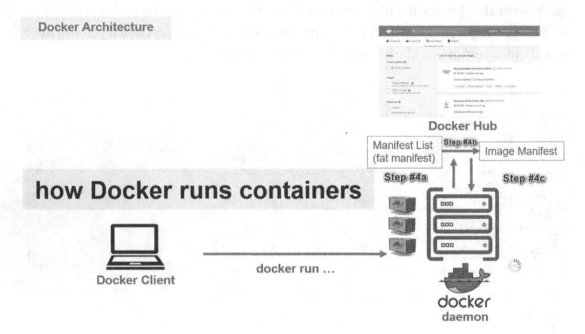

Figure 5-4. *Docker Hub sending the correct image based on manifests*

Let's explore the intermediate steps between Step #4 and Step #5:

1. If the Docker daemon doesn't have a local copy of the *hello-world* container image, it searches Docker Hub for the image (Step #4). The Docker daemon also sends platform information – mainly OS and CPU architecture – to Docker Hub and queries for manifest.

2. If a "fat" manifest exists, Docker Hub searches it for the section that matches the Docker daemon's platform information (from Step #4a) and redirects the query to the corresponding image manifest (Step #4b).

3. The image manifest gets parsed, reading the corresponding filesystem layers required to build the image. Those filesystem layers are then sent to the Docker daemon (Step #4c).

4. Once the download completes, the Docker daemon created and ran a new container based on the *hello-world* image (Step #5).

The use of a fat manifest allows an image repository like Docker Hub to serve the right image to a Docker host. You wouldn't want a Linux Docker host pulling a Windows-based image from an image repository, would you? That's not going to work.

Fat Manifest?

Step #4a introduced what is called a "fat" manifest. I don't really know why it's called a "fat" manifest, but the official term is *manifest list*. Think of a manifest list as a "manifest of manifest." The idea behind having a "fat" manifest is to provide seamless user experience for multi-architecture support, the true essence behind "write once, deploy anywhere" principle that Java used to brag about. With a "fat" manifest, I don't need to worry about finding the correct image name and tag combinations that will work for my current platform. For example, I can run the `docker run hello-world` command across different operating systems and different CPU architectures.

Let's examine the "fat" manifest for the *hello-world* image using the *docker manifest* command. Since this is an experimental command, you need to enable the DOCKER_ CLI_EXPERIMENTAL environment variable using the *export* command. Run the following commands to examine the manifest list for the *hello-world* image. Figure 5-5 shows a snippet of the different architectures that the *hello-world* image supports and the fields that define it.

```
export DOCKER_CLI_EXPERIMENTAL=enabled
docker manifest inspect hello-world
```

```
emsarmiento@CENTOSDOCKER01:~                                           —   □   ✕

[emsarmiento@CENTOSDOCKER01 ~]$ export DOCKER_CLI_EXPERIMENTAL=enabled
[emsarmiento@CENTOSDOCKER01 ~]$ docker manifest inspect hello-world
{
    "schemaVersion": 2,                                          mediaType for "fat" manifest
    "mediaType": "application/vnd.docker.distribution.manifest.list.v2+json",
    "manifests": [                                               mediaType for image manifest
      {
          "mediaType": "application/vnd.docker.distribution.manifest.v2+json",
          "size": 524,
          "digest": "sha256:92c7f9c92844bbbb5d0a101b22f7c2a7949e40f8ea90c8b3bc396879d95e899a",
          "platform": {
             "architecture": "amd64",                   content digest of the image manifest:
             "os": "linux"                                     Linux on AMD64 image
          }
      },
      {
          "mediaType": "application/vnd.docker.distribution.manifest.v2+json",
          "size": 525,
          "digest": "sha256:1e44d8bca6fb0464794555e5ccd3a32e2a4f6e44a20605e4e82605189904f44d",
          "platform": {
             "architecture": "arm",                     content digest of the image manifest:
             "os": "linux",                                     Linux on ARM image
             "variant": "v5"
          }
      },
      {
          "mediaType": "application/vnd.docker.distribution.manifest.v2+json",
          "size": 524,
          "digest": "sha256:d1fd2e204af0a2bca3ab033b417b29c76d7950ed29a44e427d1c4d07d14f04f9",
          "platform": {
             "architecture": "arm",
             "os": "linux",
             "variant": "v7"
          }
```

Figure 5-5. Fat manifest for the hello-world image

The "fat" manifest for the *hello-world* image tells us that we can run the container on several OS and CPU architecture combinations – Linux on x86 and amd64, Windows 10 Build 10.0.17134.885, and Linux on ARM, among others. Imagine running a Docker container on a Raspberry Pi device.

Note   I wish this was the case with SQL Server on containers. Unfortunately, the Microsoft documentation specifically mentions "x64-compatible only" processor types for SQL Server 2017 and higher on Windows Server and Linux. Gone are the days when SQL Server ran on non-x64 platforms like the DEC Alpha. However, Azure SQL Database Edge looks promising for ARM-based Linux devices. Check out *https://azure.microsoft.com/en-us/services/sql-database-edge/* for more details. It's still in the early days of development.

What gives this away as a "fat" manifest are the following fields:

- *mediaType*: This will have the value application/vnd.docker. distribution.manifest.list.v2+json.

- *schemaVersion*: This will have a value of 2.

The "fat" manifest is optional – you can create a Docker image without it. If it doesn't exist, Step #4a is skipped and the Docker daemon's query is sent directly to the image manifest (Step #4b). An example of this is the SQL Server on Linux image. Since it was specifically created for the Linux on amd64 platform, the *mediaType* field will only show an image manifest. Refer to the following *mediaType* value to distinguish it from a "fat" manifest:

> *"mediaType": "application/vnd.docker.distribution.manifest.*
> *v2+json"*

Run the following commands to examine the image manifest for the *SQL Server on Linux* image. Figure 5-6 shows a snippet of the SQL Server on Linux image manifest.

```
export DOCKER_CLI_EXPERIMENTAL=enabled
docker manifest inspect mcr.microsoft.com/mssql/server:2017-CU14-ubuntu
```

Figure 5-6. *Manifest for the SQL Server on Linux image*

I didn't say I like working with JSON data. But the reality is that JSON is a very popular data interchange format that even SQL Server included support for it starting with SQL Server 2016. Good thing there are alternatives. A tool that you can use to query whether or not a Docker image has a "fat" manifest without having to deal with all those JSON data is the *mquery* utility. It also tells you, if a "fat" manifest exists, what other platforms are supported. For more information on the *mquery* utility, check out *https://github.com/estesp/mquery*.

Run the following command to check the SQL Server on Linux image using the *mquery* utility. Keep in mind that this will also pull the corresponding image that contains the tool. Figure 5-7 displays the output of the command, confirming that the SQL Server on Linux image does not have a "fat" manifest (Manifest List: No) and only supports Linux on the amd64 platform.

```
docker run mplatform/mquery mcr.microsoft.com/mssql/server:2017-CU14-ubuntu
```

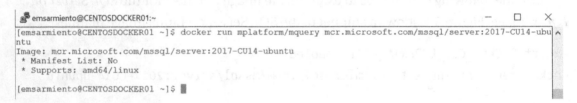

Figure 5-7. *Running the mquery tool against the SQL Server on Linux image*

If you run the tool against the official Linux Ubuntu image, you will see the different platforms it supports, as shown in Figure 5-8. Most of the Docker official images now support multiple architectures.

```
[emsarmiento@CENTOSDOCKER01 ~]$ docker run mplatform/mquery ubuntu:latest
Image: ubuntu:latest
 * Manifest List: Yes
 * Supported platforms:
   - linux/amd64
   - linux/arm/v7
   - linux/arm64
   - linux/386
   - linux/ppc64le
   - linux/s390x

[emsarmiento@CENTOSDOCKER01 ~]$
```

Figure 5-8. *Running the mquery tool against the official Ubuntu image*

Image Manifest

If a "fat" manifest exists, inside it is the *manifests* field that contains a list of image manifests for the different platforms that it supports, like a pointer to the image manifest. If it doesn't exist, what you get when you run the *docker manifest inspect* command is the *image manifest*. The image manifest provides the details of the different filesystem layers needed to build the image and a configuration that tells the Docker daemon how to piece together all those layers to run a container. Think of the different filesystem layers as Lego pieces and the image manifest as the building instruction manual (that's how memorable my very first Happy Meal was). The generic Lego pieces are unaware of how they are related to one another. Only the building instruction manual has the details that connect them all so you can build a Star Wars Millennium Falcon. You can even create your own Lego structure (Docker image) from the available pieces (filesystem layers) so long as you also create your own building instruction manual (image manifest) – even if the manual is just in your head. The process of pulling a Docker image from a repository consists of retrieving the image manifest and the filesystem layers.

Run the following *docker inspect* command to explore the low-level details of the *hello-world* image. Note that you are inspecting an image, not a container. You can use the *docker inspect* command to inspect both the image and the container. But we're only interested in the image at this point.

```
docker inspect hello-world
```

If you scroll down the output to the *Layers* section, it will tell you how many filesystem layers this image has. Figure 5-9 shows the *hello-world* image as having only one filesystem layer.

```
        },
        "Name": "overlay2"
    },
    "RootFS": {
        "Type": "layers",
        "Layers": [
            "sha256:af0b15c8625bb1938f1d7b17081031f649fd14e6b233688eea3c5483994a66a3"
        ]
    },
    "Metadata": {
        "LastTagTime": "0001-01-01T00:00:00Z"
    }
}
]
```

Figure 5-9. *The hello-world image with one filesystem layer*

Tip   Don't be confused between the *docker manifest inspect* and the *docker inspect* commands. They may both have the same *inspect* subcommand but they function differently. If you want to explore a manifest – either a "fat" manifest or image manifest – use the *docker manifest inspect* command. If you want to explore low-level details of a Docker object such as an image or a container, use the *docker inspect* command. Too bad they both return results in a JSON array. There's just no escaping the pervasiveness of JSON.

Recall the output of the docker run hello-world command as shown in Figure 5-10. It is consistent with the number of filesystem layers pulled from the Docker Hub.

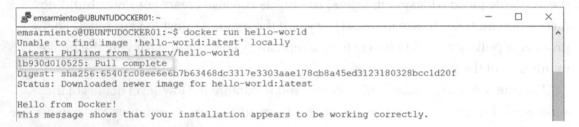

```
emsarmiento@UBUNTUDOCKER01: ~                                    —    □    ×
emsarmiento@UBUNTUDOCKER01:~$ docker run hello-world
Unable to find image 'hello-world:latest' locally
latest: Pulling from library/hello-world
1b930d010525: Pull complete
Digest: sha256:6540fc08ee6e6b7b63468dc3317e3303aae178cb8a45ed3123180328bcc1d20f
Status: Downloaded newer image for hello-world:latest

Hello from Docker!
This message shows that your installation appears to be working correctly.
```

Figure 5-10. *Running the hello-world container, pulling one filesystem layer*

Similarly, you can run the following command to explore the SQL Server on Linux image:

```
docker inspect mcr.microsoft.com/mssql/server:2017-CU14-ubuntu
```

Figure 5-11 shows the *Layers* section with nine filesystem layers, also consistent with the number of filesystem layers shown in Figure 5-1.

```
emsarmiento@CENTOSDOCKER01:~                                                    —   □   ×

f:/var/lib/docker/overlay2/2e086f90806648f08f91e1ad5278b37afcceb571fca7875b3f671c31ef6fb61b/diff:/var/li
b/docker/overlay2/d5d922b57065f74c94b27b5216793720fd3f3e1114c22f5befe45ddc69f276c3/diff:/var/lib/docker/
overlay2/021be9f89d6f778ba3e727dff1bb2234f0969817cb6880f543f689f3bd52a92f/diff:/var/lib/docker/overlay2/
a598cb26e4d598b322e555bc62afcb1fd4e42b8afc8c888fa9dcd4c72f3eac93/diff:/var/lib/docker/overlay2/93b9b1831
37b70978bbccabea095ec6ff5e2f895344fff1e6390435af588315a/diff",
              "MergedDir": "/var/lib/docker/overlay2/c01f24c48875811594b71f4fbe22e0ef89614e9c8f24a7fc0
55fa6862e1f0947/merged",
              "UpperDir": "/var/lib/docker/overlay2/c01f24c48875811594b71f4fbe22e0ef89614e9c8f24a7fc05
5fa6862e1f0947/diff",
              "WorkDir": "/var/lib/docker/overlay2/c01f24c48875811594b71f4fbe22e0ef89614e9c8f24a7fc055
fa6862e1f0947/work"
          },
          "Name": "overlay2"
      },
      "RootFS": {
          "Type": "layers",
          "Layers": [
              "sha256:644879075e24394efef8a7dddefbc133aad42002df6223cacf98bd1e3d5ddde2",
              "sha256:d7ff1dc646ba52a02312b535446d6c9b72cd09fda0480524e4828554efb2f748",
              "sha256:686245e78935e73b737c9a82111c3c7df35f5529d06ce8c2f9a7cd32ec90b456",
              "sha256:d73dd9e652956dccbbef716de4b172cc15fff644cc92fc69d221cc3a1cb89a39",
              "sha256:2de391e51d731ba02b708038a7f98b7103061b916727bcd165e9ee6402f4cdde",
              "sha256:d33a8ef9dea5016c8647174b5580425f021385b9ab87453cd7508587c030305c",
              "sha256:911ad08015cfe167b552e1c330220f90e4ff82f572bfb309f7e3afab619d71fc",
              "sha256:d8ae8f5c696757597c1fc44e2755f1cf55041f924848a34eb500092b6af3b6d4",
              "sha256:ff6a9e5f1dd51c05977b17c46e04c114264df6725b5cfdb799b5887b7d8691e4"
          ]
      },
      "Metadata": {
          "LastTagTime": "0001-01-01T00:00:00Z"
      }
  }
]
[emsarmiento@CENTOSDOCKER01 ~]$
```

Figure 5-11. *Filesystem layers of the SQL Server on Linux image*

Check out *https://docs.docker.com/registry/spec/manifest-v2-2/* for additional information regarding manifests. Although the image manifest is the only one relevant to us working with SQL Server on containers, knowing that you can run a Docker container on multiple platforms gives you an idea on what's possible. Who knows, Microsoft may decide to run SQL Server on other platforms other than x64 in the future.

Content Digest

In the wild world of the Internet, it would be unwise for you to download anything without validating its integrity and authenticity. You wouldn't know if the contents have been maliciously tampered with or modified as part of a change request. This is where the concept of a content-addressable storage comes in. Content-addressable storage is used to store information so it can be retrieved based on its content, not location. It uses a cryptographic hash function's digest that is generated from the content. How this works is that a hash function is generated based on the contents of a file – or in Docker's case, the filesystem layer. The generated hash is called the *content digest*. Since the content digest is a hash of the filesystem layer's contents, changing the contents in the layers requires changing the content digest.

So, when you run a *docker pull* or a *docker run* command, the content digest is included as part of the return code. Docker Hub sends the filesystem layers that have the same content digest as the ones defined in the image manifest. Once downloaded, the Docker daemon reruns the hash and verifies if the content digest of the filesystem layers is the same as the one defined in the image manifest. This guarantees the integrity and authenticity of the filesystem layers that make up the image regardless of where they are stored – be it on Docker Hub or your own container registry.

Distribution Hash

I wish I can say that the digest values in the image manifest are the same as what you get from the *Layers* section of the output from the *docker inspect* command. That would make it easy for us to identify which digest corresponds to which layer just by looking at both the image manifest and the *Layers* section. Unfortunately, it's more complicated than that. Just have a look at the hash in the image manifest for the SQL Server on Linux image and compare it to the *Layers* section, as shown in Figure 5-12.

```
emsarmiento@CENTOSDOCKER01:~                                           —   □   ×

[emsarmiento@CENTOSDOCKER01 ~]$ docker manifest inspect mcr.microsoft.com/mssql/server:2017-CU14-ubuntu
{
        "schemaVersion": 2,
        "mediaType": "application/vnd.docker.distribution.manifest.v2+json",
        "config": {
                "mediaType": "application/vnd.docker.container.image.v1+json",
                "size": 5531,
                "digest": "sha256:644ca19cb10df461d8ed47ecafd1bd627dc856f8e053840e6c84572d112a3838"
        },
        "layers": [
                {
                        "mediaType": "application/vnd.docker.image.rootfs.diff.tar.gzip",
                        "size": 42215182,
b1"                     "digest": "sha256:59ab41dd721a1d353bb77e39468417d8b74e5a9f669d09d37ab4a5c73f0949
                },
                {
                        "mediaType": "application/vnd.docker.image.rootfs.diff.tar.gzip",
                        "size": 855,
43"                     "digest": "sha256:57da90bec92ca4bf7c5e0aad0a1b0304e2b1460d7847717e4c2a29eaaccfe9
                },
                {
                        "mediaType": "application/vnd.docker.image.rootfs.diff.tar.gzip",
                        "size": 626,
b3"                     "digest": "sha256:06fe5753062556f7c9614562c50146e92d5a57928f153315ffdcb1460bf024
                },
                {
                        "mediaType": "application/vnd.docker.image.rootfs.diff.tar.gzip",
```

```
        "Type": "layers",
        "Layers": [
                "sha256:644879075e24394efef8a7dddefbc133aad42002df6223cacf98bd1e3d5ddde2",
                "sha256:d7ff1dc646ba52a02312b535446d6c9b72cd09fda0480524e4828554efb2f748",
                "sha256:686245e78935e73b737c9a82111c3c7df35f5529d06ce8c2f9a7cd32ec90b456",
                "sha256:d73dd9e652956dccbbef716de4b172cc15fff644cc92fc69d221cc3a1cb89a39",
                "sha256:2de391e51d731ba02b708038a7f98b7103061b916727bcd165e9ee6402f4cdde",
                "sha256:d33a8ef9dea5016c8647174b5580425f021385b9ab87453cd7508587c030305c",
                "sha256:911ad08015cfe167b552e1c330220f90e4ff82f572bfb309f7e3afab619d71fc",
                "sha256:d8ae8f5c696757597c1fc44e2755f1cf55041f924848a34eb500092b6af3b6d4",
                "sha256:ff6a9e5f1dd51c05977b17c46e04c114264df6725b5cfdb799b5887b7d8691e4"
        ]
]
```

Figure 5-12. *Comparing the digest values for the SQL Server on Linux image layers*

That's because when you are working with files across the network, a form of file compression is implemented to improve network bandwidth and storage space requirements. It's the same thing when working with other file types on the Internet. But compressing a file changes its content and, as a result, also changes its content digest. Surely, this would be an issue when you are pushing and/or pulling the filesystem layers because the content digests no longer match – the hash verification would fail.

To address this issue, a *distribution hash* is generated. Distribution hashes are generated after the filesystem layers are compressed. Every single filesystem layer used to build an image will be compressed and distribution hash generated. The distribution hash for each filesystem layer is what gets written in the image manifest. Once the distribution hashes have been written in the image manifest, the image can now be pushed to Docker Hub or other container registries.

The hash that you see in the *Layers* section when you run the *docker inspect* command for the image is the uncompressed hash – the content digest – of the filesystem layer. Meanwhile, the hash value in the *digest* field of the image manifest is that of the compressed filesystem layer – the distribution hash. Given the details of how the content digest and distribution hashes work with manifests, Docker images, and filesystem layers, Figure 5-13 presents a better picture of the SQL Server on Linux image manifest shown in Figure 5-6. Also, run the following command to display the details of the SQL Server on Linux image:

```
docker images mcr.microsoft.com/mssql/server:2017-CU14-ubuntu
```

Figure 5-13. *Content digest and distribution hashes for the SQL Server on Linux image*

Your Docker Host's Local Filesystem

Once the filesystem layers required to build the image have been downloaded into your Docker host's local filesystem, the Docker daemon cooks up its magic to assemble the pieces so you can run a container. Well, only the assembling of the pieces is true in that statement. But it may seem like magic when you do think about what is going on under the covers. Let's have a look at the different components that make this magic happen.

Union Filesystem

Working with Docker containers and how they work with the filesystem require an understanding of *union filesystems*. A union filesystem allows you to take different filesystem layers and create a union of their contents, with the topmost layer overriding any similar files found in the layers below. The simplest way I can describe this without overwhelming you with the technical details is like writing something – like ABC – on a transparent tape. I can stick another layer of transparent tape on top of the existing one with a totally different writing – like DEF. I'll stick another layer above the topmost layer with a different writing – like GHI. When I look at the layers of transparent tape from the top, what I would see is a single layer with the writing ABCDEFGHI, assuming you didn't write directly on top of the transparent tape layer below it. From Docker's point of view, all of these layers of transparent tape are what make up an image. Regardless of how many layers there are, there's just one image.

The way a union filesystem is implemented is through storage drivers. In Linux, the most common ones are OverlayFS and AUFS (formerly known as AnotherUnionFS until it was renamed to advanced multilayered unification filesystem). AUFS was the default storage driver in earlier versions of Docker. Newer installations leverage *overlay2*, which is an improved version of OverlayFS.

Files, Directory Names, and Symbolic Links

Since each filesystem layer that gets pulled from Docker Hub is stored in the Docker host's local filesystem, it makes sense for you to know where they are stored so you can examine them later on for performing administrative tasks such as cleaning up your drive, managing images, moving files around, and the like. You also need to know what the files are and how they are referenced.

The location of the filesystem layers in the local disk depends on the storage driver that you are using. Run the following command on a Linux host to find the installed storage driver:

```
docker info | grep -w 'Storage Driver:'
```

Run the following command on a Windows Server host to find the installed storage driver:

```
docker info | Select-String "Storage Driver"
```

Figure 5-14 shows the storage driver for Linux and Windows Server hosts, respectively.

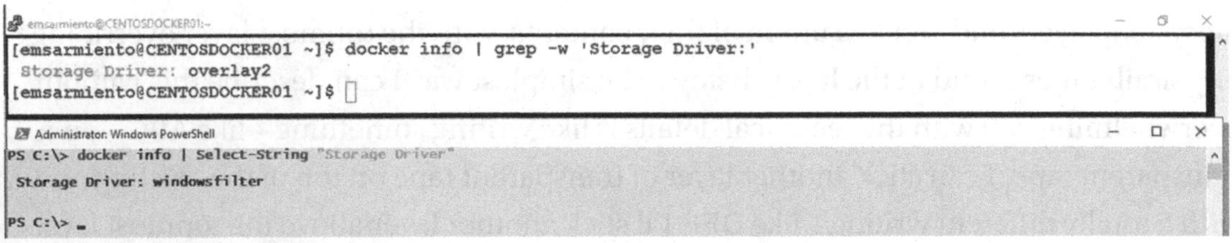

Figure 5-14. *Displaying Docker storage drivers*

On a Linux host, you can find the filesystem layers in the */var/lib/docker/aufs* directory if you are using AUFS or */var/lib/docker/overlay2* directory if you are using overlay2. On a Windows Server host, it's on *C:\ProgramData\docker\windowsfilter*. Remember that the *C:\ProgramData* is a hidden folder so you might not see it through Windows Explorer unless you have it configured to display hidden items.

Let's explore the contents of the */var/lib/docker/overlay2* directory on a Linux host. You would need *sudo* privileges to explore the */var/lib/docker* directory and everything in it. Remember to prefix your commands with *sudo*. The following examples run as *root* to simplify the commands. I also cleaned up my Linux host so it only contains the SQL Server on Linux image.

Refer to Figure 5-15. We'll keep using the `ls -l` command to list the files and directories in Linux. Inside the *overlay2* directory are nine directories that have 64-character hex strings as names. Each of them represents the filesystem layers of the SQL Server on Linux image. I also wish there was an easy way to correlate the directory names with the hash of the image layers that you get when you pull the image layers.

Unfortunately, the directory names are neither the content digest of the uncompressed layers nor their distribution hash. They are based on a randomly generated "cache id" that the Docker daemon keeps track of where the layers' contents are on disk. Let's park this concept here for a minute and come back to it later.

```
emsarmiento@CENTOSDOCKER01:/var/lib/docker/overlay2                          –  □  ×
[root@CENTOSDOCKER01 overlay2]# ls -l
total 4
drwx------. 3 root root   30 Aug  4 19:24 06eaa3c437eeba370a3fcf317ff3309cad1f87d4875823287d98e2a4a617322b
drwx------. 4 root root   55 Aug  4 19:24 181cf8b59f294362982feb5c34b3111c83771337be9da27d5ab7e3b7b869b3e8
drwx------. 4 root root   55 Aug  4 19:24 37023615aa0228bc2ecc4639d971806430d2967b9afd8819b927c16768e8fe82
drwx------. 4 root root   55 Aug  4 19:24 3c41b3611ba38f280198138681c65f86c30a8f0bef04f35257698498f500493a
drwx------. 4 root root   55 Aug  4 19:24 4d82cf4ad32e2555ac3f5852a335406e1a84aa70c11b21e2f4e35c140c223616
drwx------. 4 root root   55 Aug  4 19:24 551ebc14fd0fda8d3eaf8a3ce1eb07ae8b5f03db858a0289fdd9d4254dab5609
drwx------. 4 root root   55 Aug  4 19:24 70f09ad1f2b74ca2cde84d1377839488e31e04458392bfb7bcc13f2927cc9082
drwx------. 4 root root   55 Aug  4 19:24 92e3c43506014db9778446e3a21d9663428302a49e4ae3f7b654acc2952249c0
brw-------. 1 root root 253, 0 Jul 23 22:26 backingFsBlockDev
drwx------. 4 root root   55 Aug  4 19:24 f9440d8359c64bfb7b525b293d08a4195623bea7d90d82bede2cc2886e010911
drwx------. 2 root root 4096 Aug  4 19:24 l
[root@CENTOSDOCKER01 overlay2]# █
```

Figure 5-15. *Displaying /var/lib/docker/overlay2 directory*

There's also another directory named *l* (lowercase L). This directory contains the shortened layer identifiers as *symbolic links*. In Linux, a symbolic link is a text file whose content is a path to another file or directory in the form of an absolute or relative path and that affects pathname resolution. Think of it as a shortcut in Windows. The big difference is that a symbolic link in Linux can act like a substitute for a directory or a file, whereas a shortcut in Windows is just a regular file that has a reference to a destination file or folder. Figure 5-16 displays the content of the */var/lib/docker/overlay2/l* directory.

```
emsarmiento@CENTOSDOCKER01:/var/lib/docker/overlay2/l                          –  □  ×
[root@CENTOSDOCKER01 l]# pwd
/var/lib/docker/overlay2/l
[root@CENTOSDOCKER01 l]# ls -l                           symbolic link
total 0
lrwxrwxrwx. 1 root root 72 Aug  4 19:24 2YO42XXOU7E2ATZNCX7GOOKUBI -> ../92e3c43506014db9778446e3a21d9663428302a49
e4ae3f7b654acc2952249c0/diff
lrwxrwxrwx. 1 root root 72 Aug  4 19:24 AKAY7CCWAWIQUPHTGHJMUB4X55 -> ../3c41b3611ba38f280198138681c65f86c30a8f0be
f04f35257698498f500493a/diff
lrwxrwxrwx. 1 root root 72 Aug  4 19:24 GAJDAYEWW5D53XFXPVIYW5PEAO -> ../4d82cf4ad32e2555ac3f5852a335406e1a84aa70c
11b21e2f4e35c140c223616/diff
lrwxrwxrwx. 1 root root 72 Aug  4 19:24 GG3HHXWNHGMCM4JLYH5GETBT2X -> ../70f09ad1f2b74ca2cde84d1377839488e31e04458
392bfb7bcc13f2927cc9082/diff
lrwxrwxrwx. 1 root root 72 Aug  4 19:24 H3KQTH4VTDYYTWYUQX4PCDUI6Q -> ../181cf8b59f294362982feb5c34b3111c83771337b
e9da27d5ab7e3b7b869b3e8/diff
lrwxrwxrwx. 1 root root 72 Aug  4 19:24 OHPRELSZ7HQRQSWK52WSSH5GPW -> ../06eaa3c437eeba370a3fcf317ff3309cad1f87d48
75823287d98e2a4a617322b/diff
lrwxrwxrwx. 1 root root 72 Aug  4 19:24 SGXJVNVMWUQZIN5PSGY7SKVYGJ -> ../37023615aa0228bc2ecc4639d971806430d2967b9
afd8819b927c16768e8fe82/diff
lrwxrwxrwx. 1 root root 72 Aug  4 19:24 SX5CTIIFSSOUH7PGM5J2A6K5LU -> ../551ebc14fd0fda8d3eaf8a3ce1eb07ae8b5f03db8
58a0289fdd9d4254dab5609/diff
lrwxrwxrwx. 1 root root 72 Aug  4 19:24 YDML67BTE2UAGGUNDLD7DWI2ND -> ../f9440d8359c64bfb7b525b293d08a4195623bea7d
90d82bede2cc2886e010911/diff
[root@CENTOSDOCKER01 l]# █
```

Figure 5-16. *Inside the /var/lib/docker/overlay2/l directory*

The 26-character symbolic link points to the path after the ->. For example, the symbolic link 2YO42XXOU7E2ATZNCX7GOOKUBI points to the *92e3c43506014db977 8446e3a21d9663428302a49e4ae3f7b654acc2952249c0/diff* directory. So far, so good.

But remember, these are not hashes. These are cache id values that the Docker daemon uses to keep track of where the layers' contents are on disk. To find out which directory maps to this cache id, we need to search for this cache id value inside a file named *cache-id*. This file contains the directory name that contains the filesystem layer. And it's inside one of the directories in */var/lib/docker/image/overlay2/layerdb/sha256*. Run the following *grep* command to search for files inside the */var/lib/docker/image/ overlay2/layerdb/sha256* directory that contain the cache id value you're looking for. For the symbolic link 2YO42XXOU7E2ATZNCX7GOOKUBI, I'll just use the first 12 characters of the directory name.

```
grep -Ril "92e3c4350601"
```

The following parameters are used with the *grep* command:

- *R*: Recursive; I want *grep* to search for the content within the files inside the directory and subdirectory.

- *i*: Ignore case.

- *l*: Displays the filename and not the result.

Figure 5-17 displays the output of the *grep* command. Note that the 64-character hex string directory name is now the content digest of the filesystem layer. You also get the file named *cache-id*.

Figure 5-17. *The cache-id file containing the directory name of the symbolic link*

Run the following *cat* command to display the contents of this *cache-id* file. Be aware of the path to the file. I'm running the command from inside the */var/lib/docker/image/ overlay2/layerdb/sha256* directory. Figure 5-18 shows the cache id value representing the directory name.

```
cat 98fc4d5421178c7be7d5718d2d44abba8053dc5c712e51658fe5b872675b4f7a/cache-id
```

Figure 5-18. *The cache-id value corresponding to the directory name*

Be sure to use the values that you get in your Linux host when exploring these directories and files. But I'll stop right here before we end up going down the rabbit hole of hashes translated into cache ids and into directory names and what have you. For now, it's enough to know where the filesystem layers are stored on disk and how the Docker daemon keeps track of where they are. If you really want to dig deeper on Docker's local storage architecture, check out *https://programmer.group/docker-learning-image-s-local-storage-architecture.html*.

There are a few more files to be aware of:

- */var/lib/docker/image/overlay2/repositories.json*: Stores information of all pulled images in your local disk.

- */var/lib/docker/image/overlay2/imagedb/content/sha256/<hex value>*: The filenames inside this directory are the image IDs of the images you pulled; they are the basis for when you run some of the Docker commands like *docker inspect* and *docker history*.

- */var/lib/docker/image/overlay2/distribution/diffid-by-digest/ sha256/<hex value>*: The filenames inside this directory are the mappings between the content digest and the distribution hash (based on the *docker manifest inspect* command) of the filesystem layers you pulled.

There are still more of these files and directories, most of them undocumented. I'll leave them for you to poke around and figure out on your own. But don't mess around with them unless you know exactly what they are for.

Note   The names of directories can change should you decide to delete and repull all of the filesystem layers and images in your Docker host. What doesn't change is the hash of the filesystem layers. The hashes are what make the images immutable.

Also, Windows does not have an */* folder. The folders in the *C:\ProgramData\ docker\windowsfilter* are the cache id values themselves, not symbolic links. Plus, everything else about the filesystem structure is the same – except they are on *C:\ ProgramData\docker*.

Stitching Layers: Assembling the Image

Once the filesystem layers are stored on disk and identifiers defined, the Docker daemon starts piecing them together to form a complete image. The manifest tells the Docker daemon which filesystem layers are needed to build the image and run a container. This is also where the storage driver works with the Docker daemon to build a unified view of the different filesystem layers. I'll describe how this is done using the *overlay2* storage driver since this is the default storage driver on Linux.

You've seen how the filesystem layers are stored as directories in the */var/lib/docker/ overlay2/* directory, named using their corresponding cache id. Recall the image in Figure 5-1 where it displays the different filesystem layers that make up the SQL Server on Linux image. The lowest layer in the image contains the following:

- A file named *link*. This contains the symbolic link between the cache id value and the directory containing the contents of the layer.

- A directory named *diff*. This contains the contents of the layer.

The next and succeeding layers in the image also contain the following in addition to the *link* file and *diff* directory:

- A file named *lower*. This file contains the symbolic link to the layer below it (parent).

- A directory named *merged*. A view that contains the unified contents of itself and the layer below it. This directory gets created under a new directory that represents the read-write layer (container), not the read-only filesystem layer.

- A directory named *work*. A directory that overlay2 uses internally.

How a Union FileSystem Works

To better understand how Docker leverages the storage driver to build the image, let's use the *mount* command to create directories as layers and "mount" them as a union filesystem layer. First, create the directories – lower, diff, merged, work. Be sure you are logged in using your user account so you don't mess around with any Docker-related files and folders. Run the following command to create the directories using the *mkdir* command:

```
mkdir lower diff merged work
```

Next, let's create a file inside the *lower* directory. This directory will function as the lowest/base layer. Run the following command to create a file named *fileInLower.txt* with the provided text:

```
echo "LOWER: This file is in the LOWER directory" > lower/fileInLower.txt
```

Now, run the following *mount* command to unify the directories we created:

```
sudo mount -t overlay -o lowerdir=lower,upperdir=diff,workdir=work none
merged
```

We're using the *overlay* filesystem type and the *merged* directory as the location of the unified view. Since we are not mounting any device but a directory, we use *none* as a placeholder. To verify, run the following command to display the mount that you just created as shown in Figure 5-19:

```
mount | grep overlay
```

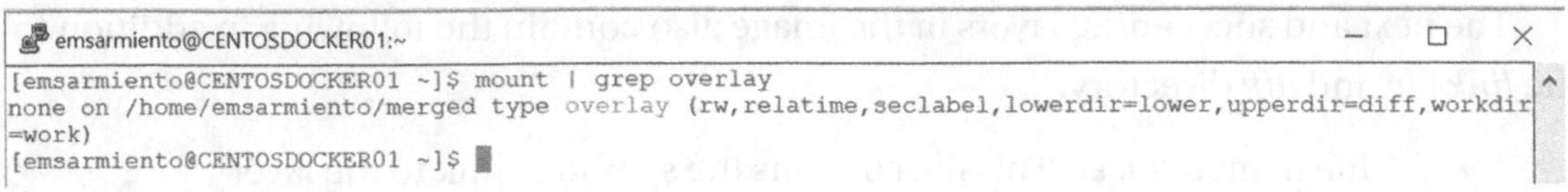

```
emsarmiento@CENTOSDOCKER01:~                                    —    □    ×
[emsarmiento@CENTOSDOCKER01 ~]$ mount | grep overlay
none on /home/emsarmiento/merged type overlay (rw,relatime,seclabel,lowerdir=lower,upperdir=diff,workdir
=work)
[emsarmiento@CENTOSDOCKER01 ~]$
```

Figure 5-19. *Properties of the newly created mount*

You now have a file in the *lower* directory and a *merged* directory that displays a unified view of all directories. It's time to test out the union filesystem. Create a new file in the *merged* directory.

echo "MERGED: This file is in the MERGED directory" > merged/fileInMerged. txt

When you browse the contents of the *merged* directory, you will see the file you created in the *lower* directory and the one you just created in the *merged* directory, as shown in Figure 5-20.

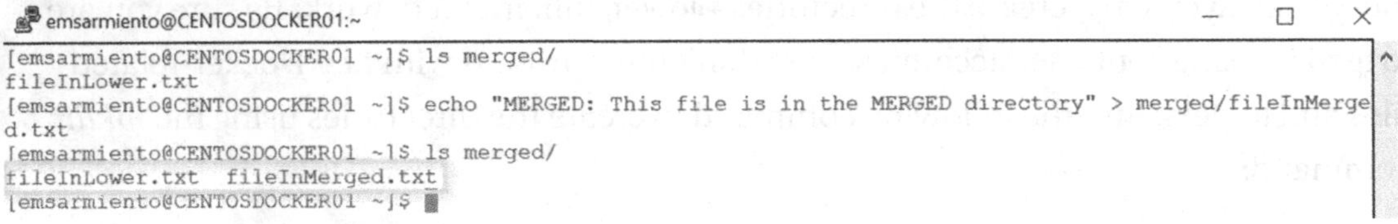

```
emsarmiento@CENTOSDOCKER01:~                                    —    □    ×
[emsarmiento@CENTOSDOCKER01 ~]$ ls merged/
fileInLower.txt
[emsarmiento@CENTOSDOCKER01 ~]$ echo "MERGED: This file is in the MERGED directory" > merged/fileInMerge
d.txt
[emsarmiento@CENTOSDOCKER01 ~]$ ls merged/
fileInLower.txt   fileInMerged.txt
[emsarmiento@CENTOSDOCKER01 ~]$
```

Figure 5-20. *Union filesystem in action*

This is just one aspect of how a unified filesystem works and how Docker leverages it to create a read-write filesystem layer for the container. You still have other aspects like working with read-only filesystem layers and working with multiple filesystem layers. A great resource on how OverlayFS works and how Docker leverages it to build images based on filesystem layers can be found here: *http://blog.programster.org/ overlayfs*.

Traversing the Layers

Let's find the lowest layer in the image and the succeeding layers above it. All the layers have the *lower* directory – except for the lowest layer (why would it if it's the lowest layer, duh). Let's use this information to search for the directory inside */var/lib/ docker/overlay2/* that does not have a *lower* directory. You could manually search every directory to find the one that does not have the *lower* directory (or the one that only has the *link* file and *diff* directory), like how you would with Windows Explorer. But that's time-consuming. Instead, run the following command to do so:

```
find -maxdepth 1 -type d '!' -exec test -e "{}/lower" ';' -print
```

The *find* command is used to search the */var/lib/docker/overlay2/* directory and uses the following arguments:

- *maxdepth*: The number of levels to traverse below the starting point. A value of 1 means we only want to find the directory one level below.

- *type*: Find a specific type. A value of *d* means we want to find directories.

- *!*: The NOT operator. We want to evaluate the condition after the operator and check if it is the opposite. In this example, we are looking for folders that DO NOT contain the *lower* directory.

- *exec*: Parameter of the *find* command to perform actions on files or folders that match the search expression.

- *test*: Used for evaluating conditional expressions. The *-e* parameter evaluates whether the *lower* directory exists. The {} represents the current name of either a file or directory being processed.

- *print*: Parameter of the *find* command used to print the name of the current file or directory.

Figure 5-21 shows the result of running the command. Since we know that the *l* directory contains the symbolic links, it's safe to say that the other directory is the lowest layer. You can verify by listing the contents using the *cat* command. Note that only the *diff* directory and the *link* file are there. Also, if you look at the contents of the *link* file, it displays the cache id value, which is a symbolic link to the directory.

```
emsarmiento@CENTOSDOCKER01:/var/lib/docker/overlay2                      —    □    ×
[root@CENTOSDOCKER01 overlay2]# find -maxdepth 1 -type d '!' -exec test -e "{}/lower" ';' -print
./1
./06eaa3c437eeba370a3fcf317ff3309cad1f87d4875823287d98e2a4a617322b
[root@CENTOSDOCKER01 overlay2]# ls 06eaa3c437eeba370a3fcf317ff3309cad1f87d4875823287d98e2a4a6173
22b/
diff  link
[root@CENTOSDOCKER01 overlay2]# cat 06eaa3c437eeba370a3fcf317ff3309cad1f87d4875823287d98e2a4a617
322b/link
OHPRELSZ7HQRQSWK52WSSH5GPW root@ls -l 1/
total 0
lrwxrwxrwx. 1 root root 72 Aug  4 19:24 2YO42XXOU7E2ATZNCX7GOOKUBI -> ../92e3c43506014db9778446e
3a21d9663428302a49e4ae3f7b654acc2952249c0/diff
lrwxrwxrwx. 1 root root 72 Aug  4 19:24 AKAY7CCWAWIQUPHTGHJMUB4X55 -> ../3c41b3611ba38f280198138
681c65f86c30a8f0bef04f35257638498f500493a/diff
lrwxrwxrwx. 1 root root 72 Aug  4 19:24 GAJDAYEWW5D53XFXPVIYW5PEAO -> ../4d82cf4ad32e2555ac3f585
2a335406e1a84aa70c11b21e2f4e35c110c223616/diff
lrwxrwxrwx. 1 root root 72 Aug  4 19:24 GG3HHXWNHGMCM4JLYH5GETBT2X -> ../70f09ad1f2b74ca2cde84d1
377839488e31e04458392bfb7bcc13f2927cc9082/diff
lrwxrwxrwx. 1 root root 72 Aug  4 19:24 H3KQTH4VTDYYTWYUQX4PCDUI6Q -> ../181cf8b59f294362982feb5
c34b3111c83771337be9da27d5ab7e3b7b869b3e8/diff
lrwxrwxrwx. 1 root root 77 Aug  4 23:55 LUEKZ4WNI6BT7Q6JAOIPUPVJLU -> ../304ee9a31fe14401ab9942d
229ef4fb5fc470284b4209acbb0c4adc12c07f392-init/diff
lrwxrwxrwx. 1 root root 72 Aug  4 19:24 OHPRELSZ7HQRQSWK52WSSH5GPW -> ../06eaa3c437eeba370a3fcf3
17ff3309cad1f87d4875823287d98e2a4a617322b/diff
lrwxrwxrwx. 1 root root 72 Aug  4 19:24 SGXJVNVMWUQZIN5PSGY7SKVYGJ -> ../37023615aa0228bc2ecc463
9d971806430d2967b9afd8819b927c16768e8fe82/diff
lrwxrwxrwx. 1 root root 72 Aug  4 23:55 SUFXETGW632STY3LLYR6Q3LDSK -> ../304ee9a31fe14401ab9942d
229ef4fb5fc470284b4209acbb0c4adc12c07f392/diff
lrwxrwxrwx. 1 root root 72 Aug  4 19:24 SX5CTIIFSSOUH7PGM5J2A6K5LU -> ../551ebc14fd0fda8d3eaf8a3
ce1eb07ae8b5f03db858a0289fdd9d4254dab5609/diff
```

Figure 5-21. *Displaying the lowest layer*

After finding the lowest layer, we can start searching the other directories to find the succeeding layers. Again, you can either do a manual search or automate the process. But how do you know which is the next filesystem layer after the lowest? From the definition, the *lower* file of the next filesystem layer after the lowest contains only one symbolic link to the layer below it – the lowest/base layer. The one after it will have two and so on and so forth. If you look at the *lower* file of the topmost layer of the SQL Server on Linux image, you will see eight entries of the symbolic links. Figure 5-22 shows the *lower* file of the topmost layer. OK, I cheated and manually searched for the file. But you don't have to.

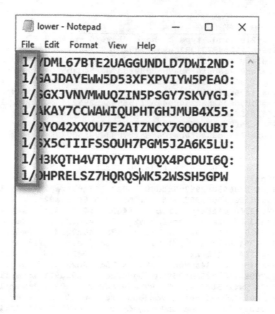

Figure 5-22. *The lower file of the topmost layer*

If you observe the contents of the file, the existence of the characters "l/", which refer to the relative path of the symbolic links to the directory, precedes the symbolic links. We can use this to count the number of "l/" characters in each of the *lower* files to figure out the sequence of filesystem layers stacked one on top of the other. Run the following command to do so. It's a little bit crude but it does the trick. The concept is similar to finding the lowest layer except that this one searches the *lower* file for the "l/" characters and displays each line. Figure 5-23 displays the output of the command.

```
find -type f -name "lower" -print0 | xargs -0 grep -o 'l/'
```

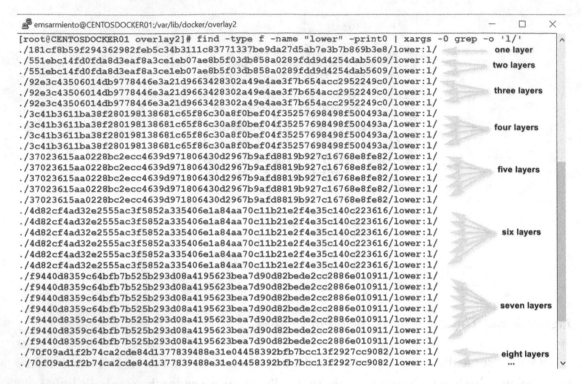

Figure 5-23. *Displaying the lines of the lower files in each directory with the "l/" characters*

Reconstructing the filesystem layers for the SQL Server on Linux image in Figure 5-1 using the directory names, it would look like Figure 5-24.

Figure 5-24. *SQL Server on Linux image with image layers using directory names*

The Container Layer

We spent a lot of time digging deep into the read-only filesystem layers of the image because that sets you up to understand the read-write filesystem layer that is the container. Recall that a container is simply a thin read-write layer that sits on top of the read-only layers. After the Docker daemon builds the read-only filesystem layers for the image from the contents of the directories, it creates the thin read-write layer for the container. This read-write layer gets created inside the */var/lib/docker/ overlay2* directory, with the same file structure and link references as the read-only layers.

Modifying data in the container happens in this read-write layer. This is made possible via the *copy-on-write* (CoW) strategy. Go back to how the union filesystem works. The *diff* directory of the read-write layer has the contents of the container. If you perform a change on a file that exists on any of the read-only filesystem layer, the union filesystem will perform a *copy_up* operation to copy the file from the *diff* directory of the filesystem layer containing the file to the *diff* directory of the container. Once the file has been copied, the change is then performed. Subsequent changes made to the file will be written to the *diff* directory of the read-write layer. But unlike SQL Server where it copies data pages (or extents, depending on the number of data pages affected) to a database snapshot when a record is modified, Docker copies the entire file. This makes it inefficient working with large, write-intensive processes like relational databases. Containers that write a lot of data will require more disk space on the read-write layer. Dealing with storage requirements of write-intensive applications like relational databases will be covered in *Chapter 7*.

Note I only used database snapshots in SQL Server as an illustration to showcase how the copy-on-write strategy works similarly with containers. However, the write process is reversed. With SQL Server database snapshots, the original data is written in the snapshot and is not modified, giving you a point-in-time view of the database. With containers, the original file is written in the read-write layer and is the one being modified.

Deleting data in a container involves creating a *whiteout* file in the *diff* directory of the read-write layer. A *whiteout* file in a union filesystem is a special file with a *.wh.* extension similar to those whiteout correction tapes you see in office supply stores. It's like painting a file white so it appears to be gone from the point of view of the container. You can't see it but it's there, just beneath the white paint.

Much like stopping a running virtual machine, stopping a container does not remove the read-write layer. Everything that Docker wrote on the read-write layer remains in the local disk. The only time the directory of the read-write layer gets deleted from disk is when you delete the container. Imagine creating user databases in your SQL Server instance in a container. The data and log files get created on the read-write layer. If you delete the container, the SQL Server data and log files get deleted as well. We need to be able to deal with SQL Server databases in a way that is outside the container. We'll cover this in more detail in *Chapter 7*.

Summary

This chapter covered how Docker images and containers work under the covers from the storage point of view. We've looked at how the filesystem layers are stored on disk with the use of content digests and distribution hashes, how they are referenced by the Docker daemon to create an image using a union filesystem, and how a container is simply a thin, read-write filesystem layer sitting on top of the read-only layers. In the next chapter, we'll look at the most common administrative tasks that you'll perform when working with SQL Server on containers.

CHAPTER 6

Managing and Administering Containers

Never be afraid to take on a really tough problem. When you solve it, the benefits will be that much greater.

—Carl Gerstacker

Working with digital audio workstations (DAW) as a musician has created a lot of opportunities for creating music. When I was learning how to play the piano, all I knew was the 88 different keys that I could play across the keyboard. As I progressed into playing with different bands, it became impractical for me to always ask for a venue that had an analog upright piano. Besides, there was no way I would carry a 300-lb piano with me during performances. That's when I decided to invest in a lightweight digital synthesizer.

As I was getting ready for one of our performances, I noticed the keyboard player of the next band set up his MacBook Pro and plugged it into the digital synthesizer. The mere presence of a MacBook Pro working alongside a musical instrument got me curious. I'd never seen this before. I'm pretty sure he was not about to write a Python script during the performance. So, I asked the guy about his setup. He explained how the software on his MacBook Pro created different sounds that he used when playing. He let me listen to the sound of a piano layered with a beautiful violin and strings to evoke a feeling of tranquility, as if spending a quiet afternoon near the lake. An arpeggiated techno sound can evoke an upbeat feeling and can make you move your feet. It's a totally different world of music. I decided to try it out and played around with a copy of the Ableton Live software on my MacBook Pro. I was hooked. I was making my own sound samples, audio tracks, loops – anything that would expand my musical creativity. My setup now included the MacBook Pro together with my digital synthesizer.

© Edwin M Sarmiento 2020
E. M. Sarmiento, *The SQL Server DBA's Guide to Docker Containers*,
https://doi.org/10.1007/978-1-4842-5826-2_6

But working with any new tools comes with its own set of challenges. I now have to worry about managing the large audio files that my DAW created, moving them around so as to avoid filling up my main hard drive. I also have to keep a list of configuration settings that I need when playing at different venues and different equipment. And the more audio files I create, the more I need to properly name them so I know what they are and how I use them. The last thing I want is to be fumbling around trying to find an audio file that I need right in the middle of a performance.

I did say working with any new tools and technology comes with its own set of challenges. The same is true working with Docker – or any technology you might get your hands on. This chapter will cover the most common tasks that you will perform as someone who manages Docker, tasks such as creating, starting, and stopping SQL Server on containers. In the previous chapters, you've already been introduced to some of the *docker* commands that we will be using. So, you should be familiar with them at this point. We'll also look at making configuration changes to the Docker daemon outside of the default. I won't be covering any SQL Server administrative tasks as I would assume you're already familiar with that. You're a SQL Server DBA after all, aren't you?

Configuring the Docker Daemon

Like your default SQL Server installation, the configuration settings that you got from the default Docker installation work just fine. But there are configuration settings that you can change to enhance the overall experience working with Docker as a SQL Server administrator.

There are two ways to configure the Docker daemon. The first one is by using flags when starting the Docker daemon, like using startup parameters in SQL Server. The second one is by using the *daemon.json* configuration file.

To illustrate the use of these two options, let's say you want to test out new Docker daemon features. Unless you are using the Edge Channel – version that contains new features but isn't fully tested – of the Docker daemon, all experimental features are turned off. You certainly don't want to deploy a non-stable version in a production environment.

Working with dockerd

To enable flags when starting the Docker daemon, run the *dockerd* command and pass the corresponding flag. Using the preceding example to enable experimental features, run the following command. Just like a Windows service, the Docker daemon should be in a stopped state before running this command:

```
sudo dockerd -experimental
```

Note the use of *sudo* when starting the Docker daemon using the *dockerd* command – you need *root* privileges on Linux. And, similar to starting SQL Server using the command line, you need to open another terminal session to interact with Docker after starting the daemon using *dockerd*. Otherwise, you might end up terminating the process when you quit the current terminal session.

You can do the same thing on Windows but without *sudo*.

A full list of the available flags and options when working with *dockerd* is available at *https://docs.docker.com/engine/reference/commandline/dockerd/*. On Windows, it's on *https://docs.microsoft.com/en-us/virtualization/windowscontainers/manage-docker/configure-docker-daemon#configure-docker-on-the-docker-service*.

Working with daemon.json

The *daemon.json* file contains configuration settings for your Docker daemon. By default, the *daemon.json* file does not exist. You have to manually create it to set custom configuration on your Docker daemon.

On Linux, the file should be stored in the */etc/docker* directory. On Windows, it should be in the *C:\ProgramData\docker\config* folder.

Tip   If the *daemon.json* file already exists, be sure to make a copy of the file prior to making modifications to it. Having a backup of a configuration file before making modifications is always a great idea. After all, if the configuration changes didn't produce the desired effect, having a backup that you can use to roll back the change is a lot faster than trying to remember what you did a few minutes before making the change.

You can use your favorite text editor to create the *daemon.json* file and simply copy it to the appropriate directory on your Docker host. On Linux, you need to have *root* privileges to copy the file to the */etc/docker* directory.

Using the same example earlier of enabling experimental features on your Docker daemon, add the following content to it:

```
{
    "experimental": true
}
```

After creating and updating the file, restart the Docker daemon. Run the following command on Linux to do so:

```
sudo systemctl restart docker
```

On Windows, it's just like how you would restart any Windows service.

Tip   Don't be overwhelmed when working with the Linux filesystem. You don't always have to be on the command line when you're just getting started. Tasks like creating, copying, or modifying files can be done using a Windows-based app. I use a tool called WinSCP for this. I will create the file on my Windows machine using a text editor and use WinSCP to copy it to a Linux machine. You do need *root* privileges on Linux when working on most configuration settings. Refer to *Appendix A* for installing and configuring WinSCP to connect to a Linux machine.

Be sure to revert the changes if you don't need to enable the experimental features on your Docker daemon. A full list of configuration options that you can add to the *daemon.json* file can be found at *https://docs.docker.com/engine/reference/commandline/dockerd/#daemon-configuration-file*. On Windows, it's on *https://docs.microsoft.com/en-us/virtualization/windowscontainers/manage-docker/configure-docker-daemon#configure-docker-with-a-configuration-file*.

This is just a very simple example of how to use either the *dockerd* command or the *daemon.json* file to make configuration changes to your Docker daemon. The real value comes from knowing how to use these two ways to configure the Docker daemon.

Note   You might be wondering, "which one do I use to make configuration changes to my Docker daemon?" To answer this question, think back to how you use startup parameters vs. *sp_configure* in SQL Server. If you are going to make a one-time change as part of a troubleshooting exercise, you use startup parameters in SQL Server; the -m parameter for single-user mode, the -T to specify trace flags, or the -f to start with minimal configuration. If you want to make permanent configuration changes like enabling backup compression, setting recovery interval, and so on, you use *sp_configure* (although you might argue that some configuration settings are only available via startup parameters, while some are only available via *sp_configure*). Similarly, use *dockerd* for one-time changes and *daemon.json* for permanent changes.

Changing the Default Image and Container Directory

One of the most common issues that I see when working with Docker is the challenge of dealing with disk space. Isn't this the same thing that we deal with as SQL Server DBAs? You run out of disk space because your database files keep growing or your backup files are taking up too much space. This is usually caused by an oversight or lack of planning. But with emerging technologies such as Docker that usually get adopted first in development and test environments, planning isn't even considered until the platform becomes mission critical (remember how you were forced to upgrade those Microsoft Access databases to SQL Server?). When you're getting started, lack of disk space wouldn't be much of an issue for you. Eventually, it will.

Recall from *Chapter 5* that the default Docker root directory is in the */var/lib/docker/overlay2* directory on Linux and *C:\ProgramData\docker\windowsfilter* folder on Windows. The Docker images you pulled from Docker Hub together with the container files will be stored in these directories. You can change these default locations by modifying the *daemon.json* file on Linux and adding the following to it:

```
{
    "data-root": "/mnt/docker",
    "storage-driver": "overlay2"
}
```

The */mnt/docker* directory will become the new location for all the images and containers. Be sure that the directory exists prior to configuring the new Docker root directory.

Here are the steps to change the default Docker root directory on Linux:

1. Stop the Docker daemon:

    ```
    sudo systemctl stop docker
    ```

2. Modify the *daemon.json* file to include the preceding settings.

3. Start the Docker daemon:

    ```
    sudo systemctl start docker
    ```

The same steps apply to Windows. Just change the */mnt/docker* directory to a valid Windows directory such as *C:\\mnt\\docker* (notice the use of two backslashes instead of one because a backslash character is interpreted differently in the Go language) and remove the line *"storage-driver": "overlay2"*. And, of course, using either the Services management console or the command line to stop and start the Docker service.

You can verify that the changes have taken effect by running the `docker info` command as well as pulling a new image and reviewing the contents of the */mnt/docker/overlay2* directory. Figure 6-1 shows the new Docker root directory on a CentOS Linux host.

```
emsarmiento@CENTOSDOCKER01:/mnt/docker                                    —  □  ✕
[root@CENTOSDOCKER01 docker]# docker info | grep Dir:
Docker Root Dir: /mnt/docker
[root@CENTOSDOCKER01 docker]# docker pull mcr.microsoft.com/mssql/server:2017-latest-ubun
tu
2017-latest-ubuntu: Pulling from mssql/server
59ab41dd721a: Pull complete
57da90bec92c: Pull complete
06fe57530625: Pull complete
5a6315cba1ff: Pull complete
739f58768b3f: Pull complete
ea9100c8982e: Pull complete
dfc476bbacd5: Pull complete
109325643a8b: Pull complete
2d9ca38a89c8: Pull complete
Digest: sha256:e235aaa983f2ab339de6b7846e93080ad0351cd553cd32d31d5232ccef3a7cbf
Status: Downloaded newer image for mcr.microsoft.com/mssql/server:2017-latest-ubuntu
mcr.microsoft.com/mssql/server:2017-latest-ubuntu
[root@CENTOSDOCKER01 docker]# pwd
/mnt/docker
[root@CENTOSDOCKER01 docker]# ls -l
total 4
drwx------.   2 root root   24 Aug 15 19:35 builder
drwx------.   4 root root   92 Aug 15 19:35 buildkit
drwx------.   2 root root    6 Aug 15 19:35 containers
drwx------.   3 root root   22 Aug 15 19:35 image
drwxr-x---.   3 root root   19 Aug 15 19:35 network
drwx------. 12 root root 4096 Aug 15 19:40 overlay2
drwx------.   4 root root   32 Aug 15 19:35 plugins
drwx------.   2 root root    6 Aug 15 19:35 runtimes
```

Figure 6-1. *New Docker root directory on CentOS Linux host*

Figure 6-2 shows the new Docker root directory on a Windows Server host together with contents of the *daemon.json* file.

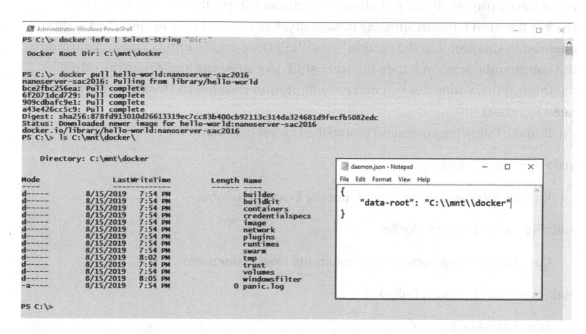

Figure 6-2. *New Docker root directory on Windows Server host*

Changing the default Docker root directory creates a new directory structure but does not remove the previous one. This also means that Docker becomes unaware of the previous directory containing all the pulled images and created containers – they are still there. If you want to reuse all the image layers to avoid pulling them again and reclaim disk space, move the entire */var/lib/docker* directory to the new directory prior to restarting the Docker daemon. Otherwise, you'll be duplicating image layers and using up more disk space. Docker is not going to tell you whether or not an image already exists after you configure a new root directory – it is no longer aware of the old root directory.

Use the following command on Linux to move the entire */var/lib/docker* directory to the new directory (on Windows, it's a simple copy and paste). Be sure to create the target directory first before running the command.

```
mv /var/lib/docker/* /mnt/docker/
```

Add this command between Steps #2 and #3. If it's a brand-new installation with no pulled images, you can skip this step.

Stopping and Restarting the Docker Daemon

I may have jumped ahead and already mentioned stopping and restarting the Docker daemon without showing it. Actually, I've covered how to start the Docker daemon in Chapter 3 in the section "Installing Docker on CentOS Linux." Learning the command comes in handy for other stuff, like stopping and restarting other daemons. Plus, whenever you make configuration changes to Docker, you would need to restart it.

Run the following command to stop the Docker daemon:

```
sudo systemctl stop docker
```

Run the following command to start the Docker daemon:

```
sudo systemctl start docker
```

Run the following command to restart the Docker daemon:

```
sudo systemctl restart docker
```

See, that was easy.

Configure the Docker Daemon for Remote Access on CentOS Linux

So far, we've been connecting to the Docker daemon remotely on a Linux host using an SSH client. While you may consider this "remote access," the fact that the Docker CLI client and the Docker daemon are still on the same host means the two are interacting locally. True remote access is when you have the Docker CLI client interacting with a remote Docker daemon, calling the Docker API from a different machine. An example of this is using the Docker CLI client on a Windows machine and connecting to a Docker daemon on a Linux host. By default, the Docker daemon binds to a Unix socket instead of a TCP/IP port. In order to access the Docker daemon remotely, you need to configure it to listen on an IP address and specific port number.

Here's a high-level overview of the process involved in configuring remote access to the Docker daemon on Linux:

1. Configure remote access to the Docker daemon with the *systemd* unit file.

2. Protect the Docker daemon socket by configuring mutual TLS encryption.

3. Update the *daemon.json* to include the settings for mutual TLS encryption.

4. Enable firewall port to allow traffic to Docker daemon.

Configure Remote Access to the Docker Daemon with the *systemd* Unit File

Instead of using either *dockerd* or the *daemon.json* file, we will use *systemd* to configure remote access to the Docker daemon. The Docker documentation mentions setting the *hosts* array in the *daemon.json* file to allow remote access to the Docker daemon. Unfortunately, I've tested as many possible variations as I can based on the documentation without any luck. So, I tried other approaches mentioned in the documentation. This is where using *systemd* comes in.

systemd provides a standard process for controlling programs and processes on Linux. It's an initialization system and service manager that includes features like on-demand starting of daemons, parallel processing at boot, and process tracking using Linux control groups. An initialization system is a daemon process that starts as soon as the computer starts and continues running until it is shut down. In *systemd*, a *unit* refers to any resource that the system knows how to control. These resources are defined using configuration files called unit files. You can define how these resources are managed on the system with the use of unit files. Other than using *dockerd* flags and daemon.json, the Docker daemon can also be configured with the use of *systemd* unit files.

> **Note**   I didn't include using *systemd* as a way to configure the Docker daemon because it requires an understanding of Linux internals. Since the Docker daemon is just like any other daemons running on Linux, the way you configure Docker using *systemd* is no different from how you would configure other daemons. But be very careful. Choose only one way to configure the Docker daemon. Configuring Docker using either *systemd*, the *dockerd* flags, or *daemon.json* can cause conflicts that can prevent the Docker daemon from starting.

For this task, we will use *systemd* to make changes to the default Docker configuration:

1. Run the following command to create an override file for the Docker daemon using the default text editor on Linux. An override file is a way to change the behavior of a daemon without modifying its corresponding *systemd* unit file. The *systemctl edit* command ensures that the override settings are properly loaded.

   ```
   sudo systemctl edit docker.service
   ```

2. Add the following content in the file and save it:

   ```
   [Service]
   ExecStart=
   ExecStart=/usr/bin/dockerd -H fd:// -H tcp://172.28.106.158:2376
   ```

   Substitute the provided IP address with the IP address of your CentOS Linux Docker host. Also, the default port numbers that the Docker daemon listen on are 2375 (unencrypted) and 2376 (encrypted). Port 2376 will be used for secure communications between the Docker CLI client and the Docker daemon.

   The -H flag binds the Docker daemon to a listening socket, either a Unix socket or a TCP/IP port. You can specify multiple -H flags to bind to multiple sockets/ports, like in the example provided.

   Don't be confused about the *ExecStart* parameter specified twice. There are parameters that need to be cleared out before setting the new override value. The *ExecStart* parameter is one of them.

3. Run the following command to reload the *systemd* unit file:

    ```
    sudo systemctl daemon-reload
    ```

4. Finally, restart the Docker daemon:

    ```
    sudo systemctl restart docker
    ```

Once completed, the Docker daemon is now configured to listen on a TCP/IP port and can be accessed remotely. You can check the status of the Docker daemon to verify as shown in Figure 6-3.

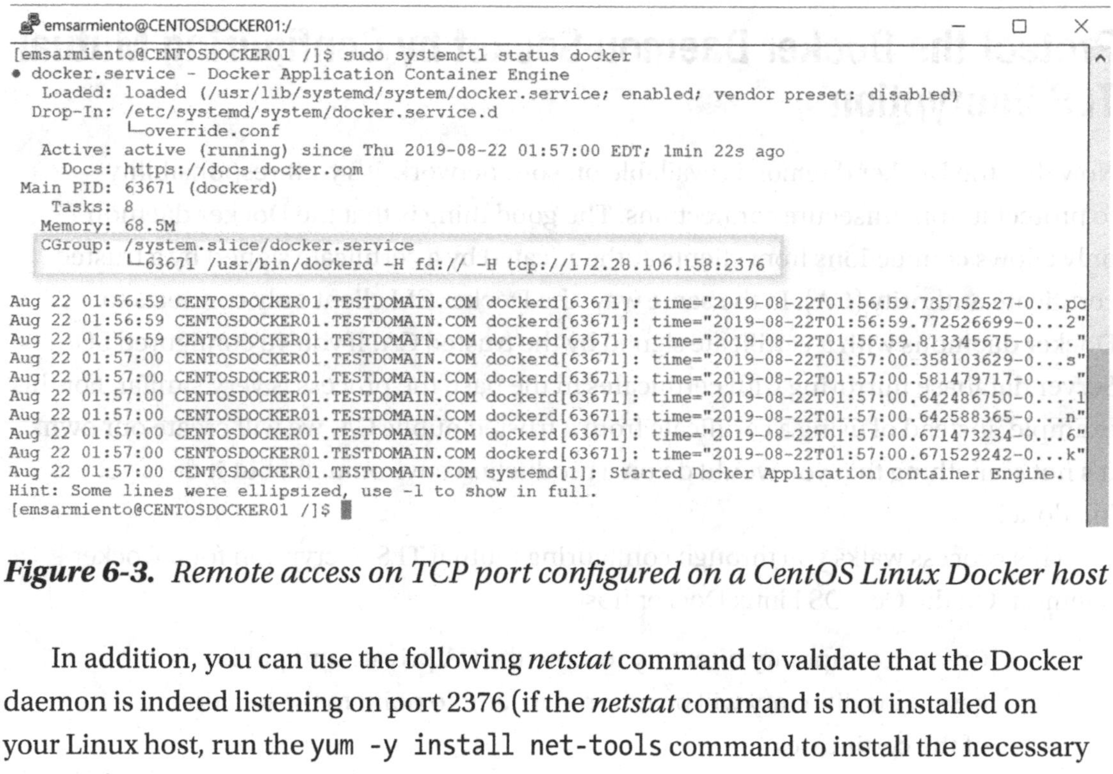

Figure 6-3. *Remote access on TCP port configured on a CentOS Linux Docker host*

In addition, you can use the following *netstat* command to validate that the Docker daemon is indeed listening on port 2376 (if the *netstat* command is not installed on your Linux host, run the yum -y install net-tools command to install the necessary package):

```
sudo netstat -lntp | grep dockerd
```

You definitely need to know how to use *vi* – the default text editor on Linux – for this. Otherwise, use your favorite text editor on Windows to create the override file named *override.conf.* You can then copy the *override.conf* file using WinSCP to the */etc/systemd/ system/docker.service.d/* directory. You need to manually create the *docker.service.d* directory if you didn't use the *systemctl edit* command.

Tip   Earlier in the chapter, I mentioned the use of *dockerd* with flags or the *daemon.json* file to make configuration changes to the Docker daemon. I wish that was always the case. But my experience working with open source software has taught me to expect several challenges. One of them is inconsistencies with how things are done. Configuring the Docker daemon for remote access is an example. Inconsistencies are expected when working with open source software. I'm just setting the right expectations in case you get frustrated.

Protect the Docker Daemon Socket by Configuring Mutual TLS Encryption

Now that the Docker daemon is available on your network, it's your responsibility to protect it from unsecure connections. The good thing is that the Docker daemon only allows connections from clients authenticated by a certificate signed by a trusted certificate authority (CA). In the same way, the Docker CLI client only connects to Docker daemons with a certificate signed by the trusted CA. If you've configured SQL Server database mirroring with certificates in the past, the process is very similar. For this example, instead of using a certificate from a trusted public CA, we will create our own. It's not something that you would do on a production environment, but it does get the job done.

This process walks you through configuring mutual TLS encryption for a Docker daemon. On the CentOS Linux Docker host

1. Create a temporary directory to store the CA private and public keys. This directory will be referred to later to point to the location of the certificates.

   ```
   mkdir /tmp/dockerTLS
   cd /tmp/dockerTLS
   ```

2. Run the following *openssl* command to create the CA private key. When prompted, provide the passphrase for the private key.

   ```
   openssl genrsa -aes256 -out ca-key.pem 4096
   ```

3. Run the following *openssl* command to create the CA public key. When prompted, provide details to identify the public key. Figure 6-4 provides an example of this. For the *Common Name* field, be sure to provide the hostname that you use to connect to your Docker daemon and can be resolved in the network. In this example, the fully qualified domain name (FQDN) of my CentOS Linux Docker host is *CENTOSDOCKER01.TESTDOMAIN.COM*.

```
openssl req -new -x509 -days 365 -key ca-key.pem -sha256
-out ca.pem
```

```
emsarmiento@CENTOSDOCKER01:/tmp/dockerTLS                              —    □    ×
[emsarmiento@CENTOSDOCKER01 dockerTLS]$ openssl req -new -x509 -days 365 -key ca-key.pem -sha256 -out ca
.pem
Enter pass phrase for ca-key.pem:
You are about to be asked to enter information that will be incorporated
into your certificate request.
What you are about to enter is what is called a Distinguished Name or a DN.
There are quite a few fields but you can leave some blank
For some fields there will be a default value,
If you enter '.', the field will be left blank.
-----
Country Name (2 letter code) [XX]:CA
State or Province Name (full name) []:ON
Locality Name (eg, city) [Default City]:Ottawa
Organization Name (eg, company) [Default Company Ltd]:15C Inc
Organizational Unit Name (eg, section) []:IT
Common Name (eg, your name or your server's hostname) []:CENTOSDOCKER01.TESTDOMAIN.COM
Email Address []:assist@LearnSQLServerHADR.com
[emsarmiento@CENTOSDOCKER01 dockerTLS]$ ▮
```

Figure 6-4. *Details for the CA public key*

4. Run the following *openssl* command to create the server key:

```
openssl genrsa -out server-key.pem 4096
```

5. Run the following *openssl* command to create the certificate signing request. Be sure that the *Common Name* value matches the Docker daemon's hostname that you provided in Step #3.

```
openssl req -subj "/CN=CENTOSDOCKER01.TESTDOMAIN.COM"
-sha256 -new -key server-key.pem -out server.csr
```

6. Run the following command to create an extensions configuration file. Since TLS connections can be made through IP address as well as FQDN, the IP addresses need to be specified when creating the certificate. The extensions configuration file will contain the

FQDN of the Linux Docker host, its IP address, and the loopback
IP address so you can still connect to the Docker daemon locally
via a TCP port.

```
echo subjectAltName = DNS:CENTOSDOCKER01.TESTDOMAIN.COM,IP:172.28.
106.158,IP:127.0.0.1 >> extfile.cnf
```

7. Run the following command to append the extensions
   configuration file and add the extended usage attributes so that the
   Docker daemon's key can only be used for server authentication:

```
echo extendedKeyUsage = serverAuth >> extfile.cnf
```

8. Run the following *openssl* command to sign the public key with
   the CA and pass it the extensions configuration file:

```
openssl x509 -req -days 365 -sha256 -in server.csr -CA ca.pem -CAkey
ca-key.pem -CAcreateserial -out server-cert.pem -extfile extfile.cnf
```

You should have the following files in the */tmp/dockerTLS* directory as shown in
Figure 6-5.

```
emsarmiento@CENTOSDOCKER01:/tmp/dockerTLS                                    —    □    ×
[emsarmiento@CENTOSDOCKER01 dockerTLS]$ ls -l
total 28
-rw-rw-r--. 1 emsarmiento emsarmiento 3326 Aug 22 02:34 ca-key.pem
-rw-rw-r--. 1 emsarmiento emsarmiento 2171 Aug 22 02:45 ca.pem
-rw-rw-r--. 1 emsarmiento emsarmiento   17 Aug 22 03:08 ca.srl
-rw-rw-r--. 1 emsarmiento emsarmiento   82 Aug 22 03:02 extfile.cnf
-rw-rw-r--. 1 emsarmiento emsarmiento 1972 Aug 22 03:08 server-cert.pem
-rw-rw-r--. 1 emsarmiento emsarmiento 1610 Aug 22 02:53 server.csr
-rw-rw-r--. 1 emsarmiento emsarmiento 3243 Aug 22 02:50 server-key.pem
[emsarmiento@CENTOSDOCKER01 dockerTLS]$
```

Figure 6-5. *Files created after completing all the steps*

Now we're ready to work on the Docker CLI client. For this example, the Docker CLI
client is also running on a CentOS Linux machine named *CENTOSDOCKERCLIENT*.
On the CentOS Docker client machine

1. Create a temporary directory to store the CA private and public
   keys. This directory will be referred to later to point to the location
   of the certificates.

```
mkdir /tmp/dockerTLS
cd /tmp/dockerTLS
```

2. Run the following *openssl* command to create the client key:

```
openssl genrsa -out key.pem 4096
```

3. Run the following *openssl* command to create the certificate signing request:

```
openssl req -subj '/CN=client' -new -key key.pem -out client.csr
```

4. Run the following command to create an extensions configuration file to make the client key suitable for client authentication:

```
echo extendedKeyUsage = clientAuth > extfile-client.cnf
```

5. Copy the *ca.pem* and *ca-key.pem* files that you generated on the Docker daemon's host machine to the */tmp/dockerTLS* directory on the client machine. You can use WinSCP or the *scp* command on Linux to do so. You should have the following files in the */tmp/ dockerTLS* directory as shown in Figure 6-6. Don't proceed to the next step unless you have all the files available.

```
emsarmiento@CENTOSDOCKERCLIENT:/tmp/dockerTLS
[emsarmiento@CENTOSDOCKERCLIENT dockerTLS]$ ls -l
total 28
-rw-rw-r--. 1 emsarmiento emsarmiento 3326 Aug 20 08:18 ca-key.pem
-rw-rw-r--. 1 emsarmiento emsarmiento 2171 Aug 20 08:18 ca.pem
-rw-rw-r--. 1 emsarmiento emsarmiento   17 Aug 22 03:29 ca.srl
-rw-rw-r--. 1 emsarmiento emsarmiento 1899 Aug 22 03:29 cert.pem
-rw-rw-r--. 1 emsarmiento emsarmiento 1582 Aug 22 03:20 client.csr
-rw-rw-r--. 1 emsarmiento emsarmiento   30 Aug 22 03:29 extfile-client.cnf
-rw-rw-r--. 1 emsarmiento emsarmiento 3243 Aug 22 03:17 key.pem
[emsarmiento@CENTOSDOCKERCLIENT dockerTLS]$
```

Figure 6-6. *Files created after completing all the steps*

6. Run the following *openssl* command to generate the signed certificate, passing the public key, private key, and the extensions configuration file. When prompted, provide the passphrase for the CA private key.

```
openssl x509 -req -days 365 -sha256 -in client.csr -CA ca.pem
-CAkey ca-key.pem -CAcreateserial -out cert.pem -extfile extfile-
client.cnf
```

We now have all the files that we need to establish mutual TLS encryption between the Docker CLI client and the remote Docker daemon. But we're not done yet.

Update the daemon.json to Include the Settings for Mutual TLS Encryption

We have to tell the Docker daemon to enforce encrypted and authenticated remote connections. The following configuration options will be added to the *daemon.json* file:

- *tlsverify*: A value of *true* enforces encrypted and authenticated remote connections.

- *tlscacert*: The Docker daemon will only trust certificates signed by this CA.

- *tlscert*: The path to TLS certificate file.

- *tlskey*: The path to TLS key file.

Add the following content to the *daemon.json* file and save it. Note the path of the files you generated on the Docker host.

```
"tlscacert": "/tmp/dockerTLS/ca.pem",
"tlscert": "/tmp/dockerTLS/server-cert.pem",
"tlskey": "/tmp/dockerTLS/server-key.pem",
"tlsverify": true
```

After updating the *daemon.json* file, restart the Docker daemon:

```
sudo systemctl restart docker
```

Enable Firewall Port to Allow Traffic to Docker Daemon

You didn't need to worry about the firewall when you were connecting to the Docker daemon locally using the Docker CLI client. That's because you were already logged in on the machine via SSH (on port 22) and running commands locally. Enabling remote access to the Docker daemon means you need to open port 2376 on the Linux firewall.

Run the following command to enable the firewall to allow remote connections on port 2376. By default, FirewallD is the firewall solution available on CentOS Linux.

```
sudo firewall-cmd --zone=public --add-port=2376/tcp --permanent
```

Run the following command to reload the new firewall rule added:

```
sudo firewall-cmd --reload
```

After enabling the firewall port, use TELNET to test connectivity to port 2376.

Testing Remote Client Connectivity

The ultimate test, of course, is when you can run commands from a Docker CLI client that connects to a remote Docker host. Run the following command to connect to a remote Docker host. Be sure you are in the */tmp/dockerTLS* directory so you don't have to provide the absolute path to the public key, the signed certificate, and the client key.

```
docker --tlsverify --tlscacert=ca.pem --tlscert=cert.pem --tlskey=key.pem
-H=172.28.106.158:2376 info
```

The -H parameter points to the IP address of the remote Docker host. Alternatively, you can use the hostname or the FQDN provided that it can be resolved on the network. Figure 6-7 shows a Docker CLI client running on *CENTOSDOCKERCLIENT* connecting to a remote Docker host running on *CENTOSDOCKER01*.

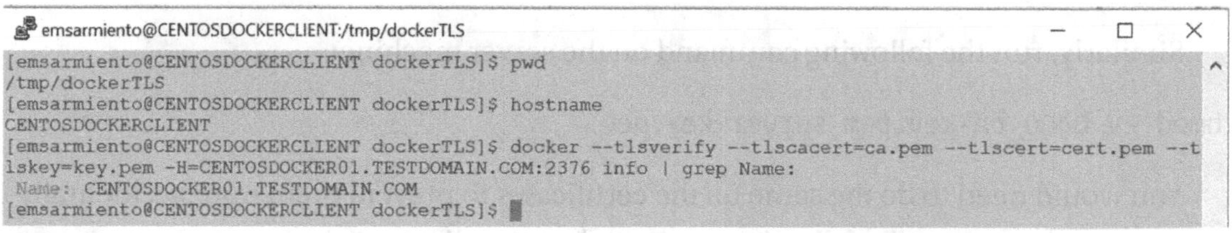

Figure 6-7. *Docker CLI client connecting to a remote Docker host*

You can also avoid repeatedly providing the remote connection–related parameters when you run *docker* commands by setting the environment variables in your current session using the *export* command. Run the following commands prior to running any *docker* commands. Figure 6-8 shows setting the environment variables and running *docker* commands to a remote Docker host.

```
export DOCKER_TLS_VERIFY=1
export DOCKER_HOST=tcp://172.28.106.158:2376
export DOCKER_CERT_PATH=/tmp/dockerTLS/
```

```
emsarmiento@CENTOSDOCKERCLIENT:/                                                    —    □    ×
[emsarmiento@CENTOSDOCKERCLIENT /]$ export DOCKER_TLS_VERIFY=1
[emsarmiento@CENTOSDOCKERCLIENT /]$ export DOCKER_HOST=tcp://CENTOSDOCKER01.TESTDOMAIN.COM:2376
[emsarmiento@CENTOSDOCKERCLIENT /]$ export DOCKER_CERT_PATH=/tmp/dockerTLS/
[emsarmiento@CENTOSDOCKERCLIENT /]$ docker info | grep Name:
  Name: CENTOSDOCKER01.TESTDOMAIN.COM
[emsarmiento@CENTOSDOCKERCLIENT /]$ docker images
REPOSITORY                        TAG              IMAGE ID        CREATED         SIZE
mcr.microsoft.com/mssql/server    2017-CU14-ubuntu 644ca19cb10d    5 months ago    1.38GB
hello-world                       latest           fce289e99eb9    7 months ago    1.84kB
[emsarmiento@CENTOSDOCKERCLIENT /]$ 
```

Figure 6-8. Setting environment variables to connect a Docker CLI client to a remote Docker host

Cleanup

After configuring the client and server for TLS mutual authentication, you no longer need the certificate signing requests. You can proceed to delete the *client.csr* and *server. csr* files on the client and server machines, respectively. You can do the same for the extensions configuration files – **extfile-client.cnf** and **extfile.cnf**.

Also, to prevent your keys from accidentally being overwritten, remove their write permissions. Run the following command on the client machine to make the keys only readable by your user account:

```
chmod -v 0400 ca-key.pem key.pem
```

Similarly, run the following command on the server machine:

```
chmod -v 0400 ca-key.pem server-key.pem
```

You would need to do the same on the certificates to prevent them from accidentally being overwritten. Run the following command on the client machine to make the certificates only readable by your user account:

```
chmod -v 0400 ca.pem cert.pem
```

Similarly, run the following command on the server machine:

```
chmod -v 0400 ca.pem server-cert.pem
```

The process to configure a Docker CLI client running on Windows will be the same. But since OpenSSL isn't natively available on Windows, it has to be installed manually. Refer to *Appendix A* to install and configure OpenSSL on a Windows workstation.

Once you're inside the OpenSSL command prompt, you can run the same commands as the one you used for Linux but without the *openssl* command. For example, the command `openssl genrsa -out key.pem 4096` should just be written as `genrsa -out key.pem 4096`. Figure 6-9 shows a Windows 10 machine running the Docker CLI client connecting to a Linux Docker host. Pay attention to the -H parameter, though. The format is similar to the one defined in the DOCKER_HOST environment variable. Also, instead of using the *export* keyword, use the *set* keyword to define the environment variables.

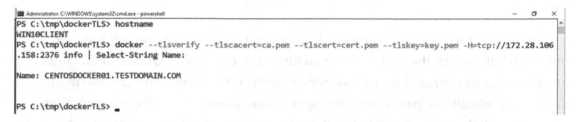

Figure 6-9. *Docker CLI client on a Windows 10 host connecting to a remote Linux Docker host*

Configure Docker CLI Bash Completion

They say the laziest IT professionals are the former developers who became sysadmins. That may have a hint of truth in it as is my experience. I switched from Visual Basic to C#.NET because Visual Studio had IntelliSense in 2005. When Monad (original name for PowerShell) came out, I immediately converted all my VBScript-based administrative scripts to take advantage of the tab autocomplete feature in the PowerShell command shell. I'm always thinking of ways to make my life easier.

This leads me to configuring the Docker CLI bash completion. Bash completion allows you to use tab autocomplete when writing your *docker* commands. While this was originally intended for developers, there's nothing stopping you from using it to make administering Docker a lot easier. You do need to enable bash autocompletion on your Linux distribution prior to using the Docker completion script.

On Ubuntu, run the following command to refresh the package database and install the bash autocompletion package:

```
sudo apt update
sudo apt install bash-completion
```

On CentOS, run the following command:

```
sudo yum -y install bash-completion
```

Once bash autocompletion is enabled, place the Docker completion script in the /etc/bash_completion.d/ directory by running the following command. Be sure to run this command every time you update Docker:

```
sudo curl https://raw.githubusercontent.com/docker/docker-ce/master/
components/cli/contrib/completion/bash/docker -o /etc/bash_completion.d/
docker.sh
```

Log out of your current session and log back in again. You can try typing *docker images m* followed by the TAB. It saves you time from typing the SQL Server on Linux image name *mcr.microsoft.com/mssql/server:2017-CU14-ubuntu*. You can also use it to display the available parameters for a specific command. For example, try running *docker run* – followed by the TAB. It will display all the available parameters for the *docker run* command.

Starting and Stopping Containers

You've already had an experience running a container in *Chapter 4*. Using the *docker run* command is the fastest way to start a container. It pulls the image if it doesn't yet exist in the local disk and starts it. The different parameters you pass to the *docker run* command determine how the container runs. We've already covered the most common parameters that you will use when running SQL Server on containers in *Chapter 4* so just refer to those.

A good practice is to pull all the images you need on your Docker host using the *docker pull* command so it doesn't take time to run or start a container. Once pulled, you can pre-create containers using the *docker create* command. The following command creates a SQL Server on Linux container without running it. It's almost the same command that we used in *Chapter 4* but without the *-d* parameter (detached mode).

```
docker create -e "ACCEPT_EULA=Y" -e "SA_PASSWORD=mYSecUr3PAssw0rd" -p
1433:1433 --name sqldevlinuxcon01 -h linuxsqldev01 mcr.microsoft.com/mssql/
server:2017-CU14-ubuntu
```

You won't see a created container just by running the docker ps command. You need to use the *-a* parameter with the docker ps command to display all the containers, regardless of their state. If you want to be more specific, you can use the *-f* parameter of the docker ps command to filter by specific conditions. The following command displays all created containers:

```
docker ps -a -f status=created
```

You can then use the following *docker start* command and just pass either the container name or the ID:

```
docker start sqldevlinuxcon01
```

Stopping a container is as easy as running the *docker* stop command and passing either the container name or the ID:

```
docker stop sqldevlinuxcon01
```

You might be tempted to run a *docker kill* command to kill a running container. Don't. This is a SQL Server instance on a container we're talking about, not just any random app. Recall that SQL Server must be properly shut down in order to commit or roll back all transactions, write all dirty pages to disk, and then write an entry in the transaction log. Running a *docker kill* command will prevent SQL Server from performing a clean shutdown and can potentially cause data loss or – even worse – data corruption. A *docker stop* command will gracefully send a SIGTERM signal (request for termination) to the process running inside the container, in this case, SQL Server. It's the proper way to shut down SQL Server on a Linux environment.

Also, remember that stopping a container does not remove it from the Docker host. This is the reason why you cannot create another container with the same name. If you want to create another container with the same name that you used before, you need to delete it first.

Tip   You're starting to see the benefit of using the *--name* parameter with the *docker run* command. We used the name of the container – sqldevlinuxcon01 – on both the *docker start* and *docker stop* commands instead of the container ID. This makes it easy to work with containers instead of relying on the system-generated IDs. When creating SQL Server containers, always use the *--name* parameter with the *docker run* command.

A trick that you can use is to display all the containers and their corresponding container ID using the -q parameter as shown in the following command:

```
docker ps -a -q
```

You can then pass this to either the *docker start* or *docker stop* command to start or stop all containers, respectively, as shown in the following:

```
docker start $(docker ps -a -q)
```

Deleting Containers and Images

If you want to clean up your Docker host, deleting old and unwanted containers, the *docker rm* command is what you need. However, you won't be able to delete a running container. The container must be stopped first before you can delete it, as shown in the following command:

```
docker stop sqldevlinuxcon01
docker rm sqldevlinuxcon01
```

There are a lot of examples on the Internet (and even the Docker documentation) that demonstrate the use of the *-f* parameter with the *docker rm* command to stop and delete a container at the same time. Avoid this temptation. Using the *-f* parameter with the *docker rm* command is like running a *docker kill* command and would cause SQL Server to abruptly terminate.

Dealing with images is something else. Remember that containers are simply a read-write filesystem layer that sit on top of the image's read-only filesystem layer, which means you can delete all the containers that are based on the image without affecting the image. However, when you delete an image, you will no longer be able to create a new container unless the image is made available on the Docker host by pulling it again from a repository. Similarly, you won't be able to delete an image when it is in use by a running container. You have to stop and delete all of the containers using it before you can delete the image. The following commands show how to delete an image using the *docker rmi* command, following the sequence of events – from stopping and deleting a container to deleting the image:

```
docker stop sqldevlinuxcon01
docker rm sqldevlinuxcon01
docker rmi mcr.microsoft.com/mssql/server:2017-CU14-ubuntu
```

Interacting with Running Containers

I mentioned in *Chapter 4* that I'm not a big fan of logging in to servers and interacting with them directly. I would rather connect to them remotely unless I really need to for troubleshooting purposes – same thing with containers. But in case I really need to, I use the *docker exec* command. This allows me to run a command inside a running container. Let's say I want to run a bash shell inside my existing SQL Server on Linux container so I can check the filesystem structure. Run the following *docker exec* command with the *-i* (interactive) and *-t* (pseudo-terminal) parameters, passing the command (bash) that you want to run. Figure 6-10 shows how the terminal changed from *CENTOSDOCKER01* (the name of my Linux Docker host) logged in as myself to *linuxsqldev01* (the name of the SQL Server on Linux container) logged in as root. I can now interactively work with the container from an operating system point of view.

```
docker exec -it sqldevlinuxcon01 bash
```

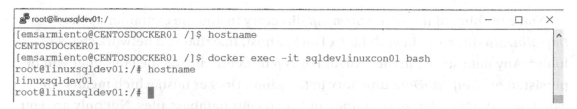

Figure 6-10. *Running bash on a running container*

Similarly, you can run the following command to run a PowerShell command shell inside a SQL Server on Windows container:

```
docker exec -it sqldevwincon01 powershell
```

In the past, terminating the bash or PowerShell shell will also terminate the container. Not anymore. However, it's still a good practice to exit the interactive shell by pressing Ctrl+PQ.

Sharing Files Between Host and Container

There might be some cases where you have files on your Docker host that you want to share with the container. For example, you may want to restore a backup of a SQL Server database on the SQL Server instance inside a container. You can copy the backup file in a directory on your Docker host and make it available to your container. This is where the *-v* or *--volume* parameter of the *docker run* command comes in. First, create a */tmp/dbData* directory in your Linux Docker host. Then, copy your database backups in that directory. Using the following command, mount the */tmp/dbData* directory on the Linux Docker host to the */var/opt/mssql* directory inside the container. It's the same *docker run* command we've been using except that this one has the *-v* parameter.

```
docker run -e "ACCEPT_EULA=Y" -e "SA_PASSWORD=mYSecUr3PAsswOrd" -p
1433:1433 --name sqldevlinuxcon01 -d -h linuxsqldev01 -v /tmp/dbData:/var/
opt/mssql mcr.microsoft.com/mssql/server:2017-CU14-ubuntu
```

You can think of the */var/opt/mssql* directory inside the container as the */tmp/dbData* directory in your Linux Docker host, like that of a network shared folder. Any data stored in the */var/opt/mssql* directory inside the container will be persisted on */tmp/dbData* directory in the Linux Docker host, which means you can delete the SQL Server container and keep your database files. Not only are you sharing data and files between the Linux Docker host and your container, you're also persisting the data created inside your container. More details about this coming up in *Chapter 7*.

Once the */tmp/dbData* directory has been mounted in the container, the SQL Server instance can access the backup files inside it. You can, then, restore the backup on the SQL Server instance inside the container. Of course, since the */var/opt/mssql* directory inside the container points to the */tmp/dbData* directory in the Linux Docker host, every database you create will also be stored in the */tmp/dbData* directory. You can test this out by restoring the database backup followed by deleting the container. Figure 6-11 shows the contents of the */tmp/dbData* directory in the Linux Docker host after deleting the SQL Server container.

```
emsarmiento@CENTOSDOCKER01:/tmp/dbData                                    —   □   ×
[emsarmiento@CENTOSDOCKER01 dbData]$ ls -l
total 285256
drwxr-xr-x. 2 root       root              156 Aug 30 17:28 data
-rw-rw-r--. 1 emsarmiento emsarmiento 201411072 Jun  5  2006 DemoSalesDBBackupOriginal.bak
drwxr-xr-x. 2 root       root              248 Aug 30 17:24 log
-rw-rw-r--. 1 emsarmiento emsarmiento   6803456 Jul  7  2017 NorthwindBackup.bak
-rw-r-----. 1 root       root          75497472 Aug 30 17:28 northwnd.ldf
-rw-r-----. 1 root       root           8388608 Aug 30 17:28 northwnd.mdf
drwxr-xr-x. 2 root       root               25 Aug 30 16:41 secrets
[emsarmiento@CENTOSDOCKER01 dbData]$
```

Figure 6-11. *Sharing data between Linux Docker host and the container*

Run the following command on Windows to create a container and map the
C:\dbData folder on the Windows Docker host to the *C:\dbData* folder inside the
container. The folder doesn't have to exist inside the container, it will get created in
the process of running the container. Note the use of a forward slash (/) instead of a
backslash (\) to define the path. In the past, only the forward slash character worked
when defining the path due to how the Go language interpreted the character. Now,
you can use both. I use forward slash just to be consistent with both Windows and
Linux paths.

```
docker run -e "ACCEPT_EULA=Y" -e "SA_PASSWORD=mYSecUr3PAsswOrd" -p
1433:1433 --name sqldevwincon01 -d -h winsqldev01 -v  C:/dbData:C:/dbData
microsoft/mssql-server-windows-developer
```

Another way to share files between the host and the container is by using the
docker cp command. Using the same example, run the following command if you
wanted to copy the */tmp/dbData/NorthwindBackup.bak* file from your Linux Docker
host inside the *sqldevlinuxcon01* container. You can use either the container ID or
the container name, but I prefer using the container name so I know exactly what I'm
working with.

```
docker cp /tmp/dbData/NorthwindBackup.bak sqldevlinuxcon01:/var/opt/mssql/
data
```

On Windows, just replace the path with the proper Windows directory path, taking
into account the forward slash instead of the backslash.

```
docker cp C:/dbData/NorthwindBackup.bak sqldevwincon01:C:/
```

You can also do the reverse and copy a file – in this case, the *testDB.bak* file – from the container into the Linux Docker host using the following command:

```
docker cp sqldevlinuxcon01:/var/opt/mssql/data/testDB.bak /tmp/dbData/
```

There's clearly more than one way to share files between your Docker host and container.

Configuring Container Resources

By default, a container has no resource constraints. It can use as much of a given resource as the host's kernel scheduler allows. This is not a good thing as far as SQL Server is concerned. We know that SQL Server will use up as much memory resource as is available in the system. Similarly, it will take up all available CPU cores. Think about how that would affect your licensing (not a big deal if this was a test environment and you're only running Enterprise Evaluation, Developer, or Express Editions). But if you've licensed all the CPU cores on your Docker host, no need to worry about SQL Server licensing.

The way you configure CPU and memory resources that your container consumes is similar to how you assign resources to virtual machines. Using the *docker run* command, add the *--cpus* parameter to assign the number of CPU resources your container can use and the *--memory* parameter to set the maximum amount of memory (you could argue that this can be done with *sp_configure* inside SQL Server, but it would be a lot better if this was done at the container level since you cannot run multiple SQL Server instances in the same Linux host). In my test environment, my Linux Docker host is configured to have 4 CPU cores and 8GB of memory, as shown in Figure 6-12.

```
 Profile: default
Kernel Version: 3.10.0-957.21.3.el7.x86_64
Operating System: CentOS Linux 7 (Core)
OSType: linux
Architecture: x86_64
CPUs: 4
Total Memory: 7.62GiB
Name: CENTOSDOCKER01
ID: BPYY:5RBB:FU7Q:VQAE:Y5G3:YVMG:C2PB:GQHI:TVUJ:GY4E:F3RM:NJBJ
Docker Root Dir: /var/lib/docker
Debug Mode: false
Registry: https://index.docker.io/v1/
Labels:
Experimental: false
```

Figure 6-12. *Configured hardware resources for Docker host*

Running the following *docker stats* command with the formatting provided displays the CPU and memory utilization for my SQL Server on Linux container while running multiple queries, as shown in Figure 6-13. Clearly, it is taking up most of the CPU and memory resources (using up all 7.62GB memory) available on the Docker host.

```
docker stats sqldevlinuxcon01 --format "table {{.Name}}\t{{.CPUPerc}}\t
{{.MemUsage}}"
```

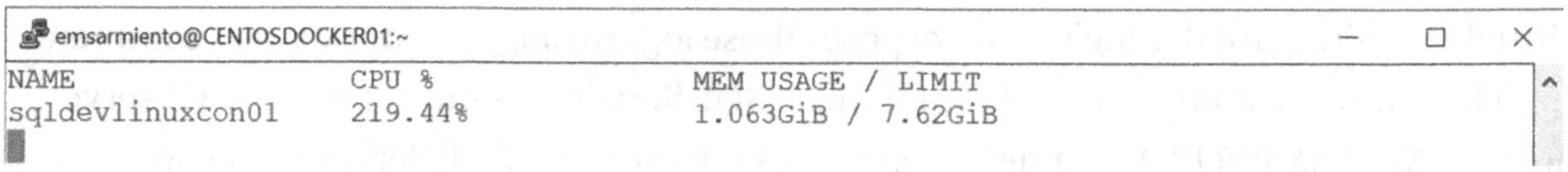

```
emsarmiento@CENTOSDOCKER01:~                                          —    □    ×
NAME                 CPU %              MEM USAGE / LIMIT
sqldevlinuxcon01     219.44%            1.063GiB / 7.62GiB
```

Figure 6-13. *Container resource utilization*

Run the following command to create and run the SQL Server on Linux container, assigning only 2 CPUs and 4GB of memory using the *--cpus* and *--memory* parameters, respectively:

```
docker run -e "ACCEPT_EULA=Y" -e "   SA_PASSWORD=mYSecUr3PAssw0rd"
-p 1433:1433 --name sqldevlinuxcon01 -d -h linuxsqldev01 --cpus="2"
--memory=4g mcr.microsoft.com/mssql/server:2017-CU14-ubuntu
```

After restricting the amount of CPU and memory resources that the container can use, rerunning my queries on the SQL Server instance displays the new resource utilization using the *docker stats* command, as shown in Figure 6-14. Of course, the results of your tests depend on a lot of different factors – hardware configuration, SQL Server instance configuration, database schema, indexes, queries, and so on. This is just to demonstrate how you can configure container resource utilization.

```
emsarmiento@CENTOSDOCKER01:~                                          —    □    ×
NAME                 CPU %              MEM USAGE / LIMIT
sqldevlinuxcon01     57.94%             2.73GiB / 4GiB
```

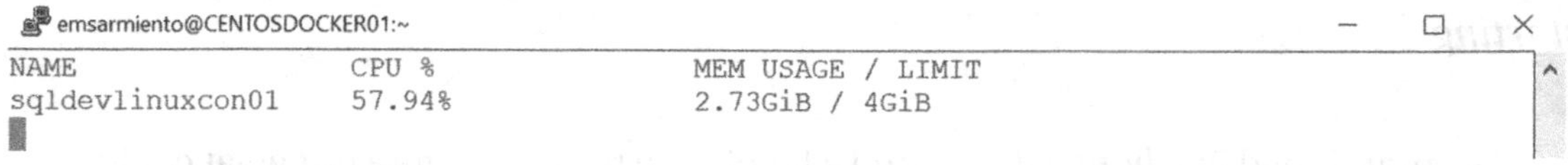

Figure 6-14. *After configuring container CPU and memory resource utilization*

Additional ways to configure container resource utilization are available at *https:// docs.docker.com/config/containers/resource_constraints/*.

Exploring the Container Logs

In *Chapter 4*, I talked about how failing the SQL Server password complexity policy can prevent the container from starting. If it was running on a Windows or Linux host, I could have easily opened the SQL Server error log using a text editor to check for possible causes. But because the SQL Server error log is inside the container, there's no way I can access it unless the container is started or the */var/opt/mssql* directory is mounted on the Linux Docker host. It's like trying to access the SQL Server error log inside a stopped virtual machine. Good thing Docker exposes those logs through the *docker logs* command.

The following command will create a new SQL Server on Linux container. Observe how the *SA_PASSWORD* parameter value does not meet the SQL Server password complexity policy.

```
docker run -e "ACCEPT_EULA=Y" -e "SA_PASSWORD=password12" -p 1433:1433
--name sqldevlinuxcon01 -d -h linuxsqldev01 mcr.microsoft.com/mssql/
server:2017-CU14-ubuntu
```

If you check the status of all the containers using the docker ps -a command, you will see that the container exited immediately, as shown in Figure 6-15.

Figure 6-15.   *SQL Server on Linux container terminating immediately after starting*

As I mentioned in *Chapter 4*, I wasted a lot of time trying to figure out what could have caused the container to stop. It wasn't until I reviewed the logs that I found out what the real problem was. Use the *docker logs <container name>* command to review the SQL Server error logs generated inside the container, as shown in Figure 6-16. After finding out that the real issue has something to do with the *SA_PASSWORD* parameter value, I made the necessary modifications and reran the command.

```
emsarmiento@CENTOSDOCKER01:~                                      —   □   ×

[emsarmiento@CENTOSDOCKER01 ~]$ docker logs sqldevlinuxcon01
2019-08-31 00:40:33.80 Server      Setup step is copying system data file 'C:\templatedat
a\master.mdf' to '/var/opt/mssql/data/master.mdf'.
2019-08-31 00:40:33.86 Server      Did not find an existing master data file /var/opt/mss
ql/data/master.mdf, copying the missing default master and other system database files. I
f you have moved the database location, but not moved the database files, startup may fai
l. To repair: shutdown SQL Server, move the master database to configured location, and r
estart.
2019-08-31 00:40:33.87 Server      Setup step is copying system data file 'C:\templatedat
a\mastlog.ldf' to '/var/opt/mssql/data/mastlog.ldf'.
2019-08-31 00:40:33.88 Server      Setup step is copying system data file 'C:\templatedat
a\model.mdf' to '/var/opt/mssql/data/model.mdf'.


2019-08-31 00:40:35.60 spid17s     ERROR: Unable to set system administrator password: Pa
ssword validation failed. The password does not meet SQL Server password policy requireme
nts because it is not complex enough. The password must be at least 8 characters long and
 contain characters from three of the following four sets: Uppercase letters, Lowercase l
etters, Base 10 digits, and Symbols..
2019-08-31 00:40:35.60 spid5s      Starting up database 'msdb'.
2019-08-31 00:40:35.60 spid20s     Password policy update was successful.
2019-08-31 00:40:35.61 spid23s     Always On: The availability replica manager is waiting
 for the instance of SQL Server to allow client connections. This is an informational mes
sage only. No user action is required.
2019-08-31 00:40:35.61 spid17s     An error occurred during server setup. See previous er
rors for more information.
2019-08-31 00:40:35.61 spid9s      Starting up database 'mssqlsystemresource'.
2019-08-31 00:40:35.61 spid17s     SQL Trace was stopped due to server shutdown. Trace ID
 = '1'. This is an informational message only; no user action is required.
2019-08-31 00:40:35.63 spid9s      The resource database build version is 14.00.3076. Thi
s is an informational message only. No user action is required.
2019-08-31 00:40:35.65 spid9s      Starting up database 'model'.
[emsarmiento@CENTOSDOCKER01 ~]$ ▮
```

Figure 6-16. *Running docker logs to explore the SQL Server error logs*

Note   Unlike in Linux, failing the SQL Server password complexity policy on Windows does not terminate the container nor does it create an entry in the SQL Server error log. The container will continue to run but it won't allow you to log in using the *sa* credentials that you provided. You're going to need your DBA skills to log in interactively to the container using the *docker exec* command and start the SQL Server instance in single-user mode so you can change the *sa* password.

You can also use the *docker logs* command with the *-f* parameter to review the SQL Server error log – in real time. I find it a much better approach than running *sp_readerrorlog* when troubleshooting SQL Server–related issues since I can see exactly what is going on while it is happening. It's like having a live trace in the SQL Server error log. Figure 6-17 shows using both *sp_readerrorlog* and the *docker logs* command side by side.

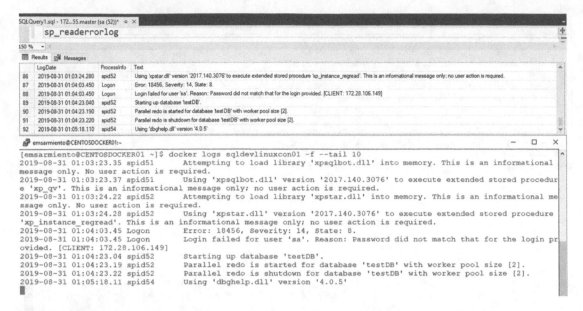

Figure 6-17. *sp_readerrorlog vs. the docker logs command to explore the SQL Server error logs*

Reviewing the Status of the Docker Daemon

Knowing the status of the Docker daemon is also key to making sure it runs smoothly. It can also lead you to finding out issues should you need to perform some troubleshooting. After installing the Docker daemon on a Linux host in *Chapter 3*, one of the things we did was to check its status using the following command. The *-l* parameter displays the entire message without truncating them with ellipses. Figure 6-18 shows the status of the Docker daemon on a Linux host.

```
sudo systemctl status docker -l
```

```
emsarmiento@CENTOSDOCKER01:/                                          —   □   ×

[emsarmiento@CENTOSDOCKER01 /]$ sudo systemctl status docker -1
● docker.service - Docker Application Container Engine
   Loaded: loaded (/usr/lib/systemd/system/docker.service; enabled; vendor preset: disabl
ed)
   Active: active (running) since Fri 2019-08-30 23:59:50 EDT; 6h ago
     Docs: https://docs.docker.com
 Main PID: 1222 (dockerd)
    Tasks: 15
   Memory: 146.2M
   CGroup: /system.slice/docker.service
           ├─ 1222 /usr/bin/dockerd -H fd:// --containerd=/run/containerd/containerd.sock
           └─19401 /usr/bin/docker-proxy -proto tcp -host-ip 0.0.0.0 -host-port 1433 -con
tainer-ip 172.17.0.2 -container-port 1433

Aug 30 23:59:46 CENTOSDOCKER01 dockerd[1222]: time="2019-08-30T23:59:46.435764848-04:00"
level=info msg="pickfirstBalancer: HandleSubConnStateChange: 0xc0006bd130, CONNECTING" mo
dule=grpc
Aug 30 23:59:46 CENTOSDOCKER01 dockerd[1222]: time="2019-08-30T23:59:46.436986036-04:00"
level=info msg="pickfirstBalancer: HandleSubConnStateChange: 0xc0006bd130, READY" module=
grpc
Aug 30 23:59:46 CENTOSDOCKER01 dockerd[1222]: time="2019-08-30T23:59:46.517565342-04:00"
level=info msg="[graphdriver] using prior storage driver: overlay2"
Aug 30 23:59:46 CENTOSDOCKER01 dockerd[1222]: time="2019-08-30T23:59:46.634377591-04:00"
level=info msg="Loading containers: start."
Aug 30 23:59:48 CENTOSDOCKER01 dockerd[1222]: time="2019-08-30T23:59:48.954503626-04:00"
level=info msg="Default bridge (docker0) is assigned with an IP address 172.17.0.0/16. Da
emon option --bip can be used to set a preferred IP address"
Aug 30 23:59:49 CENTOSDOCKER01 dockerd[1222]: time="2019-08-30T23:59:49.695938806-04:00"
level=info msg="Loading containers: done."
Aug 30 23:59:49 CENTOSDOCKER01 dockerd[1222]: time="2019-08-30T23:59:49.901218916-04:00"
```

Figure 6-18. *Display the status of the Docker daemon in Linux*

Since Docker is just like any other Linux daemon, it also sends its logs to the *systemd* journal. You can think of *systemd* journal as the Windows event log. You can access all the system events from the *systemd* journal by running the following command:

```
sudo journalctl
```

But given that it contains all system events and logs, it can be a bit overwhelming. We only want the system logs from the Docker daemon. To display the Docker daemon logs from the *systemd* journal, run the following *journalctl* command. You can also pass the *-o verbose* parameter if you want to display a more detailed information for each entry.

```
sudo journalctl -u docker
```

These are stored in the */var/log/syslog* file on Ubuntu or */var/log/messages* file on CentOS. You can retrieve Docker-related events using the following command. Just replace the appropriate filename depending on your Linux distribution. Figure 6-19 displays Docker-related events when you run the command on a CentOS Docker host.

```
sudo cat /var/log/messages | grep docker
```

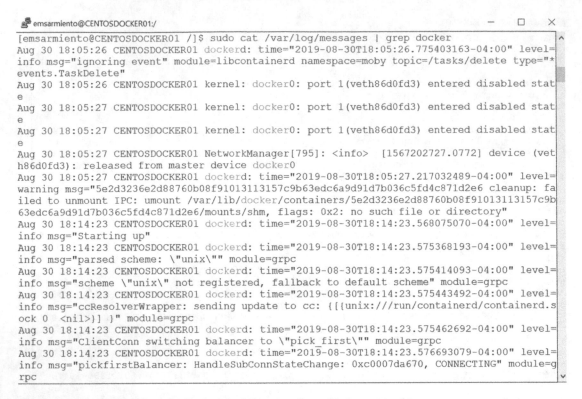

Figure 6-19. *Display the status of the Docker daemon in Linux*

On a Windows host, since the events are written to the Windows event log, you can filter the application logs to only display event sources from *docker*. Alternatively, you can use the following PowerShell command:

```
Get-EventLog -LogName Application -Source Docker
```

Summary

We've covered a lot of ground in this chapter as far as managing Docker and containers is concerned. But that's not all of it. It's just enough to get you started on managing containers and the Docker host from a SQL Server DBA's point of view. As you do more work with Docker, you'll get more involved with the Linux operating system. I'm sure you've learned a lot about Linux since *Chapter 3*. And we're just scratching the surface. I can guarantee that you'll be working with the Linux filesystem, configuring daemons, managing system resources, and much more by the time you finish this book. You have no other choice but to be really good with Linux when you do more work with SQL Server running in a Docker container.

In the section "Sharing Files Between Host and Container," I covered the use of volumes to make a directory on the Docker host available inside the container. The next chapter will cover this in more detail and how to manage and persist data inside a container for stateful applications, specifically SQL Server. Besides, how good is a relational database if you can't persist data in it? We'll make sure that doesn't happen to your SQL Server databases inside containers.

## CHAPTER 7

Persisting Data

The faintest ink is more powerful than the strongest memory.

—a Chinese proverb

Immediately after getting settled in on my desk, I asked my Sunday school teacher for some sheets of paper and crayons. It's not that I like writing, it's just one of the very few things that I can do as a sick kid. According to my doctor, I can't play rough, I can't do sports, I can't even laugh hard (that's what I was told). So, it's reading books, playing the piano, and writing – or scribbling, because I can't even read my own handwriting.

My Sunday school teacher handed me a Magic Slate, and, according to her, it's a reusable drawing device. My 4-year-old brain tried to comprehend what it was and how it worked. Besides, all I knew at that point were pencil – sometimes crayons – and paper. I was told that I can draw on it, lift the sheets of filmy paper to erase my drawing, and do it over and over and over again as many times as I want. It came with a stylus but my fingernails were good enough to scribble with. So, I started scribbling and drawing. I wrote my name on it. I even tried to draw one of the kids' face while being as detailed as I can. It's interesting how we both ended up laughing when I showed him my artistic sketch.

Our laughter was broken when he lifted the sheet of filmy paper on the Magic Slate. My drawing, the one that took me hours to carefully sketch, was all gone in less than the time I was able to say "Ben!" (if you're reading this, sorry, Ben. Somebody had to be thrown under the bus, and I happen to be the one telling the story). I was devastated. How could that ever happen? I busted out crying until my Sunday school teacher approached us and asked what happened. As I was trying to explain the disappearing act that my drawing did, she reminded me that it was how the Magic Slate worked.

© Edwin M Sarmiento 2020
E. M. Sarmiento, *The SQL Server DBA's Guide to Docker Containers*,
https://doi.org/10.1007/978-1-4842-5826-2_7

You write on it and erase everything by lifting the sheet of filmy paper. It was designed that way. It took me a good half an hour to finally settle down and ask for paper and crayons. I went back to what I knew worked and vowed not to touch the Magic Slate ever again. Or so I thought.

Before you get too involved with deploying your SQL Server databases on containers, I want to make sure you get one thing straight: Docker containers were originally designed specifically to be stateless. That means they do not have data persistence and they can't maintain data when they're either moved to another server (in case you decide to deploy a Docker Swarm cluster with multiple hosts) or the container is destroyed. As SQL Server database professionals, that's a big no-no. We want to store and persist data. We want to protect it, back it up, and make sure it's there when we need it. How can this Docker thing be right for SQL Server or any type of data storage platform?

I could have skipped writing this chapter if that was the case. But I didn't. This chapter covers working with stateful applications like relational databases in containers. I'll introduce you to Docker volumes, how to work with them, and using volumes to store SQL Server database files. Once you've gone through the configuration, you will see how Docker containers can be used for stateful applications and SQL Server, in particular.

Stateful vs. Stateless Applications

I mentioned in the previous section that Docker was originally designed to be stateless. Stateless applications are those that do not save client data generated in one session for use in the next session. Imagine getting a haircut from your favorite barber every other week. Being stateless means you're always telling your barber how you would like your haircut every time you visit. Your barber does not keep a record of your preferred hairstyle, nor your favorite chair in the shop, nor give you their signature scalp massage with shampoo; you get the picture.

In contrast, stateful applications are those that do save client data generated in every session and use that data the next time the client makes a request. This is your barber preparing your favorite chair and the shampoo that will be used for their signature scalp massage and already set to do your preferred hairstyle the minute you walk into the shop. All this information about you and your preferences are stored and persisted in your barber's brain. However, you might argue that the brain is a temporary storage because if your barber decides to go on vacation, you would have to tell the replacement barber everything about your preferences. A better way to store this information is to write it on a piece of paper for all barbers to access – or if the shop is sophisticated enough, a customer relationship management (CRM) system that has a back-end database.

I'm pretending to know all about hairstyles and barbershops but I really don't. I haven't seen a barber in 10 years. Don't judge me.

Containers Are Ephemeral and Immutable

One of my favorite scenes in the movie *The Matrix Reloaded* is about Neo having a conversation with the Oracle. And while the philosophical ideas conveyed in their discussion fascinate me more, this specific Q&A in their dialog caught my attention. The conversation went like this:

> *Neo: And why would a program be deleted?*

> *The Oracle: Maybe it breaks down. Maybe a better program is created to replace it – happens all the time.*

I'm not sure if this conversation was the inspiration behind these two tenets of containers: ephemeral and immutable. But it sure is a great way to explain how they apply to containers.

Ephemeral means that containers are short-lived – temporary. Immutable means that containers are unchanging; the state and contents cannot be modified after they are created. Just like how the Oracle explained to Neo why a program would be deleted, an app can malfunction or upgraded to provide additional functionality. And the Oracle was right, it does happen all the time. But the way we have been dealing with software running on servers in the past to address these two possible outcomes has been so unlike Neo. When an app malfunctions or needs an upgrade, we don't delete it. We move it to a different server – or to a different virtual machine (VM). We maintain, patch, update, migrate, and so on. The servers running the app have a longer lifecycle and are constantly updated – but seldom deleted. We carry them over to the next version of the software, bringing with it all the baggage and junk that could potentially affect stability and performance of the app. It's no wonder an upgrade or a migration project takes so much time and resources.

Containers, on the other hand, have a very short lifecycle. Want a new version of the app running on a container? Simple. Don't update the container. Just delete and deploy a new one with the new version of the app. Sounds too simplistic? You will have to wait until later in the chapter to see this in action.

How Cloud Providers Implement Infrastructure-as-a-Service

Have you ever wondered how cloud service providers like Amazon Web Services (AWS), Microsoft Azure, or Google Cloud Platform can easily scale up a VM with very minimal downtime? They'll tell you to choose a larger VM size and reboot the machine. That's it. At first, I was skeptical about this whole "scale-up-with-minimal-downtime" approach because it goes against everything I knew about upgrading and scaling up servers. I spent years doing this as a data center engineer, and it sure didn't take a few minutes – especially for SQL Server with large databases. So, I tried it on both Microsoft Azure and AWS. Figure 7-1 illustrates how cloud service providers conceptually do this scale-up approach for VMs.

Figure 7-1. *How scaling up a VM happens on the cloud with minimal downtime*

I was shocked. It does work as published. But I'm still not 100% convinced. I took everything I knew about scaling up servers running SQL Server databases and started doing thought experiments (you know, the ones that we do to pretend we're smarter than the average DBA). Here are the facts.

SQL Server databases are simply files – MDF, NDF, and LDF files – that the database engine accesses to read and write data. These files are stored on a storage subsystem attached to a server with compute resources – CPU and memory. If I need to scale up a server to increase compute capacity with minimal downtime, I usually have another server available with the same version and edition of both the operating system and SQL

Server installed. I would then start to replicate the databases across the machines either by using database mirroring or log shipping. If I have the storage resources available, I'll replicate the storage subsystem – while keeping the SQL Server database engine stopped on the target machine – instead of just replicating the databases. Once I'm ready to cut over to the scaled-up machine, I'll just stop the source machine, complete the replication process, and start the SQL Server database engine on the target machine. Stopping the SQL Server database engine on the source machine allows it to cleanly shut down all the databases and then terminates the service. This involves either committing or rolling back transactions, writing all dirty pages to disk, and then writing an entry into transaction log. Starting the SQL Server database engine on the target machine allows it to run recovery – reading the transaction log and either committing or rolling back transactions before bringing the databases online. This is how SQL Server works since the beginning. So, nothing new here.

Tip   The article "Understanding Logging and Recovery in SQL Server" contains more information on the internals of SQL Server when it comes to logging and recovery. This is foundational information, and the concepts apply to all commercial relational database management systems other than SQL Server. Check out the article at *https://docs.microsoft.com/en-us/previous-versions/technet-magazine/dd392031(v=msdn.10)*.

Remember what I said about thought experiments? What if instead of having two separate storage subsystems – one for the source and another for the target machine – to store the database files, we simply decouple it from the server? What if instead of having it directly attached to the server, we simply have a pointer to the storage? The server can access the remote storage, and the SQL Server database engine can access the files. Decoupling the compute from the storage allows you to perform a scale-up process with minimal downtime because all you need to do is redirect the new compute to the old storage. And isn't this already available in SQL Server 2012 – storing database files in an SMB file share? What about SQL Server 2014 – storing database files in Azure Blob storage?

Note   When asked what my secret is for keeping up with and mastering new technology, my typical response has been "don't forget the old." It's interesting to see how these new technology features are either improvements of or a combination of old technologies. Take SQL Server Always On Availability Groups as an example. It's a combination of database mirroring and Windows Server Failover Clustering – both of which have been available since SQL Server 2005 (earlier for failover clustering). What about the readable secondary replicas? It's a real-time implementation of row versioning, again, a feature that's been available since SQL Server 2005. The filestream feature that was introduced in SQL Server 2008? It's the backbone for In-Memory OLTP. I can go on and on with the different features introduced in every new version of SQL Server, and I can find their roots in an old feature. Either Microsoft has already seen the future and is leading the market into their direction or they're really good at maximizing their existing technology investments. I think it's a brilliant strategy. And I guess my Sunday school teacher knew something about technology even before the Oracle had that conversation with Neo. She kept telling me this very famous verse from the Holy Book: "History merely repeats itself. It has all been done before. Nothing under the sun is truly new."

Ah, so that's how they do it. Figure 7-2 illustrates how cloud service providers conceptually do this scale-up approach for VMs by decoupling the compute from the storage.

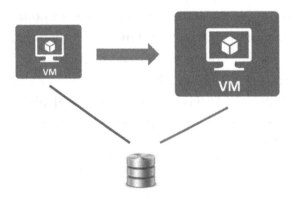

Figure 7-2. *Decoupling compute from storage allows for scaling up a VM with minimal downtime*

When you think about it, we've been using this approach for decades, since the early 2000s when storage area networks (SAN) were introduced. The server (compute) runs the app and the data is stored outside of it – the storage. Doing this thought experiment reminded me of a migration project that we did back in 2006 for a large SQL Server 2000 failover clustered instance (FCI). Since a SQL Server FCI has the compute decoupled from storage, we managed to replace one of the problematic failover cluster nodes fairly quick by attaching it to the existing SAN and joining it to the cluster with proper validation, of course. It also reminded me of another data center migration project I did back in 2010. Following the workflow sequence described earlier plus replicating the storage subsystem across geographical locations allowed me to move more than 400+ SQL Server physical machines from a data center in Los Angeles to another in Las Vegas in less than an hour.

Since a VM is just a filesystem format stored on disk with metadata to represent the compute resources – CPU, memory, network – it's so much easier to scale it up. Just redirect the storage from the old VM into the new VM. Cloud service providers can do this with an automated workflow process under the covers, including steps to properly stop and start the SQL Server service on the source and target VMs, respectively, so long as the underlying hardware has the appropriate compute resources to support the new VM.

Docker Volumes

The concept behind containers being ephemeral and immutable together with decoupling compute from storage is what allows Docker to run stateful applications like relational databases. Despite having been originally designed to run stateless applications, storing data outside of the containers allows you to leverage their ephemeral and immutable nature while being able to store data if and when you decide to delete programs. I mean, containers.

Recall in *Chapter 5* that a container consists of a filesystem layer stored on the local storage of the Docker host. The filesystem layer is what makes up the container and is tied to its lifecycle. The filesystem layer – including the data you store inside it – gets created when you create the container and deleted when you delete the container. Pretty straightforward, isn't it? To decouple the compute from the storage, we need an object that exists outside of the container. Enter Docker volumes.

A Docker volume is an object that represents a filesystem outside of the container. It is a directory outside of the container's union filesystem and exists as normal directory with files on the Docker host's filesystem. Docker volumes are the preferred way to persist data generated and used by containers. I like to think of Docker volumes as a network shared folder – it looks like a folder inside the operating system (container) but is external to it. Volumes being outside of the container allow you to add as much data into it without affecting the size of the container, which are perfect for SQL Server databases. And because it is an object that exists outside of the container, it is managed using its own `docker volume` subcommand. For example, you can run the following command if you want to create a Docker volume. Be sure to provide a meaningful name. Otherwise, Docker will assign a 64-character GUID value for the name. I'm sure you don't want to see more of those 64-character GUID value names after reading *Chapter 5*.

```
docker volume create samplevolume
```

By default, creating a Docker volume creates a directory on the host, which is located in */var/lib/docker/volumes* in Linux and *C:\ProgramData\docker\volumes* on Windows.

After creating the Docker volume, you can inspect the metadata by using the `docker volume inspect` command here:

```
docker volume inspect samplevolume
```

Figure 7-3 displays the metadata of the created Docker volume on both Windows host and Linux host. Pay attention to the following:

- *Driver*: This displays the name of the storage volume driver. By default, Docker will create volumes with the built-in local driver. This means that the volumes will only be available to containers on the host they are created on.

- *Mountpoint*: This displays the full path of the directory in the Docker host's local filesystem. When you attach the volume to a container, any data generated in the container will be stored here.

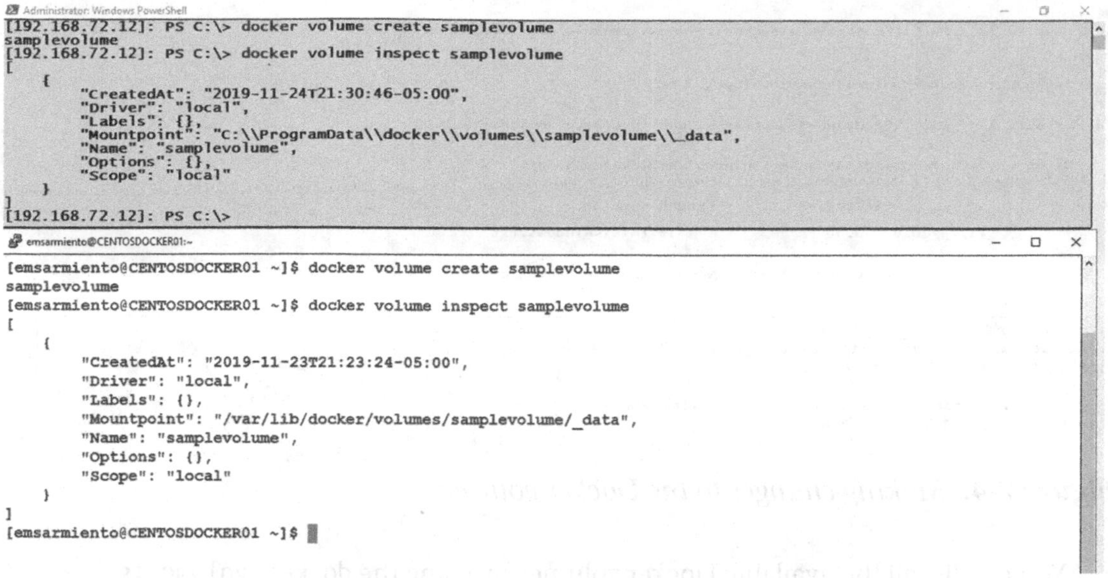

Figure 7-3. *Creating and inspecting Docker volume metadata*

Because Docker volumes are simply directories in the filesystem layer, I can add and modify files in these directories directly from the host without having to run a container.

Tip   Always keep permissions in mind when working on Linux. Unlike in Windows where I can access the *C:\ProgramData\docker\volumes* directory simply by being a member of the local administrator group, that's not the case in Linux. The *root* user owns the */var/lib/docker/volumes* (and everything else in the */var/lib/docker*) directory. In order to directly access the directories and make any changes, you need to have *root* privileges. You either switch to *root* or prefix commands with *sudo*.

Figure 7-4 shows a simple file that I copied to the Docker volume on both the Linux host and Windows host. Keep in mind that I do not currently have any running containers.

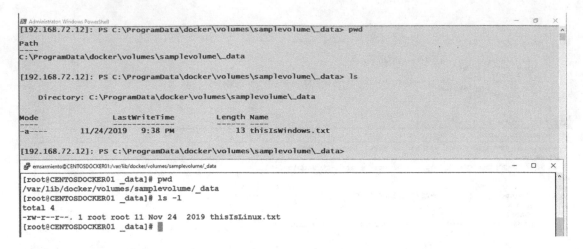

Figure 7-4. *Making changes to the Docker volume*

You can list all the available Docker volumes by using the `docker volume ls` command. Finally, you can delete a specific Docker volume by using the `docker volume rm` command like the one here:

```
docker volume rm samplevolume
```

I won't delete the volume that I created here. I'll use it with a container and mount it as a volume in the next section.

You can display the list of available subcommands for managing Docker volumes by running the `docker volume` command as shown in Figure 7-5.

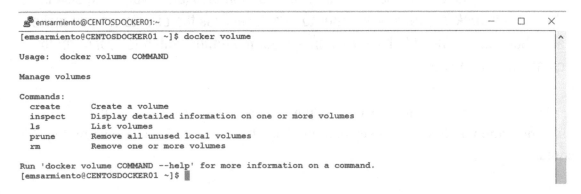

Figure 7-5. *List all commands for managing Docker volume*

Attach Volumes to Containers

Let's use the Docker volumes created in the previous section and attach them to a container. For a Linux container, I'll use a CentOS 7 image and attach the *samplevolume* volume to it. Use the *--mount* parameter of the *docker run* command as shown in the following. I'm passing a *-it* parameter (*i* for interactive and *t* for pseudo-TTY or a terminal session) so I can inspect the filesystem inside it. The *--mount* parameter of the *docker run* command uses *key=value* pairs that are easy to understand. In the example provided, *source* is the name of the Docker volume and *target* is the directory inside the container.

```
docker run --mount source=samplevolume,target=/tmp/dockervolume -it
centos:7
```

You will see the *thisIsLinux.txt* file that was copied into the volume before the container was created. Figure 7-6 displays the file as seen from inside the container.

```
@45340a1df526:/tmp/dockervolume                                                                    -  □  ×
[emsarmiento@CENTOSDOCKER01 /]$ docker run --mount source=samplevolume,target=/tmp/dockervolume -it centos:7
[root@45340a1df526 /]# cd /tmp/dockervolume/
[root@45340a1df526 dockervolume]# ls -l
total 4
-rw-r--r--. 1 root root 11 Nov 25  2019 thisIsLinux.txt
[root@45340a1df526 dockervolume]# ▮
```

Figure 7-6. *Attaching a volume to a Linux container and displaying its contents*

For a Windows container, I'll use the Windows Server 2016 Nano Server image and attach the *samplevolume* volume to it. But instead of using the *--mount* parameter of the *docker run* command, I'll be using the *-v* (or *--volume*) parameter. This is the supported way of attaching volumes in Windows Server containers. Refer to *https://docs. microsoft.com/en-us/virtualization/windowscontainers/manage-containers/ persistent-storage* on how to deal with persistent storage in Windows Server containers.

```
docker run -v samplevolume:c:\dockervolume -it microsoft/nanoserver:sac2016
powershell
```

You will see the *thisIsWindows.txt* file that was copied into the volume before the container was created, as shown in Figure 7-7.

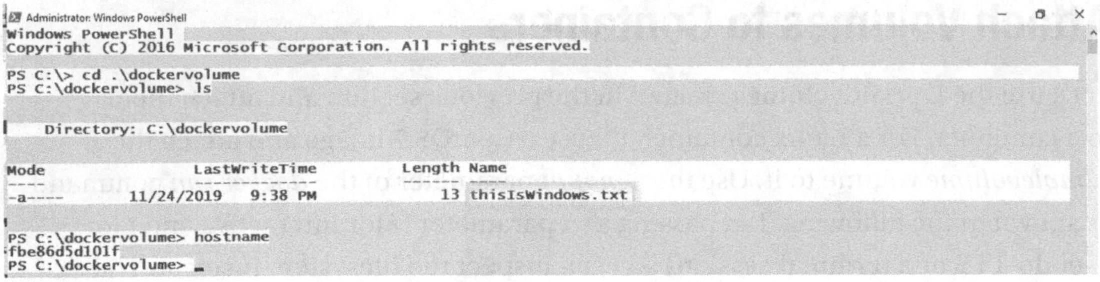

```
Administrator: Windows PowerShell                                        -  □  ×
Windows PowerShell
Copyright (C) 2016 Microsoft Corporation. All rights reserved.

PS C:\> cd .\dockervolume
PS C:\dockervolume> ls

    Directory: C:\dockervolume

Mode                LastWriteTime         Length Name
----                -------------         ------ ----
-a----        11/24/2019     9:38 PM          13 thisIsWindows.txt

PS C:\dockervolume> hostname
fbe86d5d101f
PS C:\dockervolume> _
```

Figure 7-7. *Attaching a volume to a Windows container and displaying its contents*

To -v or to --mount

You might be wondering what's the difference between the *-v* and the *--mount* parameters of the *docker run* command aside from the support between Windows Server containers and Linux containers. The *-v* parameter came in first, so you'll see more of its usage in documentation and online resources. The *--mount* parameter was only introduced in Docker version 17.06. Originally, the *-v* parameter was used for stand-alone containers, and the *--mount* parameter was used for services in Docker Swarm. Now, you can use the *--mount* parameter for both. Also, the *--mount* parameter syntax is easier to understand with its explicit use of *key=value* pairs. Just look at the sample docker run command to attach a volume on a Linux container.

Both parameters will create the directory on the Docker host in case it doesn't already exist. But they won't tell you if the volume that you are trying to attach to a container already exists. This is fine for any other type of app but certainly not for SQL Server. Imagine a SQL Server on Linux container using a volume to store both system and user databases. If you start up a new container and attach the existing volume that another SQL Server container is already using, you'll get an *Error 17113* as shown in Figure 7-8 with an *Access is denied* error message. That's because the *sqlservr* process from the existing container already has an exclusive lock to the system database files used to run the SQL Server instance.

```
emsarmiento@CENTOSDOCKER01:/var/lib/docker/volumes/samplevolume/_data/data        —   □   ×

[root@CENTOSDOCKER01 data]# docker logs f54b1784ffb6
2019-11-24 13:56:41.60 Server          Microsoft SQL Server 2017 (RTM-CU14) (KB4484710) - 14.0.3076.1 (X64)
           Mar 12 2019 19:29:19
           Copyright (C) 2017 Microsoft Corporation
           Developer Edition (64-bit) on Linux (Ubuntu 16.04.6 LTS)
2019-11-24 13:56:41.61 Server          UTC adjustment: 0:00
2019-11-24 13:56:41.61 Server          (c) Microsoft Corporation.
2019-11-24 13:56:41.61 Server          All rights reserved.
2019-11-24 13:56:41.61 Server          Server process ID is 28.
2019-11-24 13:56:41.61 Server          Logging SQL Server messages in file '/var/opt/mssql/log/errorlog'.
2019-11-24 13:56:41.61 Server          Registry startup parameters:
           -d /var/opt/mssql/data/master.mdf
           -l /var/opt/mssql/data/mastlog.ldf
           -e /var/opt/mssql/log/errorlog
2019-11-24 13:56:41.62 Server          Error: 17113, Severity: 16, State: 1.
2019-11-24 13:56:41.62 Server          Error 5(Access is denied.) occurred while opening file '/var/opt/mssq
l/data/master.mdf' to obtain configuration information at startup. An invalid startup option might have
caused the error. Verify your startup options, and correct or remove them if necessary.
[root@CENTOSDOCKER01 data]#
```

Figure 7-8. *Attaching a volume to a new SQL Server container that is already being used by an existing SQL Server container*

It is recommended to use the *--mount* parameter for new deployments unless you are deploying SQL Server on Windows containers, or any Windows Server containers, for that matter. For more information, refer to the Docker documentation on using volumes at *https://docs.docker.com/storage/volumes/*.

Sharing Volumes Between Containers?

While I was researching about how to share data between containers, the topic of Docker volumes came up a lot. This isn't surprising, given that even Docker recommends it. When you read the documentation on using volumes, this is one of the items listed as an advantage: *Volumes can be more safely shared among multiple containers.*

Wait, what? Docker, the creator of the Docker container runtime engine, is telling you to use volumes so you can share them among multiple containers? You've got to be kidding me! And everyone else is saying the same thing.

Having already done thought experiments to understand the "scale-up-with-minimal-downtime" approach I mentioned in an earlier section, I decided to again gather what I knew about SQL Server and filter the statement about Docker volumes to see if it makes sense. So here goes. The SQL Server database engine initiates an exclusive lock to the database files for access. It does so because part of being able to use a database is opening all the files that belong to it and performing recovery. If the SQL Server database engine has an exclusive lock on all of the database files, there's no way another process – like another SQL Server database engine – could gain exclusive access

145

to the same set of database files. There's a reason why Microsoft recommends excluding the SQL Server database files from antivirus scanning: to make sure that the files are not locked when the SQL Server process must use them. And don't get me started with third-party tools that bypass the SQL Server APIs to quiesce the database files while performing backups. The very tools that you thought were there to protect you are the very ones causing disasters.

Given that the SQL Server process requires an exclusive lock on the database files, it doesn't make sense to have multiple SQL Server containers accessing the same volume. I repeat: it doesn't make sense to have multiple SQL Server containers accessing the same volume. Remember the error message in Figure 7-8? I hope I made myself very clear.

To Docker's defense, since containers were originally designed for stateless applications, the practice of having multiple containers access the same volume makes total sense. Let's say you have a logging module for all of your applications. The logging module can be implemented in a container and write the log files in a volume that can be shared across multiple logging containers. Since most logging applications are predominantly write intensive with very minimal read access (until after an auditor who wakes up on the wrong side of the bed decides to ask for a detailed audit report), storing the log files in a single volume has the benefit of a "single-source-of-truth" for all the logs. Plus, you don't have to do any of those extract-transform-load (ETL) or extract-load-transform (ELT) processes since all of the data is stored in one place – the volume.

It does bear repeating: it doesn't make sense to have multiple SQL Server containers accessing the same volume.

Leveraging Volumes with SQL Server on Containers

In *Chapter 6*, I highlighted the use of volumes in the section "Sharing Files Between Host and Container." Now that you understand Docker volumes and how they work, it is clear that this is how we persist data with SQL Server running in containers.

Run the following command on a Linux host to attach the created volume *samplevolume* to a SQL Server on Linux container:

```
docker run -e "ACCEPT_EULA=Y" -e "SA_PASSWORD=mYSecUr3PAssw0rd"
-p 1433:1433 --name sqldevlinuxcon01 -d -h linuxsqldev01 --mount
source=samplevolume,target=/var/opt/mssql mcr.microsoft.com/mssql/
server:2017-CU14-ubuntu
```

The */var/opt/mssql* directory is the default SQL Server directory in Linux. This directory contains the following structure:

- *data*: Directory containing system database files, user database files, and transaction log files

- *log*: Directory containing the SQL Server error log files, the default trace files, and default Extended Event sessions

- *secrets*: Directory containing the Server Master Key that is generated for the SQL Server instance

During the creation of the SQL Server on Linux container, the contents of the */var/ opt/mssql* directory get copied to the container as part of the setup process. Because we are telling Docker to mount the */var/opt/mssql* directory inside the container to the *samplevolume* volume, the contents of the directory get created in the Docker host's local filesystem – */var/lib/docker/volumes/samplevolume/_data*. And just like in Figure 7-6, you will see the *thisIsLinux.txt* file that was copied into the volume before the container was created. Figure 7-9 displays the file as seen from inside the Docker host's filesystem together with the contents of the */var/opt/mssql* directory.

```
[root@CENTOSDOCKER01 _data]# pwd
/var/lib/docker/volumes/samplevolume/_data
[root@CENTOSDOCKER01 _data]# ls -l
total 8
drwxr-xr-x. 2 root root  200 Nov 24 08:52 data
drwxr-xr-x. 2 root root 4096 Nov 24 17:40 log
drwxr-xr-x. 2 root root   25 Nov 24 08:51 secrets
-rw-r--r--. 1 root root   11 Nov 24 2019 thisIsLinux.txt
[root@CENTOSDOCKER01 _data]#
```

Figure 7-9. *Contents of the mounted volume to a SQL Server on Linux container*

With the container up and running, I can create a sample user database in SQL Server, and the database files will get created in the *samplevolume* volume. Figure 7-10 shows the database files as seen from inside the container filesystem and from the Docker host's filesystem. And, yes, I did create a sample database named *sampleDB*.

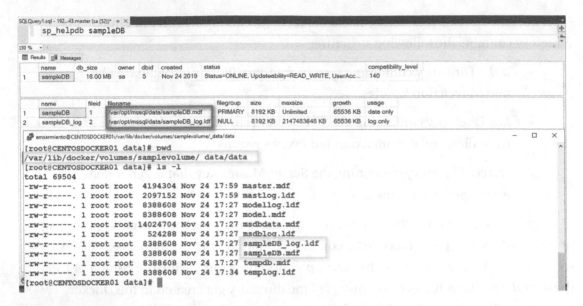

Figure 7-10. *SQL Server database files getting created in volumes*

Keep in mind that because the default SQL Server directory in Linux is what we mounted to a volume, both the system and user databases will get created in the same location. But nothing is stopping you from keeping the default database file location for system databases and just using a volume for user databases. Run the following command on a Linux host to attach the created volume *samplevolume* to a SQL Server on Linux container, using the */tmp/dbdata* directory inside the container as the user database file location. Be sure to stop and remove the existing SQL Server on Linux container so you can reuse the container name and port number.

```
docker run -e "ACCEPT_EULA=Y" -e "SA_PASSWORD=mYSecUr3PAssw0rd"
-p 1433:1433 --name sqldevlinuxcon01 -d -h linuxsqldev01 --mount
source=samplevolume,target=/tmp/dbdata mcr.microsoft.com/mssql/server:2017-
CU14-ubuntu
```

In my example, I also cleaned up the SQL Server–related contents of the *samplevolume* volume and just kept the *thisIsLinux.txt* file. Deleting the container does not delete the contents of the volume. Remember, the volume exists outside of the container. I also used the following CREATE DATABASE command to create the sample database. Note the use of the *target* directory – */tmp/dbdata*.

```
CREATE DATABASE [sampleDB]
ON PRIMARY
(NAME = N'sampleDB', FILENAME = N'/tmp/dbdata/sampleDB.mdf')
 LOG ON
(NAME = N'sampleDB_log', FILENAME = N'/tmp/dbdata/sampleDB_log.ldf')
```

Figure 7-11 shows the system databases inside the default SQL Server directory and the sample user database inside the *samplevolume* volume.

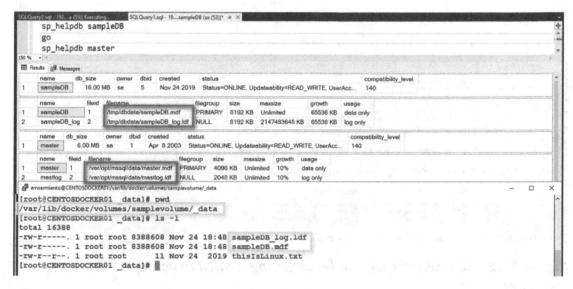

Figure 7-11. *SQL Server user databases getting created in volumes*

In fact, this is how the SQL Server on Windows container is configured. Unlike the SQL Server on Linux container where the entire */var/opt/mssql* directory is copied to the container, the publicly available SQL Server on Windows container still leverages the default SQL Server directory – *C:\Program Files\Microsoft SQL Server\MSSQL{nn}. MSSQL*. Mounting a volume to a SQL Server on Windows container will only create the target directory inside the container filesystem, it won't change the default database file location because the SQL Server instance is already installed.

Run the following command on a Windows Server host to attach the created volume *samplevolume* to a SQL Server on Windows container, using the *C:/dbdata* directory inside the container. Again, be sure to stop and remove the existing SQL Server on Windows container so you can reuse the container name and port number.

```
docker run -e "ACCEPT_EULA=Y" -e "SA_PASSWORD=mYSecUr3PAsswOrd" -p
1433:1433 --name sqldevwincon01 -d -h winsqldev01 -v samplevolume:C:/dbdata
microsoft/mssql-server-windows-developer
```

Figure 7-12 shows the Windows container equivalent of system databases inside the default SQL Server directory and the sample user database inside the *samplevolume* volume.

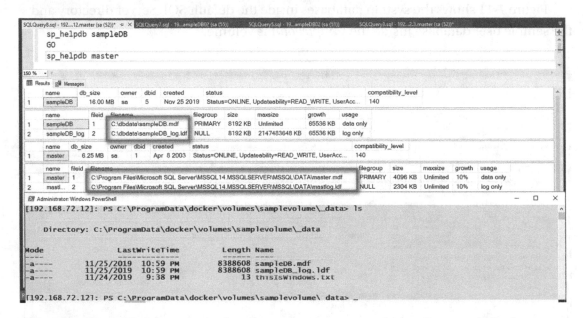

Figure 7-12. *SQL Server user databases getting created in volumes – Windows container*

Note   You can modify the default SQL Server database file location on a SQL Server running on a container – either on Windows or Linux. You do this by creating a custom SQL Server image instead of using the publicly available images from Microsoft. Chapters 9 and 10 cover how to create a custom SQL Server image for Windows and Linux, respectively.

I've seen customers deploy SQL Server databases like this – system databases are stored on a different location than the user databases. And I've also seen customers who deploy SQL Server databases – both system and user – in the same location. Neither is right nor wrong, nor is one a best practice while the other isn't. But there's a benefit to keeping both the system and user databases in the same location. You'll see a really good example in the next section.

Removing a container does not remove the volume. Because the volume exists outside of the container, you don't have to worry about somebody accidentally deleting a container and wiping out all of the databases inside it – not that you have to worry about it because it never happens.

Despite the fact that volumes are objects that exist outside of containers, you won't be able to delete a volume while an existing container is using it. Good luck with that. Docker knows when a volume is attached to a container and will not allow you to remove it, even if you use the -*f* parameter of the docker volume rm command. Figure 7-13 shows my attempt at deleting the *samplevolume* volume that my SQL Server on Windows and Linux container is using. The error message also shows the CONTAINER ID value of the container using it.

Figure 7-13. *Docker preventing deletion of a volume attached to a running container*

Make sure you keep track of which volumes your SQL Server containers are using. You don't want to end up attaching an existing volume that another SQL Server container is already using to a new one. Even in today's world of continuous integration, continuous delivery, and DevOps, there's no substitute to proper process and documentation.

Smart SQL Server In-Place Upgrade

The way we update or upgrade SQL Server in the past was to download the cumulative update (yes, Microsoft no longer releases service packs starting with SQL Server 2017) and install them on the SQL Server instance. The installation process will stop the SQL Server service, apply the binaries, and start the SQL Server service. This applies to both SQL Server on Windows and Linux.

This process is risky and can affect your service-level agreements (SLAs). For one, the amount of downtime your SQL Server instance will require depends on the length of time that the whole update process runs. I've seen cases in the past where a SQL Server service pack installation took as much as an hour or even longer. This is unacceptable for systems with very tight SLAs. Also, in case the installation of the update didn't go as planned, the rollback process can range from annoying to absolutely painful. Remember the times when you had to restore all of your database backups because the service pack installation failed?

In the previous section, I hinted on a really great benefit of keeping the system and user databases in the same location: fast updating of SQL Server instances. Remember how we can decouple the compute from the storage? Instead of installing the SQL Server updates, how about switching the compute with a new version of SQL Server? Let me show you.

Run the following command on a Linux host to attach the created volume *samplevolume02* to a SQL Server on Linux container. We'll attach the default directory for SQL Server on Linux – */var/opt/mssql* – to the volume. Again, be sure to stop and remove the existing SQL Server on Linux container so you can reuse the container name and port number.

```
docker run -e "ACCEPT_EULA=Y" -e "SA_PASSWORD=mYSecUr3PAssw0rd"
-p 1433:1433 --name sqldevlinuxcon01 -d -h linuxsqldev01 --mount
source=samplevolume02,target=/var/opt/mssql mcr.microsoft.com/mssql/
server:2017-CU14-ubuntu
```

Create a sample database so you can verify that the system and user databases are created and stored in the *samplevolume02* volume. Figure 7-14 shows the SQL Server version of the image I used – SQL Server 2017 with CU14 (14.0.3076.1) – and the database version number of the sample database (869).

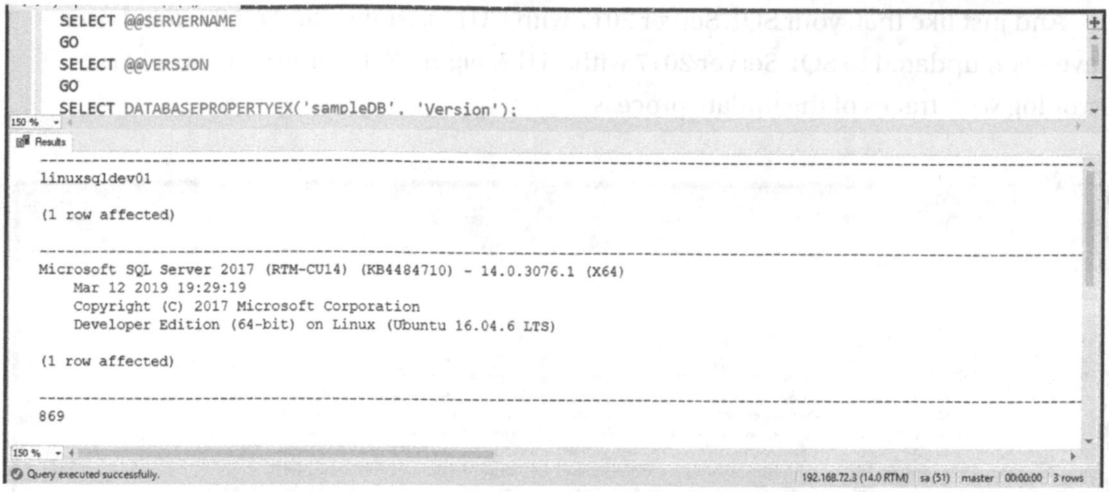

```
SELECT @@SERVERNAME
GO
SELECT @@VERSION
GO
SELECT DATABASEPROPERTYEX('sampleDB', 'Version');
```

Results

```
-------------------------------------------------------------------------
linuxsqldev01

(1 row affected)

-------------------------------------------------------------------------
Microsoft SQL Server 2017 (RTM-CU14) (KB4484710) - 14.0.3076.1 (X64)
    Mar 12 2019 19:29:19
    Copyright (C) 2017 Microsoft Corporation
    Developer Edition (64-bit) on Linux (Ubuntu 16.04.6 LTS)

(1 row affected)

-------------------------------------------------------------------------
869
```

Query executed successfully.   192.168.72.3 (14.0 RTM) sa (51) master 00:00:00 3 rows

Figure 7-14. *SQL Server version of the image and database version number*

In preparation for the update, I'll pull the publicly available SQL Server 2017 with CU17 image from the Microsoft Container Registry. This way, I don't have to include the time it takes to pull the image as part of my maintenance window. My effective downtime will only include switching between containers and updating SQL Server.

```
docker pull mcr.microsoft.com/mssql/server:2017-CU17-ubuntu
```

I will use this image to create a new container running SQL Server 2017 with CU17. At this point, my SQL Server 2017 databases are still up and running and have not experienced any downtime. The process outlined here is how I will upgrade my SQL Server 2017:

1. Stop the existing SQL Server on Linux container:

   ```
   docker stop sqldevlinuxcon01
   ```

2. Create a new SQL Server on Linux container with a new name – *sqldevlinuxcon02* – based on the SQL Server 2017 with CU17 image. Attach the *samplevolume02* volume to this new container. I'm reusing the same port number and hostname.

   ```
   docker run -e "ACCEPT_EULA=Y" -e "SA_PASSWORD=mYSecUr3PAssw0rd"
   -p 1433:1433 --name sqldevlinuxcon02 -d -h linuxsqldev01 --mount
   source=samplevolume02,target=/var/opt/mssql mcr.microsoft.com/
   mssql/server:2017-CU17-ubuntu
   ```

And just like that, your SQL Server 2017 with CU14 instance and all the databases have been updated to SQL Server 2017 with CU17. Figure 7-15 shows the SQL Server error log with traces of the update process.

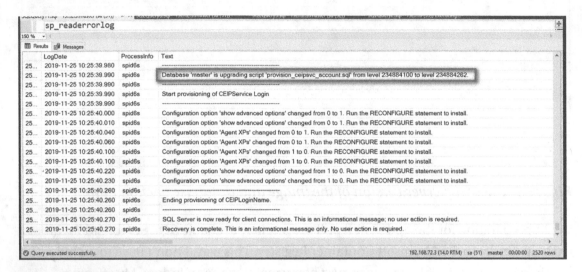

Figure 7-15. *SQL Server error log while updating the container*

Rerunning the same query used in Figure 7-14 now yields a different SQL Server version number – 14.0.3238.1 – but with the same database version number, as shown in Figure 7-16.

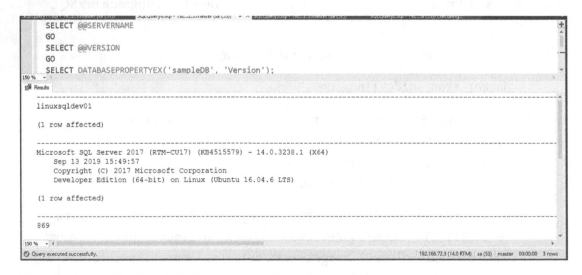

Figure 7-16. *Updated SQL Server on Linux container*

154

Note   Should you decide to upgrade your SQL Server 2017 on Linux container to SQL Server 2019, you need to start with having the SQL Server 2017 container with non-root user. Microsoft made modifications to how SQL Server on Linux containers are deployed to minimize security risks. The process within most Docker containers run as a *root* user. The *root* user in the container is also the same *root* user on the Linux host machine. This basically means if the container is compromised, the Linux host also gets compromised. Remember the SQL Server service account that has local administrator privileges on the Windows machine? Or the one that has an Active Directory domain admin privileges?

Upgrading your existing SQL Server 2017 on Linux containers is not as simple as running a new SQL Server 2019 container and mounting the existing volume to it. Because the SQL Server 2017 on Linux container ran as *root* by default, the *root* user owns all SQL Server folders and files in the volume. Ownership of folders and files must be reassigned to the non-root user in order for SQL Server to start. For additional information, refer to the process of building and running non-root SQL Server 2017 containers at *https://docs.microsoft.com/en-us/sql/linux/sql-server-linux-configure-docker?view=sql-server-2017#buildnonrootcontainer.*

I didn't delete the SQL Server 2017 with CU14 container so I can use it as a rollback plan. The container still exists and is in a *Stopped* state. That's the reason I created a new container with a new name – *sqldevlinuxcon02* – Docker cannot create a new container with the same name as an existing one, unless you delete the old and create a new one with the same name as what I've been doing in the previous exercises. Should the update process fail, I can revert to the SQL Server 2017 with CU14 container as fast as I switched to the SQL Server 2017 with CU17 container.

But make no mistake. There's still no substitute for good-old backups. While it is very easy and fast to perform a SQL Server update with containers, the fact is that the database files are not locked while you stop the existing container and create a new one. This can potentially cause other processes on the Docker host to acquire an exclusive lock to the SQL Server database files in between the update process. Use either the native SQL Server backups or any supported SQL Server on Linux VDI client to back up the databases prior to performing an update.

Summary

In this chapter, I've pointed out some of the things you need to watch out for when working with SQL Server on containers. While containers were originally designed for stateless applications and to be ephemeral and immutable, decoupling the storage from the compute using Docker volumes allowed containers to run stateful applications like SQL Server. The examples provided demonstrate using Docker volumes to store SQL Server databases and leverage them for operational tasks like updating the database engine with minimal downtime.

In the next chapter, I'll cover working with SQL Server on Linux in preparation for creating your own SQL Server on Linux images. As a SQL Server DBA, I'll assume that you already have the basic knowledge of how SQL Server on Windows works so I'll just point out the key differences on how it works on Linux.

I'll end this chapter with the final words that the Oracle left with Neo: "Be there, at that exact time, and you will have a chance." When the right time comes, your preparation will make way for you.

## CHAPTER 8

Working with SQL Server on Linux

Policies are many, Principles are few, Policies will change, Principles never do.

—Dr. John C. Maxwell

As the staff at the rental car company handed me the keys, she briefly explained how they only have manual transmission cars available. She assumed I didn't know how to drive a stick shift car just because I had a driver's license from North America. I had to tell the story of how my elder brother taught me how to drive when I was 15 with a 1986 Suzuki Samurai jeep. Her face immediately lit up when I told her about the jeep – it was what her family drove when she was a kid. I guess the simple mention of the jeep brought up amazing childhood memories with her family.

She completed the paperwork and gave me directions to the parking lot where I can pick up the rental car. As I was approaching the car, I noticed something strange. "Why are people walking on the other side of the street?", I asked myself. Or maybe I was still trying to get acquainted to the city after being on the plane for almost 12 hours. "That's just jetlag," I told myself. But it got even more weird when I opened the door of the car – it's a right-hand drive vehicle. That's when I realized it wasn't weird at all. I was in the UK and people here drive on the other side of the road. This is their normal.

I didn't really have any issues with driving on the other side of the road. Living in Singapore for three-and-a-half years taught me how to deal with taking the bus, walking on the street, and even riding on the passenger side of a car – on the other side of the road. "No big deal," I thought, "How hard can it be?". I knew how to drive a stick shift car, and I knew how to deal with being on the other side of the road. I was wrong. Driving out of that parking lot made me feel like I was a student driver all over again. The frustrations of stalling, when I was about to come near a speed bump, slow turning a corner, or even driving forward as I start the car. You know that feeling of knowing what to do – because you've been doing it your entire life – but couldn't? It took me around 2 days to finally find my rhythm and drive normally. I started to like it. But, then, I had to return the car.

If you've been working with SQL Server your entire career, I can understand your reluctance with even thinking about running it on Linux. You've built your entire career on working with Windows – both your work computer and the servers you manage. You know the shortcuts, you wrote scripts, and you're very comfortable fixing issues (there's a reason you're the computer tech support guy during family holiday gatherings). I'm guessing you're thinking of joining the ranks of thousands of IT professionals who retired knowing how to manage Windows servers only. And I don't blame you. Large enterprises run mission-critical SQL Server databases on Windows servers. And that is already taking too much of your time. Why move to Linux?

The reality is that businesses are already starting to move their SQL Server databases to Linux after Microsoft announced support for it back in 2017. Given that Docker was originally a developer for the Linux operating system, the move to run SQL Server on Docker containers was the next logical step. So, while you're still reluctant to even look at the penguin icon, your career will depend on it.

This chapter covers working with SQL Server on Linux. We'll look at the architecture and setup experience. We'll compare running SQL Server on Windows vs. Linux. And we'll write simple Linux bash scripts. The goal of this chapter is to give you a good understanding of what it takes to create a custom SQL Server on Linux image that you can deploy as a container. And I can guarantee you, it won't be as stressful and frustrating as driving a stick shift car in the busy streets of London.

SQL Server on Linux Architecture

In Chapter 1, I told the story of how I found out about Project Helsinki in one of the executive roundtables at the annual Microsoft MVP Summit. Immediately after that announcement, I started asking questions regarding how the SQL Server engineering team managed to pull off an almost impossible task of porting SQL Server to Linux. My limited understanding of Oracle made me assume that Microsoft engineers had to rewrite the entire code base to support running SQL Server on Linux. Besides, Oracle had a different code base for Windows and Linux. How did the engineering team manage to release SQL Server on Linux given the very short timeframe?

Project Drawbridge

I like history. I wish I did when I was still in school. But history gives us an opportunity to learn from and possibly leverage the work that others have already done. So, I asked one of the engineers from the SQL Server team about how it all started. Over several bottles of our preferred beverages, he talked about Project Drawbridge, a research project within Microsoft that explored the concept of application sandboxing. While the project ran in 2011, the concept of application sandboxing isn't new. Remember how the Unix V7 allowed processes to run in isolation back in 1979? That's how old this concept is. The idea behind it is to limit (or isolate) the environment in which a certain code can execute. This project was designed to sandbox Windows-based applications. It addresses the same kind of problems that hypervisors solve but with a much lower overhead and disk footprint compared to a full-blown virtual machine. Think of it this way. You can download an application on the Internet and install it on your computer without it taking over your operating system. It's the same concept behind running applications on mobile devices. And you can have the same user experience regardless of the device and the version of the operating system.

Project Drawbridge combines two core technologies – the library operating system and a picoprocess. The library operating system is a collection of application programming interfaces (APIs) and dynamic link libraries (DLLs) that an application needs from the operating system in order to run. But instead of loading the entire copy of the operating system, only a refactored version of the operating system containing functions that the application needs is loaded and ran in the same address space (user mode vs. kernel mode). The reality is that while the Windows operating system provides a ton of features and functionalities, applications don't necessarily need all of them. Think mini-Windows. The picoprocess is a process-based isolation container with a minimal kernel API surface. You can think of these two core technologies as condominium units inside a large apartment building. The condominium unit (picoprocess) has the utilities like electricity, water, and ventilation (library operating system) that a tenant (application) needs to live in that space. But the condominium unit cannot exist on its own. It must exist within the context of the apartment building (computer hardware plus operating system). Tenants can come and go without disturbing other tenants in the building. And it's much faster for tenants to come and go within the condominium units instead of waiting for an entire apartment building to be built.

The utilities tap into the main supply of the apartment building. But in order for the utilities to reach the apartment building, you need a central distribution system. Electrical distribution systems for electricity, pump and tank for water distribution, and centralized HVAC systems. This allows the owner of the apartment building to change to a different utility company should the need arise. Changing to a different utility company has minimal to no effect to the tenants other than maybe rate changes in their utility bills. In the context of Project Drawbridge, this is the platform abstraction layer (PAL).

Note   I'm oversimplifying these concepts to avoid diving deep into the technical details of their implementation. My goal is not to explore the details of how operating systems work but rather to provide just enough information to explain how SQL Server on Linux was made possible given resources and time constraints. Two great resources on the high-level architecture of how the different pieces work together to make this work are the video *Drawbridge: A new form of virtualization for application sandboxing* on Channel 9 at `https://channel9.msdn.com/Shows/Going+Deep/Drawbridge-An-Experimental-Library-Operating-System` and the published research paper *Rethinking the Library OS from the Top Down* at `www.microsoft.com/en-us/research/wp-content/uploads/2016/02/asplos2011-drawbridge.pdf`.

When you start to think about it, Project Drawbridge sounds a lot like containers.

SQLOS and SQLPAL

If you've been a SQL Server DBA for a while, you probably recall the significant change in the architecture between SQL Server 2000 and SQL Server 2005. Like other applications, SQL Server 2000 and earlier versions leveraged Windows for hardware resource management – things like thread scheduling, memory management, and I/O handling. Remember the famous UMS.DLL (SQL User Mode Scheduler DLL) file? This limited SQL Server's ability to better handle hardware resources for scalability, especially given the advancements in hardware capabilities in the early 2000s. To take advantage of the hardware improvements for improved performance and scalability, the SQL Server engineering team decided to decouple that dependency on Windows for hardware resource management. Enter SQLOS.

SQLOS is SQL Server's attempt to bring the hardware resource management within its user mode process. It's like SQL Server's own PAL into Windows. SQLOS provides operating system services such as a non-preemptive scheduling, memory management, exception handling, and the like. You can read more about the introduction of SQLOS in SQL Server 2005 and the rationale behind it at *https:// blogs.msdn.microsoft.com/slavao/2005/07/20/platform-layer-for-sql-server/*. But while SQLOS provided abstraction into Windows, it's still not a true operating system abstraction layer. SQLOS had to be rewritten in order to allow SQL Server to run on different operating systems other than Windows, making it a true PAL regardless of operating system.

Luckily, the team working on Project Drawbridge already had a rough prototype ported on Linux. The idea to merge components that already existed in Project Drawbridge and SQLOS plus the rough prototype for Linux made porting SQL Server on Linux a reality given the limitations and constraints. Thank goodness they didn't have to rewrite all the SQL Server source code written for the past two-and-a-half decades. What came out of that effort was an evolved version of SQLOS, combining the library operating system from Project Drawbridge together with SQLOS. They called it SQL Platform Abstraction Layer (SQLPAL). This allowed the SQL Server team to utilize much of the executable SQL Server code written for Windows to run on Linux. They also created a host extension layer, an abstraction layer that interacts directly with the operating system. To make everything the same for both Windows and Linux, the team came up with a host extension layer for Windows and for Linux. I guess this was done to make it easy to maintain the source code for SQL Server regardless of the underlying operating system. Given all the details that make SQL Server on Linux possible, Figure 8-1 shows my interpretation of a very high-level diagram of the architecture. You will see similar diagrams available from the documentation, but I try my best to illustrate complexities using visuals so I can understand them better.

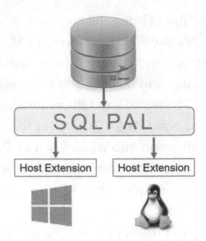

Figure 8-1. *High-level architecture that made SQL Server on Linux a reality*

I'm sure Slava Oks and his team were not even thinking about porting SQL Server to Linux back in 2005 when they worked on SQLOS. It just magically happened.

Tip   Chapter 1 of the Apress book *Pro SQL Server on Linux* by Bob Ward covers this in more detail.

Difference Between SQL Server on Windows vs. Linux

Having gone through the previous section "SQL Server on Linux Architecture," it's pretty obvious that there really isn't any difference between SQL Server running on Windows and on Linux – it's the same database engine. The SQL Server engineering team made every effort to use the same code base on both platforms. However, due to the long history of development for the Windows platform, SQL Server will definitely have more supported features on Windows than on Linux. For example, when SQL Server 2017 came out, transactional and merge replication were not available yet. Transactional replication is already supported on SQL Server 2019, but merge replication still isn't. As later versions are released, you bet that the features will be the same for both platforms. It's just a matter of time. Refer to the documentation at *https://docs.microsoft.com/ sql/linux/sql-server-linux-editions-and-components-2017* for a complete list of supported features for SQL Server 2017 on Linux and *https://docs.microsoft.com/en-us/sql/linux/sql-server-linux-editions-and-components-2019* for SQL Server 2019 on Linux.

From my experience, the biggest difference that you'll see will be your personal experience. When you've worked with SQL Server your entire career and have spent your working hours on a rich graphical user interface like the Microsoft Management Console interacting with the operating system, working on the command line like you've been doing running Docker commands can really feel very awkward. You'll hear yourself say, "this task is way easier on Windows." Or when you can't run a command because you forgot to request for *root* privileges, you'll whisper a few "#&%@$#%!" words as you hit the keys on your keyboard. On the other hand, if you've also been managing other database platforms running on Linux and have written shell scripts to automate boring tasks, running SQL Server on Linux will be like a heaven-sent gift, wondering why Microsoft didn't do this years ago. Your personal experience, preference, and even biases will highlight those differences. But once you're inside SQL Server Management Studio, you won't be able to tell the difference.

Installing SQL Server on Linux

Here's something that most SQL Server DBAs will say is the biggest difference between SQL Server on Windows and on Linux: setup experience. On Linux, there's no *setup. exe*, no SQL Server Installation Center, nor the *New SQL Server stand-alone installation or add features to an existing installation* link. How do you click and type and drag and select and...? But if you've deployed hundreds – or even thousands – of SQL Server instances, I'm sure you hate the wizard-driven setup experience. You probably have a batch file that calls *setup.exe* and passes all the parameters you need to install SQL Server. Maybe you have a *ConfigurationFile.ini* file stored in a central repository that you access as part of running *setup.exe*. The only times I use the SQL Server Installation Center are when I have to create a new (or validate an existing) *ConfigurationFile.ini* file or demonstrate how it is used to install SQL Server.

This section is divided into two parts – installing SQL Server on Linux manually and using a script to perform an unattended installation. The goal is to give you an idea of how the installation process works in preparation for creating a custom SQL Server on Linux Docker image. But nothing is stopping you from using the steps outlined in the following to automate deployment of SQL Server on Linux on either a physical machine or virtual machine.

Manual Installation

In Chapter 3, I walked you through installing Docker on two different Linux distributions – CentOS and Ubuntu. Similarly, I'll walk you through the process of installing SQL Server on both CentOS and Ubuntu so you can create a custom SQL Server on Linux Docker image that can run on either distribution. Recall that the publicly available SQL Server on Linux images from Microsoft were created using Ubuntu. You may want to create a custom SQL Server on Linux Docker image running on either Red Hat Enterprise Linux/RHEL (or CentOS like what I'm using in this book) or SUSE Linux Enterprise Server so you can standardize on a specific Linux distribution. You're free to install SQL Server on a supported Linux distribution. A list of these supported Linux distributions is available at *https://docs.microsoft.com/en-us/sql/linux/sql-server-linux-setup?view=sql-server-ver15#supportedplatforms*.

Let's start with installing SQL Server on CentOS. Similar to installing Docker on Linux, you need to tell your Linux system where to download the Microsoft SQL Server Red Hat (because CentOS is based on RHEL) repository configuration file. Be sure to specify the version of SQL Server that you want to download. Run the following command to download the Microsoft SQL Server Red Hat repository configuration file for SQL Server 2017:

```
sudo curl -o /etc/yum.repos.d/mssql-server.repo https://packages.microsoft.com/config/rhel/7/mssql-server-2017.repo
```

Run the following command to download the Microsoft SQL Server Red Hat repository configuration file for SQL Server 2019. Notice the subtle difference. I'll give you a hint – it's the SQL Server version.

```
sudo curl -o /etc/yum.repos.d/mssql-server.repo https://packages.microsoft.com/config/rhel/7/mssql-server-2019.repo
```

After you download the repository configuration file, run the following command to install SQL Server. This will download the SQL Server installation packages for RHEL (don't worry, they're compatible with CentOS). Once the download completes, it will automatically run the installation.

```
sudo yum install -y mssql-server
```

After the package installation completes, run the */opt/mssql/bin/mssql-conf* script with the following *setup* parameter to configure SQL Server using the default configuration. Follow the prompts to choose your SQL Server edition and set the *sa* password.

```
sudo /opt/mssql/bin/mssql-conf setup
```

Be careful with the choice of edition. If you intend to use this for development and testing purposes, Developer Edition is free and has all the capabilities of Enterprise Edition. Choosing Developer Edition means you intend to deploy Enterprise Edition in production. Don't make the mistake of deploying Developer Edition on development environments and eventually deploying on Standard Edition in production due to licensing cost. While SQL Server 2019 Standard Edition on Windows is almost at par with the available features on Enterprise Edition, it's not the same with SQL Server on Linux.

That's it. It's that simple. Installing SQL Server on RHEL or CentOS only requires running three commands. Well, actually four if you consider enabling the SQL Server daemon to start on system boot, which you'll have to do on an Ubuntu system as well. The following command is how you do that:

```
sudo systemctl enable mssql-server
```

On the other hand, installing SQL Server on Ubuntu includes additional steps and uses the *apt-get* command instead of the *yum* command. We'll start with importing the public GPG keys on the local Ubuntu Linux system. Run the following *curl* command to download and import the public GPG keys:

```
curl https://packages.microsoft.com/keys/microsoft.asc | sudo apt-key add -
```

Next, you need to add the Microsoft SQL Server Ubuntu repository to your Ubuntu Linux system. The following command is specific to SQL Server 2017:

```
sudo add-apt-repository "deb [arch=amd64] https://packages.microsoft.com/
ubuntu/16.04/mssql-server-2017 xenial main"
```

The following command is specific to SQL Server 2019:

```
sudo add-apt-repository "deb [arch=amd64] https://packages.microsoft.com/
ubuntu/16.04/mssql-server-2019 xenial main"
```

> **Note**   Recall the */etc/apt/sources.list* file described in Chapter 3. This file contains the list of APT software repositories, the location of the packages that you want to install on your Ubuntu Linux system. The previous command simply adds an entry in the file for the Microsoft SQL Server Ubuntu package. But you might be wondering where I got that value. The value to add to the */etc/apt/sources.list* file using the *add-apt-repository* command is from the `https://packages.` `microsoft.com/config/ubuntu/16.04/mssql-server-2017.list` file. You can download the specific list file for the version of SQL Server on Ubuntu package that you want to install.

After adding the Microsoft SQL Server Ubuntu repository to the */etc/apt/sources. list* file, you can run the following command to install SQL Server. Because you have made modifications to your Ubuntu system by adding the Microsoft SQL Server Ubuntu package repo, you need to run the `apt-get update` command prior to installing SQL Server:

```
sudo apt-get update
sudo apt-get install -y mssql-server
```

After the package installation completes, run the *mssql-conf* script with the following *setup* parameter to configure SQL Server using the default configuration. Follow the prompts to choose your SQL Server edition and set the *sa* password.

```
sudo /opt/mssql/bin/mssql-conf setup
```

If you observe the installation process, it consists of running some commands and passing parameter values. If you can combine all the steps in a script, you can automate the installation process and not have to type responses to prompts. That's the idea behind unattended installation.

Unattended Installation

Performing an unattended installation of SQL Server on Linux requires an understanding of running scripts in Linux. I'll save the details of how to run scripts on Linux at a later section. This section will describe what goes into the script for performing an unattended installation.

Recall how you manually installed SQL Server on both CentOS and Ubuntu systems. You run several commands that consist of parameters. If you look at the command to install SQL Server on both CentOS and Ubuntu – *sudo yum/apt-get install -y mssql-server* – you will see a *-y* parameter. This is a parameter that all package managers use, and it assumes that the answer to any question which would be asked during the installation process is *yes*. This also allows users to perform installation without user interaction. I usually do the manual installation several times before I perform an unattended installation to see exactly what the package is asking me to do that requires a *yes/no* response. I certainly don't want a prompt that asks, "have you killed anyone recently?" and carelessly typing *yes*. I may not be a lawyer but I try my best and read the fineprint when installing software on my computer or smartphone.

Similarly, you can pass different parameters when running the */opt/mssql/bin/mssql-conf* script as part of the setup process. These parameters, also called *environment variables*, are described in *https://docs.microsoft.com/en-us/sql/linux/sql-server-linux-configure-environment-variables?view=sql-server-linux-2017* for SQL Server 2017 (the list is similar for SQL Server 2019). Recall the environment variables passed to the *docker run* command in *Chapter 4*. They are the same environment variables and can be used to configure SQL Server on Linux during the setup process so as not to require user interaction. If you took note of the manual installation process, there are three prompts that required user input:

- *MSSQL_PID*: Similar to the PID parameter when installing SQL Server on Windows – either the product ID or the SQL Server edition. If not specified, it will default to Developer Edition.

- *ACCEPT_EULA*: I'm sure you already know this by now.

- *MSSQL_SA_PASSWORD*: The *sa* login's complex password.

Given these three environment variables, you can run the */opt/mssql/bin/mssql-conf* script with their corresponding values as shown here:

```
sudo MSSQL_PID=Enterprise ACCEPT_EULA=Y MSSQL_SA_
PASSWORD='mYSecUr3PAssw0rd' /opt/mssql/bin/mssql-conf setup
```

Note   I've seen examples from Microsoft documentation, blog posts, and sample codes on GitHub of running the */opt/mssql/bin/mssql-conf* script as part of the setup process using the *-n* parameter. One example can be found on *https:// docs.microsoft.com/en-ca/sql/linux/sample-unattended-install-redhat?view=sql-server-ver15#sample-script*. Refer to the line *echo Running mssql-conf setup...* where it shows the /opt/mssql/bin/mssql-conf -n setup code with the environment variables. The *-n* (also *--noprompt*) parameter does not prompt the user and uses environment variables or the default settings during the installation. My curious mind wanted to know if there is any difference in behavior so I tested running the command with and without the *-n* parameter. It turns out that there really is no difference between the two. So, to save on a few keystrokes and several bytes of characters, I opted not to use the *-n* parameter in my unattended installation.

Combining all the commands on a CentOS Linux system to

- Download the Microsoft SQL Server Red Hat repository configuration file for SQL Server 2017

- Download and install the SQL Server installation packages for RHEL

- Run the */opt/mssql/bin/mssql-conf* script with the *setup* parameter and environment variables

- Enable the SQL Server daemon to start on system boot

your script will include the commands as shown in the following:

```
sudo curl -o /etc/yum.repos.d/mssql-server.repo https://packages.microsoft.
com/config/rhel/7/mssql-server-2017.repo
sudo yum install -y mssql-server
sudo MSSQL_PID=Developer ACCEPT_EULA=Y MSSQL_SA_PASSWORD='mYSecUr3PAssw0rd'
/opt/mssql/bin/mssql-conf setup
sudo systemctl enable mssql-server
```

Going through the steps in performing the manual installation of SQL Server on an Ubuntu Linux system, the corresponding script to perform an unattended installation will include the commands as shown in the following:

```
curl https://packages.microsoft.com/keys/microsoft.asc | sudo apt-key add -
sudo add-apt-repository "deb [arch=amd64] https://packages.microsoft.com/
ubuntu/16.04/mssql-server-2017 xenial main"
sudo apt-get update
sudo apt-get install -y mssql-server
sudo MSSQL_PID=Developer ACCEPT_EULA=Y MSSQL_SA_PASSWORD='mYSecUr3PAssw0rd'
/opt/mssql/bin/mssql-conf setup
sudo systemctl enable mssql-server
```

Even running these commands and providing the password to run them as *sudo* give you some form of unattended installation. But we're not done yet. You have to wait until later in the chapter to have a fully automated script that will perform an unattended installation of SQL Server on Linux.

Configuring the Firewall

Depending on your Linux system configuration, you may need to configure the Linux firewall to allow remote connections to SQL Server. Linux systems use *iptables*, a rule-based firewall that comes preinstalled on most Linux distributions. It uses the concept of network address translation (NAT) and packet filtering to control network access to the system. But given the open source nature of Linux, many have attempted to build utilities and tools to make managing it a lot easier – hence, the availability of these utilities. For instance, the default system firewall on RHEL and CentOS 7 and higher is *FirewallD*. *FirewallD* exposes *iptables* via an API and allows administrators and developers to easily configure firewall settings using a command-line tool called *firewall-cmd*. You can learn more about *FirewallD* from `https://firewalld.org/`. On the other hand, Ubuntu uses a command-line tool called *UFW* (short for uncomplicated firewall) that directly interacts with *iptables*. You can learn more about *UFW* from `https://help.ubuntu.com/community/UFW`. Fun fact, you can install *FirewallD* on an Ubuntu system if you prefer. This makes it easier to standardize management of system firewall across these two Linux distributions. But where's the fun in that? I won't go into the details of how *iptables, firewalld, firewall-cmd*, and *ufw* work. I'll just provide enough information to allow you to configure remote connectivity to your SQL Server on Linux using the tools available for your specific distribution.

Let's start with CentOS. First, run the following command to check whether *FirewallD* is running or not. Figure 8-2 shows the status of a running *FirewallD* daemon on a CentOS Linux system.

```
sudo systemctl status firewalld
```

```
emsarmiento@CENTOSSQL01:~                                                    —  □  ×
[emsarmiento@CENTOSSQL01 ~]$ systemctl status firewalld
● firewalld.service - firewalld - dynamic firewall daemon
   Loaded: loaded (/usr/lib/systemd/system/firewalld.service; enabled; vendor preset: enabled)
   Active: active (running) since Thu 2019-12-12 23:19:38 EST; 6 days ago
     Docs: man:firewalld(1)
 Main PID: 3664 (firewalld)
   CGroup: /system.slice/firewalld.service
           └─3664 /usr/bin/python -Es /usr/sbin/firewalld --nofork --nopid

Dec 12 23:19:37 CENTOSSQL01 systemd[1]: Starting firewalld - dynamic firewall daemon...
Dec 12 23:19:38 CENTOSSQL01 systemd[1]: Started firewalld - dynamic firewall daemon.
[emsarmiento@CENTOSSQL01 ~]$ █
```

Figure 8-2. *FirewallD running on a CentOS Linux system*

Next, run the following *firewall-cmd* command with the corresponding parameters to open TCP port 1433 from the firewall:

```
sudo firewall-cmd --zone=public --add-port=1433/tcp --permanent
```

A key feature of *FirewallD* is the concept of zones. Every other feature is bound to a zone, and this describes the trust level for a connection, interface, or source address binding. *Public*, the zone used for this command, means you do not trust the other computers on the network, and only incoming traffic to TCP port 1433 will be allowed. The *--permanent* parameter means you want to permanently apply this firewall rule. But just because you configured it doesn't mean it is automatically applied nor will it be persisted during system restarts. Another concept in *FirewallD* is the separation of runtime configuration vs. the permanent configuration. Runtime configuration is what the firewall is currently using to manage the rules and can be lost when the firewall rules are reloaded or the system is rebooted. Permanent configuration is stored in the *iptables* and loaded during system startup or when firewall rules are reloaded. This means you can make temporary changes to the firewall rules and load them in the runtime configuration. If you remove the *--permanent* parameter, you will be able to temporarily connect to the SQL Server instance on Linux remotely. But once the system is restarted or the firewall rules reloaded, the connection will be blocked because the firewall rule is lost. Also, because the *--permanent* parameter was used with the command, the firewall rule only exists as a permanent configuration, not a runtime configuration, and won't take effect immediately. To apply the firewall rule, run the following command to reload it as a new runtime configuration:

```
sudo firewall-cmd --reload
```

A simple TELNET test on port 1433 to your CentOS Linux system will verify if the firewall rule has been applied. You can also run the following command to display runtime configuration of the opened ports in the firewall. Figure 8-3 displays the opened TCP port 1433.

```
sudo firewall-cmd --list-ports
```

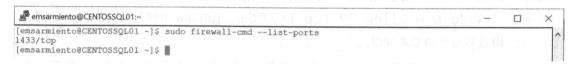

Figure 8-3. *List opened ports in the system firewall*

Didn't I say we'll use a different tool for Ubuntu systems? Run the following commands to check the status of *UFW*. Figure 8-4 shows the status of the *UFW* daemon on an Ubuntu Linux system. But unlike *FirewallD*, *UFW* is disabled by default. Note the *Status: inactive* message.

```
sudo systemctl status ufw
sudo ufw status
```

```
emsarmiento@ubuntusql01: ~                                          —    □    ×
emsarmiento@ubuntusql01:~$ sudo systemctl status ufw
● ufw.service - Uncomplicated firewall
   Loaded: loaded (/lib/systemd/system/ufw.service; enabled; vendor preset: enabled)
   Active: active (exited) since Thu 2019-12-19 13:57:10 PST; 3h 24min ago
 Main PID: 419 (code=exited, status=0/SUCCESS)
   CGroup: /system.slice/ufw.service

Warning: Journal has been rotated since unit was started. Log output is incomplete or unavailable.
emsarmiento@ubuntusql01:~$ sudo ufw status
Status: inactive
emsarmiento@ubuntusql01:~$ █
```

Figure 8-4. *UFW on an Ubuntu Linux system is disabled by default*

Run the following command to enable *UFW*. When prompted, type *y* for *Yes*. This will enable *UFW* and configure to start on system boot.

```
sudo ufw enable
```

Note   A word of caution regarding the *UFW* firewall on Ubuntu. The previous chapters allowed you to connect to your Ubuntu Linux system via an SSH client. That's because the firewall is disabled by default and the system is wide open for any remote connections – including SSH on port 22. This is unlike CentOS Linux where the firewall is enabled, blocking all access except remote connection through SSH. After enabling *UFW* on an Ubuntu Linux system, no other connections will be allowed unless you define a firewall rule for it. This also means that your existing SSH session is only valid so long as you are still connected. Once you disconnect, you're locked out. Don't make the mistake of closing your existing SSH connection without enabling port 22 on the firewall. Allow SSH connections by running this command: `sudo ufw allow 22/tcp`. To validate, run another SSH session and confirm that you can connect.

After enabling *UFW* and allowing SSH connections, you can now open TCP port 1433 from the firewall by running the following command. Figure 8-5 displays the opened port numbers – 22 for SSH and 1433 for SQL Server.

```
sudo ufw allow 1433/tcp
```

```
emsarmiento@ubuntusql01: ~                                          —    □    ×

emsarmiento@ubuntusql01:~$ sudo ufw allow 1433/tcp
Rule added
Rule added (v6)
emsarmiento@ubuntusql01:~$ sudo ufw status
Status: active

To                         Action      From
--                         ------      ----
22/tcp                     ALLOW       Anywhere
1433/tcp                   ALLOW       Anywhere
22/tcp (v6)                ALLOW       Anywhere (v6)
1433/tcp (v6)              ALLOW       Anywhere (v6)

emsarmiento@ubuntusql01:~$
```

Figure 8-5. *UFW displaying all opened ports*

As I mentioned in *Chapter 4,* the ultimate test is when you can connect remotely to the SQL Server instance on Linux via SQL Server Management Studio.

A Note on the Linux Firewalls and Docker

I was tempted to cover a bit of the Linux firewall in *Chapter 4* as you were being introduced to running SQL Server on Docker and connecting to it remotely. Besides, you need to be able to connect to a server remotely in order to access its resources. But if you observe, there's nothing in the previous chapters that cover creating a firewall rule and opening port numbers to access the SQL Server instance inside the container. So, I'll ask an obvious question on your behalf. If *FirewallD* is enabled by default on a CentOS Linux system, shouldn't it be blocking all connections except for SSH? And if I enabled *UFW* on an Ubuntu Linux system, shouldn't it also block all connections except the ones I explicitly allow? However, you wouldn't be too much concerned with *UFW* on Ubuntu because it is disabled by default.

The answer lies in the magic that Docker does behind the scenes. Remember what I said about *iptables* being the rule-based firewall available on most Linux distributions? Every time you create a Docker container and configure port mapping using the *-p* parameter in the *docker run* command, Docker creates a firewall rule directly into *iptables* as part of your implementation. Docker doesn't use *FirewallD* on RHEL/CentOS nor *UFW* on Ubuntu so you won't see any information about zones or port numbers or services when you use these tools. Figure 8-6 displays the list of opened ports and services in my CentOS Docker host. Note that *firewall-cmd* only displays *ssh* and *dhcpv6-client* (for acquiring IP addresses from a DHCP server) in the list of available services. Yet querying *iptables* shows a mapping of TCP port 1433 from any source (0.0.0.0/0 IP address range) to the IP address 172.18.0.2 (this is the IP address assigned to the *docker0* network interface on my CentOS Docker host which I'll cover in more detail in *Chapter 11*). You'll see the same rule displayed on an Ubuntu Docker host when you query *iptables*.

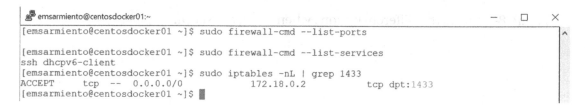

Figure 8-6. *Displaying opened ports and allowed services in FirewallD and iptables for port 1433 on a CentOS Docker host*

You can read more about this firewall rule implementation magic that Docker does at *https://docs.docker.com/network/iptables/*. They explicitly highlight not to modify the firewall rules that Docker creates in your *iptables*. In case you have security policies that prevent access from any source to your SQL Server instance inside a Docker container, talk to your network engineers on how to properly control network traffic.

Configuring SQL Server on Linux

While most of the out-of-the-box installation settings are fine, you may want to standardize your SQL Server deployments to comply with your internal best practices or maybe just to prove that you're smarter than the average SQL Server DBA. We've done this with the SQL Server Installation Center on Windows, creating a *ConfigurationFile.ini* file and using it to deploy multiple SQL Server instances with the desired configuration settings. We've also used SQL Server Configuration Manager to do it manually per instance. How do we do this with SQL Server on Linux?

The */opt/mssql/bin/mssql-conf* script can be used to set the different configuration settings for your SQL Server on Linux installation. But I haven't really described how this script is used other than using it as part of the installation process. Let's explore this script in more detail, Linux style. I briefly mentioned using Linux *man* (short for manual) pages in *Chapter 3*. While I rarely use the *man* pages for documentation nowadays due to the availability of resources on the Internet, there are cases where I couldn't find any information online about specific commands. This script is one of them. Run the following command to show how to use this script:

```
man mssql-conf
```

Figure 8-7 shows the different options when using the script.

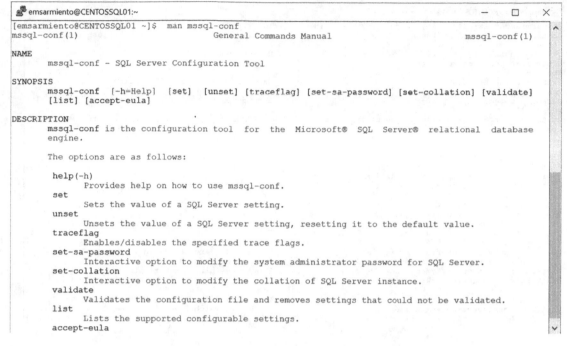

```
emsarmiento@CENTOSSQL01:~                                          —    □    ×

[emsarmiento@CENTOSSQL01 ~]$  man mssql-conf
mssql-conf(1)                    General Commands Manual                    mssql-conf(1)

NAME
       mssql-conf - SQL Server Configuration Tool

SYNOPSIS
       mssql-conf  [-h=Help]  [set]  [unset] [traceflag] [set-sa-password] [set-collation] [validate]
       [list] [accept-eula]

DESCRIPTION
       mssql-conf is the configuration tool   for   the   Microsoft®   SQL   Server®   relational   database
       engine.

       The options are as follows:

       help(-h)
            Provides help on how to use mssql-conf.
       set
            Sets the value of a SQL Server setting.
       unset
            Unsets the value of a SQL Server setting, resetting it to the default value.
       traceflag
            Enables/disables the specified trace flags.
       set-sa-password
            Interactive option to modify the system administrator password for SQL Server.
       set-collation
            Interactive option to modify the collation of SQL Server instance.
       validate
            Validates the configuration file and removes settings that could not be validated.
       list
            Lists the supported configurable settings.
       accept-eula
```

Figure 8-7. *The mssql-conf man page*

Use the *list* parameter to display all the different configurable settings, as shown in
Figure 8-8:

sudo /opt/mssql/bin/mssql-conf list

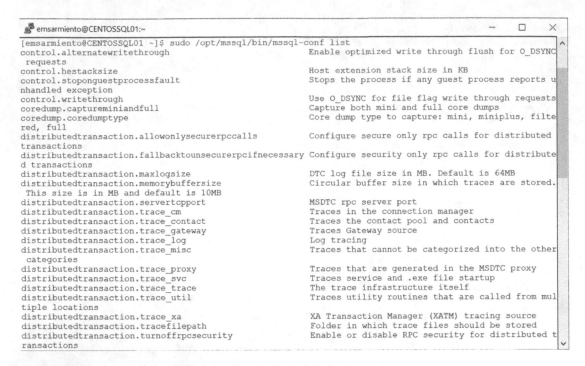

```
emsarmiento@CENTOSSQL01:~                                              —   □   ✕
[emsarmiento@CENTOSSQL01 ~]$ sudo /opt/mssql/bin/mssql-conf list
control.alternatewritethrough                    Enable optimized write through flush for O_DSYNC
 requests
control.hestacksize                              Host extension stack size in KB
control.stoponguestprocessfault                  Stops the process if any guest process reports u
nhandled exception
control.writethrough                             Use O_DSYNC for file flag write through requests
coredump.captureminiandfull                      Capture both mini and full core dumps
coredump.coredumptype                            Core dump type to capture: mini, miniplus, filte
red, full
distributedtransaction.allowonlysecurerpccalls   Configure secure only rpc calls for distributed
transactions
distributedtransaction.fallbacktounsecurerpcifnecessary Configure security only rpc calls for distribute
d transactions
distributedtransaction.maxlogsize                DTC log file size in MB. Default is 64MB
distributedtransaction.memorybuffersize          Circular buffer size in which traces are stored.
 This size is in MB and default is 10MB
distributedtransaction.servertcpport             MSDTC rpc server port
distributedtransaction.trace_cm                  Traces in the connection manager
distributedtransaction.trace_contact             Traces the contact pool and contacts
distributedtransaction.trace_gateway             Traces Gateway source
distributedtransaction.trace_log                 Log tracing
distributedtransaction.trace_misc                Traces that cannot be categorized into the other
 categories
distributedtransaction.trace_proxy               Traces that are generated in the MSDTC proxy
distributedtransaction.trace_svc                 Traces service and .exe file startup
distributedtransaction.trace_trace               The trace infrastructure itself
distributedtransaction.trace_util                Traces utility routines that are called from mul
tiple locations
distributedtransaction.trace_xa                  XA Transaction Manager (XATM) tracing source
distributedtransaction.tracefilepath             Folder in which trace files should be stored
distributedtransaction.turnoffrpcsecurity        Enable or disable RPC security for distributed t
ransactions
```

Figure 8-8. *List of configurable settings for SQL Server on Linux*

These are configurable settings on the SQL Server instance that cannot be done through T-SQL. Let's use these to show how to change some of the most common SQL Server instance configuration settings. The ones shown in the following all require restarting the SQL Server daemon so I'll skip this step and just show how it is done at the end of making all the configuration changes.

Enabling the SQL Server Agent

By default, the SQL Server Agent is disabled after installation. In fact, prior to SQL Server 2017 Cumulative Update 4, you have to install the SQL Server Agent separately using a different package. I guess the feedback (or complaints) from the community and the Microsoft MVPs has caused the SQL Server product team to include the SQL Server Agent in the *mssql-server* package. Think about having to update the SQL Server database engine and the SQL Server Agent separately. Even with proper change management process, anyone could potentially forget updating the SQL Server Agent because it's not something that we DBAs do to update SQL Server. So, your patch levels could end up being different on both. I think it's a great idea to include the SQL Server Agent as part of installing SQL Server.

Run the following command to enable the SQL Server Agent:

```
sudo /opt/mssql/bin/mssql-conf set sqlagent.enabled true
```

Configuring Default Database Data and Log Directory

The default directory for the database data and log files is */var/opt/mssql/data*. You may want to provision a dedicated storage array that contains solid-state drives and mounted as a directory on your Linux system. But before you can configure a directory as a default database data and log directory, it has to be created first and ownership changed to the *mssql* user and *mssql* group. Run the following command to create a new directory named */tmp/dbdata*:

```
sudo mkdir /tmp/dbdata
```

Next, run the following command to change the ownership of the directory to the *mssql* user:

```
sudo chown mssql /tmp/dbdata
```

You also need to change the group ownership of the directory to the *mssql* group by running the following command:

```
sudo chgrp mssql /tmp/dbdata
```

Once the directory has been created and ownership assigned, you can now set the default database data and log directory to the new location using the following commands:

```
sudo /opt/mssql/bin/mssql-conf set filelocation.defaultdatadir /tmp/dbdata
sudo /opt/mssql/bin/mssql-conf set filelocation.defaultlogdir /tmp/dbdata
```

Configuring Default Database Backup Directory

The default database backup directory is also the same as the default database data and log directory – */var/opt/mssql/data*. I like to keep my databases and backups separately for disaster recovery purposes. Similar to how you configure the default database data and log directory, you have to first create the directory and ownership changed to the *mssql* user and *mssql* group. Let's use the */tmp/dbbackup* directory as the default database backup directory. Run the following commands to perform the necessary configuration changes:

```
sudo mkdir /tmp/dbbackup
sudo chown mssql /tmp/dbbackup
sudo chgrp mssql /tmp/dbbackup
sudo /opt/mssql/bin/mssql-conf set filelocation.defaultbackupdir /tmp/
dbbackup
```

Note   In case you are wondering what the *mssql* user and *mssql* group are, these are the noninteractive login and group assigned to SQL Server nonbinary files. Think of it as the SQL Server service account on Windows. The noninteractive login runs SQL Server as a background process. But unlike the usual SQL Server service account in Windows where you can use the account and its credentials to log in to a Windows machine unless you configure it to *Log on as a service*, a noninteractive login won't be able to log in and run commands from a shell. Also, you cannot change this to any other user account. I hope this changes in future release.

Enabling Trace Flags

One of the trace flags that I enable when deploying a new SQL Server instance is trace flag *3226*. This suppresses every successful backup entry in the SQL Server error log and in the system event log. I used to filter successful backup messages from our monitoring server to avoid getting alerted every time a backup job completes. This trace flag is a lifesaver. Run the following command to enable trace flag *3226* on the SQL Server instance:

```
sudo /opt/mssql/bin/mssql-conf traceflag 3226 on
```

As all of these settings require restarting the SQL Server daemon, it makes sense to do everything at once and just restart SQL Server at the end of the configuration. Run the following command to restart SQL Server:

```
sudo systemctl restart mssql-server
```

Viewing All Instance-Level Configuration Settings

I wish there was a simple command to display all of the instance-level configuration settings other than programmatically querying the SQL Server Management Objects (SMO). What if you want to review all of the configuration settings you just did? Well, you have to manually read the */var/opt/mssql/mssql.conf* file for this. This file is where SQL Server stores the configuration changes you made and is read during startup to load configuration settings other than the defaults. I think this is better than programmatically querying SMO. Run the following command to view all of the configuration settings of the SQL Server instance. Figure 8-9 displays the instance-level configuration settings set in this section.

```
sudo cat /var/opt/mssql/mssql.conf
```

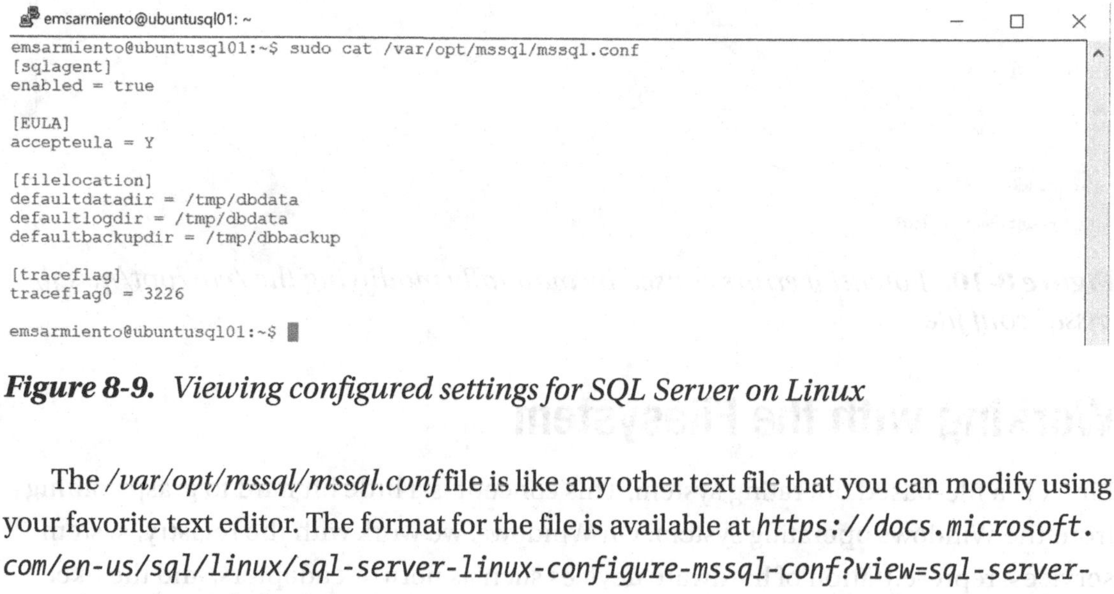

Figure 8-9. *Viewing configured settings for SQL Server on Linux*

The */var/opt/mssql/mssql.conf* file is like any other text file that you can modify using your favorite text editor. The format for the file is available at *https://docs.microsoft. com/en-us/sql/linux/sql-server-linux-configure-mssql-conf?view=sql-server-ver15#mssql-conf-format*. Should you decide to manually modify the configuration file, you need to restart the SQL Server daemon for the changes to take effect.

I'm not a big fan of manually modifying file formats because parsers could be very strict when it comes to dealing with unnecessary characters. Besides, we're humans and we're bound to make mistakes. I've done my fair share of modifying YAML, JSON, and XML files, and a simple mistake like introducing unnecessary characters in files can cost a lot of time troubleshooting issues. There's a reason the phrase "fat finger" exists in our line of work. I always use the supported tools like the */opt/mssql/bin/mssql-conf* script to make changes to files. Figure 8-10 shows the side effect of fat-fingering an extra character in the */var/opt/mssql/mssql.conf* file. Restarting the SQL Server daemon didn't tell me that there was an error loading the settings stored in the configuration file. Besides, if there was an error reading the configuration file, the parser will just ignore it and load the default values. I had to run the command `sudo /opt/mssql/bin/mssql-conf validate` to find out that there was an error in the configuration. Can you guess what the error was?

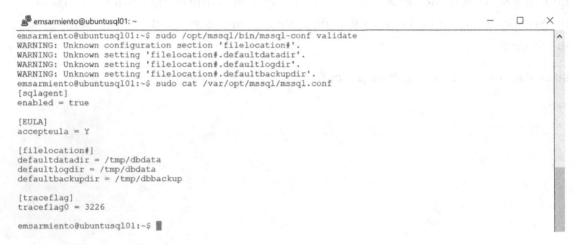

Figure 8-10. *Potential errors caused by manually modifying the /var/opt/mssql/mssql.conf file*

Working with the Filesystem

Linux is a file-based operating system. This concept is a little bit hard to grasp coming from the Windows operating system. On Windows, we work with the registry, system services, representation of hardware devices such as network adapters, and the like. On Linux (or Unix, in general), everything is a file. Your hard disk is represented by a device file. The configuration settings are stored in a file. Even the directory that contains files is a special type of file that you can read using a text editor. Recall everything you did since Chapter 3 – they all reference a file: the repo file, the package files, the filesystem layer that the container uses, the container manifest file, the symbolic link files, the *daemon.json* file, and so on. If you want to make an application behave differently, all you need to do is modify its corresponding configuration file (provided you know exactly what you're doing).

Important Directories in the Linux Filesystem

To work with a file-based operating system, you need to understand some of the basics of the filesystem. This will help you properly navigate and interact with directories and files to perform tasks such as moving files around, modifying configuration files, and so on. The following is a list of the important directories in the Linux filesystem:

- */*: The root directory. Everything in Linux is located under this directory. It's like the *C:* directory on Windows.

- */bin*: This directory contains essential user binaries (programs) that both system administrators and nonprivileged users use. Commands like *cat*, *ls*, *rm*, and so on and the shells like *bash* are in this directory.

- */boot*: Obviously, this directory contains everything required to boot the Linux system except for configuration files not needed at boot time.

- */dev*: This directory contains special or device files. I did mention that the hard drive in Linux is represented as a device file and it is stored in this directory.

- */etc*: This directory contains system configuration files and is considered the command center of your Linux system. The behavior and operation of your Linux system are stored in a configuration file found in this directory. So, be careful with messing around with the files in this directory as it can render your system unstable or even unbootable.

- */home*: This directory contains the *home* directories of all the users and is similar to the *C:\Users* directory on Windows. When you log in to your Linux system, a directory is created under the */home* directory with your username and that which you have full, unrestricted access. Your *home* directory also contains your personal configuration files.

- */lib*: This directory contains helpful library files (files used by an application or system for proper execution) needed by the system.

- */media*: This directory contains subdirectories for removable media such as CD-ROMs. I'm sure you haven't used one of these on servers in years.

- */opt*: This directory contains add-on packages that are not part of the default installation.

- */root*: This is the special *home* directory of the *root* user. Note that it is not in the */home* directory.

- */sbin*: Similar to the */bin* directory but contains essential binaries that are generally intended for system administration, typically requires *root* privileges.

- */srv*: This directory contains data for services such as Web and FTP. Not relevant to SQL Server.

- */tmp*: This directory contains temporary files, which are generally deleted during a system restart.

- */usr*: This directory contains applications and files used by users.

- */var*: This directory contains variable data like system log files, spool files, and anything that can change during normal operation of your Linux system.

When you look at the different directories created during SQL Server installation, you'll start to see the purpose behind their locations. The common ones are

- */opt/mssql/bin*: Directory containing the SQL Server binary file, the *mssql-conf* script, and other scripts used for dealing with SQL Server dump files.

- */var/opt/mssql*: Directory containing the SQL Server data and log files, secrets, and the *mssql.conf* configuration file. Variable data of the packages in */opt* must be installed in */var/opt/<subdirectory>*. Because the MDF, LDF, error log files, Extended Events, and so on are variable data that change over time while the SQL Server database engine is running.

File Permissions

File permissions in Linux play an important role in administration as well as application configuration. You've seen how elevating privileges to *root* allows you to perform certain administrative tasks and even opening or modifying files. But reading the output of the `ls -l` command can be overwhelming if you don't know what it means. Let's start by analyzing the output of the `ls -l` command on the */var/opt/mssql/* and */opt/mssql/bin* directories as shown in Figure 8-11. Note the use of *sudo* to list the contents of the */var/opt/mssql* directory.

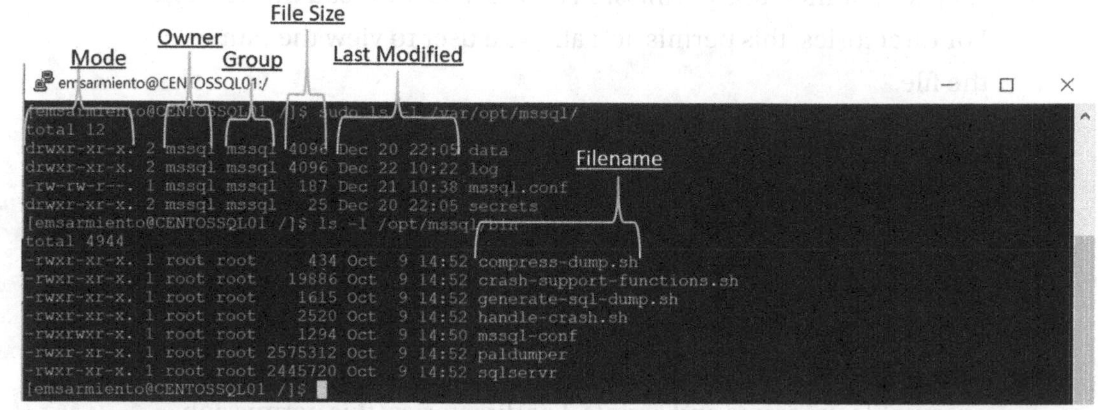

Figure 8-11. *Output of the ls -l command*

All the other attributes – *owner, group, file size, last modified,* and *filename* – are easy to understand. The one that really bothers me is the *mode* attribute. It's like some kind of code that only those who speak Klingon can understand. Let's break down the *mode* attribute even more to see how it affects the files and directories, as shown in Figure 8-12.

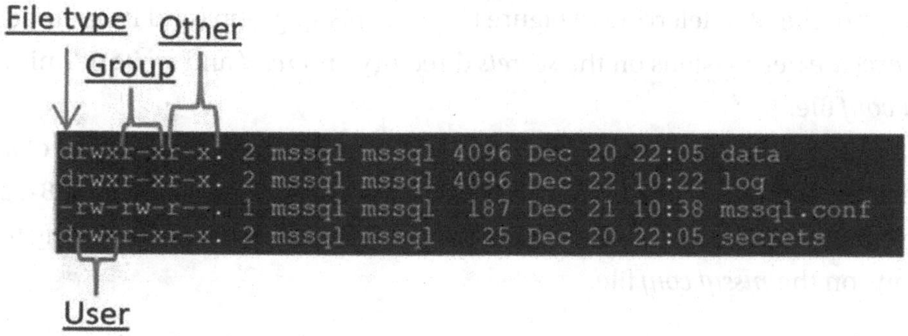

Figure 8-12. *Mode attribute of files and directories*

The first character in the *mode* represents the type. A *hyphen* (-) signifies that it is a normal file that contains data, like the *mssql.conf* configuration file. A "d" signifies a directory, like the *data*, *log*, and *secrets* directories. Keep in mind that everything in Linux is a file, even a directory. Special files, such as a directory, are identified by a nonhyphen character such as a letter. Recall the symbolic link file mentioned in *Chapter 5*, represented by an "l" character.

The next three characters in the *mode* attribute represent the permissions for a user. Let's look at the different permissions that we can assign to a file or a directory:

- *r*: Read. For files, this permission allows a user to read the contents. For directories, this permission allows a user to view the names of the file.

- *w*: Write. For files, this permission allows a user to modify and delete the file. For directories, a *write* permission allows a user to delete the directory, modify its contents (create, delete, and rename files in it), and modify the contents of files that the user can read.

- *x*: Execute. For files, this permission allows a user to execute a file (the user must also have read permission) and should be set for executable programs and scripts. For directories, this permission allows a user to access files (including their metadata) in the directory.

Referring to Figure 8-12, the *mssql* user has *read*, *write*, and *execute* permissions on the *secrets* directory but only *read* and *write* permissions on the *mssql.conf* file (the *mssql.conf* file is a normal text file that contains data and not a script like the */opt/mssql/bin/mssql-conf* file).

The next three characters in the *mode* attribute represent the permissions for the group owner of the file. Referring to Figure 8-12, the *mssql* group (and its members) has *read* and *execute* permissions on the *secrets* directory and *read* and *write* permissions on the *mssql.conf* file.

The last three characters in the *mode* attribute represent the permissions of all other users, or commonly known as the rest of the world. Referring to Figure 8-12, all other users have *read* and *execute* permissions on the *secrets* directory but only *read* permissions on the *mssql.conf* file.

Assigning Permissions to Files and Directories

Working with permissions means we also need to know the two most common commands that we need to use to assign appropriate permissions. *chown* (short for change owner) is the command to use when changing ownership of a file or directory. *chmod* (short for change mode) is the command to use to change the read, write, and execute permissions of a file or directory for owner, group, and others. The way to assign permissions with *chmod* involves two ways – the first one is by using alphanumeric characters (also known as symbolic mode) like the *r*, *w*, and *x*, while the second one is by using octal mode (and you thought you've escaped your basic computer science courses of converting decimal to octal).

Refer to changing the default database backup directory. After creating the directory, you need to change its ownership to the *mssql* user. Since you were the one who created the directory in the first place, your user account (and the group you belong to) has ownership of it. You want the *mssql* user to have permissions to read and write to the new backup directory so your database backups won't fail. Hence, the command is as follows:

```
sudo chown mssql /tmp/dbbackup
```

Here's another useful command. The *chgrp* (short for change group) command changes the group ownership of files or directories. The following command changes the group ownership of the new backup directory to the *mssql* group:

```
sudo chgrp mssql /tmp/dbbackup
```

If you only change the ownership of a file or directory but not the group, there might be inconsistencies with permissions especially if the user account does not have the same permissions as the group. User accounts can be assigned more granular permissions, but doing so requires more work. There's a reason why security groups in Windows exist. It is better to create a security group, assign permissions to it, and just add or remove users from the group. In the case of the *mssql* group, only the *mssql* user is in it and it makes sense to just assign the directory to both the user and the group for consistency.

Let's get back to assigning permissions to files and directories. If you want to create a shell script named *automateSQLinstall.sh* that would automate and configure the installation of SQL Server on Linux, you need to assign the *execute* (*x*) permissions to the file using the (+) operator. Note that using the (-) operator will revoke permissions. The following command shows a simple way to do it:

```
chmod +x automateSQLinstall.sh
```

Doing so means granting your user account, the group you belong to, and all others the *execute* permissions. Figure 8-13 shows the effective permissions after assigning the *execute* permission to the file.

```
emsarmiento@CENTOSSQL01:~/tmp                                          —    □    ×
[emsarmiento@CENTOSSQL01 tmp]$ ls -l
total 0
-rw-rw-r--. 1 emsarmiento emsarmiento 0 Dec 22 15:16 automateSQLinstall.sh
[emsarmiento@CENTOSSQL01 tmp]$ chmod +x automateSQLinstall.sh
[emsarmiento@CENTOSSQL01 tmp]$ ls -l
total 0
-rwxrwxr-x. 1 emsarmiento emsarmiento 0 Dec 22 15:16 automateSQLinstall.sh
[emsarmiento@CENTOSSQL01 tmp]$ ▉
```

Figure 8-13. *Effective permissions before and after assigning the execute permission*

Let's interpret the effective permissions on the file. The (-) symbol tells me that this is a normal file. Prior to running the `chmod +x automateSQLinstall.sh` command, the user and group named *emsarmiento* only has *read* and *write* permissions to the file. It does so because the user owns the file as a side effect of creating it. But if you notice, the user does not have an *execute* permission on the file. Unlike in Windows where a script with certain file extensions like *.vbs* or *.exe* is automatically marked for execution, file extensions on Linux don't mean anything. You have to tell Linux that the file needs to be executed in order for a specific user to run it. After running the *chmod* command, the user and group named *emsarmiento* now has *read, write,* and *execute* permissions to the file. Also, Linux automatically assigns implicit permissions where applicable. The *other* group was granted *read* permission even though I only granted *execute* permission. That's because a user needs to be able to read a file or directory before it can write to or execute it.

A more explicit way to grant the *execute* permission to the file is shown in the following, with *u=user, g=group,* and *o=other*:

```
chmod u+x,g+x,o+x automateSQLinstall.sh
```

Or this one:

```
chmod u=rwx,g=rwx,o=rx automateSQLinstall.sh
```

Clearly, there are several ways to accomplish this goal. And this doesn't even cover the octal mode yet. So, let's continue.

In octal mode, numbers represent permissions as shown in the following:

- 4 = read

- 2 = write

- 1 = execute

These values range from 0 to 7. Converting these numbers into their corresponding permissions

- 0 = ---

- 1 = --x

- 2 = -w-

- 3 = -wx

- 4 = r-

- 5 = r-x

- 6 = rw-

- 7 = rwx

Each number from 0 to 7 can be assigned to the *user*, *group*, and *other* columns. If you want to assign the *execute* permission to the file, the following command accomplishes this using the octal mode:

```
chmod 775 automateSQLinstall.sh
```

Note   This chapter is not intended to dive deep into the Linux filesystem and working with permissions. The topic alone requires an entire chapter in and of itself. The goal of this section is to provide a reference to how and why commands are used in this and other chapters. But as you can see, this topic is central to working with Linux. Remember, everything in Linux is a file and proper permissions need to be assigned for certain system processes and applications to run. You don't want to be messing around with permissions in the */var/opt* directory unless you know exactly what you're doing. I highly recommend exploring some of the available Linux titles from Apress to dive deep into the Linux filesystem and managing permissions.

Writing a Simple Linux Bash Script

What I've done in the preceding sections was simply provide the framework for creating a script to automatically install SQL Server on Linux. In fact, the title of this chapter should have been *Preparing to Automate Installation of SQL Server on Linux.* But whenever I have to deal with an automation script from a customer that performs a specific task, I get blank stares from people who have no clue how the script was written and the different tasks that it is doing. More often than not, the script was stitched together using snippets of code found online. Don't get me wrong, there's nothing wrong with stitching snippets of code found on the Internet so long as you know what it does, tested it, and properly document it. While I'm a big believer and advocate of automation, I highly emphasize the importance of process. When I worked as a data center engineer, I barely spent time on my computer. I'm either on my desk with pen and paper or on a whiteboard drawing workflows that define processes. That's because good automation is based on a solid process. So, when we did our quarterly disaster recovery exercises, all we had to do was run automation scripts and monitor the outcomes. If a specific process needs improvement, we go back to the drawing board and make modifications to meet our recovery objectives and service-level agreements. Our process-driven automation was the key behind having a very small but effective team managing hundreds of servers.

Now that we have the framework to install and configure SQL Server on Linux, it's time to write the automation script. But before we do so, we need to know how to write the script and how to execute it.

A *bash script* is a plain text file that contains a series of commands. It's called a bash script because the commands are interpreted using Bash (or **B**ourne **A**gain **Sh**ell). Bash is the default shell for most Linux distributions. In fact, you can check by running the command echo $0 in your Linux command prompt. A bash script is a fully-fledged programming language in itself. This means you can define programming constructs such as variables, functions, and conditional execution of shell commands. Any command that you can run from the command line can be used in a bash script. Normally, a bash script has a *.sh* file extension to make it clear that it is a shell script. But as I mentioned in the previous section, Linux doesn't really care about file extensions. But we humans do. And having some form of identification can immediately tell us what a file is for without opening it.

Create a simple text file on your computer. It doesn't really matter whether you create it on a Linux or Windows computer. If you can create the file on Windows and copy it later to a Linux machine, that's more than enough for now. Once you get the hang of creating and modifying files on Linux using utilities such as *vi* or *nano*, you can write your scripts inside a Linux shell terminal. I use *vi* on Linux because it is installed by default.

The first line of the file is what tells the interpreter that it is an executable file. It is known as *shebang* (or a hashbang), and it is simply the absolute path to the Bash interpreter. The first line of the file should contain the following command:

```
#!/bin/bash
```

From here onward, you can write any command that you want to run from inside the script. Recall the sequence of tasks that we outlined in the previous sections to install and configure SQL Server on Linux. On a CentOS Linux system

- Download the Microsoft SQL Server Red Hat repository configuration file for SQL Server 2017.

- Download and install the SQL Server installation packages for RHEL.

- Run the */opt/mssql/bin/mssql-conf* script with the *setup* parameter and environment variables.

- Enable the SQL Server daemon to start on system boot.

- Configure the Linux firewall to allow traffic to port 1433.

- Enable the SQL Server Agent.

- Change the default data and log file directory.

- Change the default backup directory.

- Enable trace flag 3226.

- Restart SQL Server for the configuration changes to take effect.

Be mindful of the sequence of tasks. The commands should meet the requirements for dependencies. For instance, I won't be able to configure SQL Server unless it is first installed. I won't be able to install it if the packages have not been downloaded. And I won't be able to download the packages properly unless the repo file is already available on the system. You get the picture.

Combining all the commands that we used to accomplish every single task in the list, your script should look something like this:

```
#!/bin/bash

sudo curl -o /etc/yum.repos.d/mssql-server.repo https://packages.microsoft.
com/config/rhel/7/mssql-server-2017.repo
sudo yum install -y mssql-server
sudo MSSQL_PID=Developer ACCEPT_EULA=Y MSSQL_SA_PASSWORD='mYSecUr3PAssw0rd'
/opt/mssql/bin/mssql-conf setup
sudo systemctl enable mssql-server

sudo firewall-cmd --zone=public --add-port=1433/tcp --permanent
sudo firewall-cmd --reload

sudo /opt/mssql/bin/mssql-conf set sqlagent.enabled true

sudo mkdir /tmp/dbdata
sudo chown mssql /tmp/dbdata
sudo chgrp mssql /tmp/dbdata
sudo /opt/mssql/bin/mssql-conf set filelocation.defaultdatadir /tmp/dbdata
sudo /opt/mssql/bin/mssql-conf set filelocation.defaultlogdir /tmp/dbdata

sudo mkdir /tmp/dbbackup
sudo chown mssql /tmp/dbbackup
sudo chgrp mssql /tmp/dbbackup
sudo /opt/mssql/bin/mssql-conf set filelocation.defaultbackupdir /tmp/
dbbackup

sudo /opt/mssql/bin/mssql-conf traceflag 3226 on

sudo systemctl restart mssql-server
```

I normally write comments on my script to let other people know what it is doing. I've omitted them here for brevity. The corresponding script on Ubuntu is shown here:

```
#!/bin/bash

curl https://packages.microsoft.com/keys/microsoft.asc | sudo apt-key add -
sudo add-apt-repository "deb [arch=amd64] https://packages.microsoft.com/
ubuntu/16.04/mssql-server-2017 xenial main"
sudo apt-get update
sudo apt-get install -y mssql-server
sudo MSSQL_PID=Developer ACCEPT_EULA=Y MSSQL_SA_PASSWORD='mYSecUr3PAssw0rd'
/opt/mssql/bin/mssql-conf setup
sudo systemctl enable mssql-server

sudo ufw --force enable
sudo ufw allow 22/tcp
sudo ufw allow 1433/tcp

sudo /opt/mssql/bin/mssql-conf set sqlagent.enabled true

sudo mkdir /tmp/dbdata
sudo chown mssql /tmp/dbdata
sudo chgrp mssql /tmp/dbdata
sudo /opt/mssql/bin/mssql-conf set filelocation.defaultdatadir /tmp/dbdata
sudo /opt/mssql/bin/mssql-conf set filelocation.defaultlogdir /tmp/dbdata

sudo mkdir /tmp/dbbackup
sudo chown mssql /tmp/dbbackup
sudo chgrp mssql /tmp/dbbackup
sudo /opt/mssql/bin/mssql-conf set filelocation.defaultbackupdir /tmp/
dbbackup

sudo /opt/mssql/bin/mssql-conf traceflag 3226 on

sudo systemctl restart mssql-server
```

Save the script as *automateSQLinstall.sh*. If you created the script on your Windows machine, just copy it on your Linux *home* directory. Once it is in your *home* directory, you can assign the *execute* permission on the file using the following command:

```
chmod +x automateSQLinstall.sh
```

Running the Script

Because some of the commands in the script require *root* privileges, you have to run it with *root* privileges. Either you switch to *root* before running the script or run it with *sudo*. I prefer running it with *sudo* so I don't mistakenly do something stupid while running as *root*.

Run the following command to execute the script. Note that the script file name is prefixed by the "./" characters:

```
sudo ./automateSQLinstall.sh
```

Others prefix the script file name with *bash* like the one as follows:

```
sudo bash automateSQLinstall.sh
```

I prefer the first command as it is similar to running PowerShell scripts on Windows.

An alternative to running with *root* privileges would be to change the ownership of the script to *root* to prevent password prompts. Run the following command to change the script ownership to *root* and grant the *execute* permission on the file:

```
sudo chown root:root automateSQLinstall.sh
sudo chmod 775 automateSQLinstall.sh
```

Now, run the script and watch the magic happen. Figure 8-14 shows all the configuration settings made after the script executes.

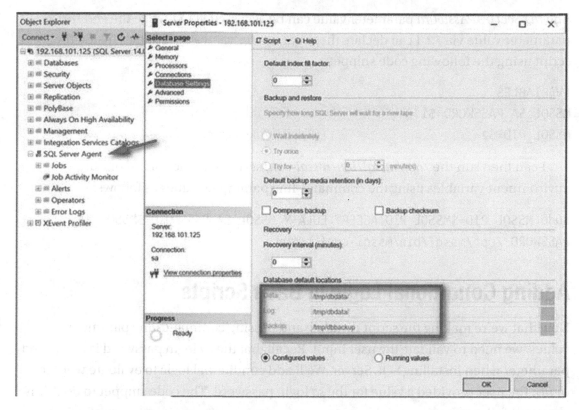

Figure 8-14. *Validating configuration changes after script execution*

Passing Parameters to the Script

While the script works as expected, I don't like the idea of hard-coding passwords in files. Anyone who can grab a hold of the script file can read the password of the *sa* login, and the SQL Server instance can potentially be compromised. What if we instead pass the *sa* login password as a command-line parameter to the script?

Like any other command-line scripts, bash scripts also accept command-line arguments as parameters. All command-line parameters can be accessed by their position number using *$*. Have a look at the following sample command:

```
sudo ./automateSQLinstall.sh mYSecUr3PAssw0rd enterprise
```

Here I'm calling the *automateSQLinstall.sh* file and passing it two command-line parameters – *mYSecUr3PAssw0rd* and *enterprise*. You might have guessed that the first parameter is the *sa* login password and the second one is the SQL Server edition. Inside the script, these parameter values can be accessed using their position numbers.

The *mYSecUr3PAssw0rd* parameter value can be accessed via *$1* while the *enterprise* parameter value via *$2*. I can declare these parameter values as variables inside the script using the following code snippet:

```
#VARIABLES
MSSQL_SA_PASSWORD=$1
MSSQL_PID=$2
```

I can then run the */opt/mssql/bin/mssql-conf* script with the corresponding environment variables using the command-line parameter values as follows:

```
sudo MSSQL_PID=$MSSQL_PID ACCEPT_EULA=Y MSSQL_SA_PASSWORD=$MSSQL_SA_
PASSWORD /opt/mssql/bin/mssql-conf setup
```

Adding Conditional Logic in Bash Scripts

Now that we're making the script dynamic and passing command-line parameter values, we need to validate the user input. Recall that the *sa* login password is a required parameter when installing SQL Server. We'll add conditional logic to evaluate whether or not the user provided a value for the *sa* login password. The code snippet to do this is shown as follows:

```
#Check if the sa password string is null or has zero length
if [ -z $MSSQL_SA_PASSWORD ]
then
  echo Environment variable MSSQL_SA_PASSWORD must be set for unattended
  install
  exit 1
fi
```

A simple *if...then* condition evaluates whether or not the *$MSSQL_SA_PASSWORD* parameter value is null or has zero length. Exit code 1 sets the script execution to failure, causing it to terminate. There's more to validating the *sa* login password such as the complexity requirements which include minimum password length, inclusion of uppercase, lowercase, non-alphanumeric characters, and base 10 digits. This is just a simple example to validate whether or not the user provided a value for the *sa* login password.

What about the edition? Since we initially provided an environment variable for the edition, we need to provide a value for it. This means we also need to evaluate whether or not the user provided a value in the command-line argument. The code snippet to do this is shown in the following. Here we're setting a default value if the user didn't provide anything – in this case, Developer Edition:

```
#Check if the edition parameter is null or has zero length
if [ -z $MSSQL_PID ]
then
  MSSQL_PID=Developer
fi
```

An updated version of the script for a RHEL/CentOS Linux system is shown in the following with parameter values and conditional logic evaluation:

```
#!/bin/bash

# VARIABLES
MSSQL_SA_PASSWORD=$1
MSSQL_PID=$2

if [ -z $MSSQL_SA_PASSWORD ]
then
  echo Environment variable MSSQL_SA_PASSWORD must be set for unattended
  install
  exit 1
fi

if [ -z $MSSQL_PID ]
then
  MSSQL_PID=Developer
fi

sudo curl -o /etc/yum.repos.d/mssql-server.repo https://packages.microsoft.
com/config/rhel/7/mssql-server-2017.repo
sudo yum install -y mssql-server
sudo MSSQL_PID=$MSSQL_PID ACCEPT_EULA=Y MSSQL_SA_PASSWORD=$MSSQL_SA_
PASSWORD /opt/mssql/bin/mssql-conf setup
sudo systemctl enable mssql-server
```

```
sudo firewall-cmd --zone=public --add-port=1433/tcp --permanent
sudo firewall-cmd --reload

sudo /opt/mssql/bin/mssql-conf set sqlagent.enabled true

sudo mkdir /tmp/dbdata
sudo chown mssql /tmp/dbdata
sudo chgrp mssql /tmp/dbdata
sudo /opt/mssql/bin/mssql-conf set filelocation.defaultdatadir /tmp/dbdata
sudo /opt/mssql/bin/mssql-conf set filelocation.defaultlogdir /tmp/dbdata

sudo mkdir /tmp/dbbackup
sudo chown mssql /tmp/dbbackup
sudo chgrp mssql /tmp/dbbackup
sudo /opt/mssql/bin/mssql-conf set filelocation.defaultbackupdir /tmp/
dbbackup

sudo /opt/mssql/bin/mssql-conf traceflag 3226 on

sudo systemctl restart mssql-server
```

And here's the corresponding script in Ubuntu:

```
#!/bin/bash

#VARIABLES
MSSQL_SA_PASSWORD=$1
MSSQL_PID=$2

if [ -z $MSSQL_SA_PASSWORD ]
then
  echo Environment variable MSSQL_SA_PASSWORD must be set for unattended
  install
  exit 1
fi

if [ -z $MSSQL_PID ]
then
  MSSQL_PID=Developer
fi
```

```
curl https://packages.microsoft.com/keys/microsoft.asc | sudo apt-key add -
sudo add-apt-repository "deb [arch=amd64] https://packages.microsoft.com/
ubuntu/16.04/mssql-server-2017 xenial main"
sudo apt-get update
sudo apt-get install -y mssql-server
sudo MSSQL_PID=$MSSQL_PID ACCEPT_EULA=Y MSSQL_SA_PASSWORD=$MSSQL_SA_
PASSWORD /opt/mssql/bin/mssql-conf setup
sudo systemctl enable mssql-server

sudo ufw --force enable
sudo ufw allow 22/tcp
sudo ufw allow 1433/tcp

sudo /opt/mssql/bin/mssql-conf set sqlagent.enabled true

sudo mkdir /tmp/dbdata
sudo chown mssql /tmp/dbdata
sudo chgrp mssql /tmp/dbdata
sudo /opt/mssql/bin/mssql-conf set filelocation.defaultdatadir /tmp/dbdata
sudo /opt/mssql/bin/mssql-conf set filelocation.defaultlogdir /tmp/dbdata

sudo mkdir /tmp/dbbackup
sudo chown mssql /tmp/dbbackup
sudo chgrp mssql /tmp/dbbackup
sudo /opt/mssql/bin/mssql-conf set filelocation.defaultbackupdir /tmp/
dbbackup

sudo /opt/mssql/bin/mssql-conf traceflag 3226 on

sudo systemctl restart mssql-server
```

You can now run the script with positional command-line arguments as shown in the following:

```
sudo ./automateSQLinstall.sh mYSecUr3PAssw0rd enterprise
```

Again, sit back, relax, and watch the magic happen.

Summary

My original intent for this chapter was to get you started with SQL Server on Linux. As a SQL Server DBA who has only worked with the Windows operating system, I understand your hesitation on working with an unfamiliar system. Now that you have an understanding of how SQL Server on Linux works, how to install and configure it, working with the Linux filesystem and permissions, and writing a simple bash script, you can no longer call yourself a Linux newbie. Give yourself a pat on the back for doing a great job of facing your fears and conquering the mighty penguin. But we're going to shift gears a bit in the next chapter and switch back to working on Windows building custom SQL Server Docker images.

## CHAPTER 9

Creating Custom SQL Server on Windows Container Images

Just because something is traditional is no reason to do it, of course.

—Lemony Snicket, *The Blank Book*

Being in private school means following certain dress codes – white collared shirt with the school logo, navy blue dress pants, and black leather shoes. Come rain or shine, school uniforms must be worn. Imagine carrying a 15-lb backpack with all your books and notebooks as you walk across the campus while the monsoon rain is pouring. It doesn't matter how good your ready-to-wear leather shoes are, they won't last an entire semester. It didn't help that ninth grader boys like playing rough and running around during recess. My mom had given me a good amount of scolding whenever I complained about my worn-out leather shoes.

That was until my brother's friend told us about custom-made leather shoes. An old man from the shoe capital of the Philippines decided to start his own business making custom leather shoes using upcycled airplane tires for the soles. I have no clue how he came up with the idea of using upcycled airplane tires for shoes or where he sourced them from (I'm pretty sure he didn't go around breaking into airports and slashing airplane tires just so he can get them). But we were not about to pass up the opportunity. We paid the old man a visit, had our measurements taken, and were told to wait for two weeks,

E. M. Sarmiento, *The SQL Server DBA's Guide to Docker Containers*,
https://doi.org/10.1007/978-1-4842-5826-2_9

because that's how long it took to make these shoes – two long weeks. That felt like eternity when you're a teen. But wait we must. And, in case you were wondering, we did pay for our shoes. They were almost twice as expensive as the ready-to-wear leather shoes that we used to get.

I put on my shoes and started running the minute I got my pair. I wanted to see if they lived up to my expectations. And I was impressed. I wore them every single day. They're not as comfortable as my previous leather shoes, but they do meet my needs. They lasted for more than several school years that I still saw them at my mom's house when I visited three years ago. I've outgrown them but they still look great and can still be worn. It just proves that you can find something that specifically meets your needs – either by finding someone who can provide it for you or by making it yourself.

The containers that we've been working with in the previous chapters were all publicly available images from registries like Docker Hub or Microsoft Container Registry (MCR). There might be cases where you need custom-built images that follow your corporate standards, meet compliance requirements, or just standardize your deployments. On the Windows side, one example could be building a SQL Server 2016 with Service Pack 2 on a Windows Server 2016 container. Only SQL Server 2017 on Windows containers are publicly available from Microsoft. On the Linux side, maybe you want to standardize on Red Hat Enterprise (or CentOS) Linux for your container operating system and not Ubuntu.

This chapter covers creating custom SQL Server on Windows images that you can deploy as containers. We will look at working with the *Dockerfile*, a text document that contains all the commands a user could run on the command line to create a custom Docker image. After creating the custom Docker image, we will deploy a container and connect to it to verify if it meets all our customization requirements.

Creating Custom Docker Images

There are two ways to create custom Docker images. The first one is to update a running container and using the *docker commit* command to create a new image that includes the changes. The idea here is that you want to make modifications to a base image and use it as a reference for your new custom image.

Let's use the publicly available SQL Server on Linux Docker images. Don't be confused. This chapter is still focused on Windows. I'm just using Linux Docker images as an example to simplify things. You'll see why later in this chapter. You can add databases in those containers and make modifications as necessary. Once you're done, you can run the following *docker commit* command to create a new image based on the changed container, with *sqldevlinuxcon01* as the name of the running container and *sqlserver2017-cu18-ubuntu-16.04-with-dbs:v2.0* as the name of the new image. As a best practice, I added a tag to the image so I can easily identify what it is.

```
docker commit sqldevlinuxcon01 sqlserver2017-cu18-ubuntu-16.04-with-
dbs:v2.0
```

Review *Chapter 5*. Running this command will create a new filesystem layer that contains the changes you made. If you run the *docker inspect* command against this new image and compare it against the one from the MCR, you'll see the new filesystem layer, as shown in Figure 9-1. Everything else looks the same.

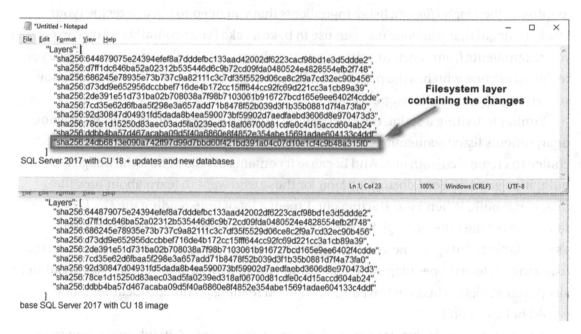

Figure 9-1. New filesystem layer added to the image containing the changes

You can use this new image to create containers that have the additional changes. Have a look at the following *docker run* command that uses the newly created image:

```
docker run -e "ACCEPT_EULA=Y" -e "SA_PASSWORD=mYSecUr3PAssw0rd" -p
1413:1433 --name sqldevlinuxcon03 -d -h linuxsqldev01 sqlserver2017-cu18-
ubuntu-16.04-with-dbs:v2.0
```

There's just one problem: the commit operation will not include any data contained in volumes mounted inside the container. If the *sqldevlinuxcon01* container was mounted on a Docker volume and your user databases were created and stored in the volume, none of those will be included. That's one of the main reasons I don't use the *docker commit* command to create custom Docker images.

Exploring the *Dockerfile*

The second – and recommended – way to create custom Docker images is by using a *Dockerfile*. A *Dockerfile* is simply a text file that contains all the commands a user could run on the command line to build a custom Docker image. It's like using the *ConfigurationFile.ini* file to deploy SQL Server using the same configuration. I like to think of the *Dockerfile* as a list of ingredients that you need to make a recipe (your Docker image) that someone else can use to bake a cake (your container). You can get your ingredients from different sources and use them to make a recipe. You can give your recipe to anyone who has the patience and creativity to bake a cake (hey, I need to say something nice about developers).

Similar to writing a script, the *Dockerfile* consists of several commands, instructions, or arguments listed sequentially to perform actions on a base Docker image of your choice to create a custom one. And because it contains details of how the image was built, it's a good piece of documentation for those who want to learn about how the image was built. When I was starting out, I spent a lot of time reading the *Dockerfile* references of the different SQL Server images on `https://github.com/microsoft/ mssql-docker`. This gave me an idea on how to build my own custom SQL Server images using my preferred operating system platform and version of SQL Server. Plus, I couldn't sleep well at night when I'm traveling so I figured reading technical documentation would help. It didn't.

You can store a *Dockerfile* on a version control system like GitHub so you can track changes made by different folks on your team. Because we are building a SQL Server environment with the required operating system and configuration, you can think of a *Dockerfile* as a way to implement *infrastructure as code*.

The File

I did say that the *Dockerfile* is simply a text file. You can use your favorite text editor to create and write the *Dockerfile*. I usually start writing it with Notepad++ on my Windows workstation. Once completed, I copy it to either a Windows Docker host, Linux Docker host, or any machine that has the Docker CLI client installed.

What I find really annoying with the *Dockerfile* is the filename itself. It must be specifically named *Dockerfile*, written with an uppercase "D", single word with no space in between, and no file extension. If you use a text editor that saves a file with a ".txt" file extension by default, be sure to remove it. I can't count the number of times that I had to troubleshoot what's wrong with my *Dockerfile* only to find out that my file had a file extension. That's why I like using Notepad++.

Tip   Well, you can actually use a different filename with a different file extension should you want to standardize your file naming convention. For example, you can use *Dockerfile* as the production-grade file while *dockerFile.dev* for use with development. The idea here is you have a proper document management strategy even for code files. After all, code files can be considered as documents. You don't just want to track and manage code changes. You also want to properly classify them so that no one on your team accidentally deploys code that are still in development. It doesn't matter if you're automating code reviews or implementing continuous integration. A proper process to minimize human errors can help improve the DevOps practice. You will see an example of how to use a different filename to build a custom Docker image later in the chapter.

The format of the *Dockerfile* looks like this:

```
#Comment
INSTRUCTION arguments
```

The *INSTRUCTION* is not case-sensitive, which I find interesting given that Docker was originally built for Linux. However, the convention is to make the *INSTRUCTION* uppercase to easily distinguish them from the arguments. Let's look at the different instructions that you can include in the *Dockerfile*. I'll define the instructions here although not all of them will be used to create a custom SQL Server on Windows image. Some of them will be used for SQL Server on Linux.

The FROM Instruction

A *Dockerfile* must begin with a *FROM* instruction, although you can argue that it can begin with a comment. The *FROM* instruction specifies the base Docker image that you want to start from (pun intended). It could be an image of the base operating system or an existing image that you want to build from. When you're building a custom golden image, the *FROM* instruction references a base operating system image. The following is the *FROM* instruction to tell the *Dockerfile* to use the Windows Server 2016 Core OS Build 14393.2972. A list of the available Windows Server Core images is available on `https://hub.docker.com/_/microsoft-windows-servercore`.

```
FROM mcr.microsoft.com/windows/servercore:10.0.14393.2972
```

Similar to running the *docker run* command, if the image in the *FROM* instruction does not exist locally on the Docker host during the build, it will be pulled from the public repository before the custom image gets created.

The LABEL Instruction

The *LABEL* instruction is a key-value pair that adds metadata to an image. Think of it as additional comments about the custom image – what base image it uses, what application runs on it, what version it is, and the like. The following is an example of how you can write a multiline *LABEL* instruction:

```
LABEL name="SQL Server 2016 with SP2 on Windows Server 2016"
LABEL version="1.00.00"
LABEL environment="dev/test"
LABEL maintainer="theawesomedbateam@testdomain.com"
```

This information is displayed in the *Labels* section output when you run the *docker inspect* command on the image you're reviewing, as shown in Figure 9-2.

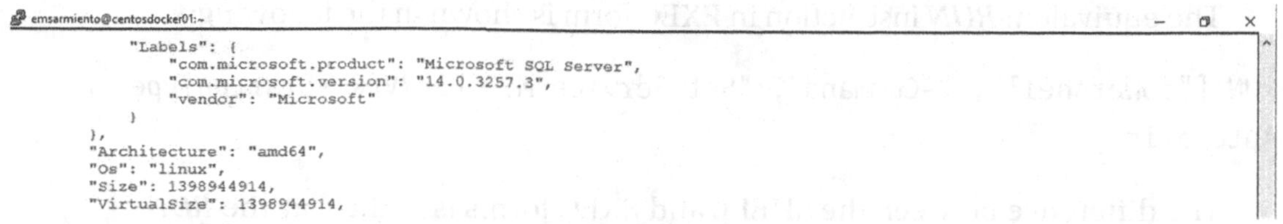

emsarmiento@centosdocker01:~

        "Labels": {
            "com.microsoft.product": "Microsoft SQL Server",
            "com.microsoft.version": "14.0.3257.3",
            "vendor": "Microsoft"
        }
    },
    "Architecture": "amd64",
    "Os": "linux",
    "Size": 1398944914,
    "VirtualSize": 1398944914,

Figure 9-2. *SQL Server on Linux image metadata having multiple LABEL instructions*

Just like any kind of documentation, you need to define standards. You don't want some of your *Dockerfile* files using the *LABEL* instruction while the rest use comments. I recommend using *LABEL* instructions as a standard in cases where someone using your custom image does not have access to the *Dockerfile*.

The RUN Instruction

Obviously, the *RUN* instruction will execute commands. This will be one of your most used instructions. You can use the *RUN* instruction in either of its two forms:

- *SHELL* form: The command is run in the operating system's default command shell – */bin/sh -c* on Linux or *cmd /S /C* on Windows.
- *EXEC* form: The command calls the executable directly without invoking a command shell. Using the EXEC form prevents possible destructive changes to the string passed to the command shell, which is common when performing string manipulation in the command line.

The *RUN* instruction is not the only one that has two forms. You'll see in later sections of this chapter that other instructions also have both the SHELL and EXEC forms.

The following is an example of using the *RUN* instruction in SHELL form. The command will use the PowerShell command shell (instead of the default *cmd.exe* shell) and set the startup type of the *MSSQLSERVER* service to automatic. In case you're wondering, Windows containers still use services unlike Linux containers where you simply run a process.

```
RUN powershell -Command (Set-Service MSSQLSERVER -StartupType Automatic)
```

The equivalent *RUN* instruction in EXEC form is shown in the following:

```
RUN ["powershell", "-Command", "Set-Service MSSQLSERVER -StartupType
Automatic"]
```

The difference between the SHELL and EXEC forms is in the way the *RUN* instruction is executed. In the SHELL form, the command is run in the context of the default shell. In the EXEC form, the command is run explicitly. Using the preceding *RUN* instruction example, the SHELL form will run the following command in the Docker image:

```
cmd /S /C powershell -Command (Set-Service MSSQLSERVER -StartupType Automatic)
```

In contrast, in the EXEC form, the command executes explicitly. Of course, we're assuming that the path to the command is defined in the system environment variables.

```
powershell -Command (Set-Service MSSQLSERVER -StartupType Automatic)
```

You can execute different commands with the *RUN* instruction so long as you can run it using the base image layer – download files, create directories, configure settings, and so on. You have the power of the base image and the capabilities of the shell environment to do anything you want.

The *RUN* instruction will execute any commands in a new read-write filesystem layer on top of the current image. This is a new, temporary container created based on the existing image. Once the command completes, the results will be committed to the image, like what was done with the *docker commit* command. This will appear as a new filesystem layer like the one shown in Figure 9-1. This new image becomes the starting point of the next instruction in the *Dockerfile*. The temporary container will then be removed. Remember the Lego pieces analogy from *Chapter 5*?

The COPY Instruction

The *COPY* instruction copies new files or directories from a source and adds them to the filesystem of the container at the path provided. Like the *RUN* instruction, it also has two forms:

- *COPY <source> <destination>*
- *COPY ["<source>", "<destination>"]*

The second form is used for paths that contain blank spaces, such as *C:/Program Files/Microsoft SQL Server*, and is mostly applicable to Windows than Linux. The files and directories must be in a path relative to the *Dockerfile*, and the *<destination>* path needs to be referenced using a forward slash (it pays to think Linux even on Windows). The following is a *COPY* instruction to copy the SQL Server 2016 Developer Edition with Service Pack 2 installation media on the machine where the *Dockerfile* is stored to the C:/SQL2016Dev_SP2 directory:

```
COPY /SQL2016Dev_SP2 C:/SQL2016Dev_SP2
```

Note   The one thing I found confusing when I was starting out was the use of forward slashes in the Docker for Windows documentation, both from Docker and Microsoft. For example, you need to write *C:\Windows\System32\cmd. exe* as *C:/Windows/System32/cmd.exe*. We've always used backslashes (\) in Windows as path separator. But since Docker was created initially for Linux, it follows Linux conventions like forward slashes (/) as path separators. If you want to use backslashes in Docker, you need to properly escape it. That's because the backslash character is used as an escape character in Linux. If you want to stick to how you've done things in Windows, you need to "escape the escape character." The preceding example would need to be written as *C:\\Windows\\System32\\cmd. exe*. Or just use forward slashes instead.

The *<source>* path must be inside the context of the build. If you are storing the *Dockerfile* in the *E:/dockerBuild* directory on your Windows machine that has a Docker CLI client, the *SQL2016Dev_SP2* directory should be inside that directory. If the *<source>* is a directory like the one in the example, only the contents – including the filesystem metadata – will be copied, not the directory. Figure 9-3 shows the filesystem structure of the build context on a Windows Docker host. I'll explain what the *start.ps1* PowerShell script is for later in the chapter.

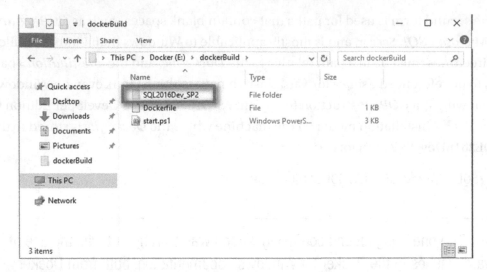

Figure 9-3. *Filesystem structure of the build context on a Windows Docker host*

On Linux, you can pass the *chown* command together with the *COPY* instruction in the format *COPY [--chown=<user>:<group>] <src>... <dest>*. This is useful since the default *COPY* instruction will always assign a UID and GID value of 0 - user and group equal to *root*. Keeping with the principle of least privilege, we don't want to assign *root* to everything. However, it's OK for *root* to have ownership of the files and directories inside the container so long as the container isn't running as *root*. An example of building a custom Docker image running SQL Server on Linux that runs as a *non-root* user is provided in *Chapter 10*.

The ADD Instruction

The *ADD* instruction is like the *COPY* instruction but with additional capabilities other than just copying from and to a filesystem. You can use the *ADD* instruction to copy from a remote location with a URL. Let's say you want to copy the *start.ps1* PowerShell script from *https://github.com/microsoft/mssql-docker/blob/master/windows/mssql-server-windows-developer/start.ps1* to C:/ of your custom SQL Server on Windows image. You can use the following *ADD* instruction:

```
ADD https://github.com/microsoft/mssql-docker/blob/master/windows/mssql-
server-windows-developer/start.ps1 /
```

You may already have an idea what the *start.ps1* PowerShell script is for. If you review the *Dockerfile* provided on *https://github.com/microsoft/mssql-docker/blob/ master/windows/mssql-server-windows-developer/dockerfile* for creating custom SQL Server on Windows image, the *start.ps1* PowerShell script is called in the last instruction – the *CMD* instruction.

I prefer making files available locally instead of copying them from a URL. I want to make sure that the file that I'm using – whether it's a script or an installation file – is free of any potential file corruption errors. I want to be able to test them manually first in my local filesystem before including them in any automated process. In fact, when I built an automated process for deploying different versions and editions of SQL Server in the past, all the installation media have already been downloaded to a network file share and manually tested. It saves you the headache of troubleshooting a failed installation because one of the CAB files is corrupted. I'm sure you've had one of those in the past while installing SQL Server.

The SHELL Instruction

The *SHELL* instruction allows the default shell used for the shell form of commands to be overridden. It is more common to use this instruction on Windows containers since Windows has both *cmd.exe* and *powershell.exe* shells. The Windows default shell is *cmd. exe*. As a PowerShell guy, I prefer using the *SHELL* instruction on Windows so I can take full advantage of the built-in cmdlets that make command execution easier. The *SHELL* instruction is written in the form *SHELL ["executable", "parameters"]*. Translating the example used in the *RUN* instruction to use the *SHELL* instruction:

```
SHELL ["powershell", "-Command", "Set-Service MSSQLSERVER -StartupType
Automatic"]
```

This makes it a lot simpler if you have a sequence of PowerShell commands that you want to run in the *Dockerfile*. Let's say you want to delete the *SQL2016Dev_SP2* directory from the container after the installation completes. You can use the *SHELL* instruction to define the default shell and use the *RUN* instruction to execute PowerShell commands:

```
#Set PowerShell as the command shell
SHELL ["powershell", "-Command"]
```

```
#Run Set-Service PowerShell cmdlet to configure MSSQLSERVER
RUN Set-Service MSSQLSERVER -StartupType Automatic

#Run Remove-Item PowerShell cmdlet to delete directory
RUN Remove-Item -Path C:/SQL2016Dev_SP2 -Recurse -Force
```

Clearly, using the *SHELL* instruction is more efficient than using the *RUN* instruction when leveraging PowerShell while building the image. And while you may start to think that the *SHELL* instruction was only written specifically for Windows containers, you can also use it on Linux to change to a different shell. But why would you want to do that inside a Linux container when the default shell can do most of the things you need?

The CMD Instruction

The *CMD* instruction allows you to set a default command and default parameters when you run a container using the *docker run* command. If you don't provide a command when running a container, this instruction is executed. However, it is overridden should you choose to run a container with a specific command. Unlike the *RUN* and *SHELL* instructions where you can have multiple of these instructions in a *Dockerfile*, only the last *CMD* instruction will be evaluated. It doesn't make sense to have multiple *CMD* instructions. Plus, you want the *CMD* instruction to execute something that runs and doesn't exit. If you execute a command that exits after completion, the container will terminate as well. You don't want the *CMD* instruction to run a service in Windows like NET START MSSQLSERVER because it will exit once the command completes, terminating the container with it. So much for running SQL Server as a service inside a container.

The *CMD* instruction comes in not two but three forms:

- *CMD ["executable", "param1", "param2"]* (EXEC form, this is the preferred form)

- *CMD ["param1", "param2"]* (as default parameters to ENTRYPOINT)

- *CMD command param1 param2* (*SHELL* form)

The following is the *CMD* instruction, in *EXEC* form, if you want to run a PowerShell script named *start.ps1* as the last instruction in your *Dockerfile*. This assumes you've already copied the PowerShell script inside the image prior to running it.

```
CMD ["powershell", "-Command", "C:/start.ps1"]
```

Running the *CMD* instruction in *SHELL* form makes it behave like the *RUN* instruction in *SHELL* form, using the default operating system command shell. If you want to run your own command, you need to express the command as a JSON array, passing the full path to the executable and enclosed in double quotes – unless you use the *WORKDIR* instruction. The following is an example of running a .NET Console application named *sampleConsole.exe* using the CMD instruction:

```
CMD ["C:/sampleConsole.exe", "--run"]
```

As I mentioned, you can override the default command defined in the *CMD* instruction when you run a container. For example, running the Windows Server 2016 Core Docker image using the *docker run* command will immediately terminate the container after creation. I couldn't find the reference *Dockerfile* that created this image to look at the *CMD* instruction. But it does terminate after creation. If I want to keep the container running, I can pass a command that doesn't exit to the container to override whatever was written in the *CMD* instruction. The following is an example of passing the `ping localhost -t` command to the *docker run* command:

```
docker run mcr.microsoft.com/windows/servercore:ltsc2016 ping localhost -t
```

The ENTRYPOINT Instruction

As if having *RUN*, *SHELL*, and *CMD* instructions aren't enough, here's another one to add to the list: the *ENTRYPOINT* instruction. The *ENTRYPOINT* instruction is used to treat a running container as if it was an executable. This is typically used when you want a container to function as a portable packaging for a specific executable without expecting the user to override that executable during runtime. It's very useful if you want your container to run the same executable every time. This means you cannot override the command with the *docker run* command. However, anything added to the end of the *docker run* command is appended to the command defined in the *ENTRYPOINT* instruction. I used to think that there was no use for the *ENTRYPOINT* instruction for SQL Server containers, until I realized that you can use this if you want to restrict the container from running anything else other than SQL Server and possibly pass parameters during startup. Besides, there's nothing stopping you from overriding the *CMD* instruction that runs the *start.ps1* PowerShell script in Windows and just running the ipconfig command. Or the SQL Server process in Linux and just run *bash*. Of course, doing that also means no more SQL Server until you restart the container and not override the *CMD* instruction.

Just like the *RUN* instruction, the *ENTRYPOINT* instruction has two forms, the EXEC (the preferred) form and the SHELL form. The following is an example of using the ENTRYPOINT instruction in EXEC form to run the SQL Server executable in Windows. Just replace the *{nn}* with the SQL Server version number you are running:

```
ENTRYPOINT ["C:/Program Files/Microsoft SQL Server/MSSQL{nn}.MSSQLSERVER/
MSSQL/Binn/sqlservr.exe"]
```

CMD vs. RUN vs. SHELL vs. ENTRYPOINT

It can be confusing to choose between these different instructions when creating your *Dockerfile*. Just remember the following:

- There is only one effective *CMD* instruction in a *Dockerfile* – only the last one will be evaluated. Use this if you want your containers to override the command defined in the *CMD* instruction.

- Use the *RUN* instruction to run commands to build your custom Docker image.

- Use the *SHELL* instruction if you want to change the default command shell and leverage it for most of your commands.

- Use the *ENTRYPOINT* instruction to prevent users from overriding the executable that you want your container to run.

- You can combine the *ENTRYPOINT* instruction with the *CMD* instruction in a *Dockerfile*. When doing so, the string in the *CMD* instruction will be appended to the *ENTRYPOINT* instruction. The *CMD* instruction needs to be the last instruction in the *Dockerfile*.

- You can run either a process or a script with either the *ENTRYPOINT* or the *CMD* instruction. If you're running a script, just make sure that it runs a process or command that doesn't exit.

The good thing about this is that building custom SQL Server images doesn't need so many configuration settings. You just need a base image and the SQL Server installation files, then configure the SQL Server instance after installation, and you're all set. You will see how these instructions are used together when we start writing the *Dockerfile*.

The WORKDIR Instruction

The *WORKDIR* instruction sets a working directory for other instructions, such as *RUN*, *CMD*, *ENTRYPOINT*, *COPY*, and *ADD*. If the *WORKDIR* does not exist in the target image during the build process, it will get created. It's very useful when you want to run an executable or a script from a custom path – define the *WORKDIR* and then run the executable relative to it. You can think of it as doing a *cd* command inside the container during the build process. This is also useful if the path to your executable is very long, like the default installation directory for SQL Server on Windows, and you don't want to repeat it all throughout the *Dockerfile*. However, using the *ENV* instruction is more appropriate to define the path since it is common to define paths as an environment variable. The following is an example of using the *WORKDIR* instruction to set the working directory to *C:/* during the build process:

```
WORKDIR /
```

Again, it pays to think Linux when doing this in Windows to minimize escaping the escape character. Get it?

The ENV Instruction

The *ENV* instruction is a key-value pair that sets a persistent environment variable that is available both during build time and container runtime. Remember those *-e* parameters you've been using in the *docker run* command?

The *ENV* instruction has two forms:

- *ENV <key> <value>*
- *ENV <key>=<value>*

I prefer using the second form – *ENV <key>=<value>* – because it is much more explicit. It also allows for setting multiple key-value pairs in a single line. The following is an example of setting a key-value pair for the SQL Server EULA and assigning the *sa* login password. I opted to show them in multiple lines to separate the two:

```
ENV SA_PASSWORD="y0urSecUr3PAssw0rd"
ENV ACCEPT_EULA="Y"
```

But they can be combined in a single line as follows:

```
ENV SA_PASSWORD="y0urSecUr3PAssw0rd" ACCEPT_EULA="Y"
```

Using Escape Characters

I don't know about you, but I don't like breaking long commands in multiple lines. My brain just looks at a command in a single line, regardless of how long it is, as if I'm writing them directly in the command line. Recall the commands I used to create the script for automated installation of SQL Server on Linux in *Chapter 8*. Every single command was written as a single line – especially the one that calls the */opt/mssql/bin/mssql-conf*.

However, some people don't like writing very long commands in a single line. They break them down into smaller chunks so they can be readable in a single page of their screen. It's like their terminal windows or command-line shells are not going to wrap the text around to the next line. I don't blame them. Looking at the computer screen for too long can cause what is known as digital eye strain (my informal research also tells me that it affects sanity). And this is where escape characters can help.

You can use escape characters in both Linux and PowerShell. A backslash is used in Linux to escape the next character from being interpreted by the shell. This is used to write a long command line in multiple lines. The following is an example of using the backslash to write the command to configure SQL Server on Linux and pass required parameters:

```
sudo MSSQL_PID=$MSSQL_PID ACCEPT_EULA=Y \
    MSSQL_SA_PASSWORD=$MSSQL_SA_PASSWORD \
    /opt/mssql/bin/mssql-conf setup
```

You can do the same with the *RUN* instruction if you want to pass the required parameters inside the *Dockerfile* instead of the *docker run* command. I prefer passing them with the *docker run* command.

```
RUN sudo MSSQL_PID=$MSSQL_PID ACCEPT_EULA=Y \
    MSSQL_SA_PASSWORD=$MSSQL_SA_PASSWORD \
    /opt/mssql/bin/mssql-conf setup
```

PowerShell uses the backtick (`` ` ``) operator for writing a very long command in multiple lines. Let's say you want to rewrite the PowerShell command example used in the *SHELL* instruction section to first check if the MSSQLSERVER service exists before setting the StartupType property; you can do it using the following sample *RUN* instruction:

```
RUN Get-Service | Where {$_.Name -eq "MSSQLSERVER"} | `
    Set-Service -StartupType Automatic
```

In addition, you can define an escape character inside the *Dockerfile*. This is very helpful especially in Windows where the directory path separator is the backslash character – the same as the default escape character used in a *Dockerfile*. That's the reason why you use a double backslash instead of a single backslash to write *C:\\ Windows\\System32\\cmd.exe*. You can change the default escape character in a *Dockerfile* by defining it as a *parser directive*. The following directive changes the default escape character in a *Dockerfile* from backslash to a backtick. This makes it consistent with PowerShell.

```
# escape=`
```

Parser directives are optional. But if you decide to use them, they must be written on top of the *Dockerfile*, even before the *FROM* instruction.

Now that we have what we need to write a *Dockerfile* for building a custom SQL Server on Windows image, it's time to put all the pieces together.

Putting the Pieces Together with a *Dockerfile*

I did mention in *Chapter 8* that I'm a big fan of processes. So, I've outlined the following process for creating a custom SQL Server 2016 Developer Edition on Windows Server 2016 Core image. The steps were patterned after the *Dockerfile* from *https://github.*

com/microsoft/mssql-docker/blob/master/windows/mssql-server-windows-developer/dockerfile to capture the required steps in creating a custom SQL Server on Windows image. Having a high-level overview of the process allows you to optimize and improve the steps and possibly replace them with your own commands and scripts.

1. Start from the publicly available Windows Server 2016 Core 10.0.14393.2972 base image from the Microsoft Container Registry.

2. Create a temporary directory inside the image to store the SQL Server 2016 Developer Edition installation files.

3. Copy the SQL Server 2016 Developer Edition installation files from your machine to the image.

4. Install SQL Server 2016 via the command line.

5. Set SQL Server service startup type to Automatic.

6. Remove the temporary SQL Server 2016 Developer Edition installation media folder from the image.

7. Switch the command shell to PowerShell in preparation for running script *start.ps1*.

8. Copy the PowerShell script *start.ps1* to the image on root directory – C:/

9. Set the current working directory for PowerShell script execution.

10. Run PowerShell script *start.ps1* when the container is started.

I mentioned the PowerShell script *start.ps1* a few times now throughout the chapter. The script does a couple of things:

- Checks for three parameters – the *sa* login password, acceptance of the EULA, and location of Azure Blob storage should you have database files that you want to attach to the SQL Server instance

- Leverages Docker secret if used to store the *sa* login password

- Goes into an infinite loop so the script does not terminate when you run the container

216

I only need the first bullet point minus attaching databases from Azure Blob storage. But I used the script to demonstrate how you can leverage the different instructions in the *Dockerfile* to build your custom image. You can download the script from *https:// github.com/Microsoft/mssql-docker/blob/master/windows/mssql-server-windows/ start.ps1*.

In preparation for the installation, I downloaded the SQL Server 2016 Developer Edition with Service Pack 2 installation media from *http://go.microsoft.com/ fwlink/?LinkID=799009*. It's up to you to download either the ISO file or the CAB file. Just make sure you properly extract the installation files into a directory named *SQL2016Dev_SP2*. And if you want to add the latest cumulative update, slipstream it into the installation media prior to installation and use the */UpdateSource* parameter when installing SQL Server from the command line. Refer to the *RUN* instruction in Step 4 in the following. Follow the filesystem structure shown in Figure 9-3.

The following is the *Dockerfile* for building the custom SQL Server 2016 Developer Edition with Service Pack 2 Cumulative Update 11 on Windows Server 2016 Core image. I'll use the item numbers as steps and identify them in the comments:

```
#Step 1
FROM mcr.microsoft.com/windows/servercore:10.0.14393.2972

#Step 2
RUN powershell -Command (mkdir C:\SQL2016Dev_SP2)

#Step 3
COPY /SQL2016Dev_SP2 C:/SQL2016Dev_SP2

#Step 4
RUN C:/SQL2016Dev_SP2/SETUP.exe /Q /ACTION=INSTALL /UPDATEENABLED=True
/UPDATESOURCE=./SQLServer2016SP2CU11 /FEATURES=SQLENGINE /
INSTANCENAME=MSSQLSERVER /SECURITYMODE=SQL /SAPWD="y0urSecUr3PAssw0rd"
/SQLSVCACCOUNT="NT AUTHORITY\System" /AGTSVCACCOUNT="NT AUTHORITY\
System" /SQLSYSADMINACCOUNTS="BUILTIN\Administrators" /
IACCEPTSQLSERVERLICENSETERMS=1 /TCPENABLED=1

#Step 5
RUN powershell -Command (Set-Service MSSQLSERVER -StartupType Automatic)

#Step 6
```

```
RUN powershell -Command (Remove-Item -Path C:/SQL2016Dev_SP2 -Recurse
-Force)

#Step 7
SHELL ["powershell", "-Command", "$ErrorActionPreference = 'Stop';
$ProgressPreference = 'SilentlyContinue';"]

#Step 8
COPY /start.ps1 /

#Step 9
WORKDIR /

ENV SA_PASSWORD "y0urSecUr3PAssw0rd"

ENV ACCEPT_EULA "Y"

#Step 10
CMD ./start -sa_password $env:SA_PASSWORD -ACCEPT_EULA $env:ACCEPT_EULA
-Verbose
```

Just by looking at the instructions in the *Dockerfile*, you can already see some potential improvements for optimization. We'll save that for later. It's time to build our custom SQL Server on Windows container.

Build the Custom SQL Server on Windows Image

Save the *Dockerfile* in the *<drive>:\dockerBuild* directory together with the *SQL2016Dev_SP2* directory and the *start.ps1* PowerShell script. You will be running the following *docker build* command in the context of that directory. We will call the new image *sql2016windev* and tag it as *v1.0*. The dot *(.)* at the end of the *docker build* command specifies the path. In this case, the *docker build* command will look at the current path and evaluate all the instructions inside the *Dockerfile* relative to the current path. If not explicitly specified, it will also tell the *docker build* command to look for a file named *Dockerfile* in that path.

```
docker build -t sql2016windev:v1.0 .
```

Figure 9-4 shows the first few lines of output from the *docker build* command.

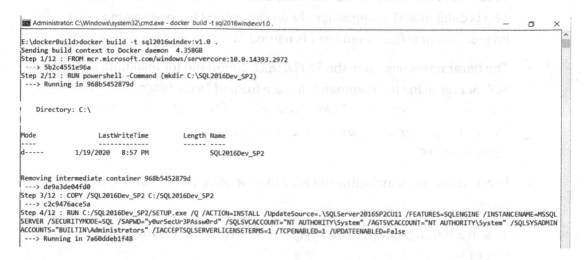

Figure 9-4. *Output of the docker build command*

Notice the following:

- The message "Sending build context to Docker daemon 4.358GB" literally means exactly what it says. The Docker CLI client is sending the entire contents of the *<drive>:\dockerBuild* directory to the Docker daemon. The reason I created the *<drive>:\dockerBuild* directory and used that as the path for building the custom image is because I only want to copy the contents of this directory to the Docker daemon. If you run the *docker build* command on your root directory – *<drive>:* – it will copy all its contents to the Docker daemon. You wouldn't want your personal MP3 files, your resume, nor your photo collection to end up on someone else's container, would you?

- Step 1/12. Didn't we only have 10 steps in the *Dockerfile*? How come the *docker build* command identified 12? That's because every instruction will create a step, including the two *ENV* instructions before Step 10. And we haven't even added a *LABEL* instruction.

- In Step 2/12, the message "---> Running in 968b5452879d" tells you that this is the temporary container that the *RUN* instruction created to run the command in this step.

- In Step 2/12, the message "---> Removing intermediate container 968b5452879d" tells you that the temporary container created in this step is deleted and changes have been committed to create a new image. This new filesystem layer is named "de9a3de04fd0".

- The parameters passed to the *SETUP.EXE* command for installing SQL Server using the command line are from *https://docs. microsoft.com/en-us/sql/database-engine/install-windows/ install-sql-server-from-the-command-prompt?view=sql- server-ver15*.

- Every instruction, including the ENV instructions, creates a filesystem layer.

- You are feeling sleepy. Your eyes are getting heavy. Now, snap out of it.

Once the build completes, you can now use the custom image to create and run a new container. Run the docker images command to see the newly built image. Figure 9-5 shows the list of the available images in my Docker host, including the one that is newly built. The size of Windows containers is the main reason I try to avoid them if I can.

```
Administrator: C:\Windows\system32\cmd.exe                                      —    □    ×

E:\dockerBuild>docker images
REPOSITORY                          TAG               IMAGE ID        CREATED         SIZE
sql2016windev                       v1.0              14d3e3d79484    45 minutes ago  19.8GB
mcr.microsoft.com/windows/servercore  10.0.14393.2972  5b2c4551e96a    8 months ago    11.1GB

E:\dockerBuild>
```

Figure 9-5. *Listing the newly built custom Docker image*

Run the following command to start using this custom image. Figure 9-6 displays validating the custom SQL Server on Windows container built – SQL Server 2016 with Service Pack 2 Cumulative Update 11 running on Windows Server 2016 Core OS Build 14393.2972.

```
docker run -e 'ACCEPT_EULA=Y' -e 'SA_PASSWORD=yOurSecUr3PAsswOrd' -p
1433:1433 --name sql-windevcon01 -d -h windevsql01 sql2016windev:v1.0
```

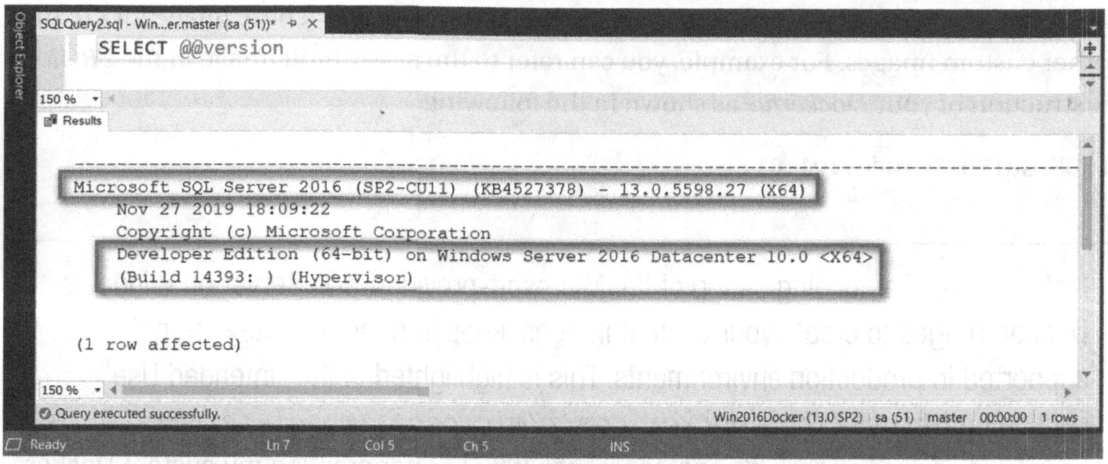

Figure 9-6. *Validating custom SQL Server on Windows Docker image*

Remember when I said you can use a different filename for the *Dockerfile*? Let's say you want to call it *dockerFile.dev* to indicate that this is what the developers will be using while *Dockerfile* will be strictly for use in production (well, production from the developers' point of view). You can use the *-f* parameter of the *docker build* command to specify the name of the file that you want to use. The following example command uses the *dockerFile.dev* file to build the custom image. The dot (.) character still tells the *docker build* command to use the current path.

```
docker build -t sql2016windev:v1.01 -f dockerFile.dev .
```

You can also pass an absolute path or a URL to the *docker build* command. The following example command uses the Microsoft-provided *Dockerfile* from GitHub to build a custom SQL Server on Linux image that runs as a non-root user. I can't use the Microsoft-provided *Dockerfile* for Windows to build a custom SQL Server on Windows image as it isn't updated – the *FROM* instruction still points to an outdated Windows Server Core image.

```
docker build -t sql2017linuxnonroot:v1.0  https://raw.githubusercontent.
com/microsoft/mssql-docker/master/linux/preview/examples/mssql-server-
linux-non-root/Dockerfile
```

Just remember that the instructions in the *Dockerfile* will be executed in the context of the current build path. Make sure all the dependencies like scripts, installation files, and so on defined in the *COPY* or *ADD* instructions are available.

Once you've built your custom image, you can now use it as a base image for creating other custom images. For example, you can refer to the newly built image in the *FROM* instruction of your *Dockerfile* as shown in the following:

```
FROM sql2016windev:v1.01
```

Note: If you're building on top of the Microsoft-provided SQL Server on Windows Docker images to create your custom images, keep in mind that they are not supported in production environments. This is highlighted in the "Intended Use" section on *https://hub.docker.com/r/microsoft/mssql-server-windows-developer/*. It's another reason why I prefer creating my custom Docker images, in this case, a SQL Server 2016 running on Windows Server 2016 image. Just make sure you're running a supported version of both Windows Server and SQL Server should you decide to roll it out in production. Windows Server 2008 and Windows Server 2008 R2 are no longer under extended support. Don't even bother.

Optimizing the Dockerfile

There are several ways you can optimize the image build process and the resulting Docker image. One of my biggest concerns is the size of the filesystem layers. It's the 11.1GB size of the base Windows Server 2016 Core image that makes me avoid using Windows containers. And that's just the operating system alone. The publicly available SQL Server on Linux image is 1.4GB. Not to mention the size of the SQL Server installation files on Windows. Figure 9-7 shows the result of the *docker history* command for the custom SQL Server on Windows image.

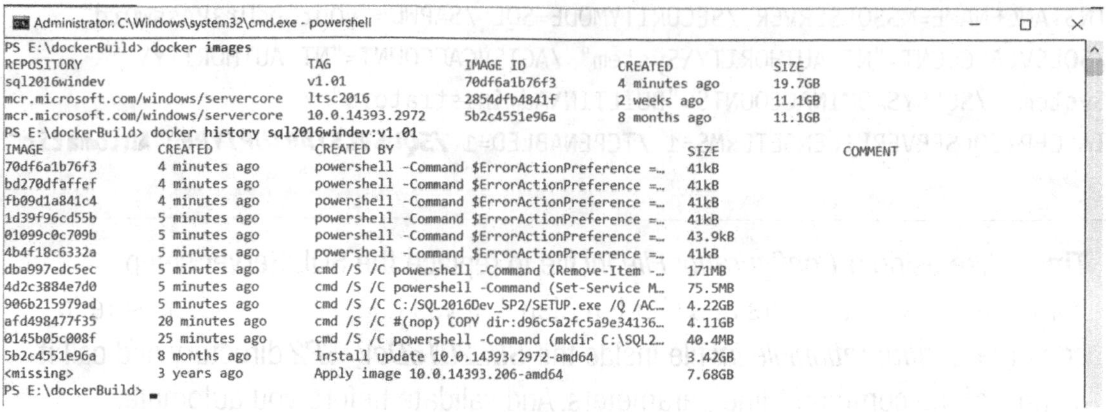

```
Administrator: C:\Windows\system32\cmd.exe - powershell                                                    —   □   ×
PS E:\dockerBuild> docker images
REPOSITORY                                   TAG                 IMAGE ID        CREATED          SIZE
sql2016windev                                v1.01               70df6a1b76f3    4 minutes ago    19.7GB
mcr.microsoft.com/windows/servercore         ltsc2016            2854dfb4841f    2 weeks ago      11.1GB
mcr.microsoft.com/windows/servercore         10.0.14393.2972     5b2c4551e96a    8 months ago     11.1GB
PS E:\dockerBuild> docker history sql2016windev:v1.01
IMAGE             CREATED           CREATED BY                                        SIZE           COMMENT
70df6a1b76f3      4 minutes ago     powershell -Command $ErrorActionPreference =…     41kB
bd270dfaffef      4 minutes ago     powershell -Command $ErrorActionPreference =…     41kB
fb09d1a841c4      4 minutes ago     powershell -Command $ErrorActionPreference =…     41kB
1d39f96cd55b      5 minutes ago     powershell -Command $ErrorActionPreference =…     41kB
01099c0c709b      5 minutes ago     powershell -Command $ErrorActionPreference =…     43.9kB
4b4f18c6332a      5 minutes ago     powershell -Command $ErrorActionPreference =…     41kB
dba997edc5ec      5 minutes ago     cmd /S /C powershell -Command (Remove-Item -…     171MB
4d2c3884e7d0      5 minutes ago     cmd /S /C powershell -Command (Set-Service M…     75.5MB
906b215979ad      5 minutes ago     cmd /S /C C:/SQL2016Dev_SP2/SETUP.exe /Q /AC…     4.22GB
afd498477f35      20 minutes ago    cmd /S /C #(nop) COPY dir:d96c5a2fc5a9e34136…     4.11GB
0145b05c008f      25 minutes ago    cmd /S /C powershell -Command (mkdir C:\SQL2…     40.4MB
5b2c4551e96a      8 months ago      Install update 10.0.14393.2972-amd64              3.42GB
<missing>         3 years ago       Apply image 10.0.14393.206-amd64                  7.68GB
PS E:\dockerBuild> _
```

Figure 9-7. *Listing the different filesystem layers for the custom SQL Server on Windows Docker image*

These file sizes affect the speed of pulling and pushing the filesystem layers as part of both the build process and the container runtime. Just running the *docker build* command with the custom *Dockerfile* took an average of 25 minutes in my test environment. And while you're not going to be running *docker build* commands every hour, you still need to worry about the image sizes and the disk space requirements.

The two common ways of optimizing the Dockerfile are by reducing the number of instructions and reducing the size of the filesystem layers. But before we look at reducing the number of instructions, let's see if we can identify some of the existing commands that can be rolled up into the other instructions. Take a look at Step 5:

```
#Step 5
RUN powershell -Command (Set-Service MSSQLSERVER -StartupType Automatic)
```

It simply calls the PowerShell command shell and sets the startup type of the *MSSQLSERVER* service to *Automatic*. We can roll this instruction up and include it as the */SQLSVCSTARTUPTYPE* parameter in Step 4 which looks something like this, with emphasis on the last parameter:

```
#Step 4
RUN C:/SQL2016Dev_SP2/SETUP.exe /Q /ACTION=INSTALL /UPDATEENABLED=True
/UPDATESOURCE=./SQLServer2016SP2CU11 /FEATURES=SQLENGINE /
```

```
INSTANCENAME=MSSQLSERVER /SECURITYMODE=SQL /SAPWD="yOurSecUr3PAsswOrd"
/SQLSVCACCOUNT="NT AUTHORITY\System" /AGTSVCACCOUNT="NT AUTHORITY\
System" /SQLSYSADMINACCOUNTS="BUILTIN\Administrators" /
IACCEPTSQLSERVERLICENSETERMS=1 /TCPENABLED=1 /SQLSVCSTARTUPTYPE="Automatic"
```

Tip   I like using a *ConfigurationFile.ini* file to replace the SQL Server setup command-line parameters and shorten Step 4. If you choose to do so, be sure to copy the *ConfigurationFile.ini* file inside the *SQL2016Dev_SP2* directory and call it as part of the command-line parameters. And validate before you automate.

The size savings for removing Step 5 – 75.5MB as per Figure 9-7 – is trivial compared to the overall size of the image. But it's a start. Evaluate existing instructions and see if you can roll them up into the other instructions. Once you've exhausted every possible instruction that you can roll up into other instructions, it's time to combine related instructions.

Take a look at Steps 4 and 6. Both use the *RUN* instruction. And since Step 2 is also a PowerShell command, why not use PowerShell as the default command shell? We can introduce a new *SHELL* instruction after Step 1 as follows:

```
SHELL ["powershell", "-Command"]
```

Because we can call Step 4 as a PowerShell command, we can combine it with Step 6 using a semicolon (;) character as follows, turning it into a single *RUN* instruction. I've also replaced the double quotes used in the parameter values of *setup.exe* to single quotes to avoid string misinterpretation. I don't want the double quotes to be interpreted as a special character within PowerShell.

```
#Step 4 and 6 combined in a single line
RUN C:/SQL2016Dev_SP2/SETUP.exe /Q /ACTION=INSTALL /UPDATEENABLED=True
/UPDATESOURCE=./SQLServer2016SP2CU11 /FEATURES=SQLENGINE /
INSTANCENAME=MSSQLSERVER /SECURITYMODE=SQL /SAPWD='yOurSecUr3PAsswOrd'
/SQLSVCACCOUNT='NT AUTHORITY\System' /AGTSVCACCOUNT='NT AUTHORITY\
System' /SQLSYSADMINACCOUNTS='BUILTIN\Administrators' /
IACCEPTSQLSERVERLICENSETERMS=1 /TCPENABLED=1 /SQLSVCSTARTUPTYPE='Automatic'
; Remove-Item -Path C:/SQL2016Dev_SP2 -Recurse -Force
```

A knowledge of the different Windows commands and PowerShell cmdlets will be helpful to know which *RUN* instructions you can combine. Refer to the list of Windows commands from *https://docs.microsoft.com/en-us/windows-server/ administration/windows-commands/windows-commands.* You can also run the Get-Command PowerShell cmdlet to retrieve all the native PowerShell cmdlets available in your Windows installation.

What else? We can remove Steps 7, 8, and 9 and the two *ENV* instructions. I really don't like the *start.ps1* PowerShell script since I already provided the required parameters – *SA_PASSWORD* and *ACCEPT_EULA* – in the *setup.exe, /SAPWD* and */ IACCEPTSQLSERVERLICENSETERMS*, respectively. Plus, I don't have any sample databases on Azure Blob storage that I need to attach. And I can replace Step 10 with a call to the SQL Server executable using the *ENTRYPOINT* instruction. The following is how the modified, trimmed down *Dockerfile* would look like:

```
#Step 1
FROM mcr.microsoft.com/windows/servercore:10.0.14393.2972

#Step 1A - switch the default command shell to PowerShell
SHELL ["powershell", "-Command"]

#Step 2
RUN mkdir C:/SQL2016Dev_SP2

#Step 3
COPY /SQL2016Dev_SP2 C:/SQL2016Dev_SP2

#Step 4 and 6 combined in a single line
RUN C:/SQL2016Dev_SP2/SETUP.exe /Q /ACTION=INSTALL /UPDATEENABLED=True
/UPDATESOURCE=./SQLServer2016SP2CU11 /FEATURES=SQLENGINE /
INSTANCENAME=MSSQLSERVER /SECURITYMODE=SQL /SAPWD='y0urSecUr3PAssw0rd'
/SQLSVCACCOUNT='NT AUTHORITY\System' /AGTSVCACCOUNT='NT AUTHORITY\
System' /SQLSYSADMINACCOUNTS='BUILTIN\Administrators' /
IACCEPTSQLSERVERLICENSETERMS=1 /TCPENABLED=1 /SQLSVCSTARTUPTYPE='Automatic'
; Remove-Item -Path C:/SQL2016Dev_SP2 -Recurse -Force

#New Step 10
ENTRYPOINT ["C:/Program Files/Microsoft SQL Server/MSSQL13.MSSQLSERVER/
MSSQL/Binn/sqlservr.exe"]
```

Figure 9-8 shows the result of the *docker history* command for the updated custom SQL Server on Windows image, including the image size difference between the first image and the new image using the modified *Dockerfile*. We've reduced the size of the image from 19.7GB to 17.9GB and from 12 instructions down to 6 instructions. Not bad.

```
Administrator: C:\Windows\system32\cmd.exe - powershell                                                    —    □    ×
PS E:\dockerBuild> docker images
REPOSITORY                              TAG                    IMAGE ID        CREATED          SIZE
sql2016windev                           v1.02                  4378718befd6    6 minutes ago    17.9GB
sql2016windev                           v1.01                  70df6a1b76f3    35 minutes ago   19.7GB
mcr.microsoft.com/windows/servercore    ltsc2016               2854dfb4841f    2 weeks ago      11.1GB
mcr.microsoft.com/windows/servercore    10.0.14393.2972        5b2c4551e96a    8 months ago     11.1GB
PS E:\dockerBuild> docker history sql2016windev:v1.02
IMAGE           CREATED          CREATED BY                                     SIZE       COMMENT
4378718befd6    6 minutes ago    powershell -Command #(nop)  ENTRYPOINT ["C:/…  41kB
24b9011c2439    6 minutes ago    powershell -Command C:/SQL2016Dev_SP2/SETUP.…  2.67GB
87d0bb412d5e    19 minutes ago   powershell -Command #(nop) COPY dir:d96c5a2f…  4.11GB
8a298eb00468    24 minutes ago   powershell -Command mkdir C:/SQL2016Dev_SP2    40.4MB
a81d6d8d53b2    24 minutes ago   powershell -Command #(nop)  SHELL [powershel…  41kB
5b2c4551e96a    8 months ago     Install update 10.0.14393.2972-amd64           3.42GB
<missing>       3 years ago      Apply image 10.0.14393.206-amd64               7.68GB
PS E:\dockerBuild>
```

Figure 9-8. *Listing the image size and the different filesystem layers after making changes to the Dockerfile*

Like I said, we can't really do much to size of the Windows Server 2016 Core base image. It is what it is. You can remove another image layer by using the LTSC2016 image instead, but you're still dealing with an 11.1GB-sized image.

I've given you several ways to reduce the number of instructions to optimize the *Dockerfile* and the resulting image. Try it out as an exercise and think of other ways that you can roll up or combine instructions.

Tip   Should there be any issues when running the *docker build* command, you will end up with a stopped container. This container represents the step from which the build failed. If you want to keep your environment clean of unwanted containers, be sure to remove these stopped containers prior to fixing the issue and rerunning the build. Use the docker ps -a command to display the container used in the failed step and the *docker rm* command to remove it. You could also use the *prune* subcommand for specific Docker objects. For example, you can run the docker image prune command to remove all images that are not tagged nor referenced by any container (also called dangling images). You can also run the docker container prune command to delete stopped containers. Refer to *https://docs.docker.com/config/pruning/* for pruning unused Docker objects.

Summary

This chapter provides the foundation for building custom Docker images using the *Dockerfile*. You can use this chapter as a reference to build any custom Docker image so long as you know the base operating system and the application that you want to run. While the examples provided were for building a custom SQL Server on Windows image, it's the same *Dockerfile* using the same instructions. You can containerize a custom ASP. NET Core application running Windows Server Core or a .NET Core application running on Linux. Additional information about the *Dockerfile* can be found on *https://docs. docker.com/engine/reference/builder/*. In the next chapter, we will explore creating a custom SQL Server on Linux image. While the steps are similar to how you build a custom SQL Server on Windows image, the concepts provided in *Chapter 8* to install and configure SQL Server on Linux will be used as a pattern. We will spice it up a bit and include running scripts that contain additional customization like creating user databases or restoring from backups.

## CHAPTER 10

Creating Custom SQL Server on Linux Container Images

The secret to learning new technologies – or just about anything – is to never forget the ones you already know.

—Edwin M. Sarmiento

In the last chapter, you've learned how to combine the different instructions in a *Dockerfile* to create a custom SQL Server on Windows container. We'll be using what we've covered in the previous chapter to create a custom SQL Server on Linux Docker image. But because Linux is a little bit different from Windows, I will be introducing additional *Dockerfile* instructions. I'll also cover more details on further customizing your SQL Server on Linux image in preparation for deploying in either a development or production environment. So, let's dive right in.

Additional *Dockerfile* Instructions

If you analyze the *Dockerfile* created in the previous chapter, the instructions used were based on our understanding of installing and configuring SQL Server on a Windows environment. In *Chapter 8*, we looked at automating the installation of SQL Server on Linux. We'll translate the bash script for automating installation and configuration of SQL Server on Linux into a *Dockerfile*. But before we do that, let's look at some of the additional instructions that we need to consider.

© Edwin M Sarmiento 2020

E. M. Sarmiento, *The SQL Server DBA's Guide to Docker Containers*, https://doi.org/10.1007/978-1-4842-5826-2_10

The EXPOSE Instruction

The *EXPOSE* instruction tells the Docker daemon that the container you run based on the image will listen on the specified network port at runtime. The default is TCP but you can choose to define whether you want the container to use a UDP port. The format of the *EXPOSE* instruction is shown in the following. I'm pretty sure you know why the specified port number is used.

```
EXPOSE 1433
```

I used to think that the *EXPOSE* instruction was intended to publish the port that the container will be listening on during runtime. After all, isn't that what the word "expose" means in the context of computer networking? But that's not the case. The *EXPOSE* instruction is merely a "hint" to tell users of the image which port will be useful when a container is created and run. The Docker daemon doesn't do anything with that instruction by itself. In fact, if you are building a custom SQL Server on Linux image, you can simply ignore the *EXPOSE* instruction – like what we did with the SQL Server on Windows image – so long as the users of your image know that it is a default configuration of SQL Server and it listens on port 1433.

I'm sure you know where I'm going with this. It's like getting a smartphone without a user manual (although you might argue that no one actually reads the user manual). If you know how to use the smartphone, you don't need a manual. But what if you don't? That's where the user manual comes in. The *EXPOSE* instruction acts as additional metadata regarding a Docker image. You can check the *ExposedPorts* value under the *Config* section when you run the *docker inspect* command on the image you're reviewing as shown in Figure 10-1.

```
emsarmiento@centosdocker01:/tmp/dockerBuild
        "DockerVersion": "1.13.0",
        "Author": "dpgswdist@microsoft.com",
        "Config": {
            "Hostname": "4dcf0239b565",
            "Domainname": "",
            "User": "",
            "AttachStdin": false,
            "AttachStdout": false,
            "AttachStderr": false,
            "ExposedPorts": {
                "1433/tcp": {}
            },
            "Tty": false,
            "OpenStdin": false,
            "StdinOnce": false,
            "Env": [
                "PATH=/usr/local/sbin:/usr/local/bin:/usr/sbin:/usr/bin:/sbin:/bin"
            ],
            "Cmd": [
                "/opt/mssql/bin/sqlservr"
            ],
```

Figure 10-1. *ExposedPorts value of a publicly available SQL Server on Linux image*

What publishes the port that the application inside the container will be listening on is the *-p* parameter of the *docker run* command. Review the *docker run* command shown in the following with emphasis on the *-p* parameter:

```
docker run -e "ACCEPT_EULA=Y" -e "SA_PASSWORD=mYSecUr3PAssw0rd" --name
sqldevlinuxcon01 -p 1433:1433 -d -h linuxsqldev01 mcr.microsoft.com/mssql/
server:2017-CU14-ubuntu
```

This is the reason why we use the *-p* parameter – to expose SQL Server's port number inside the container so we can access it via the Docker hosts' port number via port mapping. But if we haven't worked with SQL Server nor do we have any idea what SQL Server is, we wouldn't know which default port number it listens on – hence, the use of the *EXPOSE* instruction.

Another use of the *EXPOSE* instruction is if you decide to configure SQL Server to use a nondefault port, let's say port 5000. The *EXPOSE* instruction can tell the users which port to publish when running the container. But the real value of having the *EXPOSE* instruction in your *Dockerfile* is by allowing containers to talk to each other without having to publish their port numbers using the *-p* parameter of the *docker run* command. I'll cover Docker networking in more detail in *Chapter 11*.

The VOLUME Instruction

The *VOLUME* instruction creates a mountpoint with the specified name inside the container and marks it as holding externally mounted volumes. The format of the *VOLUME* instruction is shown in the following:

```
VOLUME /var/opt/mssql/data
```

The mountpoints are dynamically generated when you first run a container from the image because there is no guarantee that the volume will be available on the Docker host where you intend to run the container on. And because of the nature of Docker containers being portable, the Docker volumes created during runtime will have a GUID-like name inside */var/lib/docker/volumes* directory on the host – you cannot specify a meaningful name. These Docker volumes are called *anonymous* volumes because Docker decides where to store the files and directories. And it can be difficult to access the volume over time. Anonymous volumes are not commonly used nowadays given that we already have named volumes. Review the "Docker Volumes" section in *Chapter 7* on how to configure volumes for use with SQL Server on containers. Figure 10-2 shows the name of the Docker volume created when you run a container from an image that has a *VOLUME* instruction.

Figure 10-2. *Example of the name of a Docker volume created with the VOLUME instruction*

The USER Instruction

Back in SQL Server 2017, the *USER* instruction wasn't really meaningful given that the publicly available SQL Server on Linux images were configured to run as *root*. Given that *root* can do anything, running containers as *root* means anyone who can maliciously access containers can further exploit the host. We don't want that for security reasons. Hence, we want to run containers as a user with limited privileges.

The *USER* instruction sets the username (or UID) and optionally the user group (or GID) to use when running the container. But in order to do so, the custom image needs to have instructions that restrict execution of either the *CMD* or *ENTRYPOINT* instructions. The format of the *USER* instruction is shown in the following:

```
USER mssql
```

We'll explore this in more detail later in this chapter. For now, let's start building a custom SQL Server on Linux image.

Build the Custom SQL Server on Linux Image

We will save our *Dockerfile* in the */tmp/dockerBuild* directory of the Linux Docker host. But before we create the *Dockerfile*, let's first define the steps to install and configure a SQL Server 2017 instance in a CentOS Linux image:

1. Start from the publicly available CentOS Linux 7.6.1810. Keep in mind that CentOS is not a supported Linux distribution. I'm merely using this as an example for building development environments. If you want to deploy a SQL Server on Linux container in production, your base Linux image should be one of the supported distributions – Red Hat Enterprise Linux, SUSE, or Ubuntu.

2. Create a *repo* file containing the location of the SQL Server 2017 installation packages.

3. Install the SQL Server 2017 packages.

4. Configure SQL Server 2017 on Linux.

5. Set working directory for running the SQL Server process.

6. Run the SQL Server process.

Step 4 will contain additional details as we go through creating the *Dockerfile*. What's important is we have a high-level overview of what we need to do to create our custom SQL Server on Linux image. Let's translate the six steps outlined earlier into a *Dockerfile*.

I'll use the item numbers as steps and identify them in the comments. I've also excluded *LABEL* instructions for brevity, but make sure you include them in every *Dockerfile* you create:

```
#Step 1
FROM centos:7.6.1810
```

```
#Step 2
RUN curl -o /etc/yum.repos.d/mssql-server.repo https://packages.microsoft.
com/config/rhel/7/mssql-server-2017.repo
```

```
#Step 3
RUN yum install -y mssql-server
```

```
#Step 4
#Create the /var/opt/mssql/data directory to store the databases
RUN mkdir -p /var/opt/mssql/data
```

```
#Recursively change permissions of directories and files inside
# /var/opt/mssql and /etc/pwd from user to group
RUN chmod -R g=u /var/opt/mssql /etc/passwd
```

```
#Tell user what port this container will use
EXPOSE 1433
```

```
#Step 5
ENV PATH=${PATH}:/opt/mssql/bin
```

```
#Step 6
CMD sqlservr
```

The corresponding *Dockerfile* to use an Ubuntu Linux 16.04 base image is shown in the following. It will give you a few hints as to why I prefer RHEL/CentOS over Ubuntu. Refer to the steps to install the required dependencies in Ubuntu in *Chapter 3* and SQL Server on Ubuntu in *Chapter 8*. I've included them as Steps 1a and 1b:

```
#Step 1
FROM ubuntu:16.04
```

```
#Step 1a-install Ubuntu packages needed for installing SQL Server
```

```
RUN apt-get update && apt-get install -y curl apt-utils apt-transport-https
software-properties-common

#Step 1b-download and install public GPG keys for SQL Server
RUN curl https://packages.microsoft.com/keys/microsoft.asc | apt-key add -

#Step 2
RUN add-apt-repository "deb [arch=amd64] https://packages.microsoft.com/
ubuntu/16.04/mssql-server-2017 xenial main"
RUN apt-get update

#Step 3
RUN apt-get install -y mssql-server

#Step 4
RUN mkdir -p /var/opt/mssql/data
RUN chmod -R g=u /var/opt/mssql /etc/passwd

EXPOSE 1433


#Step 5
ENV PATH=${PATH}:/opt/mssql/bin

#Step 6
CMD sqlservr
```

Replace Step 2 with the appropriate *repo* file if you want to install SQL Server 2019. Build the custom image using the following docker build command:

```
docker build -t customsql2017centoslinux:v1.0 .
```

Didn't I say I prefer working with SQL Server on Linux images? That's because they take less time to build and consume less storage space. Figure 10-3 shows the size of this custom SQL Server on Linux image – 1.3+GB compared to the 17.9GB SQL Server on Windows image created in the previous chapter. And look at the sizes of the CentOS Linux 7.6.1810 and Ubuntu Linux 16.04 base images.

```
emsarmiento@centosdocker01:/tmp/dockerBuild                                          —    □    ×
[emsarmiento@centosdocker01 dockerBuild]$ docker images
REPOSITORY                        TAG                IMAGE ID           CREATED          SIZE
customsql2017ubuntulinux          v1.0               b0d09e31f6a4       49 seconds ago   1.32GB
customsql2017centoslinux          v1.0               d6dc25da08e6       8 minutes ago    1.31GB
ubuntu                            16.04              96da9143fb18       10 days ago      124MB
mcr.microsoft.com/mssql/server    2017-CU14-ubuntu   644ca19cb10d       10 months ago    1.38GB
centos                            7.6.1810           f1cb7c7d58b7       10 months ago    202MB
[emsarmiento@centosdocker01 dockerBuild]$ █
```

Figure 10-3. *Size of the custom SQL Server on Linux image*

Pretty straightforward, don't you think? We can build on this by adding the configuration settings we've made in Chapter 8 such as enabling the SQL Server Agent, setting trace flags, and so on as additional instructions in Step 4. We don't need to change the default locations for the database and backup files because we can run a container and mount the */var/opt/mssql* directory to a Docker volume. Also, configuring the firewall won't be necessary, Docker will work its magic to update *iptables* when you run the container. The only thing we need to worry about is setting trace flags during startup – and only if you need to. We can replace Step 6 with an *ENTRYPOINT* instruction instead of a *CMD* instruction and pass SQL Server startup parameters as part of the *docker run* command.

Let's look at several ways to tweak our custom SQL Server on Linux image by changing the *Dockerfile*. I'll only introduce specific changes to the steps so you can play around with these changes as you see fit.

Installing a Specific SQL Server Version

If you noticed, we have been installing the latest version of SQL Server that we wanted – including the latest update (CU19 for SQL Server 2017 and CU1 for SQL Server 2019 at the time of writing). While it is highly recommended to always keep your SQL Server installations updated, you may need a specific version because that's the one you've tested with your applications. Let's say you want to install SQL Server 2017 CU14 because the standardized image that you want to build needs this specific version. You certainly don't want to create a custom SQL Server on Linux image that contains anything higher than CU14. You can modify Step 3 to install a specific package that refers to the version of SQL Server that you want to install. You can check the specific SQL Server 2017 package from *https://packages.microsoft.com/rhel/7/mssql-server-2017/* (for RHEL and CentOS 7) or *https://packages.microsoft.com/ubuntu/16.04/mssql-server-2017/ pool/main/m/mssql-server/* (for Ubuntu 16.04). Or you can run the following command to list all the available packages:

```
yum --showduplicates list mssql-server #for RHEL/CentOS
apt -a list mssql-server #for Ubuntu
```

The results of this command will depend on the *repo* file you defined in Step 2. Figure 10-4 displays all the packages available for SQL Server 2017 on RHEL.

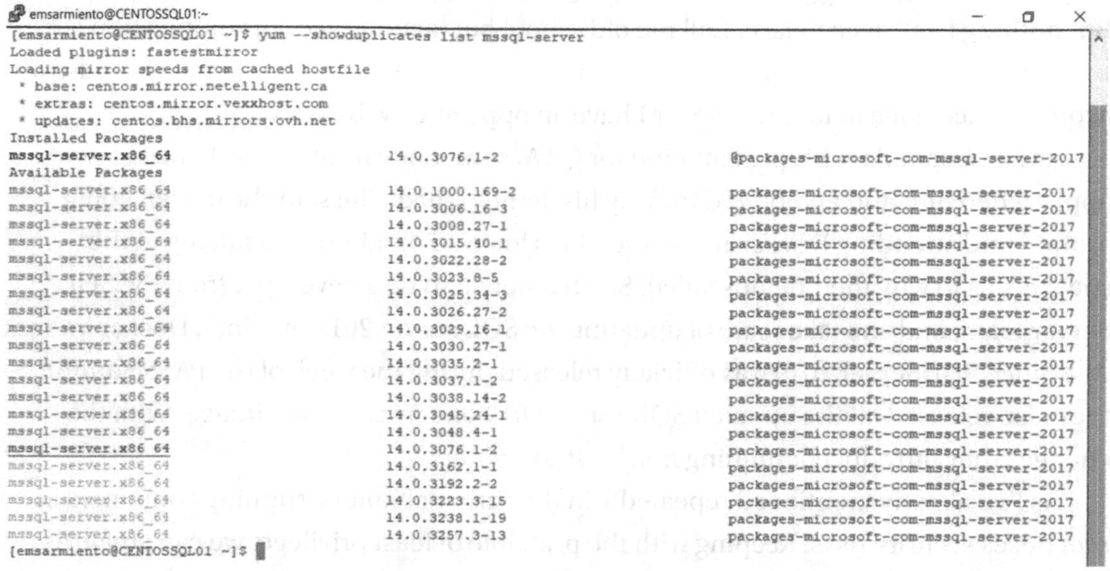

Figure 10-4. *Different packages for SQL Server 2017 on RHEL*

You can use the following command to install SQL Server 2017 CU14:

```
sudo yum install -y mssql-server-14.0.3076.1-2 #for RHEL/CentOS
sudo apt-get install -y mssql-server=14.0.3076.1-2 #for Ubuntu
```

All you have to do now is to replace Step 3 in the *Dockerfile* with the following command, replacing the appropriate package management command for the Linux distro that you're working with:

```
#Step 3
RUN yum install -y mssql-server-14.0.3076.1-2 #for RHEL/CentOS
RUN apt-get install -y mssql-server=14.0.3076.1-2 #for Ubuntu
```

Creating a Custom Image That Runs As Non-root

I attended a presentation on Kubernetes Architecture by Microsoft MVP Anthony Nocentino at the 2019 PASS Summit because it's the only way I'm 100% sure I can catch up with him in a conference this big. Most communications nowadays happen virtually – through email, instant messaging, social media, phone, or conference calls. But nothing beats face to face. Call me old school but face-to-face communication is how we build quality relationships. And I do my best to catch up with family, friends, and acquaintances face to face whenever I have an opportunity to do so.

As he wrapped up his presentation for Q&A, somebody from the audience approached him and apologized for why his demos failed. She said she'd been going around and attending Docker-related sessions focused on Linux and talking to the speakers as to why their demos failed. She happened to be a developer from the SQL Server team, and she takes care of updating the SQL Server 2019 on Linux Docker image. And since SQL Server 2019 was officially released during the week of the PASS Summit, they also released all the updated SQL Server 2019 on Linux Docker images with the changes they introduced: running non-*root* containers.

As I've already mentioned repeatedly in the earlier chapters, running containers as *root* poses security risks. Keeping with the principle of least privilege, we can create a custom SQL Server on Linux image that runs as non-*root*. The publicly available SQL Server 2017 on Linux images were all created with the assumption that the container will be running as *root*. As SQL Server 2019 was released, Microsoft also released a *Dockerfile* that contains modifications to the existing public images so they can run containers as a non-*root* user. Have a look at the *Dockerfile* here: *https://github.com/microsoft/mssql-docker/blob/master/linux/preview/examples/mssql-server-linux-non-root/Dockerfile*. We'll explore the additional instructions and what they do. Refer to the *Dockerfile* for the line numbers.

Line 10: *RUN useradd -M -s /bin/bash -u 10001 -g 0 mssql*

This instruction runs the *useradd* command to add a new user named *mssql* to the existing SQL Server 2017 on Linux image. The *-M* parameter will skip creating a home directory for the new user. The *-s* parameter specifies using the */bin/bash* as the login shell for the user. The *-u* parameter specifies the users UID value – 10001 – while the -g parameter specifies the GID value, 0. Keep in mind that this user is created inside the container, not the host.

Tip   In my testing with SQL Server 2019 (and SQL Server 2017 on Ubuntu), this instruction can cause the image build process to fail – but not so with SQL Server 2017 on RHEL/CentOS which I find weird. Part of the SQL Server on Linux installation process is the creation of a user and group named *mssql*. The *UID* and *username* values must be unique. Since the *mssql* user already exists, albeit with a different UID, the command fails. Adding a user that already exists will throw an error and cause the image build process to fail. Test accordingly. You can exclude this line when creating a custom SQL Server 2019 on Linux (or SQL Server 2017 on Ubuntu) image. However, doing so would mean accepting the *mssql* user with a different UID value (999) that gets created during the installation process. This UID value may already exist on your Linux Docker host and can cause confusion as to who is really running the container. Refer to Figure 10-10. Another option is to name it something else but use the 10001 UID value.

Line 11: *RUN mkdir -p -m 770 /var/opt/mssql && chgrp -R 0 /var/opt/mssql*

This instruction runs the *mkdir* command to create a new directory named */var/opt/mssql* with the *-m* parameter assigning 770 permissions – RWX for owner, RWX for group, and no permissions for others. The && characters simply append the *chgrp* command instead of creating a new *RUN* instruction. This looks a lot like Step 4 but with more granular permissions. Plus, appending commands instead of creating another instruction is an optimization trick that we can implement in our *Dockerfile*.

Note   If you follow the sequence of the commands in the *Dockerfile*, it's the *root* user that implicitly creates the */var/opt/mssql* directory. This means running the *chgrp* command is simply assigning the same group permissions from *root*. That's not going to work if we assign the *mssql* user to run the *sqlservr* process. Either we let the *mssql* user create the */var/opt/mssql* directory or explicitly change the ownership to the *mssql* user using the command `chown -R mssql:0 /var/opt/mssql`. The available *Dockerfile* from Microsoft works, but the image is built from an existing SQL Server on Linux image (note the *FROM* instruction isn't a base operating system image). I'm not sure if the script that they used to build the base image has already included making the *mssql* user as the owner of the SQL Server directories.

I rewrote the instruction to explicitly assign the *mssql* user ownership of the */var/opt/mssql* directory as shown in the following. I've also optimized it and combined multiple commands in a single RUN instruction instead of having multiple lines:

```
RUN mkdir -p -m 770 /var/opt/mssql && chown -R mssql:0 /var/opt/mssql &&
chgrp -R 0 /var/opt/mssql
```

Line 15: *RUN setcap 'cap_net_bind_service+ep' /opt/mssql/bin/sqlservr*

This instruction runs the *setcap* command to set Linux capabilities on a file, in this case the *sqlservr* executable. The capability *cap_net_bind_service* binds the *sqlservr* executable to a low-numbered port number (anything below 1024) without running as *root*. The +*ep* means we are assigning (the + operator) *Explicit* and *Permitted* capabilities.

Note   Linux capabilities are a security concept. They provide a process a subset of the available *root* privileges. You don't want to grant a process full *root* privileges (e.g., the docker container process), or you run the risk of exploiting that process and taking over the entire machine. A process may need special privileges to perform its function, but simply granting it *root* access is a little bit too much. So, you grant the Linux process the appropriate capability it needs to do its work. The example in Line 15 grants the *sqlservr* process the *cap_net_bind_service* capability to bind it to a low-numbered port number. It's much safer than granting it *root* privileges.

Line 19: *RUN setcap 'cap_sys_ptrace+ep' /opt/mssql/bin/paldumper*

Similar to Line 15, this instruction runs the *setcap* command to set the *cap_sys_ptrace* capability to the *paldumper* file. You can probably guess what this file is just from its name – it's a SQL Server utility to generate core dumps, mainly for troubleshooting purposes. This has to be explicitly defined because we will no longer run the container as *root*, yet we need *root* privileges to perform troubleshooting.

Line 20: *RUN setcap 'cap_sys_ptrace+ep' /usr/bin/gdb*

This is similar to Line 19 but for the *gdb* file, short for GNU debugger which is the most common debugging utility for Linux.

Line 25: *RUN mkdir -p /etc/ld.so.conf.d && touch /etc/ld.so.conf.d/mssql.conf*

This instruction creates a *ldconfig* file using the *touch* command that SQL Server will use – *mssql.conf*. The *ldconfig* command is used to create necessary links and cache for shared libraries. Shared libraries are libraries that are loaded by programs when they start. The location of these shared libraries is stored in the environment variable *LD_ LIBRARY_PATH*. The next few instructions further explain why this is needed.

Line 26: *RUN echo -e "# mssql libs\n/opt/mssql/lib" >> /etc/ld.so.conf.d/mssql.conf*

Building on Line 25, a new line containing *# mssql libs\n/opt/mssql/lib* is added to the */etc/ld.so.conf.d/mssql.conf* file. The *mssql.conf* file is read to search for the location of the shared libraries used, in this case *libs* and */opt/mssql/lib* (the *\n* is used to introduce a new line). The reason for this is because the *setcap* commands used in earlier instructions remove the *LD_LIBRARY_PATH* and other environment variables that control dynamic linking. This is for security reasons. Since you will run the container with a non-*root* user, all unsecured environment variables will be removed, rendering running *paldumper* and *gdb* during troubleshooting useless.

Line 27: *RUN ldconfig*

This instruction runs the *ldconfig* command to apply the configuration settings created in Lines 25 and 26.

Line 29: *USER mssql*

This instruction sets the *mssql* as the user when running the container.

The following *Dockerfile* integrates these lines to create a custom SQL Server on CentOS Linux image that runs as non-*root*. I've added step and line numbers as comments to identify the added instructions:

```
#Step 1
FROM centos:7.6.1810

#Step 2
RUN curl -o /etc/yum.repos.d/mssql-server.repo https://packages.microsoft.
com/config/rhel/7/mssql-server-2017.repo

#Step 3
RUN yum install -y mssql-server

#Line 10–change to a different user like mssql2 if you are
#installing SQL Server 2019 or SQL Server 2017 on Ubuntu
RUN useradd -M -s /bin/bash -u 10001 -g 0 mssql

#Modified Line 11
```

```
RUN mkdir -p -m 770 /var/opt/mssql && chown -R mssql:0 /var/opt/mssql &&
chgrp -R 0 /var/opt/mssql

#Lines 15, 19, and 20
RUN setcap 'cap_net_bind_service+ep' /opt/mssql/bin/sqlservr
RUN setcap 'cap_sys_ptrace+ep' /opt/mssql/bin/paldumper
RUN setcap 'cap_sys_ptrace+ep' /usr/bin/gdb

#Lines 25, 26, and 27
RUN mkdir -p /etc/ld.so.conf.d && touch /etc/ld.so.conf.d/mssql.conf
RUN echo -e "# mssql libs\n/opt/mssql/lib" >> /etc/ld.so.conf.d/mssql.conf
RUN ldconfig

#Tell user what port this container will use
EXPOSE 1433

#Line 29
USER mssql

#Step 5
ENV PATH=${PATH}:/opt/mssql/bin

#Step 6
CMD sqlservr
```

Save the *Dockerfile* and build the image. Once completed, you can use this custom
SQL Server on Linux image for running containers as non-*root*.

Running a Container As Non-root

By default, running a container using the *docker run* command will run it as *root*. But
now that the custom image you've built no longer runs as *root*, running a container
from the custom image means that while the *root* still owns the container's read-write
filesystem layer (the Docker daemon runs as *root* and it creates the read-write filesystem
layer), it no longer runs as *root*. Run the following *docker container inspect* command
to check the container's read-write filesystem layer. I used the *--format* parameter to
keep the result of the *docker container inspect* command clean and only display the

UpperDir directory – the directory containing the read-write filesystem layer. Replace *sqldevlinuxcon01* with the name of your container. Refer to *Chapter 5* for a quick review of the filesystem layers and their location.

```
docker container inspect sqldevlinuxcon01 --format '{{.GraphDriver.
Data.UpperDir}}'
```

Tip   The *--format* parameter is very handy for displaying only the information you need from the JSON output of the *docker container inspect* or any *docker* commands that return a JSON output. The reality is all the *docker* commands return a JSON output, hence why a lot of the commands have a *--format* parameter. It's just that the most common commands already have a template applied to them. You can format the JSON output yourself by applying a Golang package template since Docker was written using the Go programming language. Check out the Golang package template from *https://golang.org/pkg/text/template/*.

You can pass this as a parameter to the *ls* command to see the owner of the directory as shown in the following. Be sure to prefix the command with *sudo* as the *root* owns the */var/lib/docker* directory. Figure 10-5 shows the owner of the directory – it is still *root*.

```
sudo ls -ld "$(docker container inspect sqldevlinuxcon01 --format
'{{.GraphDriver.Data.UpperDir}}')"
```

Figure 10-5. *root still owns the container's filesystem layer*

But if you look at the process that runs *sqlservr* from the Linux Docker host using the following command, you will see that it no longer runs as *root*. Figure 10-6 shows the *UID 10001* as the user ID that runs the *sqlservr* process. This is the user ID we assigned when we created the *mssql* user using *Line 10* in the *Dockerfile*.

```
ps aux | grep sqlservr
```

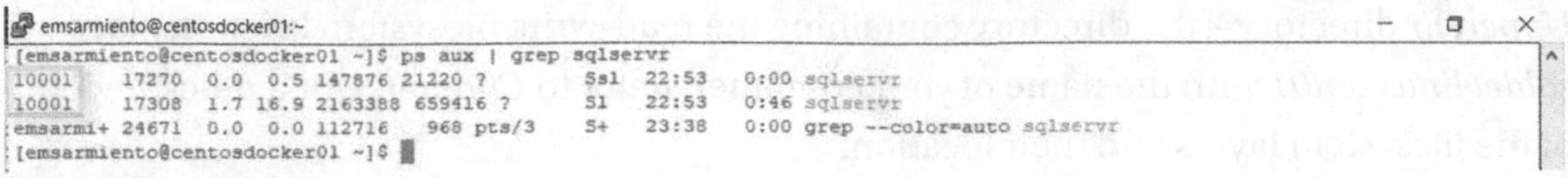

```
emsarmiento@centosdocker01:~                                                    —   □   ×
[emsarmiento@centosdocker01 ~]$ ps aux | grep sqlservr
10001    17270  0.0  0.5 147876 21220 ?        Ssl  22:53   0:00 sqlservr
10001    17308  1.7 16.9 2163388 659416 ?      Sl   22:53   0:46 sqlservr
emsarmi+ 24671  0.0  0.0 112716   968 pts/3    S+   23:38   0:00 grep --color=auto sqlservr
[emsarmiento@centosdocker01 ~]$ 
```

Figure 10-6. *UID 10001 runs the sqlservr process in the Linux Docker host*

You can confirm that the container also runs as the *mssql* user by running the following *docker exec* command passing the previous command:

```
docker exec -it sqldevlinuxcon01 ps aux | grep sqlservr
```

You can also run the following *docker container inspect* command:

```
docker container inspect sqldevlinuxcon01 --format '{{.Config.User}}
{{.Name}}'
```

Figure 10-7 shows the *mssql* user that runs the *sqlservr* process inside the container.

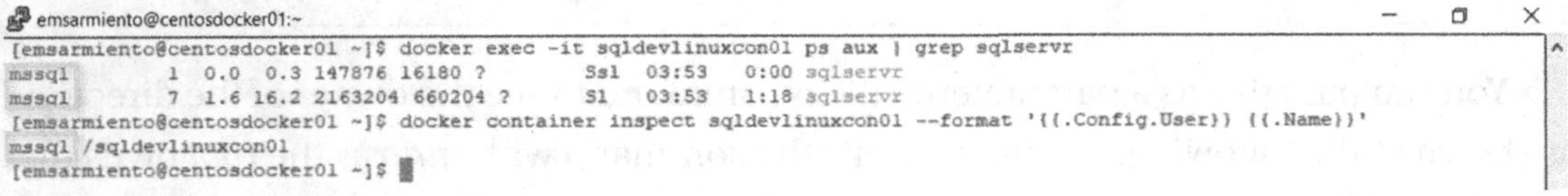

```
emsarmiento@centosdocker01:~                                                    —   □   ×
[emsarmiento@centosdocker01 ~]$ docker exec -it sqldevlinuxcon01 ps aux | grep sqlservr
mssql        1  0.0  0.3 147876 16180 ?        Ssl  03:53   0:00 sqlservr
mssql        7  1.6 16.2 2163204 660204 ?      Sl   03:53   1:18 sqlservr
[emsarmiento@centosdocker01 ~]$ docker container inspect sqldevlinuxcon01 --format '{{.Config.User}} {{.Name}}'
mssql /sqldevlinuxcon01
[emsarmiento@centosdocker01 ~]$ 
```

Figure 10-7. *mssql user runs the sqlservr process in the container*

Inspecting the container's read-write filesystem layer for the ownership of the files and directories confirms this as shown in Figure 10-8.

```
emsarmiento@centosdocker01:/var/lib/docker/overlay2/3ec7fe6d3f947c2eedca7556a8d1ecff1de74e4d3baeae47e9df3f7d32cabf52/diff          —  □  ×
[root@centosdocker01 /]# docker container inspect sqldevlinuxcon01 --format '{{.GraphDriver.Data.UpperDir}}'
/var/lib/docker/overlay2/3ec7fe6d3f947c2eedca7556a8d1ecff1de74e4d3baeae47e9df3f7d32cabf52/diff
[root@centosdocker01 /]# cd /var/lib/docker/overlay2/3ec7fe6d3f947c2eedca7556a8d1ecff1de74e4d3baeae47e9df3f7d32cab
f52/diff
[root@centosdocker01 diff]# ls -ltR
.:
total 0
drwxr-xr-x. 3 root root 17 Dec  4  2018 var                              Owned by root

./var:
total 0
drwxr-xr-x. 3 root root 19 Jan 30 18:13 opt

./var/opt:
total 0                                                              Owned by mssql user
drwxr-xr-x. 6 10001 root 59 Jan 30 19:05 mssql                          with UID 10001

./var/opt/mssql:
total 0
drwxr-xr-x. 2 10001 root 156 Jan 30 19:05 data
drwxr-xr-x. 2 10001 root 178 Jan 30 19:05 log
drwxr-xr-x. 2 10001 root  25 Jan 30 19:05 secrets

./var/opt/mssql/data:
total 53120
-rw-r-----. 1 10001 root   524288 Jan 30 19:05 msdblog.ldf
-rw-r-----. 1 10001 root  8388608 Jan 30 19:05 modellog.ldf
-rw-r-----. 1 10001 root  2097152 Jan 30 19:05 mastlog.ldf
-rw-r-----. 1 10001 root 14024704 Jan 30 19:05 msdbdata.mdf
-rw-r-----. 1 10001 root  8388608 Jan 30 19:05 tempdb.mdf
-rw-r-----. 1 10001 root  8388608 Jan 30 19:05 templog.ldf
-rw-r-----. 1 10001 root  8388608 Jan 30 19:05 model.mdf
-rw-r-----. 1 10001 root  4194304 Jan 30 19:05 master.mdf
```

Figure 10-8. *mssql user with UID 10001 owns the directories*

The reason why only the user ID value is displayed in Figures 10-6 and 10-8 is because we didn't create the *mssql* user with the corresponding user ID value on the Linux Docker host. I highly recommend creating the *mssql* user with the same UID value on the Linux Docker host so you can easily map it to the user running inside the container. Use the following command to create the user on the Linux Docker host:

```
sudo useradd -M -s /bin/bash -u 10001 -g 0 mssql
```

Rerunning the command used to show Figure 10-6 will no longer display a UID value but a user-friendly name.

The one thing that you have to be very careful of is the assignment of the UID value for the user account that you're creating inside the container. There's a reason Microsoft decided to use UID 10001 for the *mssql* user – the value is large enough to prevent any possible conflicts on the Linux Docker host. Keep in mind that the containers share the same kernel as the Docker host. The Linux kernel is responsible for managing the UID and GID space, and these are used to determine if requested privileges should be granted. When we created the *mssql* user in *Line 10* of the *Dockerfile*, the UID is checked against the Linux kernel to see if it already exists. If it does, it will just use the existing UID. If it doesn't, it gets created in an isolated UID space that only lives in the context of the container. When the container is created, the Docker daemon creates the read-write filesystem layer in the Linux Docker host via the *root* user. When we granted the *mssql* user ownership of the */var/opt/mssql* directory, the Linux kernel of the Docker host checks if a process has permissions to make modifications to the files inside the directory. The UID value is used for checking, not the username. That's why Figure 10-8 shows a UID value and not a username. However, if an existing Linux user in the Docker host has the same UID value as the one you used inside the container, the user in the Linux Docker host wins. Figure 10-9 demonstrates this. The Linux user *emsarmiento* has a UID value of 1000 in my Linux Docker host. I fat-fingered *Line 10* in the *Dockerfile* and assigned a UID value of 1000 for the *mssql* user – same as the user *emsarmiento* – instead of 10001.

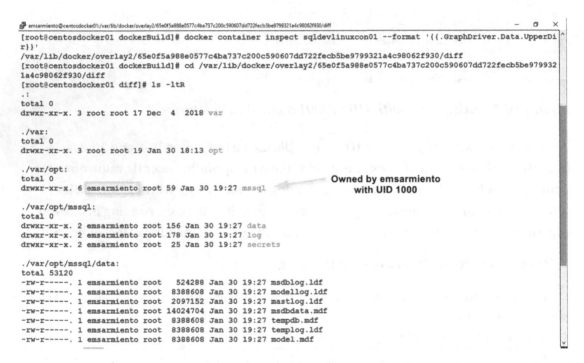

Figure 10-9. *emsarmiento user with UID 1000 owns the directories, not mssql*

You can confirm this by checking the SQL Server process running inside the container and on the Linux Docker host. Figure 10-10 shows the same UID used in the container as what's on the Linux Docker host. You might think that they're different users because of the different names. The truth is they're the same UID.

```
emsarmiento@centosdocker01:/tmp/dockerBuild                                                    —   □   ×
[emsarmiento@centosdocker01 dockerBuild]$ cat Dockerfile | grep 1000     UID of mssql user
RUN useradd -M -s /bin/bash -u 1000 -g 0 mssql                           defined in Dockerfile
[emsarmiento@centosdocker01 dockerBuild]$ cat /etc/passwd | grep 1000              UID of emsarmiento user
emsarmiento:x:1000:1000:Edwin M Sarmiento:/home/emsarmiento:/bin/bash              in the Linux Docker host
[emsarmiento@centosdocker01 dockerBuild]$ docker exec -it sqldevlinuxcon01 ps aux | grep sqlservr
mssql        1  0.0  0.5 147876 20576 ?       Ssl  00:27   0:00 sqlservr      process inside container
mssql        7  1.6 17.0 2160000 661580 ?     Sl   00:27   0:20 sqlservr
[emsarmiento@centosdocker01 dockerBuild]$ ps aux | grep sqlservr
emsarmi+  9575  0.0  0.5 147876 20576 ?       Ssl  19:27   0:00 sqlservr      process on Linux Docker host
emsarmi+  9635  1.6 17.0 2159908 661588 ?     Sl   19:27   0:20 sqlservr
emsarmi+ 13295  0.0  0.0 112712   968 pts/0   S+   19:47   0:00 grep --color=auto sqlservr
[emsarmiento@centosdocker01 dockerBuild]$
```

Figure 10-10. *Effect of using a UID on the container that already exists on the Linux Docker host*

Tip   Properly document all the users you create when building custom Docker images. This becomes helpful not only for running containers as non-*root* but also for security and auditing. In large enterprises where there is a separate team that manages the Docker infrastructure, informing them about non-*root* users running containers can help them answer security-related questions from auditors.

Non-root User and Docker Volumes

In *Chapter 7*, we looked at storing SQL Server databases in Docker volumes for persisting data. But back then, the *root* user owns the directories created inside the Docker volume. Figure 10-11 shows the directory structure and ownership of a SQL Server 2017 on Linux image running as *root* that leverages Docker volumes.

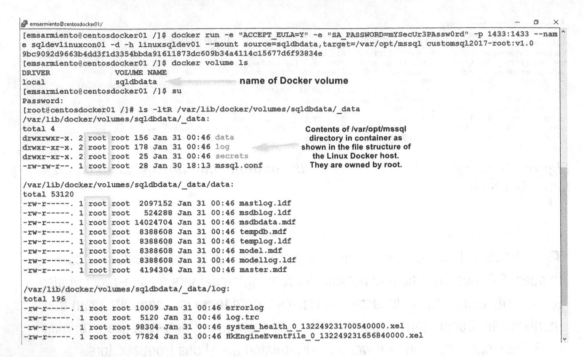

Figure 10-11. *Filesystem ownership on Docker volume when container is run as root*

Following the steps outlined in *Chapter 7* for performing a smart update or upgrade of a container that ran as *root* with another one that doesn't, you will end up with a *Permission denied (13)* error as shown in Figure 10-12. Not so smart after all, huh?

```
emsarmiento@centosdocker01:/                                                          —  □  ×
[emsarmiento@centosdocker01 /]$ docker stop sqldevlinuxcon01
sqldevlinuxcon01
[emsarmiento@centosdocker01 /]$ docker run -e "ACCEPT_EULA=Y" -e "SA_PASSWORD=mYSecUr3PAssw0rd" -p 1433:1433 --nam
e sqldevlinuxcon02 -d -h linuxsqldev01 --mount source=sqldbdata,target=/var/opt/mssql customsql2019-nonroot:v1.0
a7eb4361c2ec19984ac65fadcf2356852f6d37dd7e5a35b2360569b45f658590
[emsarmiento@centosdocker01 /]$ docker logs sqldevlinuxcon02
sqlservr: Unable to open /var/opt/mssql/.system/instance_id: Permission denied (13)
sqlservr: Unable to open /var/opt/mssql/.system//instance id: Permission denied (13)

[emsarmiento@centosdocker01 /]$ ▌
```

Figure 10-12. *Filesystem ownership error on Docker volume when a non-root container is run as root*

That's because the *sqlservr* process inside the non-*root* container is trying to access the database files inside the Docker volume that the *root* user owns. It's like running SQL Server on Windows with a specific Active Directory domain account and then changing that service account with another one that does not have read-write access to the system and user databases – SQL Server will not start.

> **Tip** If you've done this before and did not experience this issue, why are you granting the SQL Server service account administrator privileges? You're supposed to restrict permissions of the SQL Server service account, not give it unlimited access. I'm sick and tired of seeing SQL Server service accounts running as Active Directory domain administrators. Don't be one of those DBAs. Follow the guidelines in this Microsoft document to configure service accounts for SQL Server on Windows: *https://docs.microsoft.com/en-us/sql/database-engine/configure-windows/configure-windows-service-accounts-and-permissions?view=sql-server-ver15#Serv_Perm*.

Now you know why the developer from the SQL Server team was running around talking – and apologizing – to the speakers at the PASS Summit doing talks on SQL Server on Linux containers. She knew it was a ticking time bomb. And she was right. Every speaker who demonstrated how to perform an in-place upgrade of a SQL Server on Linux container failed.

The way to perform an in-place update or upgrade of a container running as *root* with another one that doesn't is to first grant the non-*root* user permissions to the directories in the Docker volume. The following is the modified version of the steps to perform a smart in-place update or upgrade of a container. This assumes that you know the non-*root* user defined in the custom image.

1. Stop the container.

2. Assign ownership of the SQL Server directories and files inside the Docker volume to the non-*root* user.

Before you proceed to update or upgrade the container, you need to set the non-*root* user as the new owner of the files inside the Docker volume. You can create a temporary container to do this assuming you don't have *root* privileges to make changes to the directory mapped to the Docker volume. The following *docker run* command runs a container using the Alpine Linux image; attach the Docker volume and run a *chown* command to change directory and file ownership to the *mssql* user with a UID value of 10001. I used the Alpine Linux image because it is very lightweight. Besides, I only need it to run the *chown* command. I used a UID value instead of a username in case it has not been created on the Linux Docker host. *sqldbdata* is the name of the Docker volume.

```
#Run a temporary Alpine Linux container, mount the Docker volume,
#and run the chown command
docker run --name temp -d --mount source=sqldbdata,target=/data alpine
chown -R 10001:0 /data

#Remove the temporary container
docker rm temp -f
```

Tip   You can also change the ownership of the directories and files directly in the Linux Docker host. The only challenge is having *root* privileges to make changes to the directory mapped to the Docker volume in the filesystem. By default, Docker volumes are created in the */var/lib/docker/volumes* directory. You can run the same *chown* command against the */var/lib/docker/volumes/sqldbdata/_data* directory. You need *root* privileges to do this.

---

3. Create a new SQL Server on Linux container with a new name – *sqldevlinuxcon02* – based on the custom SQL Server on Linux image running as non-*root* user. Attach the same volume – *sqldbdata* – to this new container and reuse the same port number and hostname.

   ```
   docker run -e "ACCEPT_EULA=Y" -e "SA_PASSWORD=mYSecUr3PAssw0rd"
   -p 1433:1433 --name sqldevlinuxcon02 -d -h linuxsqldev01 --mount
   source=sqldbdata,target=/var/opt/mssql customsql2019-nonroot:v1.0
   ```

Just remember that once you upgrade – from SQL Server 2017 to SQL Server 2019 – there's no turning back. It's not the same as updating a container with the same version but different CU where you can roll back to the previous one if things didn't work out as planned. There's really no substitute for good-old working and validated backups.

Optimizing the Dockerfile

Let's build on what we've covered in *Chapter 9* on optimizing the *Dockerfile*. However, there really isn't much to optimize when you look at the image size. Figure 10-13 shows the image layers of the custom SQL Server 2017 on Linux image that runs as a non-*root* user when you run the *docker history* command.

```
[emsarmiento@centosdocker01 /]$ docker history customsql2017-nonroot:v1.0
IMAGE              CREATED           CREATED BY                                    SIZE        COMMEN
T
42e9399a6535       3 hours ago       /bin/sh -c #(nop)   CMD ["/bin/sh" "-c" "sqlsâ¦  0B
521a46442c47       3 hours ago       /bin/sh -c #(nop)   ENV PATH=/usr/local/sbin:â¦  0B
2d6be3714337       3 hours ago       /bin/sh -c #(nop)   USER mssql                0B
a746e2c54867       3 hours ago       /bin/sh -c #(nop)   EXPOSE 1433               0B
74090c3dcbcb       3 hours ago       /bin/sh -c ldconfig                          23.9kB
f5c3d3c4f950       3 hours ago       /bin/sh -c echo -e "# mssql libs\n/opt/mssqlâ¦  28B
c52534e76439       3 hours ago       /bin/sh -c mkdir -p /etc/ld.so.conf.d && touâ¦  0B
48c7d4923c7e       3 hours ago       /bin/sh -c setcap 'cap_sys_ptrace+ep' /usr/bâ¦  6.82MB
161366096834       3 hours ago       /bin/sh -c setcap 'cap_sys_ptrace+ep' /opt/mâ¦  2.38MB
423b2f27f88c       3 hours ago       /bin/sh -c setcap 'cap_net_bind_service+ep' â¦  2.26MB
c9eda4352dce       3 hours ago       /bin/sh -c mkdir -p -m 770 /var/opt/mssql &&â¦  28B            SQL Server is
8e93bf3b5c8c       3 hours ago       /bin/sh -c useradd -M -s /bin/bash -u 10001 â¦  2.92MB          taking up
e8ab9dac20ee       9 hours ago       /bin/sh -c yum install -y mssql-server       1.11GB          most of
5e5468545834       9 hours ago       /bin/sh -c curl -o /etc/yum.repos.d/mssql-seâ¦  20.7kB         the image size
f1cb7c7d58b7       10 months ago     /bin/sh -c #(nop)   CMD ["/bin/bash"]         0B
<missing>          10 months ago     /bin/sh -c #(nop)   LABEL org.label-schema.scâ¦  0B
<missing>          10 months ago     /bin/sh -c #(nop) ADD file:54b004357379717dfâ¦  202MB
[emsarmiento@centosdocker01 /]$
```

Figure 10-13. *Listing the different filesystem layers for the custom SQL Server on Linux Docker image*

The biggest layer is the one that has the instruction to install SQL Server. And we can't really do anything about that layer unless you want to do what we did on the custom SQL Server on Windows image and delete the installation files. The way to do this is to clear the *yum cache* after installing SQL Server using the following instruction:

```
RUN yum cache all
```

But instead of adding another instruction, you can append it to Line 3 like the following command so it doesn't create an additional image layer:

```
#Step 3
RUN yum install -y mssql-server && yum cache all
```

Tip   In Linux, you can run multiple commands in a single line, like the example in *#Step 3.* You can even combine multiple different commands in a single line. You just have to separate them with a chaining operator. This is known as "command chaining," where you are stitching together multiple commands in a single line. In the preceding example, the AND operator (&&) is used. There are other command chaining operators that you can use like the semicolon operator (;), but we'll keep it simple and stick with the AND operator in *Dockerfiles.*

There won't be a huge space saving, probably around 80MB. The SQL Server on Linux packages are not as huge as the SQL Server on Windows installation files.

The other thing that you might be tempted to do is to combine Lines 25, 26, and 27 into a single *RUN* instruction. But because these are just adding capabilities to the *sqlservr*, *paldumper*, and *gdb*, you're not really saving space when you combine them in a single *RUN* instruction. You're just reducing the number of image layers.

You could eliminate the *ENV* instruction in Step 5 and include it in the *CMD* instruction in Step 6 as shown in the following:

```
CMD ["/opt/mssql/bin/sqlservr"]
```

But it's just going to be a cosmetic optimization – reducing the number of image layers but not reducing the image size. I'll leave it up to you to create a custom SQL Server on Linux image that runs as non-root and optimize it as much as you can.

Running Scripts Inside the Dockerfile

The custom SQL Server on Linux images that we've built up to this point were designed for deployment in a production environment. Notice that I didn't include the installation of the SQL Server command-line utilities. As I mentioned in *Chapter 4*, I don't like installing anything unnecessary on production servers, including client tools. For development environments, I only install the things that I really need like the SQL Server command-line utilities.

Install the SQL Server Command-Line Utilities

To install the SQL Server command-line utilities on Linux, it requires downloading a different *repo* file. You can include the following command on Step 2 of the *Dockerfile*:

```
#For RHEL/CentOS
curl -o /etc/yum.repos.d/msprod.repo https://packages.microsoft.com/config/
rhel/7/prod.repo

#For Ubuntu
add-apt-repository "deb [arch=amd64] https://packages.microsoft.com/
ubuntu/16.04/prod xenial main"
```

The updated Step 2 on your *Dockerfile* looks something like the one in the following optimized as a single *RUN* instruction:

```
#For RHEL/CentOS
RUN curl -o /etc/yum.repos.d/mssql-server.repo https://packages.microsoft.
com/config/rhel/7/mssql-server-2017.repo && curl -o /etc/yum.repos.d/
msprod.repo https://packages.microsoft.com/config/rhel/7/prod.repo
```

```
#For Ubuntu
RUN add-apt-repository "deb [arch=amd64] https://packages.microsoft.com/
ubuntu/16.04/mssql-server-2017 xenial main" && add-apt-repository "deb
[arch=amd64] https://packages.microsoft.com/ubuntu/16.04/prod xenial main"
```

The updated Step 3 will now include installing the SQL Server command-line tools on Linux as shown in the following. You need to pass the *ACCEPT_EULA* parameter with a value of *Y* to automatically respond to EULA prompts during installation. We didn't need this when we were just installing SQL Server since we're passing it as a parameter of the *docker run* command.

```
#For RHEL/CentOS
RUN ACCEPT_EULA=Y yum install -y mssql-server mssql-tools unixODBC-devel
```

```
#For Ubuntu
RUN ACCEPT_EULA=Y apt-get install -y mssql-server mssql-tools unixODBC-devel
```

Since the SQL Server command-line tools are stored in a different directory, you need to update Step 5 with an additional path as shown in the following:

```
ENV PATH=${PATH}:/opt/mssql/bin:/opt/mssql-tools/bin
```

With the SQL Server command-line tools installed on the custom SQL Server on Linux image, you can run different T-SQL scripts as part of deploying the container for the development environment.

Write the Bash Script to Check for Backups

Here's a common use case for deploying SQL Server in development environments. Let's say you want to copy database backups into Docker volumes and restore them as part of deploying your custom SQL Server on Linux image. Anyone who would run a SQL

Server on Linux container mapped to a Docker volume will automatically have those user databases ready to use. Let's start by copying your database backups in the Docker volume:

1. Create a Docker volume named sqldbdata:

   ```
   docker volume create sqldbdata
   ```

2. Copy the database backups in the Docker volume.

There are several ways to copy files into the Docker volume. But because we're assuming that you don't have *root* privileges, we'll create a temporary container to do this. This works because, by default, containers run in the security context of *root* unless you specifically configure the source image to run as non-*root*. Also, this assumes that all of your SQL Server database backup files are in the current working directory.

```
#Create a temporary container using the Alpine Linux image
#just so we can copy files into the Docker volume
docker run --name temp -d -v sqldbdata:/data alpine sleep 10000

#Copy files from the current working directory that contains
#the SQL Server database backups into the Docker volume
docker cp . temp:/data
```

3. Change ownership of the Docker volume to non-*root* user:

   ```
   #Use the temporary container to run the chown command
   #to change ownership of files in the Docker volume
   docker exec temp chown -R 10001:0 /data

   #Delete the temporary container after use
   docker rm temp -f
   ```

You could create multiple Docker volumes, each with a copy of the database backups, and just tell the users to mount the specific volume to their container. This really depends on your deployment strategy.

Because you now have the SQL Server command-line tools in your custom SQL Server on Linux image, you can run T-SQL scripts using *sqlcmd* to do anything you want as DBAs inside the container. You could write your own T-SQL script that checks for database backups and restores them and call the script from *sqlcmd*. Here's a code snippet from the bash script that loops through the database backups in the specified directory and restores them:

```
#Iterate thru all the BAK files in Docker volume
#/var/opt/mssql is mounted on Docker volume=sqldbdata
for files in /var/opt/mssql/*.bak
do
  /opt/mssql-tools/bin/sqlcmd -S localhost -U sa -P $SA_PASSWORD -d master
  -Q "RESTORE DATABASE [${files:15:-4}] FROM DISK ='$files'"
done
```

I'm sure you recognize the *sqlcmd* call with the *RESTORE DATABASE* command. You may have done something similar in the past with batch files on Windows. I'm keeping the script simple for demonstration purposes, but you can go crazy with your T-SQL scripts. The database backups are named with the format *databaseName.bak* and were all taken from a SQL Server on Linux instance with the default configuration. That way, we don't need to specify the *WITH MOVE* option when running the *RESTORE DATABASE* command. The *${files:15:-4}* inside the square brackets performs string manipulation to extract the database name. Since the */var/opt/mssql* directory in the container will be mapped to the Docker volume, the full path of the backup files will be in the form */var/opt/mssql/databaseName.bak*. There are 15 characters before the beginning of the database name (*/var/opt/mssql/*) and 4 characters after it (*.bak*). The $ symbol refers to the variable named *files* that contains the full path of the backup file. For every backup file in the specified directory, the script will generate and run the corresponding *sqlcmd* command in the following. Don't make fun of me. I still use the classic Northwind database for examples.

```
/opt/mssql-tools/bin/sqlcmd -S localhost -U sa -P $SA_PASSWORD -d master -Q
"RESTORE DATABASE [Northwind] FROM DISK ='/var/opt/mssql/Northwind.bak'"
```

I've also included a *sleep* command before running the *RESTORE DATABASE* command in the script. Remember the in-place upgrade from *Chapter 7*? Even a new deployment of a SQL Server on Linux container will look like an upgrade because it starts from the RTM release. And that takes time. The *sleep* command takes this into account and won't run the RESTORE DATABASE command until after the upgrade process completes which is roughly 2 minutes. You can bump up the wait time if you want. It's a quick and dirty way to accomplish this, but there are other ways like reading the SQL Server error log to check for a specific text like the following code snippet:

```
#Check SQL Server errorlog to see if recovery is complete
while ! grep "Recovery is complete. This is an informational message only.
No user action is required" /var/opt/mssql/log/errorlog
do sleep 10; done
```

The following is the complete bash script to check for database backups and restoring them:

```
#!/bin/bash

#Make script wait until the upgrade process completes
sleep 120

#Iterate thru all the BAK files in Docker volume
#directory /var/opt/mssql/data is mounted on Docker volume
for f in /var/opt/mssql/*.bak

do
  /opt/mssql-tools/bin/sqlcmd -S localhost -U sa -P $SA_PASSWORD -d master
  -Q "RESTORE DATABASE [${f:15:-4}] FROM DISK ='$f'"
done
```

Name the script *checkbackups_restore.sh*. You're going to need it later.

Note   Unlike in *Chapter 8* where we assigned *execute* permission on the bash script file on the Linux host, you don't need to do that here. Assigning *execute* permission on the bash script files will be done inside the custom Docker image. An additional instruction will be added in the *Dockerfile* as you'll see in the next section.

There's another bash script that you need. You can call it the "startup" script. What it does is it calls the *checkbackups_restore.sh* script and, while the script executes in the background, calls the *sqlservr* process. Recall that the last instruction in a *Dockerfile* should be something that does not terminate. Otherwise, the container will terminate as well. So, in order to run the *checkbackups_restore.sh* script and start the *sqlservr* process, we need to call them both from a startup script. The following is the code for the startup bash script. You can save this as *startup.sh*:

```
#!/bin/bash

#Start the script to restore all database backups
#from Docker volume; run script in the background
/tmp/startup/checkbackups_restore.sh &

# Start SQL Server
/opt/mssql/bin/sqlservr
```

Observe the startup script and you will notice that it is being called from inside the */tmp/startup* directory. This means that both the startup script and the *checkbackups_restore.sh* script should be in a directory named */tmp/startup* inside the container. This also means that we need to create the */tmp/startup* directory and grant *execute* permission to the *checkbackups_restore.sh* and *startup.sh* scripts. This gives you an idea on how the new *Dockerfile* would look like. Also, the "&" symbol after the script tells it to run in the background.

Run the Bash Script in the Last Instruction

Now that we have the necessary scripts, we can call the startup script as the last instruction in the *Dockerfile* as shown in the following:

```
CMD ["/tmp/startup/startup.sh"]
```

The following is the updated *Dockerfile* with comments. Note that this new custom image builds on the other custom SQL Server 2017 on Linux image with the SQL Server command-line tools installed running as non-*root*.

```
#Start from custom SQL Server 2017 on Linux image
#running as non-root with command line tools
#NOTE: Use the correct Docker image name
FROM customsql2017oncentoswithtools-nonroot:v1.0

#Create working directory
RUN mkdir -p /tmp/startup
```

```
#Copy bash scripts into working directory
# and assign the mssql user as owner
COPY --chown=mssql:0 . /tmp/startup

#Grant executable permissions to bash scripts
RUN chmod +x /tmp/startup/checkbackups_restore.sh
RUN chmod +x /tmp/startup/startup.sh

#Run startup script startup.sh
CMD ["/tmp/startup/startup.sh"]
```

Save the *Dockerfile*, the *checkbackups_restore.sh*, and the *startup.sh* files in a directory and use that directory as the build context for this new custom image. You only want these three files copied in the custom image, nothing more. Figure 10-14 shows the directory structure that contains these files.

```
[emsarmiento@centosdocker01 customSQLwithTools]$ ls -l
total 12
-rw-rw-r--. 1 emsarmiento emsarmiento 972 Feb  7 21:48 checkbackups_restore.sh
-rw-rw-r--. 1 emsarmiento emsarmiento 548 Feb  7 21:56 Dockerfile
-rw-rw-r--. 1 emsarmiento emsarmiento 167 Feb  7 21:55 startup.sh
```

Figure 10-14. *Directory structure and files for building the custom image*

Run the following command to build this new custom image:

```
docker build -t customsql2017oncentos4dev-nonroot:v1.0 .
```

And now, for the ultimate test, run a new container based on this custom image using the following *docker run* command. Be sure to use the correct image name.

```
docker run -e "ACCEPT_EULA=Y" -e "SA_PASSWORD=mYSecUr3PAssw0rd" -p
1433:1433 --name sqldevlinuxcon01 --mount source=sqldbdata,target=/var/opt/
mssql -d -h linuxsqldev01 customsql2017oncentos4dev-nonroot:v1.0
```

Mapping the Docker volume *sqldbdata* to the container means that the backup files are now accessible to the container. During startup, the container will run the *startup.sh* script which will call the *checkbackups_restore.sh* script to iterate through the BAK files in the */var/opt/mssql* directory. Since we are starting from the *customsql2017oncentoswithtools-nonroot:v1.0* custom image that already has the SQL Server command-line tools installed and *sqlservr* process running, we can call *sqlcmd* and pass it the *RESTORE DATABASE* command to restore databases from backups.

Pretty cool, don't you think?

Caution   I may have simplified the process a bit to show how you can automate deployment of SQL Server instances with user databases via containers running as non-*root*. It's pretty obvious I'm serious about security as I've mentioned in previous chapters. And I'm clearly leaving a lot of details when it comes to dealing with restoring database backups in development environments, especially those that come from production environments. Not only do you need to restrict access to both production and development environments but also implement ways to obscure sensitive data. I totally understand that developers need to work with real data to perform proper testing. But that doesn't mean we can take backups from production and just restore it in development environments. Include processes to scramble data before even taking backups. Or have a dedicated server whose purpose is to scramble data for use in development environments. You certainly don't want to end up being on tomorrow's headlines regarding security breaches.

Multi-stage Builds

I had second thoughts about including this section as it pertains more to developers than DBAs. But ever since I started doing my *SQL Server DBA's Guide to Docker Containers* workshop, I've gotten a ton of questions regarding multi-stage builds and what they are. This section gives you a high-level overview of what multi-stage builds are and how they are used. Bear with me until the end of this chapter. Pretend you're a developer reading this. I know, I'm asking too much of you.

The idea behind multi-stage builds came about due to the development practice of writing, testing, and compiling apps. Multi-stage builds are used to optimize builds and reduce size of Docker images without adding complexity. And you do this with a single *Dockerfile*. Imagine a developer writing code in his or her workstation. While the workstation has the development tools, only the compiled code is needed in a production environment. You certainly don't want your development tools included in the final custom image for the app. One major side effect of containerizing apps is producing massively large images that contain source code, compiled code, and sometimes even development tools (although, I doubt, they're as large as the SQL

259

Server on Windows images). Take a look at the following sample *Dockerfile*. I'm using the sample code from *https://github.com/microsoft/sqllinuxlabs/tree/master/containers/mssql-aspcore-example/mssql-aspcore-example-app/belgrade-product-catalog-demo* to create the custom images.

```
#Use the .NET Core with SDK on Linux image
FROM mcr.microsoft.com/dotnet/core/sdk:2.2
WORKDIR /app

#Copy csproj and restore as distinct layers
COPY belgrade-product-catalog-demo/*.csproj ./belgrade-product-catalog-
demo/
RUN dotnet restore ./belgrade-product-catalog-demo/

#Copy everything else and build app
COPY belgrade-product-catalog-demo/. ./belgrade-product-catalog-demo/
WORKDIR /app/belgrade-product-catalog-demo
RUN dotnet publish -c Release -o out
```

Building this custom image would yield a large image size, even larger than my custom SQL Server on Linux image that has the SQL Server command-line tools installed. Figure 10-15 shows the size of the custom ASP.NET web app image.

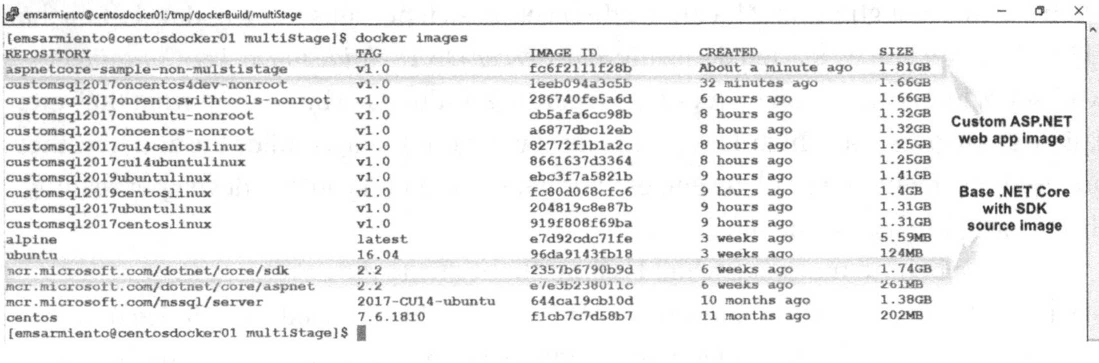
emsarmiento@centosdocker01:/tmp/dockerBuild/multiStage

```
[emsarmiento@centosdocker01 multiStage]$ docker images
REPOSITORY                              TAG                 IMAGE ID       CREATED              SIZE
aspnetcore-sample-non-mulstistage       v1.0                fc6f2111f28b   About a minute ago   1.81GB
customsql2017oncentos4dev-nonroot       v1.0                1eeb094a3c5b   32 minutes ago       1.66GB
customsql2017oncentoswithtools-nonroot  v1.0                286740fe5a6d   6 hours ago          1.66GB
customsql2017onubuntu-nonroot           v1.0                cb5afa6cc98b   8 hours ago          1.32GB
customsql2017oncentos-nonroot           v1.0                a6877dbc12eb   8 hours ago          1.32GB
customsql2017cu14centoslinux            v1.0                82772f1b1a2c   8 hours ago          1.25GB
customsql2017cu14ubuntulinux            v1.0                8661637d3364   8 hours ago          1.25GB
customsql2019ubuntulinux                v1.0                ebc3f7a5821b   9 hours ago          1.41GB
customsql2019centoslinux                v1.0                fc80d068cfc6   9 hours ago          1.4GB
customsql2017ubuntulinux                v1.0                204819c8e87b   9 hours ago          1.31GB
customsql2017centoslinux                v1.0                919f808f69ba   9 hours ago          1.31GB
alpine                                  latest              e7d92cdc71fe   3 weeks ago          5.59MB
ubuntu                                  16.04               96da9143fb18   3 weeks ago          124MB
mcr.microsoft.com/dotnet/core/sdk       2.2                 2357b6790b9d   6 weeks ago          1.74GB
mcr.microsoft.com/dotnet/core/aspnet    2.2                 e7e3b238011c   6 weeks ago          261MB
mcr.microsoft.com/mssql/server          2017-CU14-ubuntu    644ca19cb10d   10 months ago        1.38GB
centos                                  7.6.1810            f1cb7c7d58b7   11 months ago        202MB
[emsarmiento@centosdocker01 multiStage]$
```


Figure 10-15. *Size of custom ASP.NET web app image with SDK*

The 1.81GB image contains the .NET SDK, the source code, and the compiled code. We only need the compiled code and the dependencies for deploying into production – everything in the *out* directory as specified in the *RUN* instruction. What if we just use the output of this custom image instead of including everything that came with the development project? This is where multi-stage build comes in. Have a look at the following new *Dockerfile*. I've included step numbers to explain what is going on in the *Dockerfile*:

```
#Step 1: Use the .NET Core with SDK on Linux image
FROM mcr.microsoft.com/dotnet/core/sdk:2.2 AS build

#Step 2
WORKDIR /app

#Step 3: copy csproj and restore as distinct layers
COPY belgrade-product-catalog-demo/*.csproj ./belgrade-product-catalog-demo/

#Step 4
RUN dotnet restore ./belgrade-product-catalog-demo/

#Step 5 copy everything else and build app
COPY belgrade-product-catalog-demo/. ./belgrade-product-catalog-demo/

#Step 6
WORKDIR /app/belgrade-product-catalog-demo
RUN dotnet publish -c Release -o out

#Step 7:
FROM mcr.microsoft.com/dotnet/core/aspnet:2.2 AS runtime

#Step 8
WORKDIR /app

#Step 9
COPY --from=build /app/belgrade-product-catalog-demo/out ./

#Step 10
EXPOSE 5000

#Step 11
ENTRYPOINT ["dotnet", "belgrade-product-catalog-demo.dll"]
```

One thing you'll notice is the existence of two *FROM* instructions. Yes, you can have as many *FROM* instructions in a *Dockerfile* if your goal is to do multi-stage builds. Each *FROM* instruction is referenced by an index starting at 0. Step 1 can be referred to as 0, while Step 7 can be referred to as 1. For ease of reference, an alias is used. Step 1 is named as *build*, while Step 7 is named as *runtime*. Throughout the *Dockerfile*, you can reference these builds using either their index or alias. In Step 6, the output of the *RUN* instruction is the *out* directory that contains the compiled code including the dependencies. Since that's all we need to run the web app, we will use the output of Step 6 to build another custom image. In Step 7, the base image needed to run an ASP. NET Core web app is much smaller than the .NET Core with SDK image as shown in Figure 10-16. Step 9 simply copies the *out* directory generated from Step 6 into this new image. It uses *COPY --from* to copy from a separate image instead of from the local filesystem. The image could also be on either the local filesystem or from a public registry like Docker Hub or Microsoft Container Registry. Steps 10 and 11 probably look familiar to you by now. Take a look at the custom image generated by the multi-stage build: 262MB vs. 1.81GB. That's a massive difference in image size. And we're just looking at one image here. Imagine having to deal with a multi-container app designed with microservices architecture in mind.

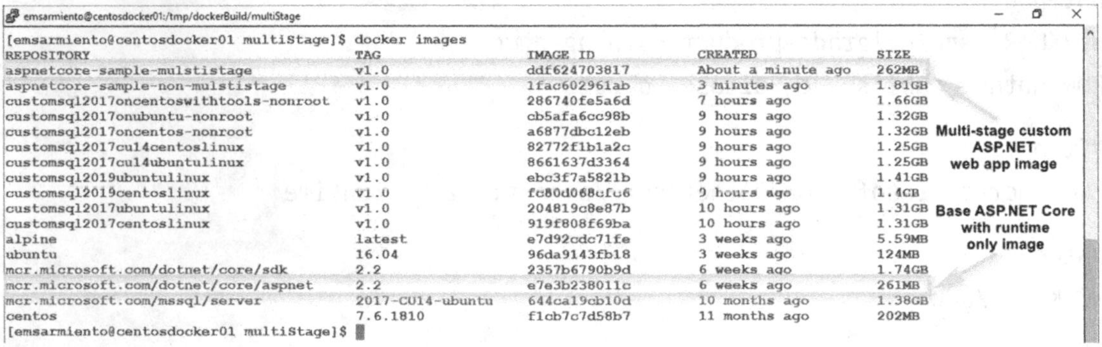

Figure 10-16. Size of custom ASP.NET web app image with just the compiled code, dependencies, and runtime

As I said, this is just a high-level overview of how to use multi-stage builds. Refer to *https://docs.docker.com/develop/develop-images/multistage-build/* if you want to learn more about multi-stage builds. In the SQL Server world, we only have one app – the SQL Server database engine. We don't need to build multi-container apps just to deploy a database. If you're thinking of multi-instance architectures like SQL Server Always On Availability Groups or SQL Server Replication, those require deploying to a high availability platform beyond a single Linux Docker host. Kubernetes is the de facto high availability and container orchestration platform for deploying such architectures. While I'd like to cover a little bit of Kubernetes, it's beyond the scope of this book. But that's going to be your next path after Docker containers.

Docker Compose and YAML Files

Last year, an attendee of my *SQL Server DBA's Guide to Docker Containers* workshop asked why I wasn't using YAML files and Docker Compose in my examples and demos. Like multi-stage builds, this is another one of those tools used for running and managing multi-container applications. It's not something SQL Server DBAs will have to deal with, but since I've already covered multi-stage builds, I might as well include this.

Remember when XML was a thing? I recall having to deal with exam questions on SQL Server certification exams that have anything to do with XML. When I was involved in the exam writing process for SQL Server 2008, I tried my best to shoot down anything XML related – because, back then, the relational database engine isn't the ideal storage for nonrelational data. Then came JSON. Whoever Jason was, he was lucky to have been chosen as a moniker for this new data interchange format. We had a guy named Jason as part of the team writing questions for the Microsoft Azure Data Platform certification exams a few years ago. We had a chuckle whenever we talk about JSON. Both XML and JSON were used to standardize data formats, hence why DBAs need to learn how to deal with them.

YAML stands for YAML Ain't Markup Language. Like XML and JSON, YAML is also used to standardize data formats. Both Docker and Kubernetes use YAML to configure containers and pods, respectively. This means working with a *Dockerfile* for customizing an image and a YAML file to describe the different containers and services that make up your app. But unlike working with a *Dockerfile* where all you need is the file to build an image, you need to install Docker Compose to work with YAML files in Docker.

Installing Docker Compose

Docker Compose still relies on the Docker engine to do its tasks. So, you can install Docker Compose directly either on the same machine as your Linux Docker host or on a development machine that can connect remotely to one. The following instructions assume you are installing Docker Compose on the same machine as your Linux Docker host.

Run the following command to download the current stable release of Docker Compose. Observe that it is copying the files into the */usr/local/bin* directory, the one meant for programs that a normal user may run:

```
sudo curl -L "https://github.com/docker/compose/releases/download/1.25.3/
docker-compose-$(uname -s)-$(uname -m)" -o /usr/local/bin/docker-compose
```

After downloading the Docker Compose package, just like dealing with a bash script, assign the *executable* permission to the file:

```
sudo chmod +x /usr/local/bin/docker-compose
```

An easy way to test if Docker Compose is installed properly is to run the following command. The current stable release at the time of writing is *1.25.3*.

```
docker-compose –version
```

Now that we have Docker Compose installed, let's look at how we can leverage it with YAML files to deploy multi-container applications.

Creating a YAML File for Multi-container Apps

I'll be using the samples from *https://github.com/microsoft/sqllinuxlabs/tree/ master/containers/mssql-aspcore-example* to demonstrate this. In case you're wondering, the ASP.NET web app that I used in the multi-stage build came from this. The app consists of a simple two-tier application – a web front end running on ASP. NET Core that connects to a back-end SQL Server database – two apps, two containers. Download all the contents so you can follow along.

I used my custom SQL Server on Linux image created in the "Running Scripts Inside the Dockerfile" section to run bash scripts inside the container that creates the user database from the *db-init.sql* script. The following code is what we will be using for the YAML file:

```
version: "3"
services:
    wfe:
        build: ./mssql-aspcore-example-app
        ports:
            - "8080:5000"
```

```
    depends_on:
        - db
db:
    build: ./mssql-aspcore-example-db
    environment:
        SA_PASSWORD: "mYSecUr3PAssw0rd"
        ACCEPT_EULA: "Y"
    ports:
        - "1500:1433"
```

Let's analyze the YAML file to understand what it is doing:

- The *version*: Line describes the version number that the Compose file will use for syntax validation. Version 3 works with the Docker engine version 1.13.0 and higher.

- The *services*: Line describes the different services that we will run for this multi-container app – the *wfe* and the *db* services. The *db* service is named in such a way as to map to the database connection string defined in the *appsettings.json* file.

- The *build*: Line is like running the *docker build* command. You're telling Docker Compose to look for a *Dockerfile* inside the *./mssql-aspcore-example-app* directory to build the image for the *wfe* service and the *./mssql-aspcore-example-db* for the *db* service.

- The *ports*: Line is like the *-p* parameter in the *docker run* command, publishing the container's TCP port to the host. The *wfe* service will use port 8080 on the Linux Docker host that will be mapped to port 5000 on the container. The *db* service will use port 1500. You can also choose to remove the *ports* definition on the *db* service, and it will default to port 1433.

- The *depends_on*: Line sets a service as a dependency for the current block-defined container. In this case, the *wfe* service depends on the *db* service. Because of this, Docker Compose will first start (or run the container that contains) the *db* service before starting the *wfe* service. It's like starting the SQL Server service before starting the SQL Server Agent service. The behavior is reversed when stopping the service.

However, Docker Compose does not wait until the container is fully ready before starting the dependent container. It just waits until the container is running. Recall that creating a new SQL Server on Linux container is like performing an upgrade because everything starts from the RTM version. You have to account for delays until the container is fully ready – hence, why I used my custom SQL Server on Linux image with the scripts.

- The *environment*: Line is like the *-e* parameter of the *docker run* command. Here, we're passing the two environment variables that we have been passing to the *docker run* command when we're running a SQL Server instance on a container.

Imagine how powerful this can be when you're dealing with multi-container apps. You can have a single YAML file to describe the entire architecture. Save the file as *docker-compose.yml* – this is the default filename that Docker Compose references just like the *Dockerfile*. But don't rush yet. Dealing with YAML files can be tricky due to the formatting. I sometimes have to use a YAML parser like this one from *https:// codebeautify.org/yaml-validator* to make sure that any error I get has nothing to do with formatting. Once you're done, run the following command. The *up* subcommand is used to build, (re)create, start, and attach containers to a service. Figure 10-17 shows what the *docker -compose* command is doing.

```
docker-compose up
```

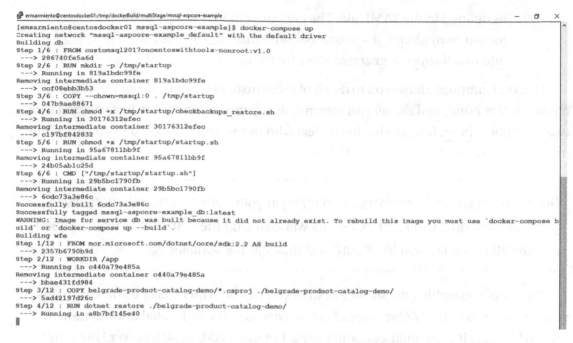

```
emsarmiento@centosdocker01:/tmp/dockerBuild/multiStage/mssql-aspcore-example                              —   □   ×
[emsarmiento@centosdocker01 mssql-aspcore-example]$ docker-compose up
Creating network "mssql-aspcore-example_default" with the default driver
Building db
Step 1/6 : FROM customsql2017oncentoswithtools-nonroot:v1.0
 ---> 286740fe5a6d
Step 2/6 : RUN mkdir -p /tmp/startup
 ---> Running in 819a1bdc99fe
Removing intermediate container 819a1bdc99fe
 ---> ccf08ebb3b53
Step 3/6 : COPY --chown=mssql:0 . /tmp/startup
 ---> 047b9ae88671
Step 4/6 : RUN chmod +x /tmp/startup/checkbackups_restore.sh
 ---> Running in 30176312efec
Removing intermediate container 30176312efec
 ---> c197bf842832
Step 5/6 : RUN chmod +x /tmp/startup/startup.sh
 ---> Running in 95a67811bb9f
Removing intermediate container 95a67811bb9f
 ---> 24b05ab1c25d
Step 6/6 : CMD ["/tmp/startup/startup.sh"]
 ---> Running in 29b5bc1790fb
Removing intermediate container 29b5bc1790fb
 ---> 6cdc73a3e86c
Successfully built 6cdc73a3e86c
Successfully tagged mssql-aspcore-example_db:latest
WARNING: Image for service db was built because it did not already exist. To rebuild this image you must use `docker-compose b
uild` or `docker-compose up --build`.
Building wfe
Step 1/12 : FROM mcr.microsoft.com/dotnet/core/sdk:2.2 AS build
 ---> 2357b6790b9d
Step 2/12 : WORKDIR /app
 ---> Running in c440a79e485a
Removing intermediate container c440a79e485a
 ---> bbae431fd984
Step 3/12 : COPY belgrade-product-catalog-demo/*.csproj ./belgrade-product-catalog-demo/
 ---> 5ad42197d26c
Step 4/12 : RUN dotnet restore ./belgrade-product-catalog-demo/
 ---> Running in a8b7bf145e40
```

Figure 10-17. *Status of Docker Compose execution*

Docker Compose does the following tasks during execution:

1. Docker will create a *bridge* network for the two containers to communicate with each other. By default, Docker Compose will create a single docker network for your app. We will cover Docker networking in more detail in *Chapter 11*.

2. Docker builds the *wfe* and *db* images based on their corresponding *Dockerfile*. Because the *wfe* is dependent on the *db*, the *db* image will be built first. Docker will only build the image if it doesn't exist yet. If it does, it will simply use the available image. By default, the image name will be in the form *directoryName_service:latest*. The image name for the *wfe* will be *mssql-aspcore-example_wfe:latest*, while the image name for the *db* will be *mssql-aspcore-example_db:latest*.

3. After building the images, Docker creates and starts the corresponding containers based on these images. It will first create and run the *db* container, followed by the *wfe* container,

as defined in the YAML file. The container names will be in the format *imageName_1 – mssql-aspcore-example_wfe_1* for the *wfe* and *mssql-aspcore-example_db_1* for the *db*.

Docker Compose allows you to do all of these instead of running *docker network create, docker build*, and *docker run* commands separately. And we're just working with two containers here. Imagine having to deal with more. And it also allows you to define infrastructure as code with the YAML file.

Note   Because the containers are running in your current terminal interactively, you can't just do a Ctrl+C to exit – this will also stop the containers. You can open another terminal session to explore and manage the containers.

I'm barely scratching the surface of what you can do with Docker Compose in this section. Refer to `https://docs.docker.com/compose/` for additional information on how to leverage it with multi-container apps. But like I said, as SQL Server DBAs, you won't be dealing with multi-container apps if all you need to do is deploy a SQL Server database. At least, you have an idea of what the developers are doing when they mention a thing or two about Docker Compose.

Summary

This chapter is an extension of the previous one on creating custom SQL Server on Docker images. And there's a reason I decided to cover more topics despite already covering the basics in *Chapter 9*. If you noticed, majority of the contents in this book revolve around Docker on Linux. Microsoft has fully invested on Linux and SQL Server is proof of that. That tells a lot about where SQL Server is headed in the future and how it will affect your career as a DBA. I see a future where most of the SQL Server deployments will be on Linux, be it on a physical machine, a virtual machine, or a container. That's why this chapter combines everything you've learned from the previous chapters when it comes to working with both Linux and Docker – from installing SQL Server on Linux to writing bash scripts. My goal is to get you ready for that future.

But we're not done yet. The next chapter covers the basics of Docker networking and explores the *bridge* network that I mentioned in more detail.

CHAPTER 11

Guide to Docker Networking for SQL Server DBAs

The expert in anything was once a beginner.

—Unknown

We IT professionals are not that good when it comes to social events. We would rather spend time on our desk fixing and troubleshooting technical issues than have that really awkward feeling of finding the right words to say during conversations just to fill in the silence. But social events, specifically professional events, provide an opportunity for growth both personally and professionally, connecting with like-minded people.

I remember attending my very first PASS Summit in Denver, CO, back in 2007. Being my very first professional event in North America, I didn't really know what to expect. I knew I had a presentation to deliver so I needed to know who the event organizers were and the logistics needed for my session. Other than knowing the T-SQL language, at least I know how to speak English to find my way around and not be that socially awkward Asian – until I was introduced to several SQL Server MVPs at the event. That was the beginning of my adventure. The MVPs made me feel like family, took really good care of me, and introduced me to opportunities that contributed to my personal and professional growth. A game of pool with SQL Server expert Aaron Bertrand established an image of me being one of the nice guys because, according to him, I let him win (not all people from the Philippines are a master of the game). It was during one of the

© Edwin M Sarmiento 2020
E. M. Sarmiento, *The SQL Server DBA's Guide to Docker Containers*,
https://doi.org/10.1007/978-1-4842-5826-2_11

conversations that I got introduced to the founders of MSSQLTips.com. A friend of mine introduced me to Dandy Weyn, a program manager at Microsoft that, to this day, has provided consulting opportunities. And a conversation with SQL Server expert Adam Machanic got me introduced to the company that helped me move to Canada in 2008.

Being connected really does open up a ton of opportunities. That goes the same for Docker containers. This chapter introduces you to the world of container networking with the goal of knowing enough details to connect your SQL Server on containers to other services and applications. The coverage will be restricted to single-host deployments since we're not covering multi-host deployments in this book. You're not expected to replace your network engineer at the end of the chapter, but you'll know a subset of what they know, enough to have intelligent conversations with them when it comes to connecting your SQL Server inside containers to the rest of the world. Besides, even with the level of details provided, we're still at a very high level as far as networking geeks are concerned.

The docker0 Bridge

Since *Chapter 4*, you've already been using Docker networking without being explicit about it. The fact that you can access the SQL Server databases inside a container from a remote machine is proof that it works. *Chapter 8* gave you a sneak peek at what's going on under the covers, with Docker manipulating *iptables* on Linux to allow traffic to and from the container's published port using the *-p* parameter of the *docker run* command. *Chapter 10* introduced you to the *bridge* network when you created a multi-container app using Docker Compose. Let's explore a little bit more of the components of Docker networking that makes all this connectivity possible.

The default installation of Docker creates a Linux bridge network on the host named *docker0*. And we've been using this bridge network since the beginning of the book. In Linux, a bridge network is used to connect two or more network segments, much like how a network switch works. This bridge network forwards traffic between the networks attached to it based on MAC addresses of the hosts. On Windows, the equivalent is the *nat* – short for network address translation – network. You can think of a bridge network as an immigration officer working on a bridge that connects two different countries. I'll use the USA-Canada border as an example to further illustrate since I regularly drive back and forth between the state of New York and the province of Ontario, passing through bridges that connect the two countries. The immigration officer has the responsibility of allowing individuals in vehicles to pass through the border, looking at the travel visa (MAC address of the destination) stamped on passports. If individuals do not have the appropriate travel visas, they won't be allowed to pass through. If you're familiar with networking terms in the world of virtualization, think of a bridge network as a *vSwitch* or a virtual switch. On Windows, the implementation of *docker0* is a Hyper-V virtual switch leveraging the Windows Host Network Service (HNS).

On top of the *docker0* bridge is an implementation of a network driver that can be customized depending on the Docker host's operating system, much like how a device driver works. This is how Docker communicates with the host operating system to implement networking capabilities that allow containers to connect to the network. Remember in *Chapter 8* how the *iptables* on Linux were updated to allow traffic to and from the running containers? That's the network driver talking to the *docker0* bridge via the Docker commands. The types of driver implemented on Docker describe the network driver used to make it work. We'll just focus on the *bridge* network since we're only covering single-host deployments. And how convenient is it that the name of the default Docker bridge network is also called *bridge*?

The *bridge* network gets a private IP address and a subnet associated with it. The subnet assigned to the *bridge* network is chosen as the first nonconflicting subnet among the following list: *172.[17-31].42.1/16, 10.[0-255].42.1/16, 192.168.[42-44].1/24.* You can inspect this by running the *ip addr* command on Linux or *ipconfig* on Windows. Figure 11-1 shows the details of the *docker0* bridge on my CentOS Linux Docker host. Keep in mind that this is mapped to the Docker *bridge* network.

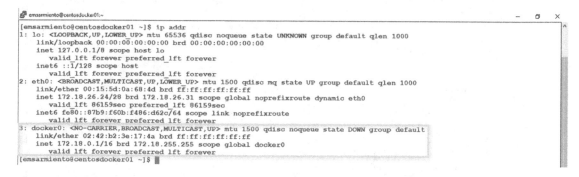

Figure 11-1. *The docker0 bridge shown as a network interface on a CentOS Linux host*

All containers attached to this *bridge* network will get an IP address in the network associated with it. In my Linux Docker host, every single container will have an IP address in the *172.18.0.0/16* network. By default, all containers have networking enabled, allowing them to make outgoing connections to other containers or other external services – including the Internet. Without specifying the *--network* parameter in the *docker run* command, it automatically connects the container to the *docker0* bridge. Since we haven't really created any other bridge network nor added the *--network* parameter in any of the *docker run* commands we used, the *bridge* network is what made all the networking possible, connecting the containers attached to it to the hosts and services attached to the external network. Also, notice the *state DOWN* value. This means there are no running containers attached to it. That will change to *state UP* if there are running containers attached.

As I mentioned, Docker provides network drivers as part of the default installation, with the *bridge* driver mapped to the *docker0* bridge. You can use the `docker network ls` command to display the available Docker networks. To inspect the network named *bridge*, you can run the `docker network inspect bridge` command. Figure 11-2 displays the default networks that come with the default Docker installation and the details of the network named *bridge*.

```
emsarmiento@centosdocker01:~
[emsarmiento@centosdocker01 ~]$ docker network ls
NETWORK ID          NAME                DRIVER              SCOPE
f8d46ddcf9be        bridge              bridge              local
8e4974121988        host                host                local
92348287b045        none                null                local
[emsarmiento@centosdocker01 ~]$ docker network inspect bridge
[
    {
        "Name": "bridge",
        "Id": "f8d46ddcf9bece5675ed763f98a2df5eaa7aac8e74d5cc3e1ba6f7ef34f77280",
        "Created": "2020-02-15T22:22:43.212630722-05:00",
        "Scope": "local",
        "Driver": "bridge",
        "EnableIPv6": false,
        "IPAM": {
            "Driver": "default",
            "Options": null,
            "Config": [
                {
                    "Subnet": "172.18.0.0/16",
                    "Gateway": "172.18.0.1"
                }
            ]
        },
        "Internal": false,
        "Attachable": false,
        "Ingress": false,
        "ConfigFrom": {
            "Network": ""
        },
        "ConfigOnly": false,
        "Containers": {},
        "Options": {
            "com.docker.network.bridge.default_bridge": "true",
            "com.docker.network.bridge.enable_icc": "true",
            "com.docker.network.bridge.enable_ip_masquerade": "true",
            "com.docker.network.bridge.host_binding_ipv4": "0.0.0.0",
            "com.docker.network.bridge.name": "docker0",
            "com.docker.network.driver.mtu": "1500"
        },
```

Figure 11-2. *Default Docker networks available and the details of the network named bridge*

> **Note**   Docker networking has its own subcommand – *docker network* – for managing Docker networks. This allows you to create, inspect, list, remove, connect, and disconnect networks. We will be using several of these subcommands throughout the chapter to illustrate their usage. A complete list of *docker network* commands is available on the Docker documentation: $https://docs.docker.$ $com/engine/reference/commandline/network/$.

Have a look at the *com.docker.network.bridge.name* value under *Options*. I'm sure you can recognize the name by now. Also, if you look at the *Containers* option, it's currently empty. It only gets populated with the names of the containers attached to it when they are running.

Virtual Network Adapters

By default, Docker creates a pair of virtual network adapters every time a container is started, one end of which is attached to the host system via the *bridge* network and the other end to the running container. Figure 11-3 shows a high-level network diagram of running containers, leveraging the default *bridge* network that connects to the *docker0* (or HNS internal NIC on Windows) bridge.

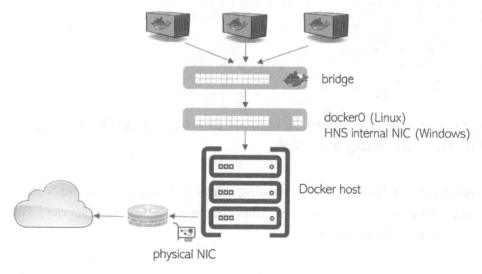

Figure 11-3. *Network diagram of running containers connected to the physical network*

> **Tip**   Nothing is stopping you from creating a container that has multiple network interfaces just like how you would with a physical or virtual machine. This is useful if you want to configure a container as a multihomed host connected to two or more networks. We'll keep it simple and just use a single network interface. After all, you're not going to replace your network engineers after finishing this chapter.

Let's explore the list of network interfaces on the Docker host after starting a container. Figure 11-4 shows a new virtual network interface named *veth2a62842@if8* attached to a running container in my Linux Docker host. Obviously, the name will be different on your Docker host. The number of virtual network interfaces created on your Docker host will depend on the number of currently running containers. Also, the name will change if you stop and restart the same container. With running containers attached to the *docker0* bridge, the value now changes to *state UP*.

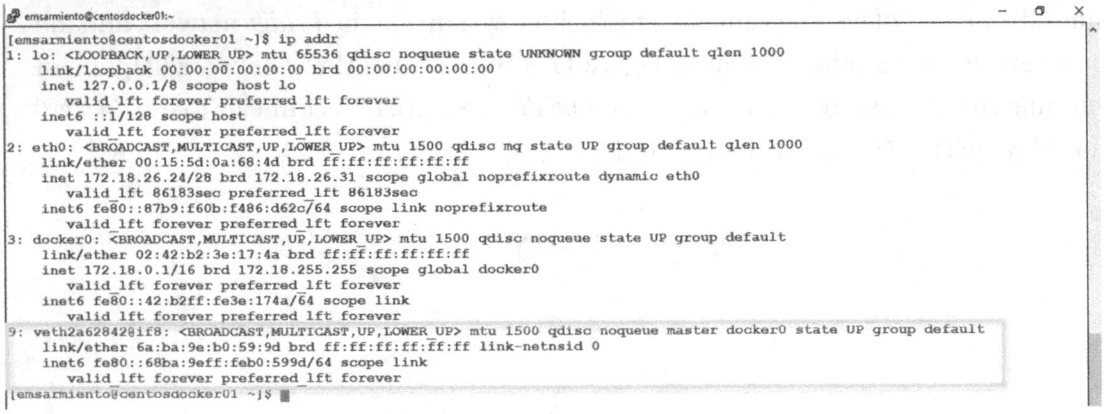

Figure 11-4. *Newly created virtual network interface on the Docker host associated with a running container*

Looking at the network diagram, running containers connected to the *bridge* network can now connect to other containers attached to it as well as services and apps available outside of the Docker host.

Working with and Exposing Ports: Running Multiple SQL Server Instances on Linux via Containers

We've been using the *-p* parameter of the *docker run* command since the earlier chapters of this book. In *Chapter 10*, we also covered the purpose of the *EXPOSE* instruction in the *Dockerfile*. The way the application inside the container is accessed from either outside of the container or locally from the Docker host is by using the *-p* parameter of the *docker run* command, which maps the port number of the container to the port number of the host. If we don't do this, the container will only be accessible to other containers connected to the same Docker network – the *bridge* network. Think about that for a second. Every SQL Server container we've created throughout the book is attached to the *bridge* network by default. And we've only been creating a single container up until *Chapter 10* when we created multi-container apps. If we didn't provide the *-p* parameter with every *docker run* command that we used, our SQL Server instances will be totally isolated – and useless. The container may have been listening on port 1433, but there's no way we can access it remotely if the port isn't published on the Docker host. Although from a security standpoint, it's the most secure SQL Server instance. You just won't be able to use it.

Port mapping is a great way to publish a container to other services and apps on external networks. However, you'll see a lot of articles and blog posts telling you not to do port mapping because it isn't scalable. Once a port on the host has already been mapped to a container, it will no longer be available to other containers. And while you have port numbers between 1024 and 65535, you must explicitly define the port numbers if you want to connect to a remote container instead of just leveraging the default values. An example of this is when you're running a web app in a container. Ports 80 and 443 are the default port numbers for connecting to a web app via HTTP or HTTPS, respectively. If you run multiple web app containers on a single Docker host, you need to map the other containers to different, nonstandard port numbers. And ordinary people like me may or may not be aware of those nonstandard port numbers.

The same is true with SQL Server. People working with SQL Server know that they can access it via port 1433. Application connection strings use the default port number, hence why you rarely see a connection string that explicitly defines a port number. But it is also true that people working with SQL Server are aware of named instances and how they leverage nonstandard port numbers. In fact, while Microsoft does not support running multiple SQL Server instances on Linux, the way you work around that limitation is by running multiple SQL Server containers on a Docker host, mapping each one of them to a different port number. The following is an example of running two SQL Server containers on the same Linux Docker host where one uses the default port 1433 while the other uses port 5000. I've highlighted the use of the -*p* parameter to illustrate this.

```
docker run -e 'ACCEPT_EULA=Y' -e 'SA_PASSWORD=yOurSecUr3PAsswOrd' -p
1433:1433 --name sql-linuxcon01 -d -h linuxsql01 mcr.microsoft.com/mssql/
server:2017-latest
docker run -e 'ACCEPT_EULA=Y' -e 'SA_PASSWORD=yOurSecUr3PAsswOrd' -p
5000:1433 --name sql-linuxcon02 -d -h linuxsql02 mcr.microsoft.com/mssql/
server:2017-latest
```

For people working with SQL Server, this is normal. We can run as many SQL Server instances as we want (well, technically, the maximum supported is 50) on the same host by leveraging named instances. In fact, this is how a lot of customers reduced their licensing costs prior to virtualization. The same concept that made running multiple SQL Server instances possible on a single host is how we can run multiple SQL Server instances on a Linux host – via containers and port mapping. Even better, you're no longer limited to a maximum of 50 SQL Server instances on the same host. You can run as many as there are ports and resources available on your Docker host.

Using the Same Port on Multiple Containers

Another way to leverage the default SQL Server port number on multiple containers running on the same Docker host is by creating a different Docker network for each container. Since each Docker network will have its own IP address range and subnet, each container can be assigned a unique IP address, allowing all of them to use port 1433. Keep in mind that a TCP or UDP port is a unique combination of an IP address plus a port number. We can reuse the same port number for a different host (or, in this case, a different container) if we are assigning a different IP address to it. The following is an example of creating a user-defined Docker network using the *bridge* driver and assigning a specific IP address to a container from that user-defined network:

```
#Step 1: Create a user-defined network named bridgenet1
docker network create -d bridge --subnet 172.19.0.1/24 bridgenet1
```

```
#Step 2: Run a container and attach it to bridgenet1
docker run --network bridgenet1 -e 'ACCEPT_EULA=Y' -e 'SA_
PASSWORD=y0urSecUr3PAssw0rd' --ip="172.19.0.2" --name sql-linuxcon01 -d -h
linuxsql01 mcr.microsoft.com/mssql/server:2017-latest
```

```
#Step 3: Create a user-defined network named bridgenet2
docker network create -d bridge --subnet 10.0.0.1/16 bridgenet2
```

```
#Step 4: Run a container and attach it to bridgenet2
docker run --network bridgenet2 -e 'ACCEPT_EULA=Y' -e 'SA_
PASSWORD=y0urSecUr3PAssw0rd' --ip="10.0.0.2" --name sql-linuxcon02 -d -h
linuxsql02 mcr.microsoft.com/mssql/server:2017-latest
```

Let's explore the sample code to understand what it is doing. In *Step 1*, we create a Docker network named *bridgenet1* using the *-d* parameter to define it using a *bridge* driver. The *--subnet* parameter defines the IP address range and the subnet mask – *172.19.0.1/24*. Any container attached to this network will have an IP address in this specific range. In *Step 2*, we create and run a new SQL Server on Linux container. Notice the use of the *--network* and *--ip* parameters instead of the usual *-p* parameter. Here, we are telling Docker to attach this container to the *bridgenet1* network and assign it a *172.19.0.2* IP address instead of relying on the *bridge* network to assign the IP address (the Docker daemon effectively acts as a DHCP server providing IP addresses to the containers attached to the *bridge* network). We do the same thing in Steps 3 and 4. Figure 11-5 shows the TCP/IP properties of the Docker host after creating the user-defined Docker networks and attaching containers to them.

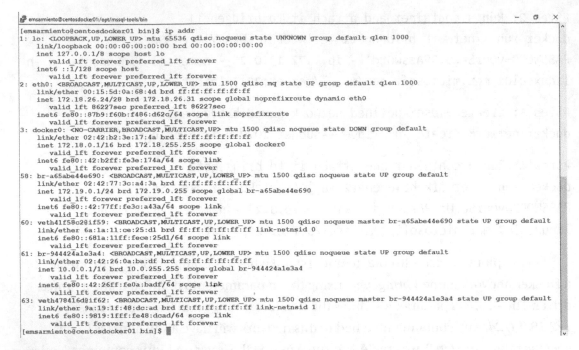

Figure 11-5. *TCP/IP settings of the Docker host after creating user-defined networks and attached containers to them*

Notice the following:

- The *docker0* bridge *state DOWN* status because there are no running containers attached to it.

- Two new Linux bridges named *br-a65abe44e690* and *br-944424a1e3a4* were created. These correspond to *bridgenet1* and *bridgenet2*, respectively. Again, names will be different on your Docker host.

- In the same way, two new virtual network adapters named *veth41f58c2@if59* and *veth478416d@if62* were created. Recall that Docker creates a pair of virtual network adapters every time a container is started, one end of which is attached to the host system via the bridge network and the other end to the running container. These virtual network adapters correspond to containers attached to *bridgenet1* and *bridgenet2*, respectively.

You can test this by connecting to the corresponding SQL Server instance on containers via their respective IP addresses, as shown in Figure 11-6.

```
emsarmiento@centosdocker01:/opt/mssql-tools/bin                                                          —  ☐  ×
[emsarmiento@centosdocker01 bin]$ ./sqlcmd -S172.19.0.2 -Usa -PyOurSecUr3PAssw0rd
1> SELECT @@SERVERNAME
2> GO

-----------------------------------------------------------------------------
--
linuxsql01

(1 rows affected)
1> SELECT local_net_address FROM sys.dm_exec_connections WHERE session_id=@@SPID
2> GO
local_net_address
-----------------------------------------------------------------------------
172.19.0.2

(1 rows affected)
1> exit
[emsarmiento@centosdocker01 bin]$ ./sqlcmd -S10.0.0.2 -Usa -PyOurSecUr3PAssw0rd
1> SELECT @@SERVERNAME
2> GO

-----------------------------------------------------------------------------
--
linuxsql02

(1 rows affected)
1> SELECT local_net_address FROM sys.dm_exec_connections WHERE session_id=@@SPID
2> GO
local_net_address
-----------------------------------------------------------------------------
10.0.0.2

(1 rows affected)
1> exit
[emsarmiento@centosdocker01 bin]$ ▉
```

Figure 11-6. *Connecting to SQL Server on containers on the same Docker host using different IP addresses*

Note   Keep in mind that while the containers are accessible via their IP addresses, you can only connect to them from the Docker host. That's because only the Docker host is aware of these new IP addresses. In order to access them remotely, you need to configure a proper route from a client machine on the network to the Docker host. Consult your network administrators on how to properly configure this to access these containers remotely.

This is a very old trick used by Internet service providers in the early days of the Internet where web servers host hundreds or more websites, each with their own domain name and IP address. Instead of spinning up hundreds of web servers, it's more cost-effective to assign multiple IP addresses to a single web server. SQL Server adopted this trick with named instances and either attached multiple network adapters on a single database server or assigned multiple IP addresses to a single network adapter. This made it possible to connect to multiple SQL Server named instances on the same host using port 1433 – same concept, different implementation. However, it's not something I recommend unless you have a strong foundation on the basics of TCP/IP or work with a system administrator who does. Troubleshooting network connectivity can be a pain with complex implementations like this.

Intra-container Communications

The *docker0* bridge is an example of a Docker *bridge* network. And while we've already covered a bit of what *bridge* networks are and what they can do, the *docker0* bridge is a bit special. Let's look at what makes intra-container communications possible using the *bridge* network.

Connecting containers to a *bridge* network allows them to take advantage of networking capabilities on the Docker host. Just like any network switch, containers connected to a bridge network can communicate with each other. However, they are totally isolated to other containers connected to other bridge networks. Figure 11-7 shows the network diagram of the user-defined bridge networks we created in the previous section.

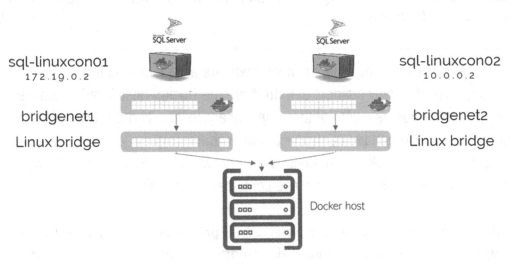

Figure 11-7. Network diagram of the user-defined bridge network created in the previous section

Because they are on two isolated networks, *sql-linuxcon01* cannot communicate with *sql-linuxcon02* and vice versa. Depending on how your network administrators designed the network, there are reasons why they would implement network segmentation – security isolation being one of the most common reasons, compliance, and quality of service (QoS), just to name a few. The same is true for deploying containers on different user-defined bridge networks. Talk to your network administrators about your network design. It is a great opportunity to understand why your network is designed the way it is. But whether the network design is simple or complex, services and applications need to talk to each other. This is where network routing and other network services like DNS come in.

Let's say we created two containers using the default bridge network, *docker0*. I did mention that the *docker0* bridge is a bit special given that while containers connected to it can communicate with each other, they can only talk to each other via IP address, not hostnames. In contrast, containers connected to a user-defined bridge network can take advantage of the built-in DNS service, allowing them to communicate with each other using either IP addresses, hostnames, or aliases. Recall the example provided in the section "Docker Compose and YAML Files" in *Chapter 10*. The following YAML file describes a bit of the networking components that make up the two containers needed for the multi-container app:

```
version: "3"
services:
    wfe:
        build: ./mssql-aspcore-example-app
        ports:
            - "5000:5000"
        depends_on:
            - db
    db:
        build: ./mssql-aspcore-example-db
        environment:
            SA_PASSWORD: "mySecUr3PAssw0rd"
            ACCEPT_EULA: "Y"
            - "1500:1433"
```

There are two services that make up the multi-container app – the *wfe* service and the *db* service. If you explore the *appsettings.json* file of the ASP.NET Core application, the database connection string specifies the database server. I've highlighted the database server name for emphasis:

```
"ConnectionStrings": {
  "BelgradeDemo": "Server=db;Database=ProductCatalog;User ID=WebLogin;
  password=SQLPass1234!"
}
```

So, how did the ASP.NET Core app know that the SQL Server on Linux container was the database server that it needs to connect to? When you ran Docker Compose to build the multi-container app, the first thing that Docker did was to create a user-defined bridge network named *<projectName>_default*. Since the name of the project is *mssql-aspcore-example*, the user-defined bridge network is named *mssql-aspcore-example_default*. Figure 11-8 shows the user-defined bridge network created as part of the multi-container app. It also shows the two containers – *mssql-aspcoreexample_wfe_1* for the *wfe* and *mssql-aspcore-example_db_1* for the *db* – attached to the bridge network with their corresponding IP addresses. So far, so good.

Figure 11-8. *User-defined bridge network created as part of the multi-container app*

But we still haven't answered the question, *how did the ASP.NET Core app know that the SQL Server on Linux container was the database server that it needs to connect to?* Because the two containers are connected to the same user-defined bridge network, the *wfe* container was able to access the *db* container via the service name as defined in the YAML file. User-defined bridge networks provide DNS name or alias resolution, in this case, aliases for the services as defined in the YAML file. Because the containers were created using Docker Compose, no hostnames were provided, unlike when we were using the *docker run* command and passing the -*h* parameter. Docker will assign the container ID as the hostname for the containers. But with the aliases defined for the services and having both containers connected to the same user-defined bridge network, they can communicate with each other using DNS name or, in this case, alias resolution. Should you decide to change the service name in the YAML file from *db* to *dbserver*, you would need to modify the connection string value in the *appsettings.json* file as well.

Putting It All Together

Using the multi-container app we built in *Chapter 10*, let's explore how the different components work together to understand the Docker networking stack, incorporating everything we've covered throughout this book. Figure 11-9 shows the network diagram of the multi-container app.

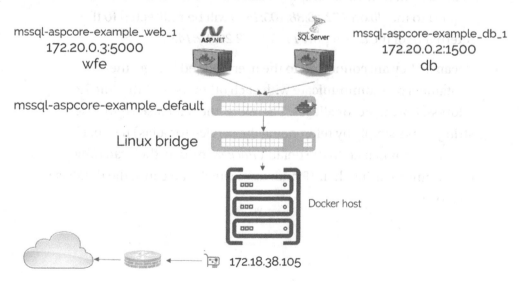

Figure 11-9. *Network diagram of multi-container app*

Since the containers are running on a single Docker host

- Both containers are connected to the *mssql-aspcore-example_default* user-defined bridge and will be assigned an IP address in the subnet *172.20.0.0/16* as shown in Figure 11-8. The IP address range will depend on what was assigned to the user-defined bridge network.

- Both containers can be accessed remotely using the Docker host's IP address with their corresponding ports. The *wfe* can be accessed via *http://172.18.38.105:5000* from any browser, while the *db* can be accessed via *172.18.38.105:1500* using your favorite SQL Server tool – SSMS, Azure Data Studio, sqlcmd, Visual Studio, and so on. This is possible even without modifying the default Linux firewall rules because the Docker daemon modifies the *iptables* behind the scenes. Recall the section "A Note on the Linux Firewalls and Docker" in *Chapter 8*.

- The *mssql-aspcore-example_default* user-defined bridge provides network address translation (NAT) for the traffic coming into the containers from the external network. This allows multiple containers to access the external network and vice versa through a single IP address – the IP address of the Docker host. A browser request to the *wfe* on *http://172.18.38.105:5000* will be redirected to the internal IP of the *wfe* on port *5000 – http://172.20.0.3:5000*. Similarly, a database request to the *db* on *172.18.38.105:1500* will be redirected to the internal IP of the *db* on port *1433 – 172.20.0.2:1433*.

- Because they are connected to the user-defined bridge, the containers can communicate with each other using either the IP address, hostname, or aliases. Therefore, the database connection string works simply by referencing the service (or alias) name. If they were connected to the default *docker0* bridge, they can only communicate using their IP addresses which can cause the database call to fail.

- As the ports are published and mapped to the Docker host, both containers can be accessed remotely. You can restrict remote access to the *db* container by removing the port mapping. If you do so, you can still access the *db* container from the *wfe* container or from the Docker host.

- We need to stop right here before you end up taking the job of your network administrator.

Since the IP address of the container wasn't explicitly defined, you can retrieve their IP addresses by using the *docker inspect* command as shown in the following, passing either the container name or ID value:

```
docker inspect <container name | ID> | grep IPAddress
```

But you wouldn't want to manually do this for all the running containers. The following command will display all the running containers with their corresponding IP addresses:

```
docker inspect --format='{{.Name}} {{range .NetworkSettings.Networks}}
{{.IPAddress}}{{end}}' $(docker ps -q)
```

Keep in mind that this only covers single-host networking. To learn more about the other types of network drivers that you can use with Docker, check out the Docker networking overview on *https://docs.docker.com/network/*.

Summary

When I was preparing the outline for this book, this chapter wasn't even on the initial draft. Until I remembered how challenging it was to deal with the network stack on anything related to the cloud. I vividly remember how I wasted hours troubleshooting issues with deploying SQL Server on AWS and Microsoft Azure only to realize that the problem had nothing to do with SQL Server – it was the network. Whether you're working with public or private cloud, understanding the fundamentals of the network stack is even more important today, especially when you're dealing with all the abstractions that the so-called networking-as-a-service provides. Hence, I included the basics of Docker networking for single-host deployments. This chapter covers how Docker leverages the Linux bridge to implement their networking capabilities, how containers are exposed to external networks via port mapping, and how it is even possible to run multiple SQL Server on Linux instances on a single Linux machine through containers even when the Microsoft documentation clearly says you can't. The truth is that the TCP/IP and networking fundamentals remain the same. Only their implementation has changed. So, the next time you're faced with a networking issue on a cloud platform like Docker, VMWare, Microsoft Azure, or AWS, go back to the basics. You'll be glad you learned the fundamentals.

APPENDIX A

Building a Personal Lab Environment

We don't stop playing because we grow old; we grow old because we stop playing.

—George Bernard Shaw

I've had the opportunity to talk to aspiring SQL Server DBAs and people who wanted to pursue a career as an IT professional. Often, they share stories of how challenging it is to find a job because of their lack of real-world experience. Theory can only do so much. They may have a computer-related degree or certification, but their lack of real-world experience is preventing them from even getting an interview. Some of them have spent years trying to get an entry-level job as a junior SQL Server DBA and are starting to lose hope. That is until I tell them about T.E.D.S.

As someone who didn't have a computer-related education, I knew early on that I would have even bigger challenges if I wanted to pursue a career in IT. No one wanted to hire me after graduation because my university transcript did not reflect your typical student. I failed 17 – not 7 but 17 – courses in my undergraduate program. Hiring managers were even surprised that I finished a five-year program in five-and-a-half years, given the number of courses I failed. But if there's one thing that my experience doing hard labor in factories has taught me, persistence and confidence can open doors of opportunities. And that's where T.E.D.S. comes in.

T.E.D.S. stands for Tech Experts Digital Sandbox. I invented the term when I was learning how to configure a Windows NT 4.0 Server while my classmates were busy studying for our power plant design final exam. My exposure with a German industrial automation company taught me that simulations, coupled with creativity, are key to

E. M. Sarmiento, *The SQL Server DBA's Guide to Docker Containers*, https://doi.org/10.1007/978-1-4842-5826-2

getting close to real-world experience. It's the rehearsals before the main performance, the practice before the real game. So, I made it an essential part of my professional growth to build simulation environments even before I got my very first job as a SQL Server DBA. In fact, I credit T.E.D.S. for getting my very first job as a SQL Server DBA. When the hiring manager asked me if I had any production DBA experience, I told him I didn't. But I knew more about SQL Server than any of their senior engineers on staff. I was hired on the spot.

The Need for a Personal Lab

A T.E.D.S. – or a personal lab – provides a powerful and safe environment to build confidence while learning new technologies. Some will argue that it isn't a real-world environment. My take on it is, with enough creativity, it can be better than some real-world environments. My very first personal lab was a barebone PC that I built for a friend. I loved building PCs when I was in college and made enough cash from it to partially support my education. First, it was as simple as installing and configuring Windows 95 on an Intel 80486–based PC with 16MB RAM. Imagine having to insert 16 floppy disks to complete the installation only to realize that the 15th disk had a bad sector. I surely don't miss those days. Then, it was Windows NT 4.0 Server. Since I couldn't afford my own PC, I used the ones I built for friends. When I learned how to connect computers to a local area network, I incorporated Active Directory and DNS – on Windows 2000 Advanced Server. I was lucky to have worked part-time at an educational institution where I had access to hardware and software that I can play around with. I was rebuilding environments almost every week – from Active Directory, DNS, networking, and SQL Server as part of the domain. And because we had to do it every week, we needed to find a way to do the work fast. Necessity drove us to adopt scripting and automation. We didn't want to be spending the whole weekend rebuilding environments for them to be ready come Monday morning.

When Microsoft bought Virtual PC and Virtual Server from a company called Connectix Corporation in 2003, they became a part of their product offerings. On the other hand, VMWare was already way ahead of the virtualization race. These technological innovations made building a personal lab more affordable. Instead of having multiple computers to build an enterprise environment, you only need one powerful computer with enough compute resources and hard disk space to run multiple virtual machines. Microsoft Virtual PC took over my T.E.D.S. environment, running a minimum of four virtual machines for Active Directory, Microsoft Exchange, SQL Server, and a Windows 2000 Workstation. I built this environment every week for a year. After getting hired as a data center engineer/DBA for a global technology company, I switched to VMWare Workstation. I was doing presentations on deploying SharePoint Server and System Center Configuration Manager for Microsoft events in Southeast Asia, running VMWare Workstation on my laptop without them even knowing (remember, this was the old Microsoft that hated everything that isn't Microsoft). The series of articles I wrote on MSSQLTips.com on building a multi-data center Windows Server Failover Cluster (WSFC) architecture was built on a very old Acer Aspire laptop that had 8GB of RAM running Windows XP Professional. It wasn't a great setup but it sure served its purpose.

When I started my own consulting practice, I searched for a portable machine that I can use when I speak at conferences. I already have my 2011 MacBook Pro with 16GB of RAM and a solid-state drive as a backup laptop running VMWare Fusion. I also added a Gigabyte BRIX barebone mini-PC in the collection. Since it's a barebone PC, I couldn't take it with me when I travel by air. Airport security would ask to power it up just like any other laptop. Without a monitor, they would have me ship it to my destination instead of carrying it with me on a flight. I didn't want to take the risk. Besides, I wanted something lighter than my MacBook Pro. So, I got myself a refurbished Dell Latitude E7480 and upgraded the RAM to 32GB. It's good enough to run eight VMs – two domain controllers, four servers for my multisite WSFC, a virtual network switch, and a Windows 10 workstation – while running PowerPoint, Word, and Ableton Live. How many SQL Server DBAs out there have a simulated environment of a multi-data center setup like this while playing music with a digital audio workstation – on their laptops? This is what I meant when I said simulation with enough creativity can be better than some real-world environments.

It was only recently when I decided to really invest in production-grade hardware. I don't recommend doing it unless you really want to focus on hardware. Besides, with everything moving to the cloud, hardware becomes irrelevant. The only reason I did it was because it was … cheap. I got a refurbished, out-of-warranty 24-core HPE DL 380 G8 machine from eBay with 128GB RAM and three disks configured with RAID-5. And it's cheaper than my Dell Latitude E7480 laptop. I've worked with production-grade hardware in the past so configuring it was no big deal, installing Windows Server 2016 with Hyper-V. Not only do I have production-grade hardware running enterprise software that emulates some of the most complex network architecture, but my T.E.D.S. also serves as additional heat source in my basement during the winter.

I share my more than 20-year journey of building and leveraging T.E.D.S. to highlight a very important point: you need one. And with virtualization and the cloud, there's no more excuse to not have one. You owe it to yourself to build a T.E.D.S. And it doesn't have to break the bank. There are evaluation copies of software available that you can download and install. Or you can invest in an MSDN Visual Studio Professional subscription so you can have access to Microsoft server software that you can use for dev/test environments. And if you have a relatively new laptop or a PC, the specifications are good enough to run the examples provided in this book. I can't emphasize the need to have a T.E.D.S. if you want to succeed as an IT professional.

Software for the Lab Environment

If you decide to build your own T.E.D.S., virtualization is the way to go unless you have the budget for a dedicated hardware just for this purpose. Choosing a virtualization platform is really a matter of preference. I'm not going to list down why you should think about capital expenditures (CapEx) like licensing and support costs, unless you're a business decision-maker for your company. But rather, choose a virtualization platform based on your professional goals (do you want to join a company that leverages VMWare ESXi?) and what your current job already uses. This makes it easy to align your learning objectives with your company's IT direction. It's a win-win situation.

Operating System

Most SQL Server DBAs work with Windows since it was the only supported platform in the past. With virtualization, you can run a supported virtualization platform of choice on an iMac running Mac OS – host SQL Server on a Windows Server operating system inside a VM on a Mac. Use an operating system that you're most familiar with. If it's Windows, stick with it. You're going to be working with Linux a lot throughout this book. And it can be frustrating to work with something you're not familiar with. We want to minimize the frustration while maximizing the learning experience.

Virtualization Platform

I use both VMWare and Hyper-V because my clients have them – and because I have access to both of them. Licensing cost can be a deciding factor especially if you're the one paying for it. VMWare has a free version – VMWare Workstation Player – that you can download and use. You can download VMWare Workstation Player from *www.vmware.com/products/workstation-player/workstation-player-evaluation.html*.

Windows 10 Enterprise, Pro, and Education has built-in Hyper-V as an optional feature, you just have to enable it. Follow the instructions on *https://docs.microsoft.com/en-us/virtualization/hyper-v-on-windows/quick-start/enable-hyper-v* to enable Hyper-V on Windows 10.

Some people prefer Oracle VirtualBox. I've tried it before but am not a big fan. I always go for platforms that have wide adoption in production environments – hence, why I opted for both VMWare and Hyper-V. But for learning purposes, it's a great platform. You can download Oracle VirtualBox from *www.virtualbox.org/wiki/Downloads*.

In order to make virtualization work, you need to have a CPU that supports it. For Intel-based processors, visit this page to check if your computer supports virtualization – *www.intel.com/content/www/us/en/support/articles/000005486/processors.html*. All processors in the Intel VT product portfolio support virtualization. For AMD-based processors, it's the AMD-V product portfolio. On top of this, virtualization support should be enabled on the BIOS. Check your computer manufacturer for instructions on how to enable virtualization support on the BIOS.

Installing CentOS Linux Server

Since most of the content in this book is focused on Linux, it helps to know how to install the operating system. We'll start with a plain-vanilla install of CentOS Linux server. I mentioned in the earlier chapters why I chose CentOS over Red Hat Enterprise Linux (RHEL) – it's free. And because it is derived from the source code of RHEL, you get the same experience as working with RHEL minus the commercial support. For mission-critical systems which need the guaranteed service-level agreement, RHEL is the choice. With CentOS, you're on your own. I have a few customers who deployed mission-critical apps on CentOS Linux because they didn't want to pay for enterprise support. And while it works for them, I don't recommend it. It's like saying you don't need health insurance because you don't ever get sick. Some people just want to reduce their operational expenditures (OpEx) without considering the risks. You're better than that. Be sure to understand the risk implications of every business decision that your company makes and be their trusted advisor that helps them make wise ones. But for development and test environments, CentOS would be good enough.

You can download the installation ISO image from *www.centos.org/download/*. Since you'll be running SQL Server on Linux in a Docker container, you need a minimum version of 7.3 – both for CentOS and RHEL – in order to be supported.

Note   In addition to the minimum supported version of the operating system needed to run SQL Server on Linux, you also need to consider the version of the container operating system in order to be supported. For example, if you decide to run a RHEL v7.4 for your Linux Docker host, your SQL Server on container should also be running RHEL v7.4. Refer to *https://support.microsoft.com/ en-us/help/4047326/support-policy-for-microsoft-sql-server* for additional information on supported configurations for running SQL Server on containers.

After downloading the installation ISO image, mount it on your VM and proceed with the installation. Figure A-1 shows the CentOS boot screen.

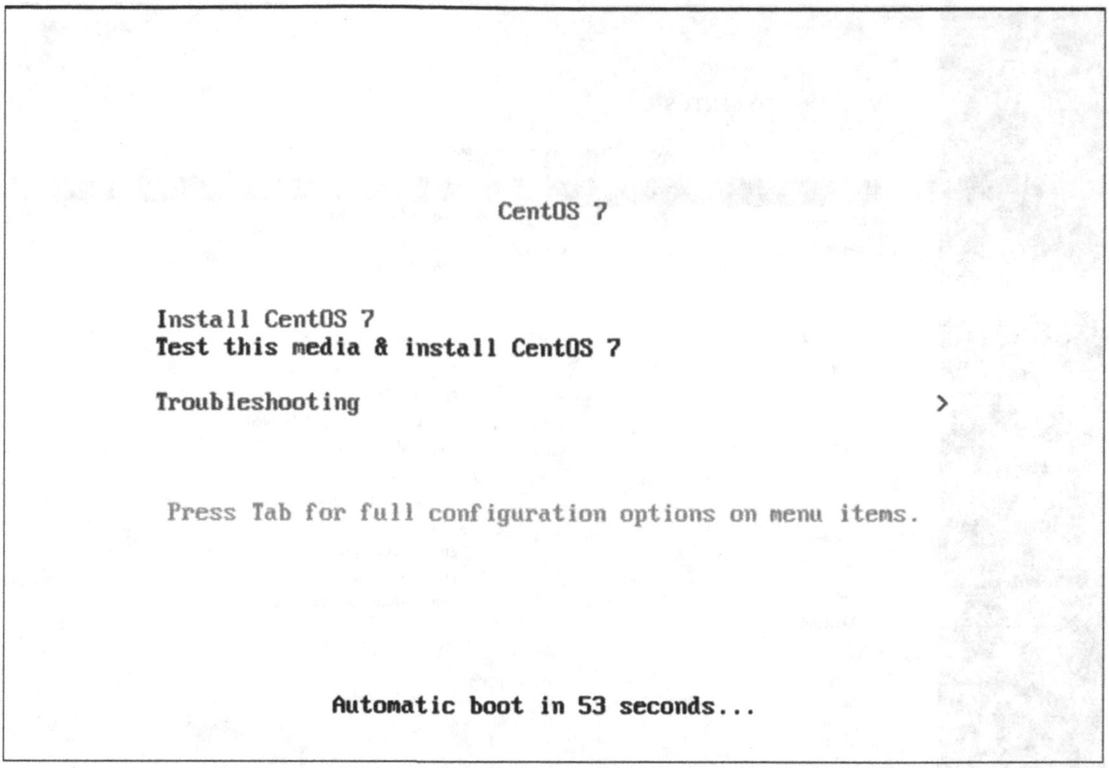

```
                            CentOS 7


          Install CentOS 7
          Test this media & install CentOS 7

          Troubleshooting                                        >



          Press Tab for full configuration options on menu items.




                    Automatic boot in 53 seconds...
```

Figure A-1. *CentOS installation boot screen*

Use your keyboard arrow keys to select the *Install CentOS 7* option to kick-start the installation process for CentOS 7.3. The next screen, as shown in Figure A-2, will prompt you to choose the language you want to use to install CentOS. The language selected here will then be used throughout the rest of the installer. I pride myself on speaking several languages other than my native Philippine language – English, American, Canadian, and Australian. But since Linux puts them all under the same name, I just choose *English (United States)* even though it technically is American.

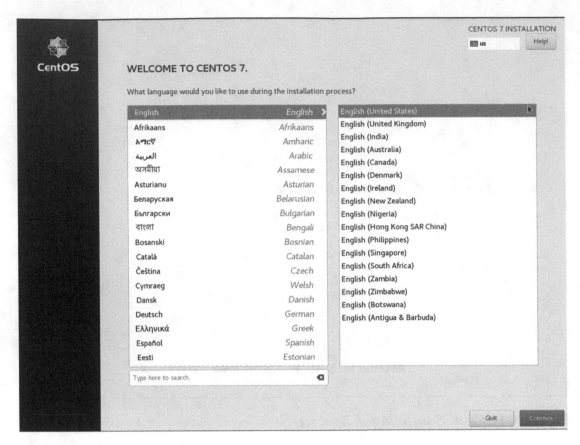

Figure A-2. *Choosing the language to use during installation*

Click *Continue* to confirm your selection and proceed with the installation. Figure A-3 shows you the *Installation Summary* page. Before you can continue with the installation, you may need to configure a few things. These will be marked with a warning icon, so you know which setting it is. One of them is the *Installation Destination* settings. Since this is a fresh installation (or when your machine contains a new disk), you will get a warning about automatic partitioning selected. Click the *Installation Destination* option under the *System* heading.

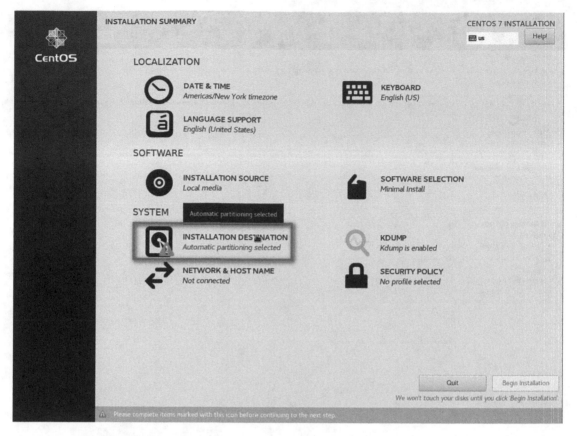

Figure A-3. *Configuring Installation Destination*

We'll simplify the configuration and accept the defaults as shown in Figure A-4. With automatic partitioning, you are telling CentOS that the selected destination disk will be automatically partitioned with the */root*, */home*, and *swap* partitions. It will also automatically create an LVM logical volume in the XFS filesystem. We're not going to configure additional disks so the default settings are fine. You don't really need to do anything here other than click the *Done* button. Unfortunately, the installation process will not continue until you do so.

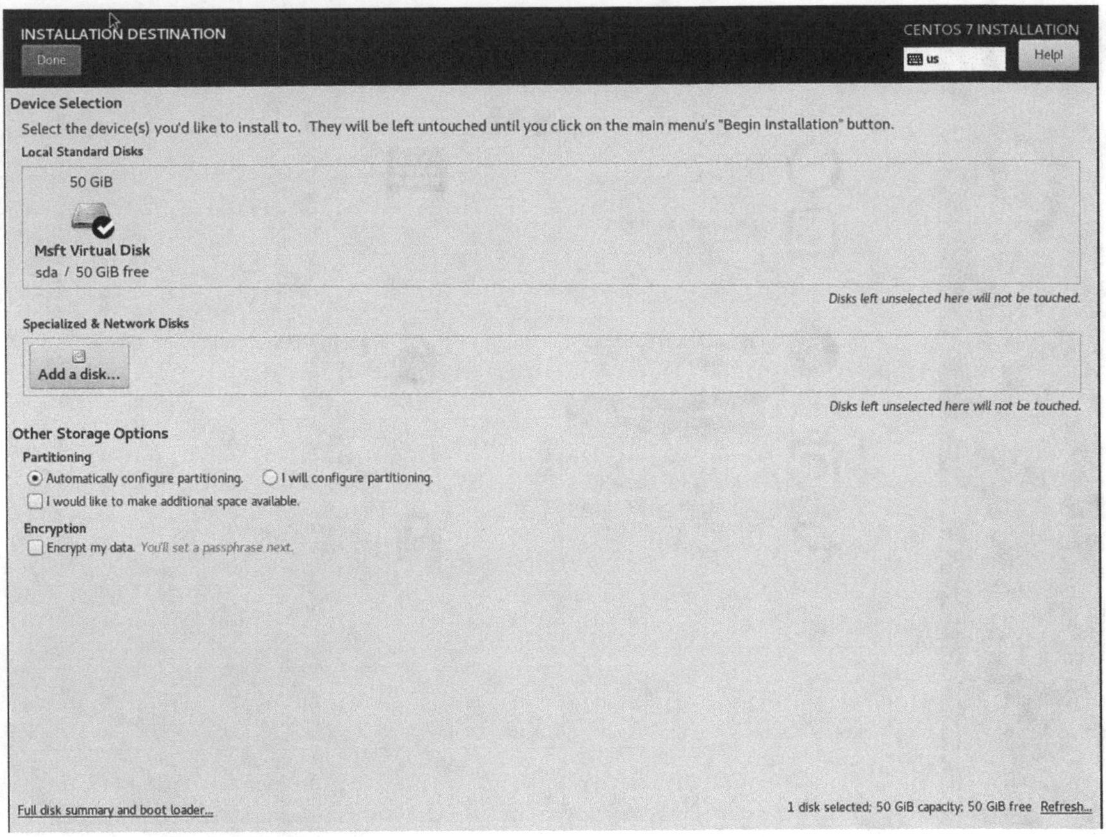

Figure A-4. *Configuring automatic partitioning under Installation Destination*

Another setting that you can configure is the *Network & Hostname* option as shown in Figure A-5. If you noticed, the status says *Not connected*. You can proceed with the installation without configuring this option, but you won't be able to access your CentOS Linux machine remotely. The machine needs to be connected to your network so you can access it remotely via SSH. Click the *Network & Hostname* option to configure the setting.

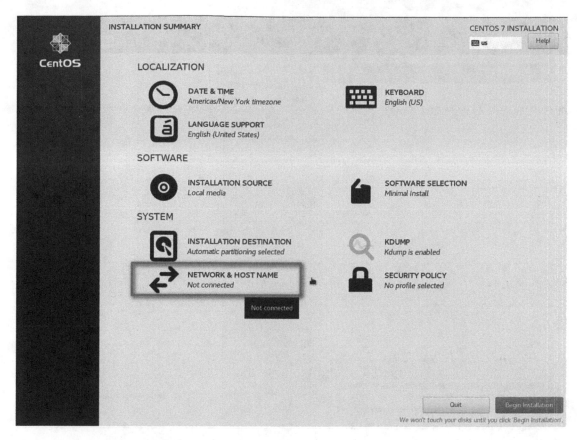

Figure A-5. *Configuring Network & Hostname*

Figure A-6 shows the *Network & Hostname* configuration page. Click the *OFF* button to change it to *ON*. Doing so will configure the CentOS Linux machine to automatically get an IP address from a DHCP server if it is properly connected to the network. Take note of this IP address. You will use it to connect to this machine remotely via SSH. If you want to configure a static IP address, click the *Configure* button. But before you do, ask your network administrators for the appropriate TCP/IP values so you don't assign one that is already used. If you're configuring this on your home network, make sure that your VM is using the physical network adapter of the computer that is connected to your router. And because you have fewer devices on your home network, the VM will be assigned the same IP address until you reboot your router. This will allow your VM to connect to the Internet. Also, change the hostname and click the *Apply* button. It's just good practice to name your servers accordingly. I use a fully qualified domain name because I integrate the servers in my lab in an Active Directory domain and leverage DNS.

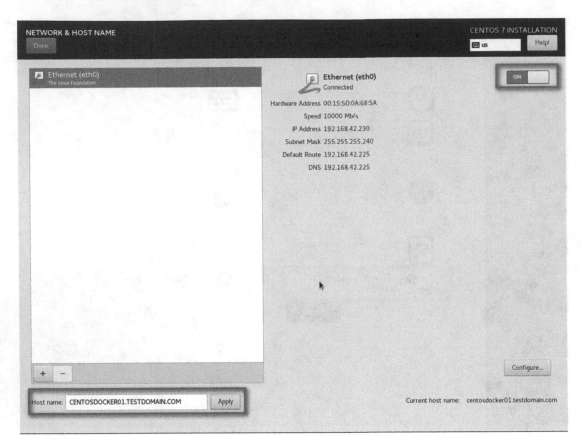

Figure A-6. *Configuring TCP/IP and hostname under Network & Hostname*

Click the *Done* button when you finish configuring the TCP/IP settings. It will take you back to the *Installation Summary* page where you can now click the *Begin Installation* button. This will take you to the *Configuration* page where you can assign a password to the *root* user and create a new user that has *root* privileges. Figure A-7 shows the *Configuration* page. Click the *Root Password* option under *User Settings* to set the *root* password.

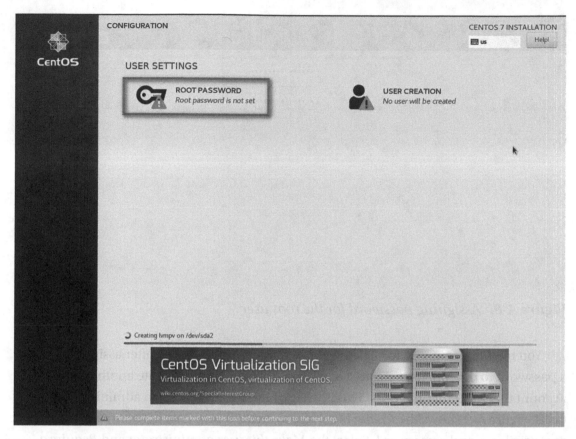

Figure A-7. *Configuring User Settings*

In Figure A-8, provide a complex password for the *root* user and don't ever forget it. I'm not going to show you how to hack the *root* user if you forget the password. So, you better take note of it. But, please, don't write it on a Post-it note and stick it to where anyone might see it. Always apply security best practices.

Click the *Done* button to close the *Root Password* page.

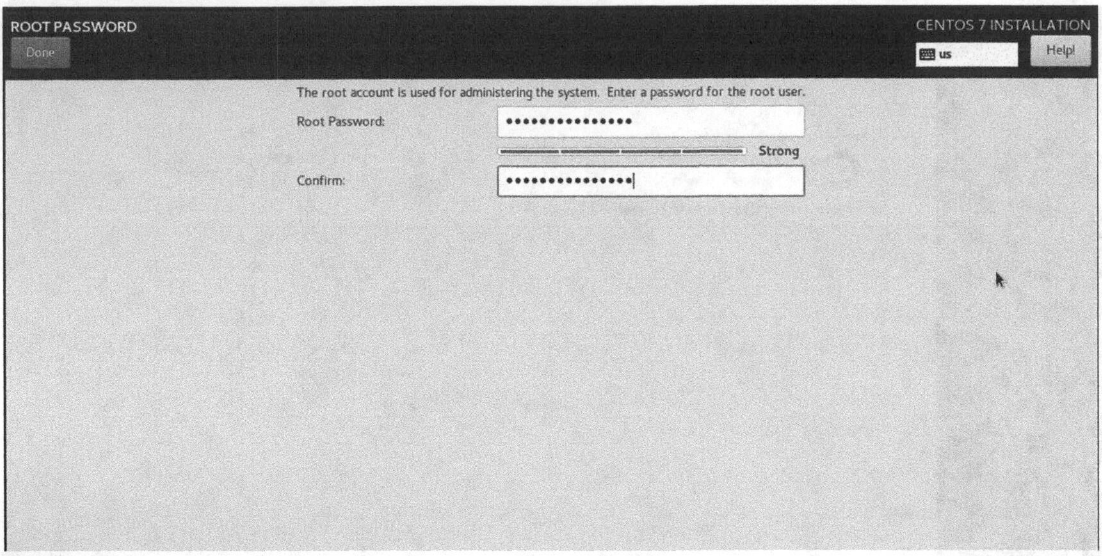

Figure A-8. *Assigning password for the root user*

You might be tempted to click the *Finish Configuration* button after assigning a password to the *root* user. Avoid it at all cost. You still need to create another user account that has *root* privileges. This is what you will use to perform administration tasks. Figure A-9 shows the *Create User* page to create a new user account; assign it *root* privileges and a password. Select the *Make this user administrator* and *Require a password to use this account* checkboxes.

Click the *Done* button to create the new user account with *root* privileges.

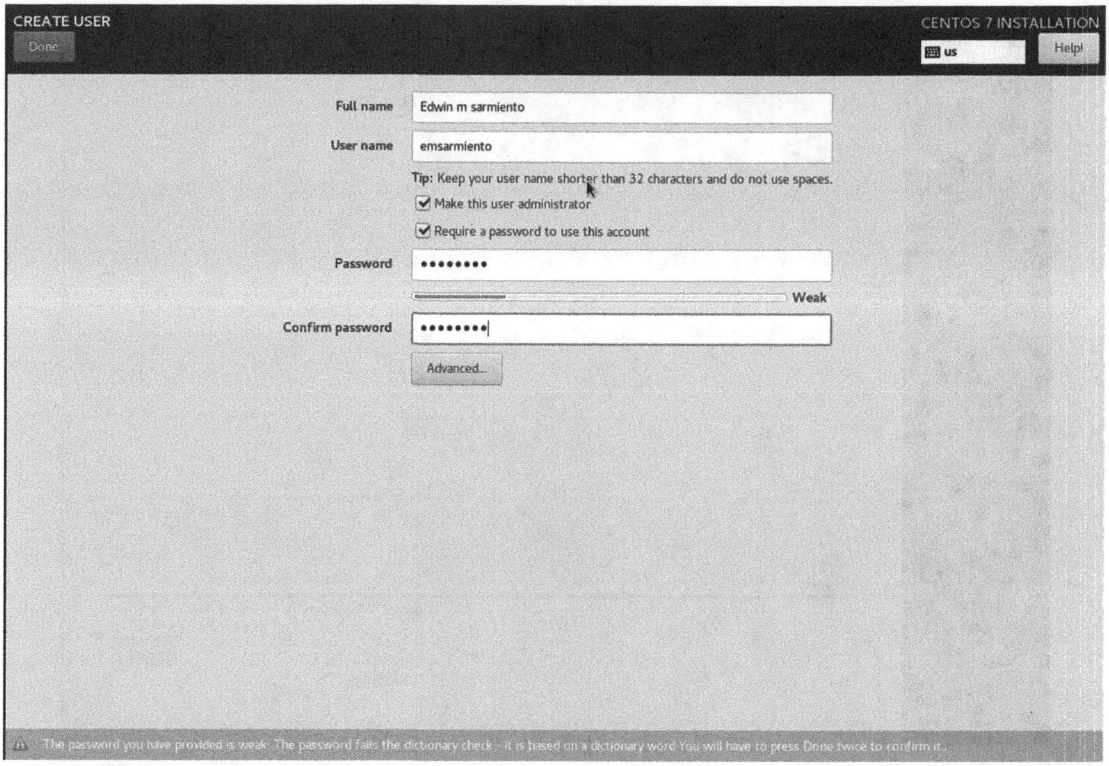

Figure A-9. *Creating a new user with root privileges*

When everything has been configured, it's time to reboot the machine. As shown in Figure A-10, click the *Reboot* button to do so. I use this example to poke fun at Linux administrators who tell Windows administrators to reboot the machine when it encounters problems, claiming that Linux doesn't need a reboot. Oh, yes it does.

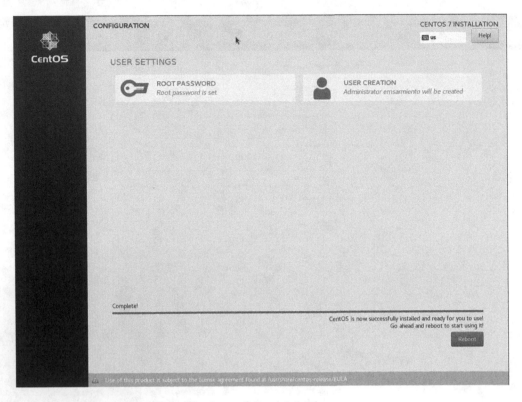

Figure A-10. *Finalizing installation of CentOS Linux*

After the machine reboots, you can test remote connectivity via SSH. We'll look at using SSH to connect to a Linux machine remotely at a later section.

Installing Ubuntu Linux Server

I'll admit, I'm a bit biased. I prefer RHEL simply because of stability, both from a technology and business perspective. It was designed with large, enterprise environments in mind. When you're dealing with mission-critical systems, the last thing you want is a stability issue caused by bug fixes. Ubuntu, on the other hand, releases package updates more frequently. That's why you'll see more of Ubuntu deployed on desktops than servers. I was surprised when Microsoft announced support for SQL Server on Ubuntu. But then, it's no different from running SQL Server Developer Edition on a Windows workstation – developers are the target audience.

You can download the Ubuntu Server installation ISO image from *http://releases. ubuntu.com/xenial/*. Since you'll be running SQL Server on Linux in a Docker container, you need a minimum version of 16.04 in order to be supported.

Tip   Just like SQL Server, Ubuntu has release codenames. Xenial Xerus is the codename for the 16.04 release, while Bionic Beaver is the codename for the 18.04 release. Release happens twice a year and, if you look at the version numbers, they're in the format *YY.MM*. So, Ubuntu Xenial Xerus (16.04) was released in April 2016, while Ubuntu Bionic Beaver (18.04) was released in April 2018.

After downloading the installation ISO image, mount it on your VM and proceed with the installation. Figure A-11 shows the Ubuntu installer language screen. If there's one thing I like about Ubuntu, it's the option to use my native Philippine language – Tagalog. But since I need to take screenshots of the installation process, I can't use that language. I did try it a few times when I first started installing Ubuntu just to get a laugh out of it. I spent more time laughing than I did installing. So much for being productive. For this installation, I'll just stick with American, I mean English.

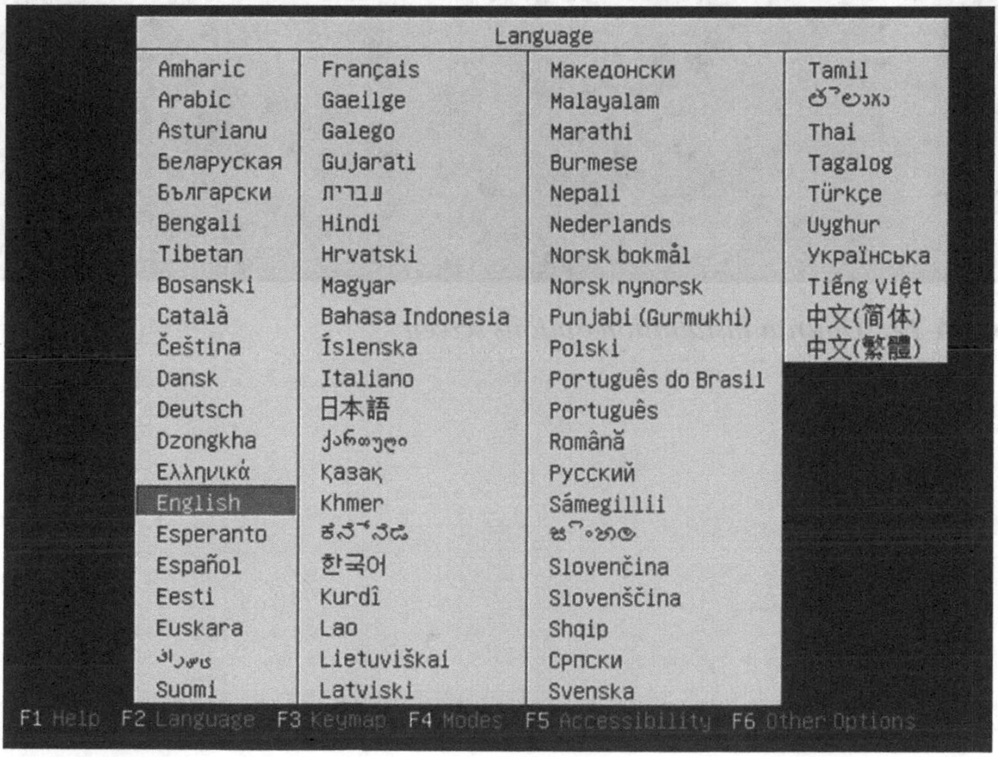

Figure A-11.   *Ubuntu installer language screen – for the installation process*

In the Ubuntu installation options screen (Figure A-12), use your keyboard arrow keys to select *Install Ubuntu Server* and hit *Enter*.

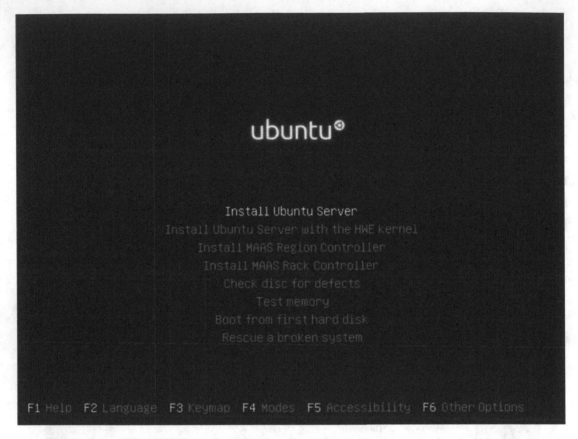

Figure A-12. *Ubuntu installation options screen*

What I find interesting is that Ubuntu will ask you again for your language of choice, as shown in Figure A-13, as if you haven't already done so in the previous selection.

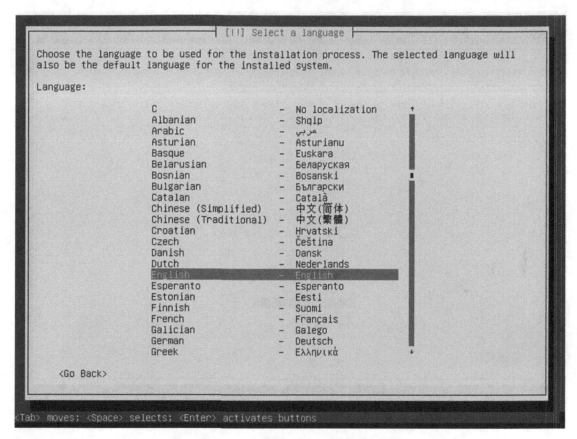

Figure A-13. *Ubuntu Select a language screen – for the operating system*

The difference between Figures A-11 and A-13 is that the former is your language of choice during the installation process, while the latter is the language of choice for the server operating system. When I think about it, how many people would actually use different languages during installation and deployment? Most of us will stick to just one language from start to finish. I don't know the rationale behind this but it is what it is. Hit *Enter* to proceed to the next screen.

In the *[!!] Select your location* screen (Figure A-14), choose your location and hit *Enter*. This will help in determining and configuring time zone.

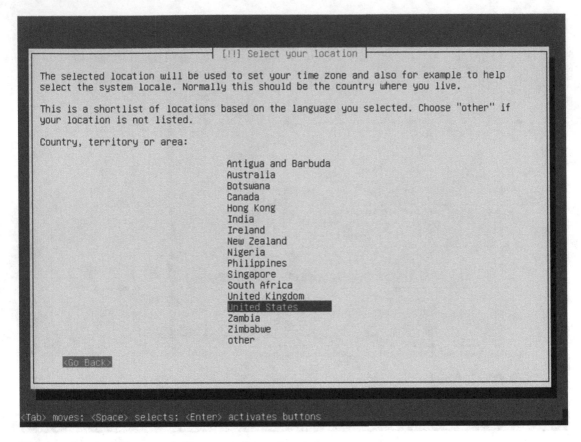

Figure A-14. *Ubuntu Select your location screen*

In the *[!] Configure the keyboard* screen (Figure A-15), select *No* and hit *Enter*. Unless you are using a special keyboard, you don't need to have Ubuntu detect your keyboard layout.

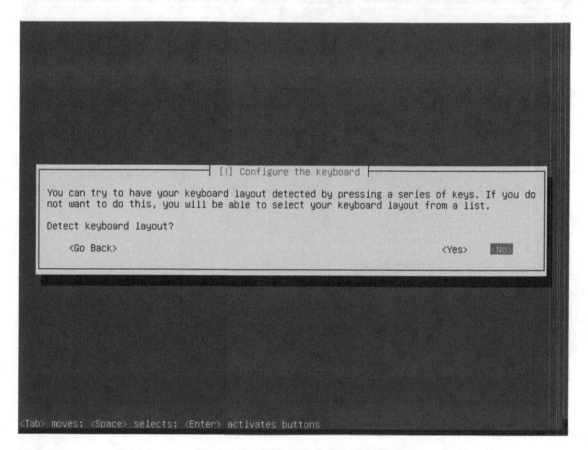

Figure A-15. *Ubuntu Configure the keyboard screen*

Still in the *[!] Configure the keyboard* screen (Figure A-16), choose the country of origin for the keyboard that you're using and hit *Enter*.

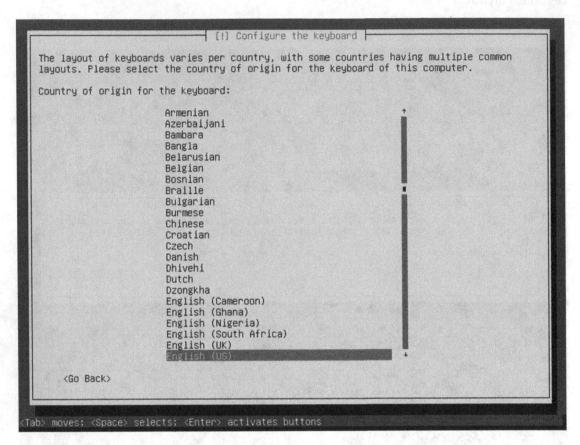

Figure A-16. *Ubuntu Configure the keyboard screen – part 2*

And still in the *[!] Configure the keyboard* screen (Figure A-17), select the keyboard that you're using and hit *Enter*. Don't worry, this will be the last one for the keyboard configuration option.

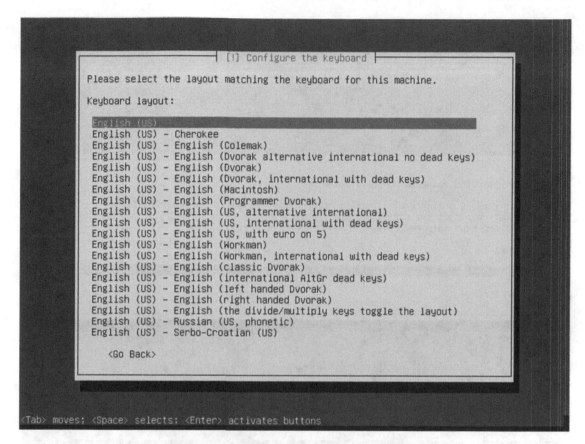

Figure A-17.   Ubuntu Configure the keyboard screen – part 3

In the *[!] Configure the network* screen (Figure A-18), provide a meaningful hostname for this server and hit *Enter*. I usually follow the Windows hostname guidelines for naming my Linux machines. This way, I won't have any issues should I decide to join the Linux machine to an Active Directory domain.

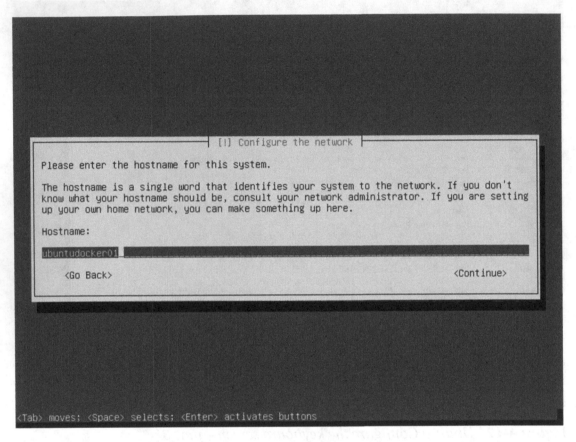

Figure A-18. *Ubuntu Configure the network screen*

In the *[!!] Set up users and passwords* screen (Figure A-19), provide a full name for the primary account that you will use to administer the server and hit *Enter*. Remember, this is not the *root* user. But you can gain *root* privileges using this user account by prefixing *sudo* to your commands.

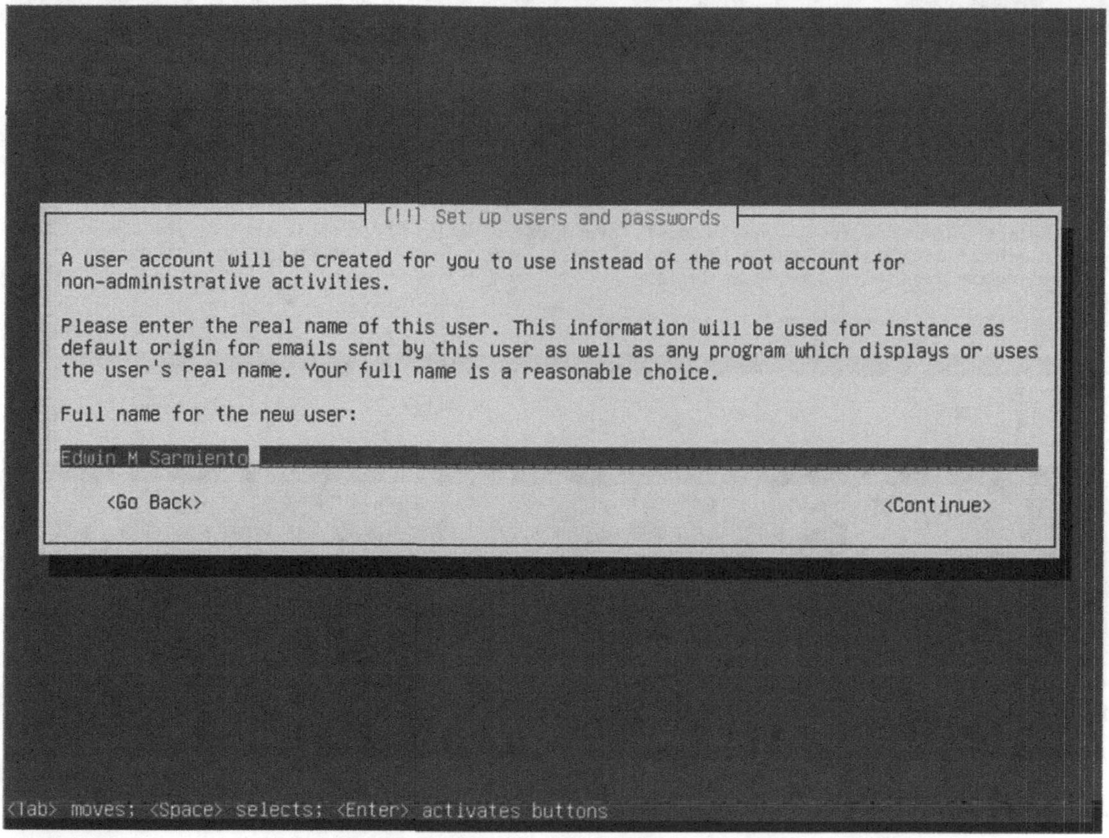

Figure A-19. Ubuntu Set up users and passwords screen

Still in the *[!!] Set up users and passwords* screen (Figure A-20), provide the account name for this user and hit *Enter*.

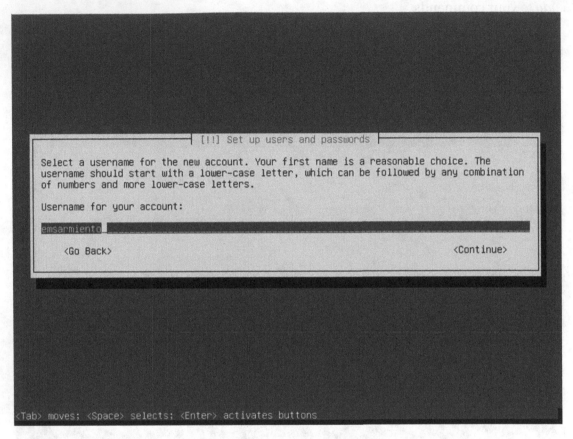

Figure A-20. *Ubuntu Set up users and passwords screen – part 2*

Still in the *[!!] Set up users and passwords* screen (Figure A-21), provide the password for this user account and hit *Enter*.

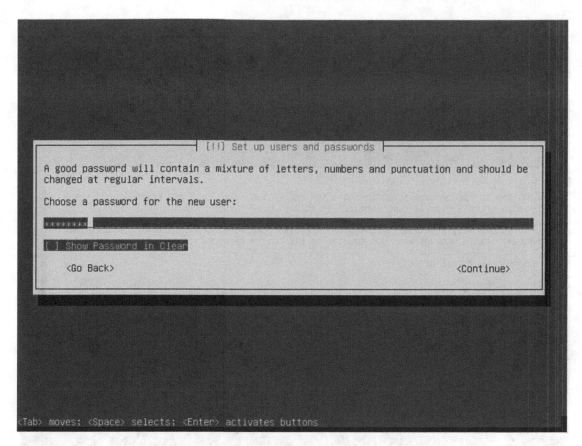

Figure A-21. *Ubuntu Set up users and passwords screen – part 3*

You will be asked to reenter the password to confirm. Once you're done, hit Enter. You will also be asked if you want your user home directory to be encrypted (Figure A-22). This isn't necessary so you can just accept the default – *No* – and hit *Enter*.

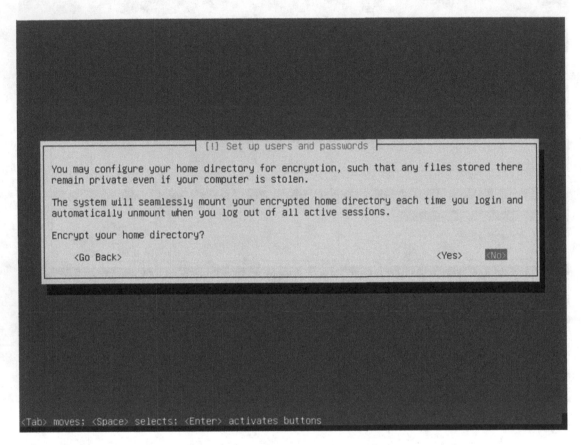

Figure A-22. *Ubuntu Set up users and passwords screen – part 4*

In the *[!] Configure the clock* screen (Figure A-23), check to see if the installer automatically picks up your physical location. If it does, hit *Enter*. This is Ubuntu's attempt to locate a network time protocol (NTP) server closest to you and set its own system clock based on it.

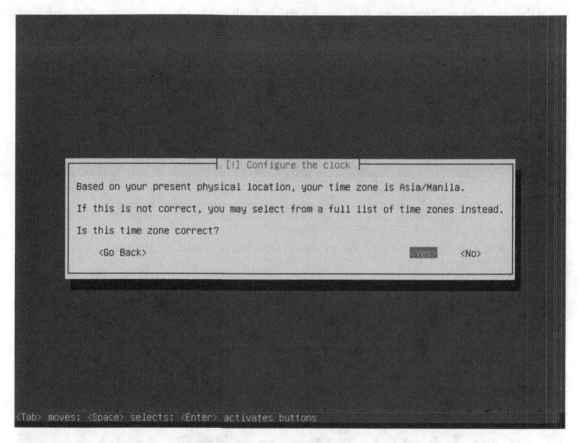

Figure A-23. *Ubuntu Configure the clock screen*

In the *[!!] Partition disks* screen (Figure A-24), the installer asks you to configure the disks. We won't be manually configuring the disks. We'll leave that for when you're the Linux systems administrator and would like to configure the disk subsystem according to the server's purpose. Normally, I would configure a disk partition that contains everything and mount a SAN volume to store the Docker image and container files. But since this is a test environment, just choose the default value *Guided – use entire disk and set up LVM* and hit *Enter*. This will allow Ubuntu to use the entire hard disk.

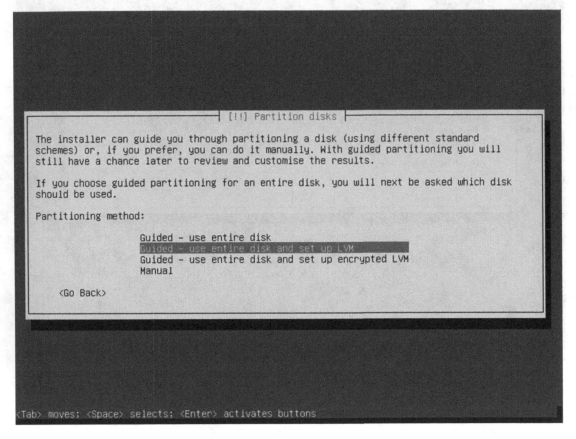

Figure A-24. *Ubuntu Partition disks screen*

Still in the *[!!] Partition disks* screen (Figure A-25), the installer asks you to confirm the disk partition that you want to configure. In this example, I only have one 50GB disk available. Hit *Enter* to choose the selected disk.

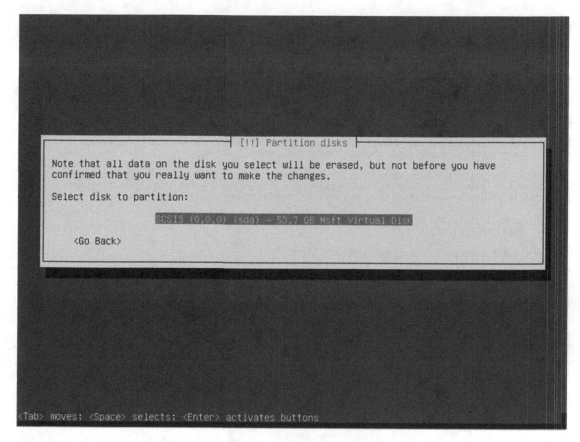

Figure A-25. *Ubuntu Partition disks screen – part 2*

Still in the *[!!] Partition disks* screen (Figure A-26), because partitioning the disk is critical, you will be asked again to confirm. Use either the arrow keys or the Tab key to select *Yes* and hit *Enter*.

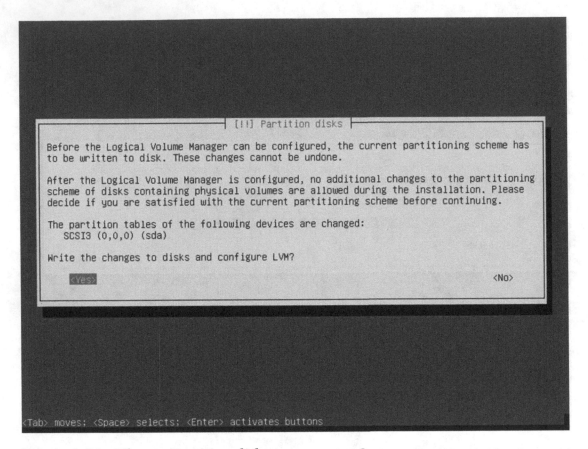

Figure A-26. *Ubuntu Partition disks screen – part 3*

Still in the *[!!] Partition disks* screen (Figure A-27), you can choose to use the entire disk or just a portion of it for the partition. As I mentioned earlier, since we're allowing Ubuntu to use the entire disk, just use the default value – the maximum size of your disk – and hit *Enter*.

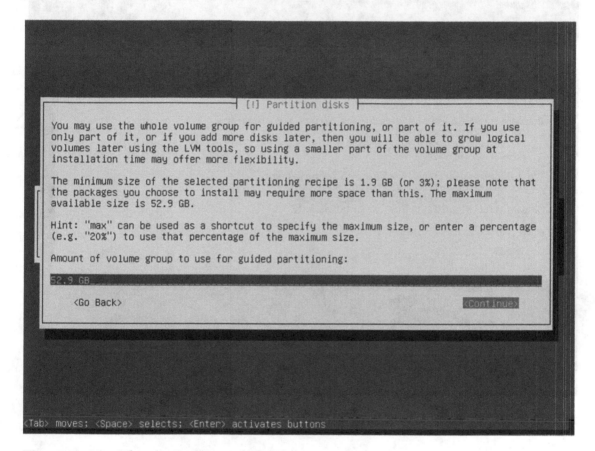

Figure A-27. *Ubuntu Partition disks screen – part 4*

I promise this will be the last *[!!] Partition disks* screen (Figure A-28). Confirm the selection by choosing *Yes* and hit *Enter*.

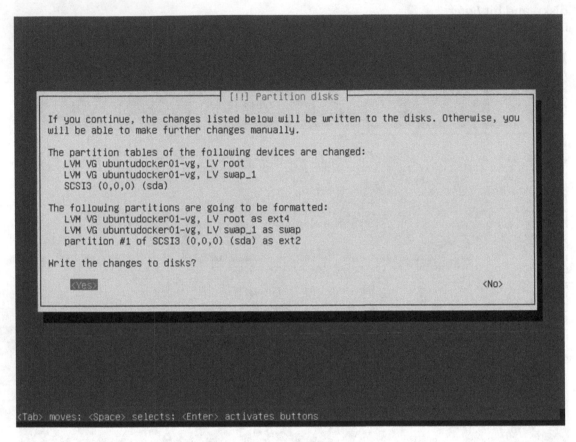

Figure A-28. *Ubuntu Partition disks screen – part 5*

In the *[!] Configure the package manager* screen (Figure A-29), leave it blank, select *Continue*, and hit *Enter*. You only provide configuration details for this section if you are accessing the Internet via an HTTP proxy.

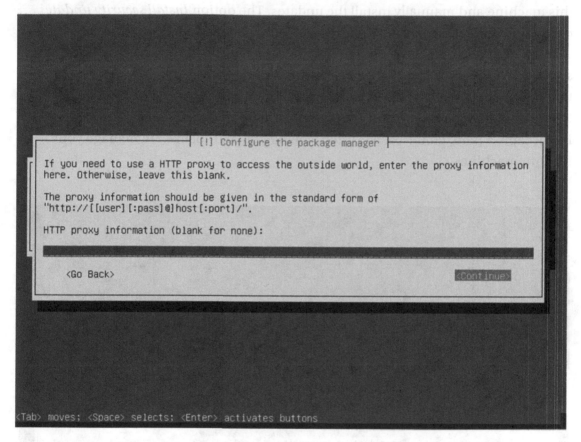

Figure A-29. *Ubuntu Configure the package manager screen*

In the *[!] Configuring tasksel* (yes, it's "tasksel", and it's not a typo because it is calling the *tasksel* command in Ubuntu) screen (Figure A-30), choose the default option *No automatic updates* and hit *Enter*. It's not that we won't be installing updates on this machine. It just means that an administrator will have to log in to this machine and manually install the updates. The option *Install security updates automatically* just means that security updates will be installed automatically without administrator intervention. I'm not a big fan of this regardless of operating system – Windows or Linux – because of the risk associated with installing updates that have not yet been tested in your environment. Any change should be tested before deploying to production. The option *Manage system with Landscape* uses Landscape, a paid, cloud-based systems management tool used to manage your Ubuntu machines.

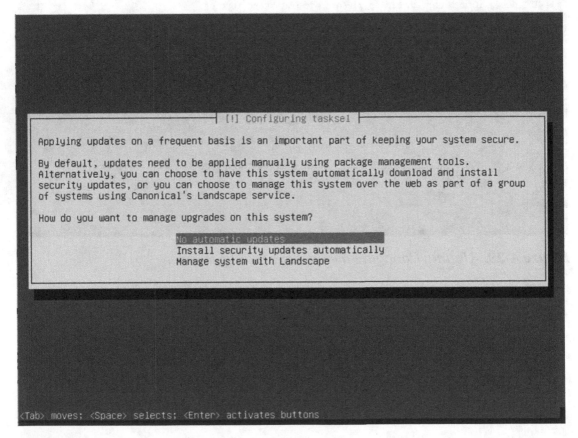

Figure A-30. Ubuntu Configuring tasksel screen

In the *[!] Software selection* screen (Figure A-31), use the arrow keys and move toward the *OpenSSH Server* option. Use the space bar to select the option, tab to move to *Continue*, and hit *Enter*. This option will install the OpenSSH Server so you can remotely log in to the Ubuntu Server via SSH. If you don't install the OpenSSH Server, you won't be able to securely connect to this machine from a remote client. If you miss this option during installation, you would need to log in locally to this machine and manually install OpenSSH Server. Imagine if this machine is on a remote data center and there are no KVM tools available to log in locally. You either have to go visit the data center or ask a data center engineer to manually install OpenSSH Server for you. So, make sure you don't forget to select this option during the installation.

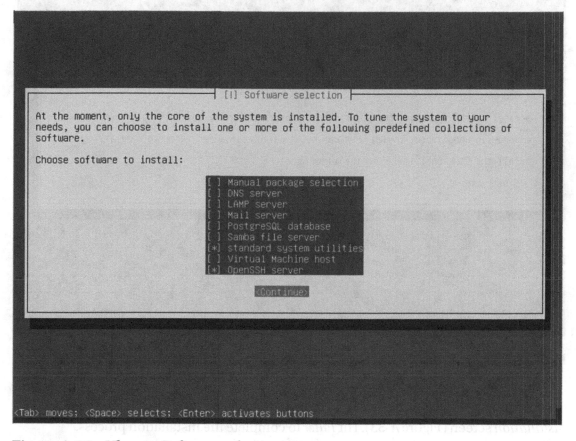

Figure A-31.   *Ubuntu Software selection screen*

In the *[!] Install the GRUB boot loader on a hard disk* screen (Figure A-32), use the arrow keys to select the *No* option and hit *Enter*. GRUB stands for *GNU GRand Unified Bootloader*. You use this if you have multiple operating systems installed on your machine, similar to how you can configure dual boot on Windows. Since this will be a dedicated Docker host machine, no other operating system will be installed other than Ubuntu (or RHEL/CentOS, if you chose that). So, we don't need GRUB.

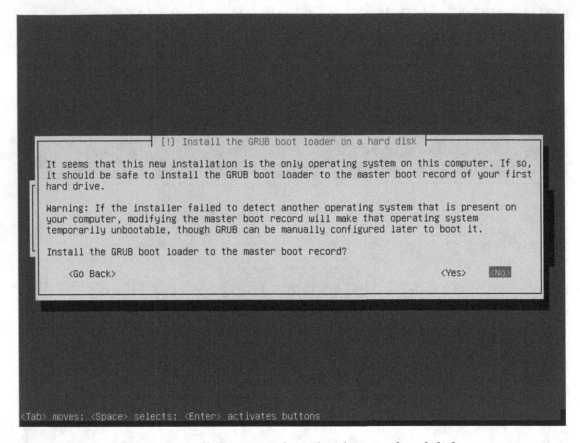

Figure A-32.   *Ubuntu Install the GRUB boot loader on a hard disk screen*

And, now we've come to the final screen in the installation – the *[!!] Finish the installation* screen (Figure A-33). Hit *Enter* to complete the installation process.

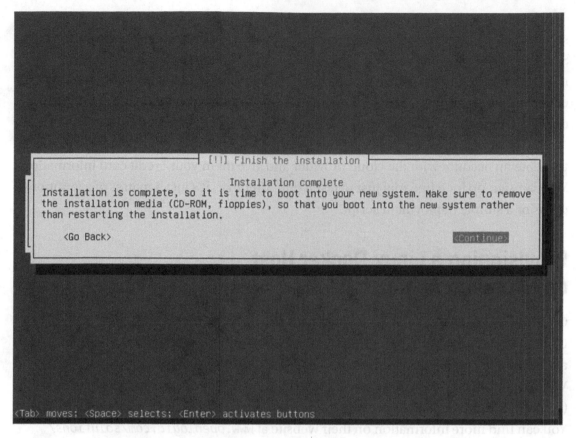

Figure A-33. *Ubuntu Finish the installation screen*

This will reboot the machine after the installation completes.

Didn't I say I'm a bit biased toward RHEL/CentOS?

Utilizing Public Cloud Resources

Knowing how to install the operating system gives you the benefit of understanding how it was configured and what pieces of software were installed in the process. If you know something should be installed – like the OpenSSH Server – but wasn't available, you know which component it is and manually install it yourself. However, if somebody did the installation for you, there's a possibility that some software that you need might be missing. And if you don't have *root* privileges, it can take a while to get the software installed. Also, if you know how to install the operating system, you can create an image template – be it on a VM or a physical machine – that can be used to standardize your deployment.

But if you don't want to provision your own hardware nor install the operating system, you can utilize public cloud resources like Microsoft Azure, Amazon Web Services (AWS), or Google Cloud Platform for your T.E.D.S. The pay-as-you-go model that the cloud provides is a very attractive alternative to having your own lab environment. Spin up a VM when you need it and, then, delete it once you're done. You only get charged for what you use.

If you want to leverage public cloud resources to build a lab environment, you need to create an account with the cloud provider and give them your credit card information. You can sign up for a free trial just to test it out. After that, it's just a matter of a few mouse clicks or a simple deployment script.

Provisioning a Linux Docker Host on Microsoft Azure

On Microsoft Azure, you have the option to deploy a RHEL 7.4 (or higher) VM or an Ubuntu Server 16.04 LTS (or higher) VM for your Linux Docker host. Since you're already paying for support as part of the subscription, it makes sense to deploy a RHEL VM image. You can also use a CentOS-based VM image from Rogue Wave Software (formerly OpenLogic). They provide a Linux VM image based on CentOS on Azure. You can find more information on their website at *www.openlogic.com/solutions/ operating-systems*. I use this a lot when delivering workshops and training classes. If you're concerned about cost, there really isn't any difference between the RHEL VM image and the CentOS-based VM image given the same VM size. I use a Standard_D2_V2 or a Standard_DS2_V2 VM image for the Linux Docker host – same thing for a Windows Docker host. If you're new to Microsoft Azure, check out their guide on *Create a Linux virtual machine in Azure* at *https://docs.microsoft.com/en-us/learn/modules/ create-linux-virtual-machine-in-azure/*. You can follow the same steps to create a Windows virtual machine in Azure.

Provisioning a Linux Docker Host on AWS

Like Microsoft Azure, Amazon AWS has a collection of Amazon Machine Images (AMI) that you can choose from. But more important is the EC2 instance size. An Amazon EC2 instance is a virtual server – a VM – in the AWS cloud. The benefit of choosing AWS is that they have a *t2.medium* sized instance – an EC2 instance with two vCPU and 4GB of RAM. For testing purposes, you don't really need a powerful machine like the Standard_DS2_V2 on Microsoft Azure. You can get away with having a 4GB RAM VM (or instance, if you're on AWS) for a Linux Docker host. If you're new to Amazon EC2, check out their guide on *Getting Started with Amazon EC2 Linux Instances* at *https://docs. aws.amazon.com/AWSEC2/latest/UserGuide/EC2_GetStarted.html*. You can follow the same steps to create a Windows EC2 instance on AWS.

Tip   AWS recommends the use of a HVM (hardware virtual machine) instance over PV (paravirtual) for best performance, especially for Linux-based EC2 instances. But like I said, we're not really that much concerned about performance for test environments. So, either of the two works. Then, it's just a matter of instance availability within your chosen region. For more information on the difference between HVM and PV virtualization for EC2 instances, check out *https://docs.aws.amazon.com/AWSEC2/latest/UserGuide/ virtualization_types.html*.

Provisioning a Linux Docker Host on Google Cloud Platform

Google Cloud Platform (GCP) is not as popular as Microsoft Azure and AWS when it comes to market share because it came in a bit late in the game and still doesn't offer as many different services and features as the other two. Plus, they don't have as many data centers as Microsoft Azure and AWS. GCP also has the same Windows and Linux – RHEL, CentOS, and Ubuntu – VM images that you can use. And like Microsoft Azure and AWS, VM size will be your primary concern when building your Docker host. GCP introduced the E2 standard machine types not too long ago to provide cost-effective VMs, which are great for running Docker hosts. Their *e2-standard-2* VMs with two vCPU and 8GB RAM are even better than the Standard_DS2_V2 VMs from Microsoft Azure when it comes to memory capacity. If you're new to GCP, check out their guide on *Creating and starting a VM instance* at *https://cloud.google.com/compute/docs/ instances/create-start-instance*.

Linux Client Tools

Once the machines are up and running, it's time to connect to them remotely. I'm sure you are very familiar with connecting to a Windows machine via Remote Desktop so I won't go into the details of how you would do it. You just need to make sure that you have the Remote Desktop feature enabled on the machine and port 3389 allowed on your firewall rules. Alternatively, you can leverage PowerShell Remoting to connect to a remote Windows machine. You just need to configure it for remote management. Refer to *https://docs.microsoft.com/en-us/powershell/module/microsoft.powershell. core/about/about_remote_requirements?view=powershell-7* on how to configure a Windows machine for remote management. Managing Windows via PowerShell Remoting sets you up for success when managing Linux remotely because everything is done via the PowerShell command line.

To connect to a Linux machine remotely, you need a secure socket shell (SSH) client that you can run from your Windows workstation.

Tip   Accessing VMs on a public cloud provider requires additional consideration. By default, firewall rules to allow inbound traffic to ports 3389 on Windows and 22 on Linux are added alongside the creation of the VM. But because the VMs are on the public Internet, they are also susceptible to attacks. Be sure to apply security recommendations from the cloud provider should you decide to deploy VMs on the cloud.

Using SSH to Connect to Linux

There are many SSH clients available that you can use to connect to a remote Linux machine. The one that I have been using since *Chapter 3* is PuTTY. PuTTY is a free, open source SSH client for Windows – one of the oldest and most popular. I've been using PuTTY for almost two decades now to remotely connect to both Unix and Linux servers. I promised never to go back to HyperTerminal on Windows 98 after I started using this tool. It's a lifesaver. You can download PuTTY from *www.chiark.greenend.org. uk/~sgtatham/putty/latest.html*.

Launch the tool after installation. Figure A-34 shows the configuration for using PuTTY to connect to a remote Linux machine.

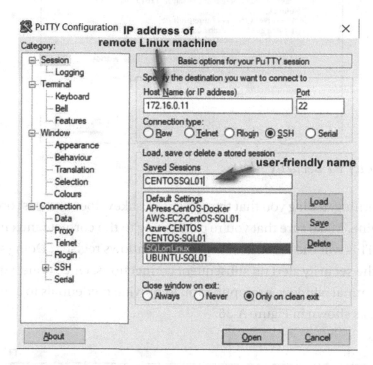

Figure A-34. PuTTY configuration screen

Provide the IP address of the remote Linux machine in the *Host Name (or IP address)* field. Recall the IP address of the CentOS Linux machine you installed as shown in Figure A-6. That's the IP address that you use for this field. You can use hostnames if you have DNS servers in your network and configured your Linux machine to leverage them. In the *Saved Sessions* field, provide a user-friendly name to easily identify this machine. Click the *Save* button to save this configuration so you don't have to keep entering the details every time you connect to the remote Linux machine. If you are connecting for the first time, PuTTY will prompt you for a security alert, as shown in Figure A-35.

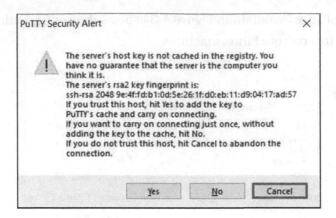

Figure A-35. *PuTTY Security Alert*

It's just a warning, telling you that the server's host key does not exist on your Windows machine. Make sure that you're connecting to the correct Linux machine and, then, click *Yes*. This will cache the host key in the Windows registry. Doing so will no longer display the security alert on subsequent connections. Once done, you will now be directed to a terminal window, prompting you to provide credentials to connect to the Linux machine, as shown in Figure A-36.

Figure A-36. *PuTTY terminal window*

Once you're connected, you're all set.

Using WinSCP for Copying Files to Linux

You'll also need to copy files to and from the Linux machine – either database backups that you need to restore on your SQL Server on Linux instance or *Dockerfile* files that you created on Windows. In *Chapter 10*, I cover creating a custom SQL Server on Docker image that includes restoring database backups. While you could use PuTTY Secure Copy (pscp) client to copy files from one Linux server to another, it can be frustrating if you're learning all of these – Docker, Linux, scp, ssh, security, permissions, and so on – at the same time. So, instead of using command-line tools for copying files to and from a Linux server, why not just use a graphical tool? Once you're comfortable using command-line utilities with Linux, you can move on to more advanced commands. In fact, you can leverage *scp* tools to automate the process of moving files around.

Windows Secure Copy (WinSCP) is a free and open source SFTP, FTP, WebDAV, Amazon S3, and SCP client for Windows (I also use it for transferring files to my Amazon S3 account). And because it's a graphical tool, you can use all the Windows tricks you've been using such as drag and drop, right-click, keyboard shortcuts, and so on. You can download WinSCP from *https://winscp.net/eng/download.php*.

Launch the tool after installation. Figure A-37 shows the configuration for using WinSCP to connect to a remote Linux machine.

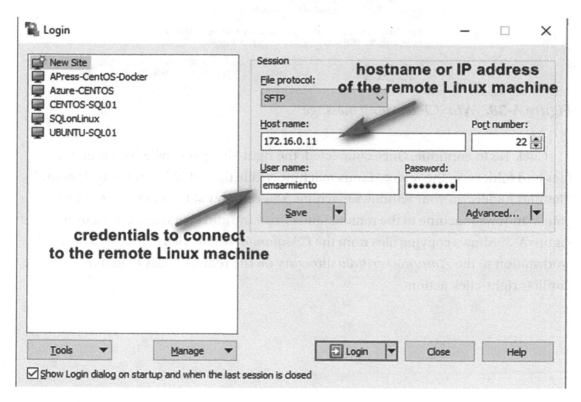

Figure A-37. *WinSCP Login window*

Similar to configuring PuTTY, provide the IP address of the remote Linux machine in the *Host name:* field. In the *User name:* field, provide the credential that has permissions to write files into the remote Linux machine. Recall the section "Working with the Filesystem" in *Chapter 8.* The user account needs to have the appropriate permissions to write files in the filesystem. And avoid the temptation to log in using the *root* user. Always follow Linux security best practices when working with filesystem permissions.

Click *Login* to log in to the remote Linux machine. Similar to using PuTTY for the first time, you'll be prompted with a warning, as shown in Figure A-38, telling you that the server host's key is not yet in the cache.

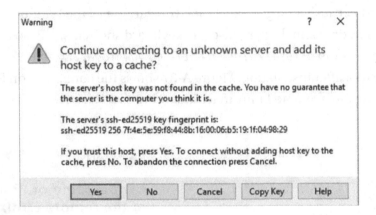

Figure A-38. *WinSCP warning message*

Click *Yes* to continue. Once connected, the right-side panel will display all the files and folders on the remote Linux machine, while the left-side panel displays the files and folders on your Windows machine. You can now start copying files from your Windows machine to the remote Linux machine and vice versa. For example, Figure A-39 shows copying files from the *C:\sqlondockerbook\ch10* on my Windows workstation to the */tmp/dockerBuild* directory on the remote Linux machine using the familiar right-click action.

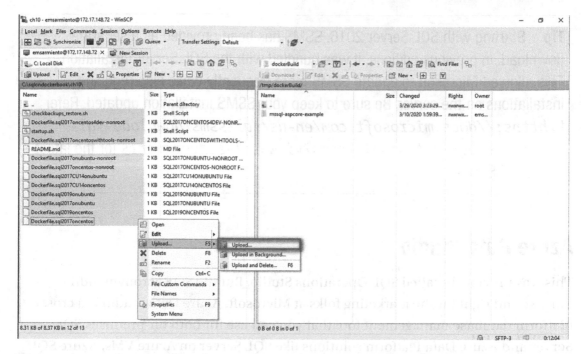

Figure A-39. *Copying files from Windows to Linux using the Upload feature*

Similarly, you can copy files from the remote Linux machine to your Windows workstation using the *Download* feature. I told you this is way easier than typing a bunch of *scp* commands just to copy files to and from a remote Linux machine.

SQL Server Client Tools

I mainly used SQL Server Management Studio (SSMS) throughout the book simply because it's what we DBAs use for managing SQL Server. But ever since Microsoft decided to embrace the culture of open source software, more tools were made available to manage SQL Server. You can continue to use SSMS but you're more than welcome to try the new tools.

Tip   Starting with SQL Server 2016, SSMS has been provided as a separate download. In previous editions, it was bundled with the SQL Server installation. This allowed Microsoft to update SSMS more frequently while also reducing installations on the server. Be sure to keep your SSMS installation updated. Refer to *https://docs.microsoft.com/en-us/sql/ssms/download-sql-server-management-studio-ssms?view=sql-server-ver15* for the latest version of SSMS.

Azure Data Studio

This was previously called SQL Operations Studio. But the SOS acronym didn't quite sound right for the marketing folks at Microsoft. Azure Data Studio is a cross-platform database management tool that you can use for both on-premises SQL Server and Azure Data Platform solutions like SQL Server on Azure VMs, Azure SQL Database, Azure SQL Data Warehouse, Azure SQL Database Managed Instance, and SQL Server 2019 Big Data Clusters. While initially designed for developers, features are constantly added to be at par with SSMS when it comes to administering SQL Server. With Azure Data Studio, you can have a consistent user experience whether you're on Windows, Linux, or a MacBook. Figure A-40 shows Azure Data Studio on Windows 10 connected to a SQL Server 2017 instance running on a CentOS Linux machine.

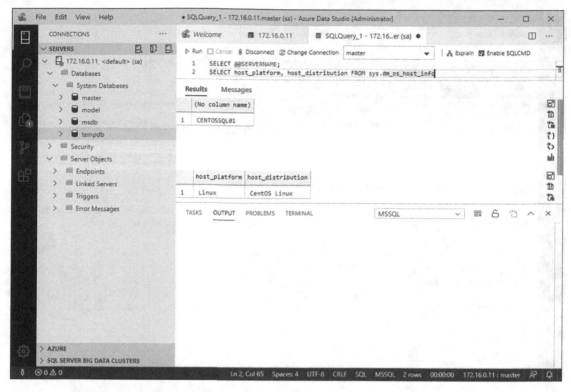

Figure A-40. *Azure Data Studio*

You can download the latest version of Azure Data Studio from *https://docs.microsoft.com/en-us/sql/azure-data-studio/download-azure-data-studio?view=sql-server-ver15*. In addition, you can install extensions to the base Azure Data Studio installation to add more functionality. As a DBA, the *Azure Data Studio Admin Pack for SQL Server* extension will be a great add-on for managing SQL Server. Figure A-41 shows how you can add the *Admin Pack for SQL Server* extension on Azure Data Studio.

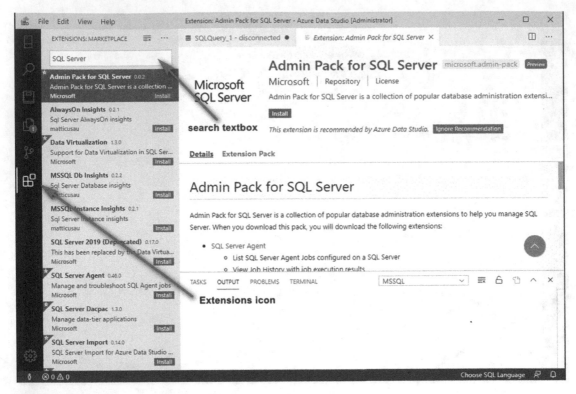

Figure A-41. *Azure Data Studio Admin Pack for SQL Server*

Just click the *Extensions* icon, type *SQL Server* in the search text box to display the extension, select *Admin Pack for SQL Server*, and click *Install*. You now have a new tool in your toolkit for managing SQL Server.

mssql-cli

mssql-cli is an interactive command-line, cross-platform tool for querying SQL Server. While not a graphical tool like Azure Data Studio, the interactive capability makes this a better command-line tool than *sqlcmd* with features like IntelliSense and syntax highlighting. Figure A-42 shows context-aware autocompletion when writing queries using *mssql-cli*.

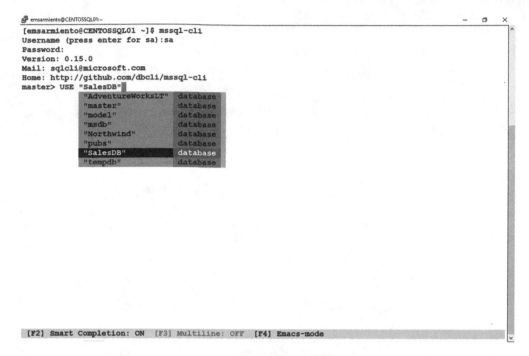

Figure A-42. *Context-aware autocompletion in mssql-cli*

For more information on how to install *mssql-cli* on your preferred operating system, check out *https://github.com/dbcli/mssql-cli/tree/master/doc/installation*.

There are other SQL Server client tools available from Microsoft. You can check them out at *https://docs.microsoft.com/en-us/sql/tools/overview-sql-tools?view=sql-server-ver15*.

Summary

Building a personal lab environment requires knowing how to install the operating system and which tools you need to get started learning the technology you've chosen, in this case, Docker. I've only laid out the essentials to get you started. As you get more involved with the technology, you'll learn more tools that you can add in your toolbox. However, avoid the temptation to get fixated with tools. Tools change, principles don't. Focus on principles when learning a new technology. Because principles are timeless, you'll find that you can apply them to every new technology that you want to learn. It's the same thing with life. Tips and life hacks come and go. But principles remain the same.

Here's to learning more about life than it is learning about technology.

Index

A

ADD instruction, 208
add-apt-repository command, 22, 32
Amazon Elastic Container Registry
     (ECR), 48
Amazon Web Services (AWS), 136,
     326, 327
AMD-based processors, 291
Application programming interfaces
     (APIs), 159
apt-get command, 22
apt-get update command, 29, 33
apt-get upgrade command, 30
apt-key command, 31
Audio files, 100
Azure Blob storage, 137, 217
Azure Data Studio, 334–336

B

Bourne Again Shell (Bash), 188
Bash script
     backups check, 253, 255–257
     conditional logic, adding, 194–197
     fully-fledged programming
          language, 188
     passing parameters, 193, 194
     plain text file, 188
     running, 192, 193
     writing, 191, 192

C

Capital expenditures (CapEx), 290
CA public key, 111
cat command, 22, 32, 88, 93
CentOS-based VM image, 326
CentOS Docker client machine, 112
CentOS Linux server, installation
     automatic partitioning,
          configuring, 296
     boot screen, 292
     configuring installation
          destination, 295
     language, choosing, 294
     network and hostname option,
          configuration, 297
     new user account, creation, 300, 301
     reboot button, 301
     root user, password assign, 300
     TCP/IP and hostname, 298
     user settings, configuring, 299
Certificate authority (CA), 110
chmod command, 186
chown command, 185
Cloud service providers, 136, 138
CMD instruction, 210–212, 236
ConfigurationFile.ini file, 163, 202
Container images, 59
Container layer, 97, 98
Container logs, 62, 126–128
Container naming conventions, 51

E. M. Sarmiento, *The SQL Server DBA's Guide to Docker Containers*,
https://doi.org/10.1007/978-1-4842-5826-2